STRATEGIC ALLIANCES

Social Movements, Protest, and Contention

Series Editor   Bert Klandermans, Free University, Amsterdam

Associate Editors   Ron R. Aminzade, University of Minnesota
David S. Meyer, University of California, Irvine
Verta A. Taylor, University of California, Santa Barbara

For more books in the series, see page 344.

STRATEGIC ALLIANCES

Coalition Building and Social Movements

Nella Van Dyke and Holly J. McCammon, Editors

Social Movements, Protest, and Contention
Volume 34

 University of Minnesota Press
Minneapolis • London

Published by the University of Minnesota Press
111 Third Avenue South, Suite 290
Minneapolis, MN 55401–2520
http://www.upress.umn.edu

Library of Congress Cataloging-in-Publication Data

Strategic alliances : coalition building and social movements /
Nella Van Dyke and Holly J. McCammon, editors.
p. cm. — (Social movements, protest, and contention ; v. 34)
Includes bibliographical references and index.
ISBN 978-0-8166-6733-8 (hc : alk. paper) —
ISBN 978-0-8166-6734-5 (pb : alk. paper)
1. Coalitions. 2. Social movements. I. Van Dyke, Nella.
II. McCammon, Holly J., 1959–
HM869.S77 2010
303.48'401—dc22
2010019710

Printed in the United States of America on acid-free paper

The University of Minnesota is an equal-opportunity educator and employer.

17 16 15 14 13 12 11 10   10 9 8 7 6 5 4 3 2 1

We dedicate this book to our children,
Seth and Hadley McCammon
and Elsa and Sadie Van Dyke

Contents

Part III. Broad Political Influences on Social Movement Coalitions

Part IV. Coalitions and Combinations of Causal Factors

Preface

Coalitions have figured prominently in both of our research agendas for some time. After a number of conversations during the past few years, including some with David S. Meyer (who finally crystallized the idea that we should pursue a collection of current research on social movement coalitions), we decided to put this book together. We knew a number of scholars conducting exciting research projects on coalitions and thought this would be a rare opportunity to bring their work together. We feel strongly that coalitions are extremely important to social movements, especially at this time in history, and an edited collection will bring greater attention to this understudied topic. Our collaboration emerged naturally from our shared belief in the importance of coalitions, but we also share an interest in explanations that consider the role of political threats and conjunctural processes in coalition formation. We wanted to bring together a volume that highlights the motivating effect of threats and illustrates the multiple paths to coalitions among social movement organizations.

We contacted researchers who were doing work on social movement coalitions as well as a number of other scholars who had published on coalitions in the past. We sought breadth in the types of movements studied, as well as in their geographic scope. The collection includes studies of antiwar, women's, panethnic, labor, militia, and environmental coalitions. Most of the research is based in the United States, but chapters look at Latin American countries, Germany, Britain, and Northeast and Southeast Asia. We divided the book into four sections, and two dominant themes emerge: first, that political threats frequently motivate coalition formation, and second, that multiple paths involving an interplay of social ties, ideologies, threats, and opportunities lead to collaboration. The book will be of interest to students and scholars of social movements, but also to activists and anyone interested in contemporary politics.

We thank our authors for allowing us to include their insightful and careful work. We appreciate their willingness to undertake several rounds of revision and a rush at the end. We may be biased, but we think that the quality of work in this collection is outstanding. We are thankful to Suzanne Staggenborg for writing a wonderful conclusion; her article on coalition work in the U.S. women's movement that was published in *Social Problems* in 1986 was groundbreaking, and we are honored that she put her stamp on this collection. We also thank Jackie Smith, who reviewed the manuscript for the University of Minnesota Press and provided many helpful comments and suggestions.

We appreciate the insightful comments on several chapters we received from the Washington State University sociology faculty research group, Daniel B. Cornfield, Larry Isaac, and Suzanne Staggenborg. And we thank David S. Meyer, who first suggested an edited volume on social movement coalitions.

Introduction:
Social Movement Coalition Formation

Nella Van Dyke and Holly J. McCammon

Political and economic changes over the past several decades have been met with a renewed emphasis from both activists and scholars on the importance of social movement coalitions. Internationally, activists are increasingly seeking collaborators across national borders in response to globalization and the rise of transnational corporations and governing bodies. These changed circumstances have created both threats and opportunities for international mobilization and coalition building (Smith 2004; Tarrow 2005). Other activists, like those in the antiapartheid movement of South Africa, driven by repression and limited opportunities at home, have reached beyond their borders for collaborators to assist in pressuring their own governments for change (Emery 2005; Keck and Sikkink 1998). Global capital's ability to move production to other parts of the globe, the emergence of flexible production, and the use of temporary subcontracting (Jenkins and Leicht 1997) have reduced labor's power and created an increasingly disorganized and spatially diffuse working class. In response, some labor activists (e.g., Mazur 2000) have called for labor to work in coalition with other groups, and the labor movement in the United States has been moved to adopt a more activism-oriented organizing style, increasingly working in coalition and attempting to mobilize new constituencies including women, minorities, and students (Bronfenbrenner et al. 1998; Cornfield and McCammon 2003; Lopez 2004; Van Dyke, Dixon, and Carlon 2007; Voss and Sherman 2000).

The development of new communication and transportation technologies has made these broad and geographically widespread collaborations possible. Activists increasingly use them to generate, in some cases, faraway alliances, and in others, massive coalitions to pursue change within their own nations and beyond. Arguably one of the largest social movement coalitions in history was assembled to protest the World Trade Organization meetings in Seattle in 1999, with over five hundred participating organizations. The success of the Seattle mobilization as well as several other global actions inspired activists to organize the first World Social Forum in 2001 in an effort to create a space where these broad alliances could be formed. Social forums now occur annually and semiannually at the national, regional, and international level. Connections nurtured at the social forums have helped create some of the largest protests in world history, such as in 2003, when millions of activists from over thirty countries organized simultaneous protests of the pending U.S. war in Iraq. This action would not have been possible without increasing partnerships and alliances among movement groups. Clearly, social movement organizational coalitions are playing a striking role in mobilizing contemporary collective action.

In spite of the importance of coalitions to social movements, they have received relatively little empirical attention from social scientists. In fact, most scholarly studies of social movements fail to recognize explicitly that many, if not most, movements are amalgamations of movement organizations. Many researchers assume that movements are simply homogeneous social entities. Instead, conceptualizing social movements as organizational clusters or coalitional networks allows us to grasp more fully the varied constituencies, ideological perspectives, identities, and tactical preferences different groups bring to movement activism. Understanding movements as coalitions also reveals that tensions can surface among groups with different cultures, practices, and goals. Such tensions make coalition formation difficult, and when coalition work is problematic, movement emergence, sustainment, and success can be stalled.

In this volume, our contributors argue that we cannot fully understand the dynamics of movement mobilization and success until we gain a more complete understanding of the factors facilitating organizational collaboration. *Strategic Alliances: Coalition Building and Social Movements* takes an important step in this direction by presenting a pioneering set of empirical studies that explore the variety of conditions that produce coalitions among social movement actors.

The chapters collected here are organized into four sections that explore questions central to understanding how social movement coalitions come about. The volume begins by asking to what degree preexisting social ties influence which groups work together. The second section explores how organizational ideologies and interests can facilitate or inhibit coalition formation.

In the third section, the authors examine the broad social and political conditions that foster coalition formation. Finally, in the fourth section of the volume, we explore ways in which these various factors combine to produce social movement coalitions. Chapters in the volume investigate coalition dynamics among a variety of social movements, including the antiwar, environmental, and labor movements as well as ethnic organizations and women's groups. Although many of the chapters investigate coalition formation in the United States, others consider coalitions in Britain, the former East Germany, East Asia, and Latin America.

The broader social movement literature has conclusively demonstrated that social ties between activists predict which individuals will become involved in social movement activity (McAdam 1988; McAdam and Paulsen 1993; Schussman and Soule 2005; Snow, Zurcher, and Ekland-Olson 1980; Taylor 1996). Research on coalitions is just beginning to establish that ties between organizations, either among individuals involved in the groups or from past organizational collaborations, also influence which organizations will participate in a coalition (Bystydzienski and Schacht 2001; Obach 2004; Rose 2000). However, research on this topic remains limited and thus far has only established that social ties are important in a few isolated cases. The studies included in the first section of this volume expand the study of social ties and coalition work to explore how social ties influence coalition formation among a variety of social movements, including the contemporary antiwar movement, nineteenth-century militias, and Northeast and Southeast Asian coalitions.

The second section of the book explores the role of ideology in coalition formation among several social movements. Existing scholarship demonstrates that cultural similarities between coalition actors (Bandy and Smith 2005) and flexible or congruent ideologies (Gerhards and Rucht 1992; Lichterman 1995) facilitate coalition formation as well as the longevity of those coalitions. Little is known, however, about the specific ideological elements that facilitate or impede coalitions. Chapters in the volume discuss the role of ideology in facilitating the formation of the AFL-CIO and also discuss how an ideology about what is "good politics" can prevent coalition formation, as it did in the case of the U.S. women's movement.

Existing scholarship demonstrates that favorable environmental conditions, including allies among political elites (Stearns and Almeida 2004), abundant financial resources, and an absence of international political conflict (Bandy and Smith 2005), support coalition formation. At the same time, however, recent studies indicate that the presence of political threats to movement goals or an antagonistic political context can also sometimes inspire coalitions to emerge (McCammon and Campbell 2002; Reger 2002; Van Dyke 2003). In the broader social movements literature, studies of the influence of political threats have tended to focus on conservative, or what scholars call "reactive," social movements (e.g., McVeigh 1999; Van Dyke and Soule 2002). In the third portion of this volume, we present research that explores whether political threats influence the formation of coalitions among a variety of social movements, including panethnic Asian coalitions and movement-party coalitions in Latin America. This work also breaks new ground by exploring the effect of economic threats on coalition formation. Other chapters consider how the structure of the institutional political system can both inhibit and facilitate coalitions among different movements.

The final section of this volume considers the interplay among different factors that influence coalition formation—how broader political and social conditions, social ties among activist groups, and the ideological orientation of movement organizations can combine to facilitate collaboration. Rarely do scholars examine how these causal dynamics interact with one another to generate social movement partnerships. It is possible, for instance, that serious threats to a group's goals may allow it to overcome ideological barriers to form an alliance with another group. One chapter included in this section considers precisely this in the Argentine women's movement. Another examines the combination of factors that enabled the rapid mobilization of the anti–Iraq war movement, while the final chapter conducts a meta-analysis of the coalition research to examine the interplay of factors that lead to coalition formation. Although virtually all of the chapters in this volume include attention to multiple factors that influence coalitions, this section centers its discussion on how broader social conditions interact with ideology and social ties to inspire collaboration.

In the following section, we provide a definition of social movement coalitions; in doing so, we identify their typical characteristics. We then review the existing research on coalitions and situate the chapters presented in this volume within the broader literature.

What Is a Social Movement Coalition?

Social movement coalitions take a variety of forms (Wilson 1973; Zald and Ash 1966). At the most basic level, a coalition can be said to exist any time two or more social movement organizations work together on a common task. Thus, coalitions can range from a simple partnership between just two movement groups to a complex network of many social movement organizations. Coalition members may work together on a single project, or they may form a more long-lasting alliance and collaborate on multiple activities over time. Coalitions are distinct from mergers, however, in that coalition partners maintain separate organizational structures. Many coalitions are created to work on a specific issue, and when efforts on the issue decline, the coalition structure dissolves. However, other coalitions may last for an extended period over many issue cycles.

Researchers have identified organizational alliances within many social movements, including within the environmental movement (Lichterman 1995; Murphy 2005; Shaffer 2000), the gay and lesbian rights movement (Adam 1995; D'Emilio 1983), the labor movement (Bandy 2004; Williams 1999), the women's movement (Ferree and Hess 1994; Gilmore 2008; Rupp and Taylor 1987; Whittier 1995), the civil rights movement (McAdam 1982; Morris 1984), the nuclear freeze movement (Hathaway and Meyer 1993; Rochon and Meyer 1997), and the New Right movement (Himmelstein 1990). Thus, social movement organizations often collaborate with other organizations focused on the same issue. However, organizations are sometimes inspired to cross movement boundaries to form coalitions. Van Dyke (2003) documents numerous instances of cross-movement coalitions between different student movement organizations over a sixty-year time span. Although the media have highlighted conflict between the U.S. labor and environmental movements, Obach (2004) shows that activists from the two camps often work together—for instance, for workplace health and safety and right-to-know laws (see also Rose 2000). Researchers studying the Industrial Areas Foundation and the Direct Action Network describe the multiracial and multiclass coalitions that form the foundations of these groups (Altemose and McCarty 2001; Polletta 2002). Meyer and Whittier (1994) examine partnerships between the U.S. women's and peace movements during the early 1980s. Hence, organizations collaborate in pursuit of a variety of goals and with many different interests in mind. Sometimes the groups involved share a narrow focus; at other times, they may share one that is broader and cuts across social movements.

The nature of the links between or among organizations can be informal, as is typically the case, or more formal (Zald and McCarthy 1980). Informal ties entail loosely coordinated actions with intermittent communication between groups. Groups may, for example, plan a joint protest event together but not pursue further collaboration. In more formalized coalition arrangements, an umbrella organization may be formed with its own staff and resources to initiate and monitor coordinated action among the member groups. Win Without War, an anti–Iraq war coalition organization described by Corrigall-Brown and Meyer in chapter 2, is an example of an umbrella organization, with a paid staff representing over forty member organizations. In such a formalized coalition arrangement, participation in the coalition may result in substantial changes in the organizational routines of member groups. Regular meetings among member groups may take place. Decision-making processes may be channeled through the coalition. Fund-raising may be coordinated with alliance partners, and protest strategies and actions for a single group may be determined by the coalition rather than by the group independently.

Whether coalition ties are formal or informal among member groups, they allow for the exchange of information between organizations (Obach 2004). Even a loose coordination of action requires such an exchange of information. For example, when groups decide to collaborate in developing a petition or letter to publish in the newspaper, they may do no more than exchange a series of e-mails. However, they must communicate and develop an agreed-upon framing of the issues for even this modest action. As Croteau and Hicks (2003) argue, developing consistent frames is a fundamental task that coalitions must accomplish.

Other actions require more resources, and groups may be motivated to collaborate in order to pool resources; this can result in a more effective pursuit of the groups' goals in that the coalition will have greater resources than any one organization (Berry 1997). However, scarcity of resources can lead to conflict if some coalition members perceive that the actions or rhetoric of more radical groups threatens funding sources, as Barkan (1986) found in his study of the Southern civil rights movement. In addition, sharing resources can also be costly for organizations. In some cases, participating organizations may contribute different amounts and kinds of resources to the coalition, and this can lead to conflict if some groups begin to sense that they are contributing more than their fair share or if some are seen as having unfair control over the coalition because of their resources. Resentments can emerge and coalitions can falter or dissolve. Bandy (2004) documents this type of conflict in his study of the Coalition for Justice in the Maquiladoras, a cross-national coalition formed to fight for reform of labor conditions in Mexico's export-oriented sector. Wealthier organizations, primarily from the United States, Canada, and Mexico City, were able to contribute more resources to the coalition and thereby tended to have more power in determining coalition strategy, while poorer organizations were often left to do more of the on-the-ground organizing. Although the coalition survived, some groups left because of these inequities.

As this brief overview demonstrates, there are benefits and costs to organizations participating in coalitions. Scholars are only beginning to identify circumstances that facilitate coalition formation, both those internal to movement groups that motivate them to form alliances and those in the broader context that sometimes compel the formation of a partnership. The chapters in this volume further our understanding of coalitions as we describe in the following pages.

Social Ties

Consistent with the general social movements literature that has emphasized the importance of social ties to social movement recruitment, coalition scholars have demonstrated that the presence of individuals with ties across organizations, what scholars have called coalition brokers or bridge builders, facilitate coalition formation (Bystydzienski and Schacht 2001; Grossman 2001; Obach 2004; Rose 2000). For example, Rose (2000) finds that bridge builders played a critical role in helping environmental, labor, and peace organizations overcome class divides that made it difficult for them to collaborate. Similarly, Grossman (2001) demonstrates that similar individuals enabled a Native American group and a rural white outdoors organization to overcome the culture, race, and class differences that had previously divided them to fight to protect natural resources in Wisconsin. Thus, the coalition literature is beginning to echo the broader social movement literature in emphasizing the importance of social ties to coalition formation. However, research on this topic is currently limited to a very small number of case studies. Chapters presented in this volume contribute to this literature by documenting the importance of social ties to coalition formation among several different social movements, including the contemporary antiwar movement, women's groups, progressive movements in Latin America, and nineteenth-century American militias.

While political and economic conditions may inspire groups to overcome barriers to collaborative work, prior social ties may shape which organizations decide to participate in a coalition. Corrigall-Brown and Meyer's work in this volume demonstrates that past organizational collaborations and the efforts of five key activists inspired particular organizations to join in the Win Without War coalition against the war in Iraq. Similarly, Guenther shows that a history of interaction and social ties between an East German town and one in Sweden led an East German women's group to seek out coalition partners in Sweden after reunification, while another East German town, lacking these ties, sought out collaborators in West Germany.

Two of the volume's chapters explore an understudied phenomenon: movements acting in coalition with state political actors. Both Almeida and Isaac demonstrate that social ties between the movements and the government are critical in the formation of these coalitions. Interestingly, the two studies examine very different coalitions. Isaac examines the formation of private militias aligned with the state against labor in the late nineteenth century, while Almeida examines coalitions between labor organizations and political parties opposing neoliberal economic reforms in five Latin American countries. Although the political parties that Almeida studies had their roots in the social movements they later worked with, which did not occur in Isaac's case, the two studies are similar in their exploration of factors that facilitate state actor–movement coalitions. They demonstrate that in two very different political contexts involving very different political issues, ties between activists and state actors facilitated coalition formation.

Interests, Identities, and Ideology

Organizations will not work with one another unless they share at least some common goals. For example, we would almost never expect to see coalitions among organizations with diametrically opposing goals, such as pro–abortion rights and opposition to abortion. Research demonstrates the importance of shared ideologies and identities to organizational collaboration (Bandy and Smith 2005; Gerhards and Rucht 1992; Lichterman 1995). For example, McCammon and Campbell (2002) show how women's suffrage groups and the Woman's Christian Temperance Union (WCTU) were able to work together once the suffragists started using arguments consistent with those used by the temperance activists. Other research demonstrates that ideological differences can inhibit coalition formation (Barkan 1986; Diaz-Veizades and Chang 1996; Gerhards and Rucht 1992). In spite of sharing common goals, many groups never work together. This suggests that the mobilizing potential of shared interests and goals is more complicated than it first appears.

Research suggests that organizations committed to a broad ideology facilitate coalition formation. Van Dyke (2003), for example, finds that the presence of multi-issue organizations on a college campus increases the likelihood that groups will work together across movement boundaries. Cornfield and McCammon's chapter in this volume adds to this literature by showing that an organization's ideology can change over time, addressing a wider set of issues, and that this can then facilitate coalition work. Their chapter presents a new quantitative method for measuring policy change and convergence over time. They demonstrate that the AFL and CIO merged only after the AFL's policy agenda broadened and converged with the more expansive policy goals of the CIO.

Groups that share similar goals may nonetheless adhere to ideological principles that make collaboration difficult. Lichterman (1995), for example, demonstrates that a belief in activism as an individual project rather than a

community effort prevented one environmental group from successfully forming alliances with other antitoxics organizations, in spite of a shared interest
in the issue and specifically valuing multicultural alliance, while an antitoxics
group that viewed activism as a community effort was successfully able to form
coalitions. Similarly, Benita Roth's contribution to this volume demonstrates
that groups sharing common goals may hold other ideological positions that
prevent coalition formation. Roth studies U.S. women's organizations from
the 1960s and 1970s and finds that although the organizations had a great
deal of ideological overlap, they actively avoided forming coalitions with other
women's groups because they believed that activism is best pursued by those
whose direct interests are at stake, and that others should not take on political action on behalf of others. Thus, ideological differences or an ideology
that suggests a noncollaborative strategy can prevent coalition formation,
regardless of external social and political conditions. Although some elements
of two groups' ideologies may overlap, they may hold other positions that
prevent collaboration.

Shared members may facilitate ideological congruence. As Staggenborg
(1986, 384) notes, "a lack of overlap in membership among diverse groups
exacerbates ideological differences, creating many disagreements and misunderstandings which might be avoided with better communication." Ferree and Roth (1998) describe how both labor groups and feminists failed to
support a strike of day care workers in West Berlin because they did not see
the connection between the issues involved in the strike and their own goals,
leading to the strike's failure. The authors argue that a lack of social ties
between the different groups produced this outcome. Barkan (1986) explores
how social distance and ideological differences led to conflict among organizations involved in the Southern civil rights movement over issues such as
communist participation, the Vietnam War, and black power. Similarly, Katja
M. Guenther's piece in this volume, described above, illustrates how a history of interaction can lead to either ideological congruence or disagreements,
which then shape who will eventually work in coalition.

Political Context

The broader social movement literature focuses on how political opportunities, including the presence of elite allies, the passage of favorable legislation
or legal decisions, and the absence of repression, inspire grassroots mobilization. Studies of the African American civil rights movement (McAdam 1982)
and other left-oriented political movements (Almeida and Stearns 1998;
Amenta and Zylan 1991; Banaszak 1996; Jenkins and Perrow 1977; Kriesi
et al. 1995; Meyer 1993) demonstrate that when political opportunities open

up for a disadvantaged group, group members begin to believe that success is possible and mobilize in higher numbers than they had previously. However, scholars are beginning to demonstrate that political threats also sometimes inspire mobilization (McVeigh 1999, 2009; Van Dyke and Soule 2002), particularly among reactive social movements such as the militia or white power movements. Groups that enjoy some level of social power and resources may mobilize when faced with a threatened loss of that power. However, the extent to which organizations on the left and the right may decide to work in coalition with other groups in response to threats remains largely unexamined. In this volume, we present research on several different social movements that suggests that threats inspire a variety of social groups to overcome barriers to collaboration, including progressive movement organizations.

Several chapters in the volume demonstrate that the structure of political opportunities, including political threats from another group gaining political power or the election of an enemy of the movement to a high governmental post, create incentives for left-oriented groups to work in collaboration. Reese, Petit, and Meyer explore how the threat of social policy contrary to movement goals can lead to coalition formation. They examine how the Bush administration's threatened war in Iraq inspired activists to activate social ties and form coalitions to mobilize in opposition. They argue that the combination of these factors enabled the coalition to mobilize a broad range of groups with unprecedented speed. Okamoto contributes to research on the role of threat and coalition by demonstrating that violent attacks on Asians increase the likelihood of panethnic Asian coalitions. Her work also makes a significant contribution by considering how ethnic and racial competition and segregation contribute to the formation of barriers to cross-ethnic collaboration.

Political threats may combine with economic crisis or with political opportunities to inspire coalition formation. In his study of party-movement coalitions in five Latin American countries, Almeida contributes to the coalition literature and the broader study of mobilization by demonstrating that groups may enjoy greater political opportunities while also facing political threats. He demonstrates that the threats associated with government austerity programs combined with the opportunities for mobilization created by democratization led to the formation of new alliances in Latin American countries. Wiest similarly shows how political threats can combine with economic crisis to inspire coalition formation. She demonstrates that the political and economic crisis in East Asian countries in the 1990s inspired organizations from the different countries to work together like never before. She adds further nuance by demonstrating that the countries of Southeast Asia, which had a history of collaboration, formed more extensive coalitions than did their neighbors in the northeast.

Thus, in contrast to the literature on threats and social movement mobilization, which has been dominated by studies of conservative or reactive social movements, the work in this volume demonstrates that political and economic threats motivate organizational coalition work among a variety of politically left-oriented social movements, including antiwar, women's, and ethnic social movements.

Another topic that has received little attention from coalition scholars is how political structure and political culture influence coalition formation. Brian Obach's chapter in this volume explores how the U.S. government's tax laws and organization of policy areas create barriers for some organizations and incentives for others to work together. For example, labor organizations and environmental groups operate within different policy domains and thus rarely come in contact with one another. They are therefore less likely to collaborate. Diani, Lindsay, and Purdue explore a related topic in their examination of how the political culture in two British cities shapes which organizations work together in coalition. They find that the protest-oriented political culture of Glasgow makes newly established, movement-oriented groups more likely to work on civic issues in coalition with other organizations, and that this often translates into social movement collaboration. A more low-key, mediation-oriented political culture in Bristol, on the other hand, is associated with few differences in the types of organizations that collaborate on civic projects, and these civic coalitions often do not lead to subsequent social movement coalitions. These two chapters, then, show that both more formal government policy structures and informal political cultures influence which organizations come into contact, which in turn shapes the frequency and composition of social movement coalitions.

Several of the volume's chapters remind us of the importance of social and political history in coalition formation. Guenther's study of coalition formation in East Germany shows how differing histories of interaction lead one East German women's group to pursue coalition work with a Swedish organization while another pursues ties with a West German group. Wiest, in comparing coalitions in Northeast and Southeast Asia, demonstrates that the political history of the two regions and the political system in the individual nations differentially shape the coalitions that form in the two regions. Thus, although political actors have agency in deciding on their strategy and strategic alliances, they do not approach these decisions with a blank slate. At any given point in time, they are influenced by their political and social histories.

Interactions among Political Context, Social Ties, and Ideology

As social movement researchers become increasingly sophisticated in their understanding of the causal processes shaping social movements, they consider that combinations of factors work together to produce movement outcomes of theoretical interest. For instance, Amenta and colleagues' (1992, 2005) political mediation model theorizes that movement policy success results from the actions of a well-mobilized social movement operating in a favorable political climate. Amenta and collaborators find that for the Townsend pension movement, the combination of a favorable political circumstance and heightened mobilization produced the movement's desired changes in policy. Similarly, in their study of the women's jury movements, McCammon et al. (2007) demonstrate that cultural conditions in the broader environment, such as legal rhetoric or opposition arguments, shape the political impact of the jury movements' frames. They too offer a causal argument of the combined effects of cultural context and movement framing.

Few coalition researchers have considered this interactive logic in exploring the circumstances that produce alliances among social movement groups. Staggenborg (1986) provides guidance in her study of coalition work among pro-choice groups, suggesting that a serious social or political threat may allow movement groups to overcome ideological differences to form coalitions. Reger's (2002) investigation of Cleveland NOW chapters provides a case in point. Cleveland's NOW members had been divided along class lines, but pro-life efforts to close local abortion clinics led to a unified, cross-class coalition among Cleveland NOW members. In the work of both of these researchers, the presence of a serious threat to the movement allowed activists to overcome significant ideological differences. Thus, their research reveals how a threat combined with ideological compatibility can work together to produce a coalition.

A unique contribution of this volume is its consideration of how various causal factors interact with one another to produce social movement coalitions. Although most of the chapters included here examine multiple factors that precipitate coalition formation, three of the volume's chapters explicitly explore the ways in which political contexts, social ties, and groups' ideological orientations may combine, resulting in a movement coalition. For instance, Borland describes how the recent political and economic crisis in Argentina, which posed a serious threat to the goals of the Argentine women's movement, inspired women's groups to overcome age-, representation-, and sexuality-based differences that had previously kept them separated. At the same time, some middle- and lower-income women's groups were never able to overcome their differences in identity and ideology in spite of sharing similar goals. Reese, Petit, and Meyer's study of the rapid mobilization of an anti–Iraq war coalition demonstrates how political threats can activate social ties and lead to mobilization. They find that movement activists who had crossed over from one movement group to another played an important role in forming the coalition. They conclude that the antiwar protests were both sudden and large due simultaneously to political threats and movement group social ties.

A final chapter in this section, authored by McCammon and Van Dyke, describes the results of a meta-analysis of coalition research. This chapter explores the combined causality of various factors identified in the literature as facilitating coalition formation, including political threats and opportunities, congruent ideologies and identities, and shared social ties. By means of qualitative comparative analysis, we identify the combinatorial and contingent conditions under which coalitions are likely to form. We find that there are multiple routes to coalition formation and that political threats, a shared ideology, and social ties often play an important role. Our results suggest that two factors, outside threats and a common ideology, may, at least in some cases, be sufficient conditions for coalition formation, while political opportunities are only a causal factor in combination with others. Thus, contrary to the emphasis in the broader social movement literature, political threats appear to be more important to coalition formation than are political opportunities.

The volume concludes with a chapter by Suzanne Staggenborg that highlights the collection's contributions and identifies areas for future research. Acknowledging that threats, and even in some cases new opportunities, can be primary causes of movement coalitions, Staggenborg encourages researchers to take the next step and begin investigating the kinds of threats and opportunities that lead to movement alliances. She also suggests that scholars pay more attention to movement communities because shared ideologies and frames (or lack thereof) as well as the structure of social ties and networks within these communities shape the ease with which coalitions can be formed and the importance of threats and leadership in generating coalition formation. In addition, Staggenborg calls for greater attention to the precise costs and benefits of coalition work for movement organizations. She also alerts us to the need for research into the organizational structures within coalitions that allow participants to mobilize resources across multiple groups, to identify leaders, and to pursue strategic action. Finally, she correctly notes that our volume, like much social movement coalition research, is focused on coalition formation rather than the outcomes of coalition work. Although studies of coalition formation remain few, research into the consequences of coalitions is even scarcer.

Conclusion

The research presented in this volume has important implications for scholarship and theory on coalitions as well as for the practice of coalition building. The work presented here makes significant empirical contributions to the literature on coalitions by demonstrating that prior social ties shape which organizations become involved in movement coalition work. Moreover, several of the chapters demonstrate that incompatible ideological elements can be sufficient to prevent a coalition from forming, even when groups share other interests. A shared history of interaction and the social ties it generates can help create congruent ideologies and pave the way for subsequent collaboration. Finally, although the movement literature reveals that political and economic threats can prompt reactive mobilization, our volume's research solidifies our knowledge that threats also can inspire progressive coalition work.

The modern era has been marked by some of the largest protests in world history. These protests, and the global justice movement that helped stage them, could not have occurred without the efforts of organizational coalitions. The work presented in this volume helps us better understand the variety of factors—an alignment of ideologies, goals, or identities; social ties generated through historic associations; and economic and political threats—that shape whether coalitions form and which organizations are likely to participate. As political and economic circumstances change, as organizations shift their ideological scope, and as social ties emerge and dissolve, so too will the shape and nature of contemporary coalitions develop and change.

Works Cited

Adam, Barry D. 1995. *The Rise of a Gay and Lesbian Movement.* New York: Twayne.

Almeida, Paul, and Linda Brewster Stearns. 1998. "Political Opportunities and Local Grassroots Environmental Movements: The Case of Minamata." *Social Problems* 45: 37–60.

Altemose, J. Rick, and Dawn A. McCarty. 2001. "Organizing for Democracy through Faith-Based Institutions: The Industrial Areas Foundation in Action." In *Forging Radical Alliances across Difference: Coalition Politics for the New Millennium,* edited by Jill M. Bystydzienski and Steven P. Schacht, 133–45. Lanham, Md.: Rowman & Littlefield.

Amenta, Edwin, and Yvonne Zylan. 1991. "It Happened Here: Political Opportunity, the New Institutionalism, and the Townsend Movement." *American Sociological Review* 56: 250–65.

Amenta, Edwin, Bruce G. Carruthers, and Yvonne Zylan. 1992. "A Hero for the Aged? The Townsend Movement, the Political Mediation Model, and U.S. Old-Age Policy, 1934–1950." *American Journal of Sociology* 98: 308–39.

Amenta, Edwin, Sheera Joy Olasky, and Neal Caren. 2005. "Age for Leisure? Political Mediation and the Impact of the Pension Movement on U.S. Old-Age Policy." *American Sociological Review* 70: 516–39.

Banaszak, Lee Ann. 1996. *Why Movements Succeed or Fail: Opportunity, Culture, and the Struggle for Woman Suffrage.* Princeton, N.J.: Princeton University Press.

Bandy, Joe. 2004. "Paradoxes of Transnational Civil Societies under Neoliberalism: The Coalition for Justice in the Maquiladoras." *Social Problems* 51: 410–31.

Bandy, Joe, and Jackie Smith. 2005. *Coalitions across Borders: Transnational Protest and the Neoliberal Order.* Lanham, Md.: Rowman & Littlefield.

Barkan, Steven E. 1986. "Interorganizational Conflict in the Southern Civil Rights Movement." *Sociological Inquiry* 56: 190–209.

Berry, Jeffrey M. 1997. *The Interest Group Society.* New York: Longman.

Bronfenbrenner, Kate, Sheldon Friedman, Richard W. Hurd, Rudolph A. Oswold, and Ronald L. Seeber, eds. 1998. *Organizing to Win: New Research on Union Strategies.* Cornell, N.Y.: ILR Press.

Bystydzienski, Jill M., and Steven P. Schacht, eds. 2001. *Forging Radical Alliances across Difference: Coalition Politics for the New Millennium.* Lanham, Md.: Rowman & Littlefield.

Cornfield, Daniel B., and Holly J. McCammon. 2003. "Revitalizing Labor: Global Perspectives and a Research Agenda." *Research in the Sociology of Work* 11: 1–20.

Croteau, David, and Lyndsi Hicks. 2003. "Coalition Framing and the Challenge of a Consonant Frame Pyramid: The Case of a Collaborative Response to Homelessness." *Social Problems* 50: 251–72.

D'Emilio, John. 1983. *Sexual Politics, Sexual Communities.* Chicago: University of Chicago Press.

Diaz-Veizades, Jeannette, and Edward T. Chang. 1996. "Building Cross-Cultural Coalitions: A Case-Study of the Black–Korean Alliance and the Latino–Black Roundtable." *Ethnic and Racial Studies* 19: 680–700.

Emery, Alan. 2005. "Revolution without the Revolution: On the Unintended Consequences of Illegitimate State Repression in South Africa." *Journal of Political and Military Sociology* 33: 209–30.

Ferree, Myra Marx, and Beth B. Hess. 1994. *Controversy and Coalition: The New Feminist Movement across Three Decades of Change.* New York: Twayne.

Ferree, Myra Marx, and Silke Roth. 1998. "Gender, Class, and the Interaction between Social Movements: A Strike of West Berlin Day Care Workers." *Gender and Society* 12: 626–48.

Gerhards, Jurgen, and Dieter Rucht. 1992. "Mesomobilization: Organizing and Framing in Two Protest Campaigns in West Germany." *American Journal of Sociology* 98: 555–95.

Gilmore, Stephanie. 2008. *Feminist Coalitions: Historical Perspectives on Second-Wave Feminism in the United States.* Champaign: University of Illinois Press.

Grossman, Zoltan. 2001. "'Let's not create evilness for this river': Interethnic Environmental Alliances of Native Americans and Rural Whites in Northern Wisconsin." In *Forging Radical Alliances across Difference: Coalition Politics for the New Millennium,* edited by Jill M. Bystydzienski and Steven P. Schacht, 146–59. London: Rowman & Littlefield.

Hathaway, Will, and David S. Meyer. 1993. "Competition and Cooperation in Social Movement Coalitions: Lobbying for Peace in the 1980s." *Berkeley Journal of Sociology* 38: 156–83.

Himmelstein, Jerome L. 1990. *To the Right: The Transformation of American Conservatism.* Berkeley: University of California Press.

Jenkins, J. Craig, and Kevin Leicht. 1997. "Class Analysis and Social Movements: A Critique and Reformulation." In *Reworking Class,* edited by John R. Hall, 369–97. Ithaca, N.Y.: Cornell University Press.

Jenkins, J. Craig, and Charles Perrow. 1977. "Insurgency of the Powerless: Farm Worker Movements (1946–1972)." *American Sociological Review* 42: 249–68.

Keck, Margaret E., and Kathryn Sikkink. 1998. *Activists beyond Borders: Advocacy Networks in International Politics.* Ithaca, N.Y.: Cornell University Press.

Kriesi, Hanspeter, Ruud Koopmans, Jan Willem Duyvendak, and Marco G. Giugni. 1995. *New Social Movements in Western Europe.* Minneapolis: University of Minnesota Press.

Lichterman, Paul. 1995. "Piecing Together Multicultural Community: Cultural Differences in Community Building among Grass-Roots Environmentalists." *Social Problems* 42: 513–34.

Lopez, Steven Henry. 2004. *Reorganizing the Rustbelt: An Inside Study of the American Labor Movement.* Berkeley: University of California Press.

Mazur, Jay. 2000. "Labor's New Internationalism." *Foreign Affairs* 79: 79–93.

McAdam, Doug. 1982. *Political Process and the Development of Black Insurgency, 1930–1970.* Chicago: University of Chicago Press.

———. 1988. *Freedom Summer.* New York: Oxford University Press.

McAdam, Doug, and Ronnelle Paulsen. 1993. "Social Ties and Activism: Towards a Specification of the Relationship." *American Journal of Sociology* 99: 640–67.

McCammon, Holly J., and Karen E. Campbell. 2002. "Allies on the Road to Victory: Coalition Formation between the Suffragists and the Woman's Christian Temperance Union." *Mobilization* 7: 231–51.

McCammon, Holly J., Courtney Muse Sanders, Harmony D. Newman, and Teresa M. Terrell. 2007. "Movement Framing and Discursive Opportunity Structures: The Political Successes of the U.S. Women's Jury Movements." *American Sociological Review* 72: 725–49.

McVeigh, Rory. 1999. "Structural Incentives for Conservative Mobilization: Power Devaluation and the Rise of the Ku Klux Klan, 1915–1925." *Social Forces* 77: 1461–96.

———. 2009. *The Rise of the Ku Klux Klan: Right-Wing Movements and National Politics.* Minneapolis: University of Minnesota Press.

Meyer, David S. 1993. "Institutionalizing Dissent: The United States Structure of Political Opportunity and the End of the Nuclear Freeze Movement." *Sociological Forum* 8: 157–79.

Meyer, David S., and Nancy Whittier. 1994. "Social Movement Spillover." *Social Problems* 42: 277–98.

Morris, Aldon. 1984. *The Origins of the Civil Rights Movement.* New York: Free Press.

Murphy, Gillian. 2005. "Coalitions and the Development of the Global Environmental Movement: A Double-Edged Sword." *Mobilization: An International Journal* 10: 235–50.

Obach, Brian K. 2004. *Labor and the Environmental Movement: A Quest for Common Ground.* Cambridge, Mass.: MIT Press.

Polletta, Francesca. 2002. *Freedom Is an Endless Meeting: Democracy in American Social Movements.* Chicago: University of Chicago Press.

Reger, Jo. 2002. "Organizational Dynamics and Construction of Multiple Feminist Identities in the National Organization for Women." *Gender and Society* 16: 710–27.

Rochon, Thomas R., and David S. Meyer. 1997. *Coalitions and Political Movements: Lessons of the Nuclear Freeze.* Boulder, Colo.: Lynne Rienner.

Rose, Fred. 2000. *Coalitions across the Class Divide: Lessons from the Labor, Peace, and Environmental Movements.* Ithaca, N.Y.: Cornell University Press.

Rupp, Leila J., and Verta Taylor. 1987. *Survival in the Doldrums: The American Women's Rights Movement, 1945 to the 1960s.* New York: Oxford University Press.

Schussman, Alan, and Sarah A. Soule. 2005. "Process and Protest: Accounting for Individual Protest Participation." *Social Forces* 84: 1083–106.

Shaffer, Martin B. 2000. "Coalition Work among Environmental Groups: Who Participates?" *Research in Social Movements, Conflict, and Change* 22: 111–26.

Smith, Jackie. 2004. "Exploring Connections between Global Integration and Political Mobilization." *Journal of World Systems Research* 10: 255–85.

Snow, David A., Louis A. Zurcher Jr., and Sheldon Ekland-Olson. 1980. "Social Networks and Social Movements: A Micro-Structural Approach to Differential Recruitment." *American Sociological Review* 45: 787–801.

Staggenborg, Suzanne. 1986. "Coalition Work in the Pro-Choice Movement: Organizational and Environmental Opportunities and Obstacles." *Social Problems* 33: 374–90.

Stearns, Linda Brewster, and Paul D. Almeida. 2004. "The Formation of State Actor–Social Movement Coalitions and Favorable Policy Outcomes." *Social Problems* 51: 478–504.

Tarrow, Sidney. 2005. *The New Transnational Activism.* New York: Cambridge University Press.

Taylor, Verta. 1996. *Rock-a-by Baby: Feminism, Self-Help, and Postpartum Depression.* New York: Routledge.

Van Dyke, Nella. 2003. "Crossing Movement Boundaries: Factors That Facilitate Coalition Protest by American College Students, 1930–1990." *Social Problems* 50: 226–50.

Van Dyke, Nella, and Sarah A. Soule. 2002. "Structural Social Change and the Mobilizing Effect of Threat: Explaining Levels of Patriot and Militia Mobilizing in the United States." *Social Problems* 49: 497–520.

Van Dyke, Nella, Marc Dixon, and Helen Carlon. 2007. "Manufacturing Dissent: Labor Revitalization, Union Summer and Student Protest." *Social Forces* 86: 193–214.

Voss, Kim, and Rachel Sherman. 2000. "Breaking the Iron Law of Oligarchy: Union Revitalization in the American Labor Movement." *American Journal of Sociology* 106: 303–49.

Whittier, Nancy. 1995. *Feminist Generations: The Persistence of the Radical Women's Movement.* Philadelphia: Temple University Press.

Williams, Heather L. 1999. "Mobile Capital and Transborder Labor Rights Mobilization." *Politics and Society* 27: 139–66.

Wilson, James Q. 1973. *Political Organizations.* New York: Basic Books.

Zald, Mayer N., and Roberta Ash. 1966. "Social Movement Organizations: Growth, Decay and Change." *Social Forces* 44: 327–40.

Zald, Mayer N., and John D. McCarthy. 1980. "Social Movement Industries: Competition and Cooperation among Movement Organizations." *Research in Social Movements, Conflicts, and Change* 3: 1–20.

I
Social Ties and the Development of Movement Coalitions

1

The Prehistory of a Coalition: The Role of Social Ties in Win Without War

Catherine Corrigall-Brown and David S. Meyer

On February 26, 2003, the day President George W. Bush sought public support for war with Iraq on prime-time television, American citizens staged a virtual march on the White House and Congress against the war. Activists reported that supporters delivered more than a million phone calls, e-mail messages, and faxes to the White House and Senate offices in eight hours. In fact, every senator's office and the White House switchboard received at least two, and often more, calls per minute, and many callers had to settle for busy signals. The goal of the march was to enable hundreds of thousands of Americans to "have their voices heard in Washington without leaving their homes and workplaces" (Win Without War 2003). This novel technique brought together concerned citizens from across the country and made it possible for many more people, regardless of their location, to express their concern about the possibility of a war in Iraq. How was this mass mobilization possible? From where did this innovative technique originate? These questions can be illuminated through an examination of the coalition of social movement organizations that created and coordinated this event, Win Without War.

Win Without War is a coalition of forty-one diverse groups opposed to the war in Iraq that engages in a range of traditional and innovative tactics, including advertising, press conferences, Internet organizing, and the virtual march on Washington. Groups whose primary identities are directed at issues of war and peace comprise slightly more than a quarter of the coalition. Like other social movements (see Van Dyke 2003), Win Without War also includes many groups whose political identities are primarily tied to other causes or constituencies (Figure 1.1).

Council for a Livable World
Fourth Freedom Forum
Peace Action
Veterans for Common Sense
Veterans for Peace
Artists United to Win Without War
Musicians United to Win Without War
Physicians for Social Responsibility
True Majority
Greenpeace
Sierra Club
American-Arab Anti-Discrimination Committee
Feminist Majority
NAACP
National Gay and Lesbian Task Force
National Organization for Women
Rainbow/Push Coalition
Soulforce
Women's Action for New Directions
Campaign for U.N. Reform
Education for Peace in Iraq Center
Global Exchange
Oxfam America
Conference of Major Superiors of Men
Leadership Conference of Women Religious
National Council of Churches
NETWORK A National Catholic Social Justice Lobby
Shalom Center
Sojourners
The Tikkun Community
Unitarian Universalist Association of Congregations
United Church of Christ
United Methodist Church General Board of Church and Society
Pax Christi USA
American Friends Service Committee
Business Leaders for Sensible Priorities
Families USA
MoveOn.org
Us Foundation
USAction
Working Assets

Figure 1.1. Member groups of Win Without War.

Win Without War is one example of large-scale coalition politics. The anti–Iraq war movement saw the development of many such coalitions internationally, and the months leading up to the war in Iraq were marked by unprecedented global protest against the planned attack. On coordinated dates in the middle of each month, from December 2002 to March 2003, millions of people demonstrated, marched, and rallied around the world. The crowds were largest in countries whose governments supported the planned war, such as in the United Kingdom, where the Stop the War coalition was active. Such coordinated and sustained international opposition to a war that had not yet started is a new development in protest politics.

To understand the creation and contours of the Win Without War coalition in the United States, we conducted twenty-six interviews with the main coalition leaders and with leaders of the member groups. These interviews ranged from fifteen minutes to an hour and a half, with most interviews lasting approximately forty-five minutes. We first interviewed the coalition's founding organizers. We next conducted interviews with leaders of the groups participating in the coalition. To identify the most appropriate contact, we asked the Win Without War organizers to name the people with whom they worked most closely in each group. In all cases, the Win Without War organizers identified individuals who were in official leadership positions (i.e., founder, chairperson, president), and we spoke with those people.

We propose that the decision of a social movement organization to join a coalition is akin to the decision of an individual to join a social movement. Although there is certainly a degree of rational calculus in this decision, as groups weigh the costs and benefits of cooperation, this rational choice has been overstated in the literature (e.g., Zald and McCarthy 1987). In fact, many elements of the decision to join a social movement coalition are not rational, at least in a narrow sense. Preexisting ties and dispositions of groups make them more or less likely to cooperate in particular coalitions, regardless of the instrumental rationality of doing so. In this way, each of the individuals and groups involved in a coalition has a history that makes them more or less available to participate in a given social movement and in a particular coalition. We seek to understand the role of this history in coalition creation through an examination of one social movement coalition, Win Without War.

We begin by reviewing past work on coalitions from a rational choice perspective, discussing the costs and benefits of joining coalitions for social movement organizations. We contend that the decision to join a social movement coalition is not discrete, but is rather the product of an accumulation of political, organizational, and leadership decisions in the past. Therefore, we claim that one must examine the role of past ties among individual activists and social movement organizations. Just as individuals have certain preexisting ties that make them more or less likely to join social movement organizations, social movement activists and organizations have preexisting ties that make them more or less likely to cooperate with one another in coalitions. To illustrate, we outline the preexisting ties of the six individuals at the original founding of Win Without War and examine how these ties created the substance and shape of this coalition.

Social Ties and Social Movement Coalitions

The act of joining a coalition for a social movement organization can be thought of as akin to the process whereby an individual joins a social movement organization, with multiple attendant considerations (Meyer and Corrigall-Brown 2005). One perspective that is given much attention in the literature is the assessment of the relative cost of participating as it is offset by the perceived benefit gained from cooperation with others. When examined through this rational choice perspective, it is clear that there are many benefits to coalition creation as a social movement tactic. Coalitions have access to a wide array of tangible and intangible resources (Benford 1993; Gray and Lowery 1998; Murphy 2005), introduce efficiencies in resource acquisition (Arnold 1994; Brown and Fox 2001; Hathaway and Meyer 1993), and can increase the political influence of member groups (Berry 1989; Staggenborg 1986).

There are also costs to participating in a coalition. Coalition cooperation can result in the loss of autonomy in decision making (Hojnacki 1997; Hula 1999), a need to alter strategies and tactical choices in compromise with partners (Hula 1999), and ideological or other conflicts with coalition allies (Arnold 1994; McCammon and Campbell 2002; Rose 2000; Staggenborg 1986). In addition, participation in a coalition can compromise organizational identity (Dalton 1994; Hathaway and Meyer 1993; Hojnacki 1997; Rose 2000) and make it more difficult to attract and maintain the support of individual members.

Clearly, groups assess the costs, risks, and benefits of participating in a coalition, but this assessment only follows an opportunity to join a particular coalition. As with individual participation in political activity, groups are generally recruited to participation (see Rosenstone and Hansen 1993 on individual mobilization), and the invitations are based on a group's identity, resources, affiliations, and reliability. There are many reasons why social ties facilitate recruitment to social movement organizations for individuals or social movement coalitions for organizations. Social movement activities are usually embedded in dense relational settings (Diani 2005), and the probability that individuals will join an organization depends on the number and strength of social network ties that connect group members to each other and to nonmembers (McPherson et al. 1992). In this way, integration into structural networks pulls individuals into social movements (McAdam 1986), and for this reason, individuals who are integrated into their community are more likely to engage in protest (Useem 1998).

For example, Morris (1981) finds that the Southern sit-in movement of the 1960s developed out of preexisting social networks such as churches, colleges, and protest organizations. These preexisting social structures provided the resources and communication networks that were critical to the spread of the movement. In her study of the women's movement, Freeman (1975) also finds that communication networks were important in that those women who were not connected into networks did not mobilize. These personal networks of friends provide individual incentives to participate (Opp and Gern 1993). They may also raise the personal costs for not participating. In addition, participation after recruitment is higher for those members who have more pre- and postrecruitment ties with other social movement organization (SMO) members (Barkan, Cohn, and Whitaker 1995).

Social ties are crucially important in the process of recruiting individuals to participate in social movements, and past research has repeatedly found that individuals rarely participate in protest and other political activities unless they are explicitly asked to do so (Klandermans 1997; Rosenstone and Hansen 1993; Verba, Schlozman, and Brady 1995). Many studies show that the presence of a network tie to someone already engaged in a movement is one of the strongest predictors of individual participation in the movement (Fernandez and McAdam 1988; Gerlach and Hine 1970; Gould 1990; Marwell, Oliver, and Prahl 1988; McAdam 1986; McAdam and Paulsen 1993; Nepstad and Smith 1999; Passy and Giugni 2001; Snow, Zurcher, and Ekland-Olson 1980; Von Eschen, Kirk, and Pinard 1971). Friends or acquaintances are thus the most effective recruiters.

McAdam's (1988) study of the Freedom Summer volunteers supports the importance of social ties in social movement mobilization. He finds that those who were more central in their networks were more likely to join and continue to participate in social movements over time. Although past activism does not matter directly, it affects one's current organizational memberships and thus one's location in the network. Networks increase an individual's chance of becoming involved and strengthen activists' attempts to further their causes. There is a dynamic, diachronic element to this process: although people often become involved in specific movements or campaigns through their preexisting links, their very participation also forges new bonds, which in turn affect subsequent developments in their activist careers (Diani 2005). We posit that just as relationships between individuals help to recruit people to SMOs, they also help recruit SMOs to social movement coalitions. This is because of past relationships between individual activists and organizations.

The past relationships among individuals and groups that make up a coalition are important for two main reasons. First, these relationships highlight the path dependence of recruitment to a social movement coalition such as Win Without War. The core group at the first meeting led to other contacts, and presumably neglected other potential allies. In this way, the composition of this initial group enabled some recruitment because individuals were more likely to sign on to a coalition in which they personally knew other members. At the same time, however, the makeup of the initial group restricted the possible groups that were asked to participate early on because only past allies were contacted.

The social ties among the individuals and groups that formed Win Without War also have important consequences for the cohesion of the coalition once formed. Recruiting along existing networks and ties leads to a coalition made up of groups that come to the table with high levels of trust already established. This trust made rapid mobilization possible because groups were able to freely exchange information and share resources immediately upon the creation of the coalition, which would not have been possible among strangers. The past ties among these groups and individuals also increased the level of consensus on goals and tactics, which facilitated organizing and mobilization within the coalition.

The Web of Core Activists and Organizations in Win Without War

On October 25, 2002, David, Alistair, Susan, Melissa, Eli, and Duane, long-time friends and allies, met for a meal at a Chinese restaurant. Hours earlier, they had all been sitting in a much larger and more crowded room where the antiwar umbrella coalition United for Peace and Justice had just been founded. All agreed that the coalition was important and would lead to widespread grassroots mobilization, but they were still concerned. They were "impatient with the tedious process and lack of focus during the all day session" (Cortright 2004, 16). They were also worried that United for Peace and Justice would be just another collection of the usual suspects and would not convince mainstream America to oppose the war in Iraq. It was at that table that they decided to form another coalition that would join together large, diverse SMOs. This coalition would work on Internet campaigns and advertising and would provide a mainstream voice for opposing the war. Within days, the coalition had grown further; it eventually encompassed forty-one groups. Win Without War was born.

The initial group's frustration with United for Peace and Justice created conditions that were ripe for the birth of Win Without War. In this way, the unhappiness among the core Win Without War organizers with the large size, and consequent perceived inefficiency, of United for Peace and Justice was the impetus for the birth of a more streamlined and professional organization. However, although the large scale of United for Peace and Justice drove these activists to organize Win Without War, United for Peace and Justice provided the foundation for the recruitment of organizational allies. So although the Win Without War organizers rejected working exclusively within United for Peace and Justice, it was in fact the contacts made through past activism, such as within United for Peace and Justice, that provided the critical foundation for Win Without War.

Coalitions such as Win Without War are the result of long-standing relationships among individuals and groups, and thus the networks of individual activists are crucial for predicting participation in a coalition. Individuals who have worked together in the past (even if under different organizational labels) have the networks and trust that allow them to more easily mobilize into coalitions, bringing their current organizational ties with them.[1] To examine how individual ties work in coalition creation, we will trace the activist trajectories of the six individuals who sat around the dinner table that first night and who were crucial in the creation of this coalition. The individuals present at this initial meeting are critical players in national progressive politics in the United States. In fact, many of them have celebrity status and extensive ties in progressive communities. We examine these ties and show how they were crucial in the creation and shaping of the coalition.

David Cortright is inarguably the hub of Win Without War. A longtime antiwar activist, Cortright fought in the Vietnam War from 1968 to 1971. He spent ten years, from 1978 to 1988, as the director of the Committee for Sane Nuclear Policy, a disarmament organization. He has also served as an advisor to various agencies of the United Nations, the Carnegie Commission on Preventing Deadly Conflict, the International Peace Academy, and the John D. and Catherine T. MacArthur Foundation. He has written widely on nuclear disarmament, nonviolent social change, and the use of incentives and sanctions as tools of international peacemaking. He is currently the director of policy studies at the Kroc Institute for International Peace Studies at the University of Notre Dame and chair of the Board of the Fourth Freedom Forum.

Alistair Millar is the director of the Center on Global Counter-Terrorism Cooperation, a nonpartisan research and policy institute that works to improve internationally coordinated responses to the continually evolving threat of terrorism by providing governments and international organizations with timely, policy-relevant research, analysis, and recommendations. He is also the vice president of the Fourth Freedom Forum and director of its Washington, D.C., office. Previously Millar was a senior analyst at the British American Security Information Council, where he focused on European security issues.

Both Cortright and Millar are directors of the Fourth Freedom Forum, an organization founded by international businessperson Howard Breembeck. The group works to create "a more civilized world based on the force of law rather than the law of force" (Fourth Freedom Forum 2006). By encouraging the effective use of economic incentives and sanctions, the group works to create a more secure and peaceful future. They work in four main areas: counterterrorism, nonproliferation, sanctions and security, and nonviolent social change.

Susan Shaer, who became cochair of Win Without War, is the executive director of Women's Action for New Directions. Helen Caldicott founded this organization in 1982 as Women's Action for Nuclear Disarmament, a group active in the antinuclear mobilization of the 1980s.[2] After the end of the cold war, the group reinvented itself in light of dramatically altered political circumstances. The new formation, Women's Action for New Directions, expanded its profile and called for a redirection of federal budget priorities away from the military and toward human needs. Its expressed goals are to challenge and promote alternatives to militarism as the solution to conflict; to shift from a military-based to a civilian-based economy to address the threats to security, ensuring that human, economic, and environmental needs are met; to clean up the environmental effects of nuclear weapons production and toxic waste at all military facilities and prevent further contamination; to eliminate the testing, production, sale, and use of weapons of mass destruction; to prevent violence against women; and to increase women's political leadership to further Women's Action for New Directions' goals (http://www .wand.org/).

As well as serving as executive director of Women's Action for New Directions, Shaer directs Project Abolition, the National Council for Peace and Justice, and other national projects on arms control and disarmament. In addition to her antiwar and disarmament work, she has chaired the Massachusetts Supreme Court case to equalize educational funding, cofounded (with Congressman John Oliver) the progressive tax lobbying group Tax Equity Alliance for Massachusetts, served as president of the League of Women Voters of Massachusetts (mid-1970s to late 1980s), and sat on the national board of directors of the league. She serves on the advisory board of *Teen Voices* magazine and works with Promoting Enduring Peace and the Center on Peace and Liberty.

MoveOn.org (http://www.moveon.org/), represented at the table by Eli Pariser, was founded by Joan Blades and Wes Boyd. They shared a frustration with the partisan warfare in Washington, D.C., over the possible impeachment of Bill Clinton. On September 18, 1998, they launched an online petition to "Censure President Clinton and Move On to Pressing Issues Facing the Nation." Within days, they had over 300,000 signatures. In 1998, the MoveOn.org PAC was formed as a political action committee so that like-minded concerned citizens could influence the outcome of congressional elections and in turn the balance of power in Washington, D.C. Eli Pariser independently founded the MoveOn.org Peace campaign, in response to the Bush administration's conduct of the war on terrorism. After the September 11, 2001, attack on the World Trade Center, Pariser established a Web site with a petition calling for a restrained and multilateral response to the attacks, which was signed by over a half million people. Eli joined forces with MoveOn.org in November 2001, and since this time, he has directed MoveOn.org's campaign against the war in Iraq, tripling its membership in three years. Before his involvement in the antiwar movement, Pariser was involved in the antiglobalization movement.

Melissa Daar worked as the state political manager for Working Assets, an organization established in 1985 to help "busy people make a difference in the world through everyday activities like talking on the phone." Every time a customer uses one of Working Assets' donation-linked services (long distance, wireless, and credit cards), the company donates a portion of the charges to nonprofit groups working to build a "world that is more just, humane, and environmentally sustainable" (Working Assets 2010). To date, Working Assets reports raising more than $50 million for progressive causes. The group donates to five categories of nonprofit groups: economic and social justice, environment, civil rights, peace and international freedom, and education and freedom of expression. In 1991, Working Assets created the Citizen Action program to provide customers with timely information and easy ways to speak out on important issues.

The final person at the table was Duane Peterson. Since 1996, Peterson has been "chief of stuff" at True Majority. True Majority was founded by Ben Cohen, cofounder of Ben and Jerry's Ice Cream. It is a grassroots education and advocacy project of Priorities Inc., a nonprofit, nonpartisan group with a reported membership of more than 500,000 people. It seeks to increase federal investment in education, health care, job training, energy independence, and world hunger by eliminating unnecessary Pentagon weapons systems.

Business Leaders for Sensible Priorities,[3] another branch of Priorities Inc., is a group of 750 professional businesspeople who advocate for the allocation of more federal budget dollars to education, health care, and environmental protection.

The capsule biographies above indicate that the decision to form a new coalition to oppose the war in Iraq was almost a characteristic response of those dining together. None was new to activism, and all saw their efforts against war as being linked to a wide range of other issues. Furthermore, the distinct professional experiences each member had as an activist before Win Without War afforded a host of potential organizational and personal contacts with like-minded people.

The Coverage of Ties

The ties between the individual activists present at the first dinner meeting created the shape of Win Without War. There was a conscious attempt to "go through all the Rolodexes,"[4] and they sought to work with individuals they knew in "past incarnations." It is important to note that they did not necessarily seek out groups with whom they had previously worked, although this did happen. Instead, they relied on personal contacts with individuals and asked those individuals to bring their current organizational memberships with them. In fact, one of the key organizers notes that they "did not approach anyone blind": everyone who was contacted was known by the core organizers or "knew people who knew people."

The five individuals at the first meeting personally knew or had worked with people in an additional twenty-four of the Win Without War organizations. Although this core of five people only represents 12 percent of the final coalition, by simply including individuals these activists knew personally or with whom they had personally worked, we increase our coverage of the final Win Without War roster to 71 percent—twenty-nine of the forty-one group members. The core and their contacts make up most of this coalition. When we also take into account the ties of this second (noncore) tier, we can see clear personal connections between this group and an additional six groups. This increases our coverage of the final Win Without War roster to 85 percent. Therefore, personal ties between our core and second tier with other activists can explain the recruitment, participation, and selection of nearly all the groups that composed Win Without War. It is clear that not all individuals are as likely to be asked to join a coalition. Instead, social ties between individuals are highly predictive of which groups and individuals are targets of mobilization.

What explains the selection of the final six groups? Four of these groups came to Win Without War seeking to join. These individuals did not have direct ties with Win Without War organizers or member groups. However, because of the political context leading up to the war in Iraq, groups had an incentive to join this coalition, both because the issue was of concern to their membership and because it was the only issue getting any media attention at the time. In addition, one of these groups was sought out by Win Without War organizers because of its central role in United for Peace and Justice (Global Exchange). Win Without War organizers explicitly sought to keep ties with United for Peace and Justice by fostering overlapping connections between these two coalitions. Finally, one of these groups was chosen because of its specific connection to the issues surrounding the Iraq war (the American-Arab Anti-Discrimination Committee). This group had not been a past ally, but because of the particular nature of this campaign, the organizers were motivated to leave their network of activists to strengthen the legitimacy of their coalition.

The overlapping ties between the core six individuals were particularly dense (Figure 1.2). These ties were primarily through joint cooperation in United for Peace and Justice and the Monday Lobby Group, a weekly meeting of members of peace and security groups who share information regarding lobbying on the Hill in Washington, D.C. All five groups the original six individuals currently represent participated in United for Peace and Justice, and three of the five were in the Monday Lobby Group. These overlapping ties created a foundation for the creation of Win Without War. In addition, many of these individuals knew one another personally from past campaigns, such as the Sane Nuclear Policy/Freeze campaign, a large movement against the arms race in the early 1980s, in which Cortright played an important leadership role (Meyer 1990).

Example of Past Ties: Freeze Campaign

To illustrate the past ties between individuals that fostered the growth of Win Without War beyond the core six activists, let us examine the historical connections between activists resulting from participation in the Sane Nuclear Policy/Freeze campaign. David Cortright, one of the core founders of Win Without War, was the director of Sane Nuclear Policy from 1978 to 1988. This organization later became known as Peace Action (a coalition member), and this group's current leader, Kevin Martin, counts Cortright as a "personal friend and colleague." Bob Edgar (from the National Council of Churches) and Mary Lord (now at the American Friends Service Committee) both worked with Cortright in the Freeze campaign. In addition, Duane Shank (now at Sojourners) had worked with Cortright and Bob Musil (from

	David Cortright	Alistair Millar	Susan Shaer	Melissa Daar	Duane Peterson	Eli Pariser
David Cortright (Fourth Freedom Forum)	—	1. Work together at Fourth Freedom Forum	1. Worked on past nuclear disarmament campaigns 2. Both groups in Monday Lobby Group 3. Both groups in United for Peace and Justice	1. Both groups in United for Peace and Justice	1. Worked together at Sane Nuclear Policy/ Freeze campaign 2. Both groups in United for Peace and Justice 3. Both in Monday Lobby Group	1. Both in United for Peace and Justice
Alistair Millar (Fourth Freedom Forum)	1. Work together at Fourth Freedom Forum 2. Both groups in Monday Lobby Group 3. Both groups in United for Peace and Justice	—	1. Worked on past nuclear disarmament campaigns 2. Both groups in Monday Lobby Group 3. Both groups in United for Peace and Justice	1. Both groups in United for Peace and Justice	1. Know through David Cortright 2. Both groups in United for Peace and Justice 3. Both groups in Monday Lobby Group	1. Both groups in United for Peace and Justice
Susan Shaer (Women's Action for New Directions)	1. Worked on past nuclear disarmament campaigns 2. Both groups in Monday Lobby Group 3. Both groups in United for Peace and Justice	1. Worked on past nuclear disarmament campaigns 2. Both groups in Monday Lobby Group 3. Both groups in United for Peace and Justice	—	1. Susan's husband worked with Melissa 2. Both groups in United for Peace and Justice	1. True Majority/ Women's Action for New Directions worked in past coalitions 2. Both groups in United for Peace and Justice	1. Fight to prevent Clinton Impeachment 2. Both groups in United for Peace and Justice

Member						
Melissa Daar (Working Assets)	1. Both groups in United for Peace and Justice	1. Both groups in United for Peace and Justice	1. Susan's husband worked with Melissa 2. Both groups in United for Peace and Justice	—	1. Both groups in United for Peace and Justice	1. Both groups in United for Peace and Justice
Duane Peterson (True Majority/Business Leaders for Sensible Priorities)	1. Worked together at Sane Nuclear Policy/Freeze campaign 2. Both groups in United for Peace and Justice	1. Know through David Cortright 2. Both groups in United for Peace and Justice	1. True Majority/Women's Action for New Directions worked in past coalitions 2. Both groups in United for Peace and Justice	1. Founder of True Majority (Ben Cohen) helped launch Women's Action 2. Knew founder of Women's Action 3. Both groups in United for Peace and Justice	—	1. Met when True Majority was founded 2. Both groups in United for Peace and Justice
Eli Pariser (MoveOn.org)	1. Both groups in United for Peace and Justice	1. Both groups in United for Peace and Justice	1. Fight to prevent Clinton impeachment 2. Both groups in United for Peace and Justice	1. Both groups in United for Peace and Justice	1. Met when True Majority was founded 2. Both groups in United for Peace and Justice	—

Figure 1.2. Overlapping ties of the original six members of Win Without War.

Physicians for Social Responsibility) at Sane Nuclear Policy. In 1988, Musil gave Ben Cohen (True Majority/Business Leaders for Sensible Priorities) a peace award at Sane Nuclear Policy. Finally, Arthur Waskow (now at the Shalom Center) knew Cortright from a period when he was a fellow at the Institute for International Policy Studies in Washington. It is clear that the ties resulting from connections in this one past campaign contributed to a dense web of connections that made the creation of Win Without War possible. Even though many of these individuals are now working and active in different groups, they were able to rely on these past personal connections to mobilize into a coalition.

Example of New Ties: Take Back America Conference

The ties between the individuals and groups that came to compose Win Without War are the result of the historical social connections between individual activists, and these ties do not stop with the organization of Win Without War. They are also the foundation for future cooperation. The successful cooperation of these groups in the creation of Win Without War made it more likely that they would cooperate again in the future. One example of cooperation that occurred after the mobilization against the war in Iraq was the Campaign for America's Future. This campaign brings together prominent Americans who seek to "challenge the big money corporate agenda by encouraging Americans to speak up—to discuss and debate a new vision of an economy and a future that works for all of us" (http://home.ourfuture .org/). The Campaign for America's Future works to revitalize a progressive agenda and fights for the interests of working people. Many of the individuals representing organizations involved in Win Without War are now involved in this coalition—for example, People for the American Way, Sierra Club, USAction, MoveOn.org, Working Assets, True Majority/Business Leaders for Sensible Priorities, Women's Action for New Directions, Physicians for Social Responsibility, Veterans for Peace, NAACP, NOW, and Tom Andrews (an organizer at Win Without War). This new cooperative venture includes thirteen of the forty-one Win Without War coalition members. The campaign is a clear continuation of the cooperation and ties built and reinforced by participation in the Win Without War coalition.

Conclusion

Through an analysis of Win Without War, we show that coalitions are not de novo formations but instead are created out of existing relationships and ties that are activated in conducive political contexts. Although groups surely weigh the costs and benefits of participating in a coalition, not all groups are equally likely to join, regardless of the instrumental rationality or irrationality of doing so; nor are all groups equally likely to be recruited. Instead, some individuals and groups are more attractive, and more available, for mobilization because of past cooperation. These ties make it more likely that they will be targets for recruitment to a coalition. In addition, these ties make it more likely that they will agree to work in coalition because of high levels of trust fostered by past collaboration.

Our analysis reveals that these social ties are clearly highly influential in creating the shape and substance of social movement coalitions. In this coalition, a full 85 percent of the final list of coalition members were personally known by either the original six individuals at the organizing meeting or someone they knew personally. Individuals were not recruited based solely on the basis of the rationality of having them as coalition partners, and not all groups were equally likely to be asked to participate.

In addition, joint participation in past campaigns and coalitions, such as the Sane Nuclear Policy/Freeze campaign and the United for Peace and Justice coalition, was a place where potentially sympathetic allies could meet and create relationships. These ties later came to facilitate recruitment to Win Without War. Finally, social ties provided the foundation for future coalition creation, such as the Take Back America conference, which overlaps with the Win Without War coalition. Our analysis of Win Without War sheds light on the role of preexisting ties between groups and individual activists that lead to both the creation and the form of social movement coalitions.

To the extent that analysts view each emergence of dissent as a distinct social movement, they run the risk of distorting the reality of activist politics and oversimplifying both the origins of social movements and their ultimate effects. The case we describe here clearly demonstrates interconnections among ostensibly distinct social movement organizations. We see these connections through organizational alliances and personal affiliations that are developed through political contacts and personal or professional careers (Meyer and Whittier 1994). Movement formations respond to changes in political opportunities that make some issues more attractive or urgent for mobilization at particular times, but frequently new mobilization is the result not only of newly engaged organizations and activists, but also the redirection of existing individuals and groups. The institutionalization of a wide range of professional advocacy groups (Berry 1989; McCarthy and Zald 1977; Meyer and Tarrow 1998) affords committed people ongoing opportunities to try to change the world, if not in circumstances they choose. The results of previous campaigns, regardless of the campaigns' direct political accomplishments, generally provide a more dense institutional infrastructure and web of personal relationships available to respond to new provocations and opportunities.

Although it is analytically convenient to pick precise dates for the sudden emergence of any social movement, and certainly for any new organization or coalition, close examination of Win Without War demonstrates that it is founded on a dense web of affiliations and experiences, all shaped by prior political activism. Certainly, there is no reason to believe that other coalitions would be appreciably different on this score. The decision to respond to an invitation to join a coalition results from what is often a long process of being in a position to be invited to join. To be sure, risks, costs, and benefits are relevant, but they are calculated over a long period of time, not in the snapshot of a particular decision. Activism and coalition building represent a moving picture.

Notes

1. Importantly, activist careers generally include service in a number of different political organizations in the service of several related causes (Meyer and Whittier 1994).

2. Caldicott herself, a physician from Australia, had been working in the movement against nuclear power through a revitalized older group, Physicians for Social Responsibility (Meyer 1990), which is also a Win Without War coalition member.

3. Business Leaders for Sensible Priorities is also a coalition member.

4. All unattributed quotations are taken from interviews with twenty-six individuals who were Win Without War organizers or leaders of member organizations. To protect their anonymity, their names and the names of their organizations are not associated with individual quotations.}

Works Cited

Arnold, Gretchen. 1994. "Dilemmas of Feminist Coalitions: Collective Identity and Strategic Effectiveness in the Battered Women's Movement." In *Feminist Organizations: Harvest of the New Women's Movement,* edited by Myra Marx Feree and Patricia Yancey Martin, 276–90. Philadelphia: Temple University Press.

Barkan, S. E., S. F. Cohn, and W. H. Whitaker. 1995. "Beyond Recruitment—Predictors of Differential Participation in a National Antihunger Organization." *Sociological Forum* 10: 113–34.

Benford, Robert. 1993. "Frame Disputes within the Nuclear Disarmament Movement." *Social Forces* 71: 677–701.

Berry, Jeffrey M. 1989. *The Interest Group Society.* Glenview, Ill.: Scott, Foresman.

Brown, L. David, and Jonathan Fox. 2001. "Transnational Civil Society Coalitions and the World Bank: Lessons from Project and Policy Influence Campaigns."

In *Global Citizen Action,* edited by Michael Edwards and John Gaventa, 43–58. Boulder, Colo.: Lynne Rienner Press.

Cortright, David. 2004. *A Peaceful Superpower: The Movement against War in Iraq.* Goshen, Ind.: Fourth Freedom Foundation.

Dalton, Russell J. 1994. *The Green Rainbow: Environmental Groups in Western Europe.* New Haven, Conn.: Yale University Press.

Diani, Mario. 2005. "Networks and Participation." In *The Blackwell Companion to Social Movements,* edited by David A. Snow, Sarah A. Soule, and Hanspeter Kriesi, 339–59. Malden, Mass.: Blackwell.

Fernandez, Roberto, and Doug McAdam. 1988. "Social Networks and Social Movements: Multiorganizational Fields and Recruitment to Mississippi Freedom Summer." *Sociological Forum* 3: 357–82.

Fourth Freedom Forum. 2006. http://www.fourthfreedomforum.org/. Accessed October 21, 2006.

Freeman, Jo. 1975. *The Politics of Women's Liberation: A Case Study of an Emerging Social Movement and Its Relation to the Policy Process.* New York: David McKay.

Gerlach, Luther P., and Virginia H. Hine. 1970. *People, Power, Change: Movements of Social Transformation.* Indianapolis, Ind.: Bobbs-Merrill.

Gould, Roger V. 1990. "Social Structure and Insurgency in the Paris Commune, 1871." PhD diss., Harvard University.

Gray, Virginia, and David Lowery. 1998. "To Lobby Alone or in a Flock: Foraging Behavior among Organized Interests." *American Politics Quarterly* 26: 5–34.

Hathaway, Will, and David S. Meyer. 1993. "Competition and Cooperation in Social Movement Coalitions: Lobbying for Peace in the 1980s." *Berkeley Journal of Sociology* 38: 157–83.

Hojnacki, Marie. 1997. "Interest Groups' Decisions to Join Alliances or Work Alone." *American Journal of Political Science* 41: 61–87.

Hula, Kevin W. 1999. *Lobbying Together: Interest Group Coalitions in Legislative Politics.* Washington, D.C.: Georgetown University Press.

Klandermans, Bert. 1997. *The Social Psychology of Protest.* Oxford: Blackwell.

Marwell, Gerald, Pamela E. Oliver, and Ralph Prahl. 1988. "Social Networks and Collective Action—A Theory of the Critical Mass." *American Journal of Sociology* 94: 502–34.

McAdam, Doug. 1986. "Recruitment to High-Risk Activism: The Case of Freedom Summer." *American Journal of Sociology* 92: 64–90.

———. 1988. *Freedom Summer.* New York: Oxford University Press.

McAdam, Doug, and R. Paulsen. 1993. "Specifying the Relationship between Social Ties and Activism." *American Journal of Sociology* 99: 640–67.

McCammon, Holly J., and Karen E. Campbell. 2002. "Allies on the Road to Victory:

Coalition Formation between the Suffragists and the Woman's Christian Temperance Union." *Mobilization* 7: 231–51.

McCarthy, John D., and Mayer N. Zald 1977. "Resource Mobilization and Social Movements: A Partial Theory." *American Journal of Sociology* 82: 1212–41.

McPherson, J. Miller, Paula A. Popielarz, and Sonja Drobnic. 1992. "Social Networks and Organizational Dynamics." *American Sociological Review* 57: 153–70.

Meyer, David S. 1990. *A Winter of Discontent: The Nuclear Freeze and American Politics.* New York: Praeger.

Meyer, David S., and Catherine Corrigall-Brown. 2005. "Coalitions and Political Context: U.S. Movements against Wars in Iraq." *Mobilization* 10: 327–44.

Meyer, David S., and Sidney Tarrow, eds. 1998. *The Social Movement Society.* Lanham, Md.: Rowman & Littlefield.

Meyer, David S., and Nancy Whittier. 1994. "Social Movement Spillover." *Social Problems* 41: 277–98.

Morris, Aldon. 1981. "Black Southern Student Sit-in Movement: An Analysis of Internal Organization." *American Sociological Review* 46: 744–67.

Murphy, Gillian. 2005. "Coalitions and the Development of the Global Environmental Movement: A Double-Edged Sword." *Mobilization* 10: 235–50.

Nepstad, Sharon E., and Christian Smith. 1999. "Rethinking Recruitment to High-Risk/Cost Activism: The Case of Nicaragua Exchange." *Mobilization* 4: 25–40.

Opp, Karl Dieter, and Christiane Gern. 1993. "Dissident Groups, Personal Networks, and Spontaneous Cooperation: The East-German Revolution of 1989." *American Sociological Review* 58: 659–80.

Passy, Florence, and Marco Giugni. 2001. "Social Networks and Individual Perceptions: Explaining Differential Participation in Social Movements." *Sociological Forum* 16: 123–53.

Rose, Fred. 2000. *Coalitions across the Class Divide: Lessons from the Labor, Peace, and Environmental Movements.* Ithaca, N.Y.: Cornell University Press.

Rosenstone, Steven J., and John Mark Hansen. 1993. *Mobilization, Participation, and Democracy in America.* New York: Macmillan.

Snow, David A., Louis A. Zurcher, and Sheldon Ekland-Olson. 1980. "Social Networks and Social Movements: A Microstructural Approach to Differential Recruitment." *American Sociological Review* 45: 787–801.

Staggenborg, Suzanne. 1986. "Coalition Work in the Pro-Choice Movement." *Social Problems* 33: 374–89.

Useem, Bert. 1998. "Breakdown Theories of Collective Action." *Annual Review of Sociology* 24: 215–38.

Van Dyke, Nella. 2003. "Crossing Movement Boundaries: Factors That Facilitate Coalition Protest by American College Students, 1930–1990." *Social Problems* 49: 497–520.

Verba, Sidney, Kay Lehman Schlozman, and Henry E. Brady. 1995. *Voice and Equality: Civic Voluntarism in American Politics.* Cambridge, Mass.: Harvard University Press.

Von Eschen, Donald, Jerome Kirk, and Maurice Pinard. 1971. "Organizational Substructure of Disorderly Politics." *Social Forces* 49: 529–44.

Win Without War. 2003. Press release. February 26. http://www.winwithoutwarus.org/html/preleases/pr_022603.pdf. Accessed April 2, 2010.

Working Assets. 2010. http://www.workingassets.com/PressRoom/article.aspx?id=4. Accessed April 2, 2010.

Zald, Mayer N., and John D. McCarthy. 1987. "Social Movement Industries: Competition and Conflict among SMOs." In *Social Movements in an Organizational Society,* edited by Mayer Zald and John McCarthy, 161–80. New Brunswick, N.J.: Transaction.

2

Policing Capital: Armed Countermovement Coalitions against Labor in Late Nineteenth-Century Industrial Cities

Larry Isaac

By the late 1870s, the nascent American labor movement was becoming increasingly locked in a struggle with local employer countermovements. Many employers worked to negatively frame and actively destroy unions intent on organizing their workers. Workers often responded by striking against their bosses. These contentious relations led to the great flash points of class struggle during the Gilded Age decades of the late nineteenth century: the national rail strike (1877), the massive eight-hour strikes (1886), Homestead steelworkers' and New Orleans dockworkers' (1892) strikes, and the Pullman strike (1894), among others. Employers mobilized police (Johnson 1976), hired private detective agencies (Smith 2003), maintained full-time company armies on their own payroll (Mahon 1983; Smith 2003), relied on federal troops (Cooper 1977) and the courts (McCammon 1993), and mobilized a variety of other local organizations, including employers' associations, citizens' associations, vigilance committees, and irregular armed forces in the form of private militias (Isaac and Harrison 2006). In many urban centers, these forms of collective action were linked together, constituting coalitions with local state authorities. This chapter examines one of these forms, armed coalitions between employers and municipal governments, across several Northern industrial cities during the rise of American industrial capitalism.

There is a growing body of research on social movement coalitions, but it is nonetheless surprisingly small relative to the significance of the topic. Even less attention has been focused on state actor–social movement coalition formation, and research on countermovement–state actor coalitions is almost nonexistent (exceptions addressed below). This is especially surprising given the large body of research on the importance of elites and the state.

The extent to which the state is autonomous from capital or to which it is in fact deeply embedded in capitalist structural logic or manipulated by capitalist elites are key questions in political sociology. In social movement studies, the state typically appears as a movement target or as part of the political opportunity structure, but it seldom appears as a coalition partner with a countermovement.

I contribute to filling the latter void by illuminating a particular type of countermovement–state coalition: private organizations of businessmen[1] who formed their own militias and entered into coalitions with local governments during the latter decades of the nineteenth century. These irregular armed forces,[2] who were often men from elite families financed by the families and their business or citizens' associations, joined with state forces—police, some preexisting public militias, and the U.S. Army—to produce an augmented institutional front to counter labor mobilizations in the wake of the first national labor revolt during the summer of 1877 (Isaac 2002).

My analysis uses materials from late nineteenth-century American political history along with primary and secondary evidence for several elite militia organizations from Northern industrial cities (Chicago, Illinois; Cleveland, Ohio; Scranton, Pennsylvania; Coal Creek, Indiana). I seek to answer three basic questions. How were these organizations of irregular armed forces allied with local governments? What were the major conditions that contributed to the production of these private countermovement organization–state armed force coalitions? And what sort of historical trajectory did these coalitions follow? The answers to these questions contain important implications for the study of movement coalitions, especially countermovement–state coalitions and theories of the state more generally, and they illuminate ways in which private actors have become involved in the policing of protest movements.

Movements and Coalitions

A small but growing body of work examines both the internal dynamics of coalitions and external factors giving rise to them (Van Dyke and McCammon, this volume). Coalitions are usually conceptualized as instrumental and contingent relations, organized to pursue goals but not necessarily long-term relationships. Research on these coalition relations can be organized along three different axes: movement–movement, movement–state, and countermovement–state.

Movement–Movement Coalition Formation

Scholarly analysis of coalition formation between distinct social movements has identified a variety of conditions that facilitate this process, including cultural features of different social movement organizations (SMOs), the external political environment, and personal linkages between SMOs. Relatively similar SMO cultural dimensions further coalition formation. Specifically, evidence suggests that coalition formation between different SMOs increases when they have multi-issue agendas (Van Dyke 2003), ideological congruence (McCammon and Campbell 2002), collective identity congruence (Rose 2000), and master frame commonality (Obach 2004).

Several studies suggest that shared threats are important in fostering coalitions because threats to movements or their goals can be significant inducements for movement actors to seek partners. In their study of suffragist and Woman's Christian Temperance Union coalition formation, McCammon and Campbell (2002, 232) put it this way: "When movement actors are frustrated in attempts to achieve their goals . . . they will be more willing to seek out new strategies, including the strategy of collaboration with another movement." Likewise in her study of college student protest from 1930 to 1990, Van Dyke (2003) finds that threats played a significant role in stimulating coalition formation (see also Rohlinger 2006).

A variety of studies have pointed to the role of activists who serve to bridge two different movements. For example, Rose (2000) describes bridge builders who act as brokers between the distinct class cultures that characterize different movements, such as working-class unionists and middle-class environmental activists. Obach (2004, 206–7) points to coalition brokers who identify SMOs that have a commonality or stake in a particular issue and who reach out to provide motivation for coalition formation by engaging in frame alignment processes. Activists who straddle multiple organizational cultures are likely to be particularly well suited to this role (Isaac and Christiansen 2002, 727; Obach 2004, 209).

Movement–State Coalition Formation

Social movement–state coalitions have received little scholarly attention, but several relevant studies have appeared. Stearns and Almeida (2004) analyzed coalition formation between Japanese antipollution movement and state actors from the mid-1950s to the mid-1970s, whereby four key groups of state actors—weak state (social) agencies, oppositional political parties, local governments, and the courts—became linked in alliance with the Japanese environmental movement. According to the authors, movement–state coalition formation is dependent on state institutional structure—for example, bureaucratic development, electoral system, and state authority fragmentation. Under the assumption of a democratic state, the more highly developed the state bureaucracy, the greater the probability that a social movement will form a coalition with a state agency. Moreover, Stearns and Almeida (2004) believe that such coalitions are most likely to occur with state agencies whose primary mission is rooted in the social policy arena, such as social welfare, antidiscrimination, or labor.

The fragmentation of political authority characteristic of federalist political structures also matters for movement–state coalition prospects, according to Stearns and Almeida (2004). Because such state structures increase the number of entry points, the potential for coalitions with the state is expanded. But multiple openings are not likely to be uniformly movement receptive across governmental levels. The authors argue that local–municipal governments are more likely to offer pair-up points because of the greater volatility of local electoral politics and spatial accessibility (Sewell 2001).

What movement actors and states do with each other has potential significance for what they become. Going beyond the conventional political opportunity structure approach, Wolfson's (2001) study of the relationship between the antismoking movement and the state argues that the growth and strength of that movement was due in part to "state–movement interpenetration," a condition where "state and movement organizations have a symbiotic relationship that involves both mutual influence and mutual benefit" (Wolfson 2001, 189). Central to the tobacco control movement, according to Wolfson, was the fact that the movement nested itself inside certain state bureaucratic ports that eventually developed into an integral feature of the movement itself.

Political institutional structures do matter for state–movement coalition formation. But as we know from movement studies generally, meaning construction is also central to movement–state coalition processes, as Croteau and Hicks (2003) have demonstrated. Their key observation is that if they are to avoid the costly damage of frame disputes, coalitions must produce a "consonant frame pyramid" that simultaneously aligns individual, organizational, and coalition frames (Croteau and Hicks 2003, 265).

Countermovement–State Coalition Formation

Whenever a social movement grows in potential political and/or cultural importance, it will generate opposition, which often takes the form of another movement—a countermovement (Lo 1982; Meyer and Staggenborg 1996, 1630), a collective, organized, and sustained opposition. The conceptual literature on countermovements has little to say about coalitions generally or those specifically formed with state actors. But there are some suggestive insights. Mottl (1980, 625) hypothesized that countermovements are more likely to form from coalitions among organizations with previous links to major institutions, such as the state, which can give countermovements a re-source advantage over challenging movements (Zald and Useem 1987, 257). States shape movements (Goldstone 2003) and countermovements (Meyer and Staggenborg 1996) in a variety of significant ways. However, we know very little about when, where, how, and with what effect counter-movements enter into coalitional processes with state authorities. Very few studies have focused on the formation of coalitional relations between private countermovement organizations and public entities. This unknown terrain of state–countermovement relations has been recognized, and calls for research have appeared in work on social movement–state coalitions (Stearns and Almeida 2004, 498) and in research on the social control of protest (Earl 2004, 59, 78).

Two scholars do, however, highlight movement–state–countermovement relations. In a study examining local state response to countermovement violence across Southern states, Luders (2003) finds that the character of a movement–countermovement relationship is highly contingent on state action. In this case, the relationship in Southern states between the civil rights move-ment and the white supremacist countermovement was shaped in significant ways by the kinds of actions or inactions undertaken by local state authori-ties. In a second study, Irons (2006) focuses on the relationship between the Mississippi State Sovereignty Commission (a public entity) and the White Citizen's Council (a private countermovement organization) during the South-ern civil rights movement. Contrary to the common assumption of constant state protest control and state–countermovement relations, these relation-ships changed markedly from 1956 to 1967, giving rise to three qualitatively distinct anti–civil rights countermovement regimes. Taken together, these stud-ies suggest two important points. First, social movement scholars should focus more systematically on relations between movement–state–countermovement to illuminate ways in which countermovements may serve as third-party ad-ministrators of state policy (Luders 2003). Second, just as movement–state relations vary across time and space, state–countermovement relations can also vary across time (Irons 2006) and space (Luders 2003).

In what follows, I investigate the forms, conditions, and trajectories of private militia coalitions with local authorities against the labor movement in Northern industrial cities during the late nineteenth century. Whether private militias formed coalitions with municipal authorities in this context was largely the outcome of a combination of conditions: political opportunity in the initial form of a permissive, open (nonrestrictive) legal environment; shared crisis framing of a collective action event precipitated by workers and defined as a universal threat to business interests and public order; and several organizational features of the militias, especially elite composition and elite civic organizational network embeddedness.

Private Militias cum Municipal Governments against Labor

A combination of conditions and events motivated a resurgence of paramilitary activity across Northern industrial cities during the 1870s that would grow well into the next century. Immediate post–Civil War retreat from militarism began to fade in the face of nationalistic fervor associated with the centennial on the one hand, and labor uprisings in industrial cities on the other (Cooper 1997; Reinders 1977). But the most salient triggering event was the first national-level labor uprising in summer 1877 (Isaac 2002), which revitalized interest in both the regular army and volunteer units, or state national guards, as they were increasingly being called (Montgomery 1993, 95).

The uprising of 1877 began as a rail strike at the Baltimore and Ohio depot in Martinsburgh, West Virginia, within the context of repeated wage cuts and labor speedups. The strike spread rapidly along rail lines, igniting actions and shutdowns in scores of cities from Baltimore to San Francisco. There was, by all accounts, little union mobilization during the uprising, but emergent grassroots strike committees were widespread (Debouzy 1983). Mass mobilizations overflowed the rail lines as railroad worker strikes served as an ignition point for miners, factory workers, and cigar workers, many of the unemployed, and thousands of others sympathetic to the workers' struggle and resentful of the oligarchical character of the newly emerging corporate political economy. When authorities were mobilized to break the strike and suppress crowds, substantial violence ensued (Bruce 1959; Stowell 1999).

The big lesson for elites—businessmen, politicians, and military leaders— was the abrupt realization that the existing police and military apparatus was insufficient to deal with such large-scale mass uprisings. In the aftermath, the press published numerous articles and editorials decrying the inadequate, unreliable character of local forces and the slow response of the regular army. Federal troops did eventually suppress the uprising in many major cities, but because of conditions (limited troop strength, widespread character of the revolt, and transportation difficulties partly due to the railroad strike itself), it took the army weeks to do so in some locations. Some wealthy businessmen (e.g., Marshall Field, Chicago retail; Amasa Stone, Cleveland manufacturing and rails; and Thomas Scott, Pennsylvania railroad) advocated that Congress expand the regular army and create permanent military outposts at key locations across the urban industrial frontier, similar to the strategy used on the Western frontier against the Indians (Isaac 2002; Isaac and Harrison 2006). Although the federal version of this vision did not materialize, other forms did.

These other responses, launched by employers and government authorities, took a variety of forms in the wake of the 1877 revolt. First, at the national level, the U.S. Army was not expanded the way Field, Scott, Stone, and other industrial barons may have wished, but it was used increasingly to break strikes (Cooper 1977). Second, at the state level, public volunteer militias were expanded and reorganized in Northern industrial states (Cooper 1997). Third, there were several important responses at the local level. Some employers formed their own permanent industrial armies and retained them on their payrolls. The Coal and Iron Police, widespread throughout Pennsylvania, was the quintessential example of this strategy (Isaac and Harrison 2006; Smith 2003). Other employers relied on hired guns, such as the Pinkertons and other agencies, when conditions required such services (Isaac 2002; Isaac and Harrison 2006; Smith 2003) and when citizens' associations or vigilance committees were not sufficient. Under municipal authorities, police forces were expanded in most cities and were used against strikers and against the labor movement more generally (Johnson 1976; Smith 2003). Private independent militias were increasingly reconstituted by elite class members or were newly founded by elites in the aftermath of the uprising (Isaac 2002; Isaac and Harrison 2006). These latter countermovement organizations used against labor, mostly private independent militias and class-reconstituted public militias, provide the empirical focus of my analysis.

This study does not pretend to be comprehensive, for any assessment of nineteenth-century local military forces faces formidable challenges. The fact that the population of such organizations is unknown and that records (when they have survived) are widely dispersed across local archives and private collections present major difficulties. Thus, my strategy here is largely illustrative. I focus on several select cases, each with a different set of conditions surrounding the initial formation processes that in turn set somewhat different coalition parameters. The cases that form this purposive sample, their location, and basic aspects of their organization are illustrated in Figure 2.1. A more dynamic accounting is contained in the following case narratives of organizational and coalition formations with local government authorities.

Cleveland's First City Troop

Given the size of the city, Cleveland had a substantial military presence during the latter decades of the nineteenth century, including as many as ten public and four independent units between the late 1870s and early 1880s. Before the Civil War, the early common militia that potentially required all able-bodied male citizens to serve had given way to the all-volunteer militia. But between the end of the Civil War and the turn of the century, two general forms of volunteer militias could be found across American cities: public units, which were mobilized and financed by state political authorities, and independent organizations, which were mobilized and financed by private citizens (Isaac 2002; Uviller and Merkel 2002; Vourlojianis 2002). Of the four independent entities in the city, two were of antebellum vintage: the Cleveland Grays and their partner organization, the Cleveland Light Artillery (see Vourlojianis 2002). The two others formed in the postbellum period were the First City Troop of Cleveland and the Cleveland Gatling Gun Battery (see Isaac 2002). I focus on the First City Troop as a major example of an elite independent postbellum militia.

In the midst of the labor uprising of July–August 1877, there was concern among prominent political and industrial elites about the performance capabilities and inclinations of the existing public militias. Major General Mortimer Leggett[3] wrote General James Barnett[4] of the nature of the problem as he saw it that August: "If called out [the public militia] would be likely to fraternize with the turbulent elements."[5] Barnett agreed. He and Leggett proceeded to mobilize "leading citizens" as the Cleveland Reserve, which would support the police should labor troubles require it (Vourlojianis 2002,

---

Independent (Private) Elite Militias	
Cleveland First City Troop	Formed in fall 1877 as elite independent; remained independent for a decade before becoming incorporated into the Ohio National Guard in 1887.
Scranton City Guard	Formed as a spontaneous elite armed citizens' association in summer 1877 and became a public elite militia that fall as part of the National Guard of Pennsylvania.
Chicago First Regiment	Formed in 1874 as elite independent; became elite public militia in 1875 as part of Illinois National Guard.
Working-Class Public Militias	
Chicago Second Regiment	An independent Irish militia turned public in 1875; was left unsupported by Chicago business elite and survived by merging with another Chicago unit in 1878.
Chicago Bohemian Rifles	An independent Bohemian militia turned public in 1875; disbanded by Illinois authorities in 1877.
Wabash Guards, Snoddy Mill	A public, largely working-class militia formed (Coal Creek, Ind.) in the 1870s; disbanded by Indiana authorities in 1878.

Figure 2.1. Purposive sample of militia cases.

48). Soon after the labor uprising had passed, many of these and other leading citizens gathered to form a calvary unit, the city's first thoroughly independent elite militia of postbellum vintage. The First City Troop was formally constituted, establishing constitution, bylaws, mounts (black stallions), uniforms (patterned after those of the Prussian hussars), and other accoutrements over several meetings occurring between September 19 and October 10, 1877.[6]

Many skilled workers at the huge Cleveland Rolling Mill (more than 5,000 employees) located in the Newburgh section of Cleveland had recently joined the Amalgamated Association of Iron and Steel Workers, headquartered in Pittsburgh. Over issues of union recognition, deskilling, and unskilled immigrant workers (mostly Poles and Bohemians), the skilled workers (mostly English) struck in summer 1882. At one point, the mayor declared the eighteenth ward to be in a state of insurrection and called up several militia units—the Cleveland Light Artillery, the Cleveland Grays, the Cleveland Gatling Gun Battery (Leonard 1979, 532), and the First City Troop[7]—to suppress the strike. The Rolling Mill was one of the largest companies in Cleveland, and its financial status, altered by a strike, was a major personal concern to many Cleveland elites, including a good many who were members of the First City Troop. This was the first major local mobilization, but not the last, of armed policing forces consisting of elite industrialists and their family members to protect their financial and civic interests in alliance with municipal authorities.

First City Troop minutes indicate that an ad hoc committee was created on October 19, 1882, to obtain "a special act of the [Ohio] Legislature similar to the act relating to the Cleveland Grays." The objective here was to have several First City Troop members approach Ohio lawmakers for the purpose of sponsoring a special act legally recognizing the First City Troop, with all the privileges and responsibilities that the other high-status independent militia in the city, the Cleveland Grays, had been granted after its earlier antebellum founding. On March 27, 1883, only days after the Ohio National Guard was formally constituted, the First City Troop Legislation Committee reported their success in obtaining for the troop the enactment of H.B. 693, which legalized and specified duties and responsibilities of the First City Troop as an independent militia under Ohio law. A decade after its founding as an independent (August 29, 1887), the First City Troop voted to join the Ohio National Guard. The unit was mustered into the state military as the First Cleveland Troop of Cavalry, Ohio National Guard, on September 10, 1887.[8] In short, the First City Troop was operating without a state legal charter between 1877 and 1883, yet had formed a coalition in practice with the municipal authorities in Cleveland. The point is that recognition by the state of Ohio was not imperative for First City Troop's existence, only for the provision of certain privileges desired by members.

Scranton's Thirteenth Regiment

There are important parallels between Scranton's Thirteenth Regiment and the Cleveland organization, although the former saw much more general strike action and more violence than did Cleveland.[9] The strike actions in the Scranton area fully mobilized in late July 1877 among miners (Meadow Brook Mines and Lackawanna Iron and Coal Company), then the railroads (Delaware and Hudson; Delaware, Lackawanna, and Western), and finally the railroad shops. The governor would eventually move state militias into the city and request assistance from the U.S. Army. In the meantime, a group of about fifty Civil War veterans approached the mayor for permission to organize a citizens' protection corps, commanded by Colonel W. W. Scranton (Martin 1877, 189–222), who soon expanded the organization to two hundred armed men.

On one occasion, Colonel Scranton led a contingent of about fifty armed men from the Citizens' Protection Corps against a "rampaging mob of workingmen" during the 1877 uprising (Walker 1979, 367). In attempts to suppress the crowd, at least three workers were killed and twenty-five wounded, while three members of the Citizens' Corps were injured. Over ensuing days, Scranton became a garrison state as the First Division, the National Guard of Pennsylvania, and the Third Infantry Regiment, U.S. Army, turned the city into an armed camp.

During the aftermath of the summer 1877 uprising, prominent citizens, "the elite of the community," comprising "lawyers, doctors, a preacher, and businessmen, mechanics, employers and employees" (Hitchcock 1924, iv, 3), with most of the men from the Citizens' Protection Corps, petitioned for a permanent militia. The governor initially authorized the enrollment of fifty-five men for a military unit. But pressure grew from men of "high character," and the state adjutant general ultimately approved a battalion of four companies (Hitchcock 1924, 3). On September 17, 1877, "many of the leading citizens" of Scranton were mustered into the Scranton City Guard, National Guard of Pennsylvania (Hitchcock 1924, 3). The key mobilizing agent was Henry M. Boies, described as "President of the Moosic Powder Company, president of the Scranton Young Men's Christian Association, [and] one of the most prominent of the city's business men," as well as a member of the National Rifle Association (Hitchcock 1924, 3, 10).

The Cleveland elite citizens' mobilization led to the formation of two new independent militias, while Scranton's elite mobilization led to a new public militia affiliated with the National Guard of Pennsylvania. But the financing of the Scranton City Guards came from both public and private sources; the private contributors were primarily railroad and coal interests. Specifically, the state of Pennsylvania supplied "Springfield breech-loading military rifles and accoutrements" (Hitchcock 1924, 8), and uniforms were supplied through a public subscription, while ammunition for target practice was supplied by individual militia members. Business interests financed many other expenses, such as construction of an armory, land for a rifle range, and travel to encampments.

The legacy of the 1877 uprising motivated state legislatures to provide at least the beginnings of monetary support to organize a modern state militia, and Pennsylvania was a leader in this movement. In 1878, the state legislature passed an act to fundamentally restructure the Pennsylvania National Guard (Cooper 1997, 50). As a result of that act, the City Guard was reorganized as the Thirteenth Regiment, Third Brigade, National Guard of Pennsylvania. The City Guard was mobilized once for disturbances in the city on October 13, 1877. But, organized as the Thirteenth Regiment, the Scranton troops saw action for at least three major strikes: the Carnegie Steel strike at Homestead (1892); the Latimer miners' strike (1897); and the miners' strike across the Lackawanna and upper Luzerne counties (1902).

No other state reformed and administered its militias as quickly, effectively, or strategically as Pennsylvania. As Cooper (1997, 50), a national guard scholar, notes, "By the late 1880s, 55 percent of the Guard's 136 companies were located in the five counties that encompassed the major industrial facilities around Pittsburgh, the eastern coalfields, and the city of Philadelphia." Numerous working-class militias were disbanded (Hinshaw 2002, 12). The National Guard of Pennsylvania received better treatment from the Pennsylvania legislature and was more tightly coupled with the corporate elite than many other state forces. The state legislature greatly expanded military expenditures to provide the state militia with the best equipment and compensation, while the Pennsylvania Railroad contributed supplies and transportation (Hinshaw 2002, 12). As Cooper (1997, 50) put it, "Businessmen, lawyers, editors, corporate leaders, and prominent Republicans dominated the Keystone State officer corps more thoroughly than any other state, as demonstrated by Scranton's Thirteenth Infantry."

Chicago's First Regiment

The case of Chicago's First Regiment provides an interesting contrast to the two organizations previously described, because it formed as an independent entity before the 1877 uprising.[10] Founded in September 1874, the First Regiment was, in the words of the Illinois adjutant general, "composed of the elite of the city" (Turnbaugh 1979, 112). Growing interest among the elite in military matters associated with turbulent elements of the city (including labor), the adjutant general's report on the dismal state of militias in Illinois generally, and anticipation of the forthcoming centennial events, all stimulated interest in a new military organization. The primary players in the mobilization were wealthy business families and especially the Citizens' Association of Chicago, composed of leading businessmen. The initial enlistment in 1874 consisted of approximately 150 men, restricted to ages eighteen to twenty-five. By December, the regiment had 300 members, mainly from middle- and upper-income families. Importantly, the First Regiment excluded members of the city's other militia companies, most of whom were Irish, German, or Bohemian working class.

Turnbaugh (1979, 112) calls the organization's legal status "questionable." But the governor did approve its formation in an Illinois constitutional clause that permitted the formation of a state military force. The Citizens' Association of Chicago, a businessmen's civic organization, provided $17,000 for uniforms, and one of the association's members, General Alexander McClurg, became its first commander. The First Regiment's formal independent status was short-lived. In 1875, the state ordered all militia units be organized as the Illinois State Guard. By July 1, 1877, the general assembly passed a comprehensive military code, largely as a result of growing concern over the militant labor movement. The new law provided for the enrollment and arming of the state militia, now renamed the Illinois National Guard. Between 1875 and 1877, the initial excitement among the young elite men of the First Regiment waned, and membership dropped to 120 by the eve of the 1877 uprising. But as the anxiety associated with the labor mobilization grew, so too did the membership of the First Regiment, soon reaching 600 men, 150 percent of its full complement.

Along with Baltimore, Pittsburgh, and St. Louis, Chicago was one of the major uprising hot spots (Bruce 1959). When General Ducat, commander of the Illinois National Guard, arrived in Chicago to suppress the national strike in the summer of 1877, he directed various units, including the First Regiment, to mobilize at their respective armories. But he simultaneously disarmed some working-class units, such as the Third Regiment, also known as the Bohemian Rifles, because he suspected them to be unreliable and sympathetic to the labor uprising. At one point, there were as many as 15,000 armed forces in the city, including police, militia, and U.S. Army regulars, and ultimately an estimated twenty to thirty-five strikers, sympathizers, and rioters were killed in confrontations with these armed forces. The First Regiment was among the units that saw action during these events.

There was a substantial gap between Chicago's planned expansion and modernization of its militia and its limited public funds for that purpose. The Citizens' Association of Chicago bridged that financial gap by mobilizing funds largely from the Chicago Board of Trade and major businesses, including banks, railroads, insurance companies, and wealthy merchants like Marshall Field. The funds supplied the First Regiment with rifles, ammunition, full cavalry equipment, and a Gatling gun. In 1883, the Citizens' Association of Chicago proclaimed it had contributed more than $100,000 for city military units since the First Regiment had formed in 1874. In its annual report, the association noted "that a well-organized militia force in a large city is, at certain times, the most efficient and cheapest police that can be maintained" (Citizens' Association of Chicago 1877, 9). The association remained the financial bulwark of Chicago's militia and continued to channel funds from businesses and elite families to class-reliable militia units well into the 1880s. Next to Pennsylvania, Illinois probably benefitted most in terms of growth, reorganization, and funds stimulated by the 1877 uprising (Cooper 1997, 51).

Conditions and Trajectory of Militia–Local Government Coalitions

From the nation's founding, American political culture expressed deep concerns about large standing armies, which fostered a decentralized republican militia tradition. The compulsory common militia was the norm from the late eighteenth century through the War of 1812. But from 1812 through the Civil War, the compulsory militia dissolved and uniformed volunteer units became increasingly prevalent. These volunteer units were very much like fraternal social clubs, organized around ethnic and class lines (Reinders 1977). The small, thinly stretched regular army was mostly preoccupied with Indian patrols. This was the general political institutional structure that shaped events during the last quarter of the nineteenth century. It was more than just a fragmented federalist structure; it was an arena of volunteer, dispersed, independent roaming armies that made for a weak military within a generally weak, underdeveloped state administrative apparatus (Skowronek 1982, chap. 4).

The post–Civil War decades produced a growing contradiction between this weak, decentralized, underprepared, and underfunded volunteer militia system and the growing realities of a class-divided industrial society. In the 1870s, a series of events—the Panic of 1873, the Tompkins Square Riot (1874), the Molly Maguires (1875), the founding of the Workingmen's Party of the United States (1876), and the great labor uprising of 1877—signaled that the character and stakes of class conflict in America were changing. The forms and size of the armed policing forces of an agrarian provincial society were scattered and insufficient for the emerging urban industrial society. With weak municipal police forces and a small regular army already stretched thin, elites mobilized counterinsurgency forces by increasingly resorting to the citizen-soldier tradition that was a central part of the organizational repertoire in American culture.

Neither federal nor state authorities exerted much control over the volunteer militias in the early postbellum period; that would change in the decades leading up to the twentieth century. Because private citizens were basically free to form military organizations, independent militias could be formed in the service of narrow class interests. This process, which favored those with substantial resources, along with a changing legal regime, served to patch the fragmented armed force system (Skowronek 1982), but it did so in a heavily class-biased manner. The class character of the process operated in two basic ways over the quarter century extending from 1877 to 1903: first, in the rise of private elite militias organized as countermovement forces in coalition with local authorities against the nascent labor movement; and second, through the erosion of the universal freedom to organize military organizations without the express consent of state authorities who favored elite independent organizations but sought to eliminate independent working-class militias (Isaac 2002; Kaufman 2001). The Cleveland, Scranton, and Chicago cases that I sketched above illustrate the beginnings of these processes.

What were the key ingredients that led to successful private militia–local government coalitions? Paths to coalition formation varied in the 1870s. Figure 2.2 highlights the key local conditions that facilitated coalitions between militias and local government authorities.

Many, but not all, new organizations were formed as a result of the 1877 labor revolt, such as Cleveland's First City Troop and Scranton's City Guard. Cleveland and Scranton illustrate the birth of new independent elite and state elite militias, respectively, while Chicago (and an Indiana case described below) illustrate selective processing of existing military units so they would be reliable bulwarks in coalition against labor insurgencies. Chicago's First Regiment was an elite unit before 1877, but the city's Second Regiment (Irish) and Third Regiment (Bohemian) were working-class units that were of questionable coalition reliability. I return to these cases of questionable political reliability below.

The first three cases in Figure 2.2 share almost exclusive uniformity in common conditions associated with their coalitions with local governments, whether they were independent organizations or state militias. Laws governing military organizations, if they existed, were weak and varied from state

Militia Organization	LAWS	EVENT	FRAMES ALIGNED	ELITE CLASS	CIVIC NETWORKS	MILITARY LIAISON	COALITION FORMED
Cleveland First City Troop	Yes	Yes	Yes	Yes	Yes	Yes	Yes
Scranton City Guard	Yes	Yes	Yes	Yes	Yes	Yes	Yes
Chicago First Regiment	Yes	No	Yes	Yes	Yes	Yes	Yes
Chicago Second Regiment	Yes	No	Yes	No	No	No	Mixed (Irish)
Chicago Bohemian Rifles	Yes	No	No	No	No	No	Disbanded (Bohemian)
Wabash Guards (Coal Creek, Indiana)	Yes	No	No	No	No	No	Disbanded (working class)

Figure 2.2. Conditions facilitating militia–local government coalitions against labor. LAWS *indicates state legal environment was open to and did not outlaw the formation of independent militias (at least at the time of organizational founding);* EVENT, *militia organizational formation was triggered by the national railroad strike of 1877;* FRAMES ALIGNED, *militia and local authority frames aligned with one another agreeing that a militant labor movement was a serious threat to the social order;* ELITE CLASS, *militia organization was composed of upper class members, including business, political, and military elites;* CIVIC NETWORKS, *links existed between the militia organization and other elite civic associations; and* MILITARY LIAISON, *an upper-class military officer served as a bridge between local authorities and the militia organization.*

to state. A few states attempted to bring some order to their militia and sought to enroll a larger stable force before the summer 1877 uprising. Illinois passed such a militia law in 1875 and Ohio in May 1877.[11] So there were weak attempts to regulate state militias in some places, but there was little concern for the independent organizations on the eve of the 1877 labor actions. All six cases in Figure 2.2 are marked by a legal openness to independent militia, at least during their formative years—that is, there were no laws precluding independent militia organizations in their respective states at the time of organizational founding (LAWS in Figure 2.2).

Given the relative openness of laws across states, the key conditions that led to military unit–local government coalitions were EVENT (in part); FRAMES ALIGNED; ELITE CLASS; CIVIC NETWORKS; and MILITARY LIAISON (Figure 2.2). Class composition of militia and consonant frames were probably the key ingredients. Elite class membership was crucial for alliances with independent militias. However, there were working-class state militias that acted at the behest of industrial, political, and military elites in service of the established order. Chicago's Second Regiment, largely composed of Irish working-class men, is a case in point; it served in the street battles of summer 1877. The framing of the threat of the labor uprising given by the Second Regiment was sufficiently consistent with that of elites for the commander of the Illinois National Guard to trust their deployment. The main distinction between the treatment received by the Second Regiment compared to the upper-class First Regiment was that the former lacked ties to elite civic organizations (Board of Trade and Citizens' Association of Chicago), which meant that it was denied the needed private financial support that their upper-class counterparts received. The First Regiment was independent when initially formed, but it had officially become part of the Illinois National Guard by 1877, yet still relied on private funding for most of its expenses. This was also the case with the Scranton City Guard. Cleveland's First City Troop was totally self-sufficient. It was supported by its wealthy members until it became part of the Ohio National Guard in 1887.

Civic organizations were an important part of the process for all elite military–municipal coalitions. The Cleveland militia was linked to the Board of Trade; the Scranton City Guard was nurtured by a citizens' association and business interests; and Chicago's First Regiment was supported by the Chicago Board of Trade and the Citizens' Association of Chicago. Embedded in each of these organizational networks was at least one military liaison, an elite military officer who served as a bridge between the city officials and the militia. These men had substantial military leadership experience, and they were actively involved in business and civic affairs. In a situation framed as outright insurrection, such as the events of summer 1877, these leaders carried enormous legitimate authority across all elite circles.

By contrast, the several militia cases that failed to materialize in alliance with municipal elites lacked the key ingredients cited above. The Chicago Second Regiment was deployed in 1877 but was left to wither financially. The Third Regiment, the Bohemian Rifles, was disbanded by the commander of the Illinois National Guard in the midst of the 1877 uprising. Members of the Wabash Guards, Snoddy Mill, who had formerly been miners, were taken out of service by the Indiana adjutant general after a series of mining strikes, and the militia was later disbanded.[12] These three negative cases—Chicago Second Regiment, Chicago Bohemian Rifles, and the Wabash Guards— were state (public) militia. Yet the full contradiction between the old laissez-faire volunteer militia system and new class realities appeared most clearly in the case of independent military organizations. Here it became increasingly clear that new means of control were required.

The new means took the form of laws that gave state governors the power to decide who could form a militia and who was precluded from doing so. Working-class militias, such as the Wabash Guards of Indiana, were sources of elite anxiety in the aftermath of 1877. In *Presser v. Illinois,* the Supreme Court stipulated that "the right voluntarily to associate together as a military company or organization, or to drill or parade with arms, without, and independent of, an act of Congress or law of the State authorizing the same, is not an attribute of citizenship" (Uviller and Merkel 2002, 228).[13]

Throughout the last quarter of the nineteenth century, individual state military codes (such as the Illinois law) were reshaping traditional militia practice, and the Supreme Court sanctioned this as long as such state actions did not prohibit federal mobilization of a militia. *Presser* was the most conspicuous indication of a new trend in America that reinterpreted the Second Amendment for counterinsurgency to be deployed against labor insurgents while supporting state-controlled and elite independent armed force mobilized to intimidate and control them (Isaac 2002; Kaufman 2001, 97). The power of municipal and industrial elites in combination with the flexibility of these new militia laws "allowed officials to look the other way whenever independent military organizations served their purposes. By this means, private armies of scabs, detectives, and strikebreaking marauders could be founded for the express purpose of combating labor" (Kaufman 2001, 97). State laws and the *Presser* decision created conditions that selected in antilabor forces in armed coalition while selecting out those who might be sympathetic to the labor movement. By the early twentieth century, the elite independent militias were also largely gone, incorporated into state militias or voluntarily disbanded decades later, hardly leaving a trace. But the tradition of using state national guards to break strikes would be carried forward into the twentieth century. What began as sporadically formed local private elite–municipal coalitions in the 1870s was eventually absorbed into the federal–state military system in the early twentieth century with the passage of the Dick Act (1903) and the National Defense Act (1916).

Conclusions and Implications

Within a limited literature on social movement–state coalitions, work on countermovement–state alliances is particularly meager. This study contributes to filling this void by focusing on coalitions between local governments and countermovement organizations in the form of elite militias that were mobilized in response to the emergence of the national labor movement in the late 1870s. Although some militias were formed and financed, at least in part, by state authorities, other independent private militias were formed by local capitalists and professionals in coalitions with municipal authorities in an effort to augment policing capacities in dealing with labor uprisings and other forms of threatening mob actions.

Several key conditions contributed to the formation of independent elite militias in coalition with local authorities. At least initially, the permissive legal structure that had traditionally allowed universal formation of citizen-soldier organizations was an important institutional factor. Civic and business associations with elite military officer members were instrumental agents in bridging, activating, and legitimating this organizational form to multiple constituencies. But at the core, affinity, trust, and common goals were crucial. Capitalist class composition (elite industrialists, bankers, leading citizens) and their law-and-order counterframing of labor events (such as strikes) were necessary for the constitution of such coalitions. This is so because these organizations and coalitions were forming at precisely the moment that working-class members of militias were coming to be viewed by the better classes as potentially unreliable, a threat to private interests and public order.

Thus, the conditions that facilitated the armed citizen–local government coalitions have their parallels in studies of other movement coalitions in very different settings and involving very different collective actors. What is truly distinctive about the coalitions in this study is that they represented extensions of the local state. At least in some cases, capitalists were themselves armed policing agents operating through their own initiative and with the cooperation of the state. Although the empirical scope of this analysis is limited by the small number of independent militia–local government coalition cases I am able to describe, these cases are probably reasonably representative of other high-status independent formations that were created in Northern industrial cities at that point in American history. Although a larger case base might yield more robust and perhaps more subtle findings not apparent in this smaller-scale analysis, these results suggest important implications for scholarly analysis of coalitions in social movement studies, the state, and protest policing.

Social Movement Studies

In contrast to the observation that social movement coalitions are most likely to form within well-developed state bureaucracies (Stearns and Almeida 2004), my findings suggest that law-and-order type countermovement coalitions with authorities are most likely to form within weak and porous states—that is, those not highly developed in division of labor or geographical reach. The present findings are also different from other studies on the type of state agency with which a movement is likely to ally itself. The Japanese environmental movement (Stearns and Almeida 2004) and the U.S. antismoking movement (Wolfson 2001) both linked themselves to the social component of the state. But the independent capitalist militias formed coalitions with the executive and policing agencies of the local state. Clearly the character of the countermovement shapes where in the state a coalition forms. The larger point is that social movement/countermovement–state coalitions are creatures of the historical process of state formation itself. This means that generalizations about state–movement alliances will undoubtedly be historically contingent on at least phases of state and movement development.

My findings, similar to Stearns and Almeida (2004), suggest that state authority fragmentation associated with a federalist political structure encourages state–movement coalitions, most likely at the local level. Parallel to Croteau and Hicks (2003), I also find that the countermovement independent militia coalitions with municipalities were partly dependent on consonant frame coupling; that is, both organizations and city authorities had to define strike activity used by labor activists to be anarchy or criminal—or at least an important threat to law and order. The particular relationships that states and cities formed with armed militias during the last several decades of the nineteenth century provide an excellent example of how "countermovements may serve as third-party 'administrators' of state policies" (Luders 2003, 44), in effect operating as an extension of the state's use of coercive capacity. Consequently, it is quite likely that the state–employer countermobilization alliance against labor in the early phases of that insurgency both intensified the struggle and decisively altered the balance of power in favor of employers.

Scholars should not only pay more attention to coalitions between social movements and/or their respective SMOs, but they should also be mindful that movements operate within fields of relations that include challenging movements, countermovements, and state authorities. Social movements do not face static political environments for long. The coupling of counter-movement and state can fundamentally reshape the political opportunity structure within which a movement must operate. When resource-rich coun-termovements form alliances with state authorities, movement challengers likely face a greatly magnified opposition in both symbolic and material terms. This was surely the case for the American labor movement.

Theories of the State

Historically based analyses of different dimensions of the U.S. state tend to support, variously, the elite/capitalist class character of U.S. state policy (e.g., Domhoff 1990; McCammon 1994; Prechel 1990). Most relevant to the present analysis, Voss's (1993) study of the decline of the Knights of Labor in the late nineteenth century indicates that what truly constituted Ameri-can exceptionalism was not so much an apolitical working class, but rather a powerful employers' countermovement in tandem with a supportive state. It was the exceptional strength of employers' associations and "a state that set the rules for industrial conflict and then generally absented itself from labor disputes" (Voss 1993, 204) that made class relations so different in Amer-ica. In some historical moments, such as the ones analyzed here, the scenario for labor was actually worse than Voss suggests (see Lipold and Isaac 2009). These cases indicate that privately organized and armed leading citizens, mostly capitalists, joined forces with local public authorities to suppress chal-lenges to the public order. As they did so, these leading citizens acted as ex-tensions of the state legitimately licensed to use armed intimidation and lethal force against the challenging movement of labor. The Voss study and the present analysis highlight processes that contributed to making the cap-italist class character of the state at a very early moment in America's state formation under an industrial regime. The symbiotic relationship between ostensibly armed employer's associations and the local state transformed the state and its policing capabilities in material and symbolic terms (Loveman 2005). Decentralized independent militias eventually became integrated into an increasingly nationalized national guard system, implicating movement–countermovement struggle in state building.

Policing Protest

These militia cases also speak to the issue of policing in relation to challeng-ing social movements, an explicit focus that is rather recent in social movement studies. For example, Della Porta and Reiter (1998) have compiled an important volume on protest policing, the strength of which is the cross-national array of case studies. But the evidence presented in their cases is restricted largely to the experience of Western democracies (United States, France, Switzerland, Italy, Spain, Germany) during the historical period since the 1960s. Thus, they have little to say about the policing of protest in early periods of state formation, especially the highly neglected role of private agents in protest control (Earl 2004). At some moments in America's industrial takeoff period, capitalists as private citizens actually played an active role in policing their community for protest, either threatened or actually occurring, by labor radicals or other undesirables who might disrupt the public order. The present study illuminates ways in which people were coming to be policed for the free market during the rise of industrial capital in the Gilded Age (Montgomery 1993, chap. 2).

But what parallels and implications, if any, do these late nineteenth-century private militia–local government coalitions offer for understanding the policing of protest in the contemporary world? As accelerating processes of globalization and dominant neoliberal ideology are employed to restructure social relations of production, consumption, distribution, flow of commodities, and labor power, there are sound reasons to expect class conflicts to continue through the twenty-first century (Harvey 2005; Isaac, Harrison, and Lipold 2008; Pereira 2003; Silver 2003) and for policing of those struggles to take on new or possibly resurrected and remodeled old forms (Della Porta, Peterson, and Reiter 2006). Destabilized regimes of the global south have seen a rise in the prevalence of brutal militias, often mobilized along ethnic lines, that struggle for power by terrorizing fellow citizens. Cases are numerous and include Somalia, Rwanda, Afghanistan, Iraq, Columbia, and Argentina (see Davis and Pereira 2003). In the United States during the 1980s and 1990s, there was a wave of armed right-wing militias that were spurred on by a growing conservative political climate, antigovernment ideology, resentment over the loss of the Vietnam War, and declining economic opportunities for the working class (e.g., Berlet and Lyons 2000; Van Dyke and Soule 2002). More recently in the United States, the growing flow of illegal immigrants from south of the border and the economic squeeze ushered in by neoliberalism have contributed to spawning citizen voluntary organizations dedicated to policing the border, like Jim Gilchrist's Minutemen Project. But these organizations are not always operating in coalition with states.

There is, however, a form of irregular armed force–state coalition development in the United States that is of special significance under the rubric of the new private military contractors (Isaac and Harrison 2006; Singer 2003).

These organizations began to appear before the Iraq war but have grown substantially and have drawn attention primarily in that context. Private for-profit companies, such as Blackwater USA Inc. (now Xe Services), contract with the U.S. government to provide various services in war zones, and sometimes those services include provision of auxiliary armed forces (Singer 2003). These irregulars work in coalition with the national state as a result of conditions of insufficient troop strength and the neoliberal urge to privatize as much of the public domain as possible (see Harvey 2005), thereby expanding the wages (and profits) of war. Although the United States has a historical tendency of differentiating and bounding the functions of military units and public order policing units (although the case studies here blur that distinction), some of the military contracting organizations have been deployed in domestic policing in both the United States and abroad, and there are good reasons for anticipating more private, for-profit military companies in the years to come (Isaac and Harrison 2006). From a historical–sociological perspective, this is a curious reversal of the trend away from the use of mercenaries by Western states that became established in the nineteenth century (Avant 2000), suggesting complex nonlinear and path-reversing ways that states can develop.

One thing is certain: irregular armed forces come in a variety of forms and have often played an important role in the development of states and political cultures (Davis and Pereira 2003), and there is every reason to expect that militias and other forms of irregular armed force will continue to shape the twenty-first century. It is very likely that with continuing globalization, states will lose their grip on legitimized violence as small, mobile networks of armed forces create a shadow state array of irregular armed forces (Pereira 2003). In the process of state reformation under globalization, the likelihood of finding various kinds of irregular armed forces in coalitions with both insurgent movements and states increases. Many of these irregulars will work to disrupt and challenge their states, but some will undoubtedly form coalitions with and serve as extensions of state power. Volunteer irregular forces that join government forces to suppress movements (e.g., labor) are most likely to form early in the state formation process when the shape of monopoly over the legitimate use of force is still being defined and up for grabs, or when states are going through major restructuring as in the current period.

Max Weber's (1947, 154–56) famous observation that states lay claim to force monopoly is important, but it is also in need of significant modifications. On the one hand, it fails to say who gets to be part of that legitimated use of physical force—who is marshaled in and out when state agents are mobilized and who is defined as a legitimate state actor. On the other hand, the state's monopoly over the means of coercion is more elusive (Zack 2003) than Weberian theory would suggest. To an important extent, this is so because of the role that subtle and shifting coalitions come to play in the ongoing process of state formation. When we look carefully at the past as well as the present, we find that states are often composed of coalitions of irregulars with their regular policing and armed forces. These irregulars, such as the ones analyzed here, may be more important in shaping political cultures, states, and systems of inequality than previously thought.

Notes

I thank Holly McCammon, Nella Van Dyke, and an anonymous reviewer for useful comments on an earlier version of this chapter and acknowledge the assistance of archivists at the Chicago Historical Society, Indiana State Library, and Western Reserve Historical Society (Cleveland, Ohio). This work was supported by a Vanderbilt University College of Arts and Science research endowment, and it also benefitted from two National Endowment for the Humanities grants (FT-44785-00 and FA5404908). The views expressed herein do not necessarily reflect those of the NEH or Vanderbilt University.

1. I use the gendered term because it is consistent with the both the empirical and cultural terrain with which I am concerned here. All of my examples consist of men. The term *businessman* signified an important class-based referent to manhood during this period (see Haydu 2008, 217).

2. By irregular armed force, I mean armed forces that are collective actors "outside the conventional category of uniformed standing armed forces fighting external aggressors in the name of national sovereignty" (Davis 2003, 32).

3. After the Civil War, Mortimer Leggett moved to Cleveland and established the law firm M. D. Leggett & Company, which cofounded the Brush Electric Company, precursor to the General Electric Company (Van Tassel and Grabowski 1996).

4. James Barnett was an early member of the independent militia, the Cleveland Grays, and commanded the Cleveland Light Artillery (an artillery spin-off of the Grays) during the Civil War, attaining the rank of general. He was a founder of the Republican Party in Cleveland, served as police commissioner, and was a leading businessman and banker after the war (Van Tassel and Grabowski 1996) and a member of the Cleveland Board of Trade (pamphlet, Cleveland Board of Trade, *The Manufacturers, Trade, and Commerce of Cleveland, 1880–81* [Cleveland: Short & Forman Co., 1881], Western Reserve Historical Society).

5. Manuscript collections, Western Reserve Historical Society, General James Barnett Papers, 1845–1906.

6. Manuscript collections, Western Reserve Historical Society, Cleveland Military Units, MS 3985, series 2, container 2, folder 52; and MS 3000, series 1, container 1, folder 1.

7. Manuscript collections, Western Reserve Historical Society, Cleveland Military Units, MS 3985, series 2, container 3, volume 1 (oversized organization record book).

8. Ibid.

9. For the Scranton case, I rely primarily on the organization's historian, Hitchcock (1924), unless otherwise indicated.

10. I rely primarily on Turnbaugh (1979) for this case, unless otherwise indicated.

11. Ohio Legislature, *Laws of Ohio to Enroll the Militia, and to Organize the National Guard,* in force May 7, 1877 (Columbus, Ohio: Nevins & Myers, 1877), Western Reserve Historical Society.

12. For the Snoddy Mill, Indiana case, I rely on the *Report of the Adjutant-General of the State of Indiana to the Governor, Two Years Ending December 31, 1878.*

13. Supreme Court decision, *Presser v. Illinois,* 116 U.S., 252, 267 (1886).}

Works Cited

Avant, Deborah. 2000. "From Mercenary to Citizen Armies: Explaining Change in the Practice of War." *International Organization* 54: 41–91.

Berlet, Chip, and Matthew N. Lyons. 2000. *Right-Wing Populism in America.* New York: Guilford Press.

Bruce, Robert V. 1959. *1877: Year of Violence.* Chicago: Quadrangle Books.

Citizens' Association of Chicago. 1877. *Annual Report of the Citizens' Association of Chicago.* Chicago: Hazlitt & Redd, Printing and Publishers.

Cooper, Jerry. 1977. "The Army as Strikebreaker: The Railroad Strikes of 1877 and 1894." *Labor History* 18: 179–96.

———. 1997. *The Rise of the National Guard.* Lincoln: University of Nebraska Press.

Croteau, David, and Lyndsi Hicks. 2003. "Coalition Framing and the Challenge of a Consonant Frame Pyramid: The Case of a Collaborative Response to Homelessness." *Social Problems* 50: 251–72.

Davis, Diane E. 2003. "Contemporary Challenges and Historical Reflections on the Study of Militaries, States, and Politics." In *Irregular Armed Forces and Their Role in Politics and State Formation,* edited by Diane E. Davis and Anthony W. Pereira, 3–34. Cambridge: Cambridge University Press.

Davis, Diane E., and Anthony W. Pereira, eds. 2003. *Irregular Armed Forces and Their Role in Politics and State Formation.* Cambridge: Cambridge University Press.

Debouzy, Marianne. 1983. "Workers' Self-Organization and Resistance in the 1877 Strikes." In *American Labor and Immigration History,* edited by Dirk Hoerder, 61–77. Urbana: University of Illinois Press.

Della Porta, Donatella, and Herbert Reiter, eds. 1998. *Policing Protest: The Control of Mass Demonstrations in Western Democracies.* Minneapolis: University of Minnesota Press.

Della Porta, Donatella, Abby Peterson, and Herbert Reiter, eds. 2006. *The Policing of Transnational Protest*. Burlington, Vt.: Ashgate.

Domhoff, G. William. 1990. *The Power Elite and the State: How Policy Is Made in America*. New York: Aldine De Gruyter.

Earl, Jennifer. 2004. "Controlling Protest: New Directions for Research on the Social Control of Protest." *Research in Social Movements, Conflicts, and Change* 25: 55–83.

Goldstone, Jack A. 2003. "Bridging Institutionalized and Noninstitutionalized Politics." In *States, Parties, and Social Movements*, edited by Jack A. Goldstone, 1–24. New York: Cambridge University Press.

Harvey, David. 2005. *A Brief History of Neoliberalism*. New York: Oxford University Press.

Haydu, Jeffrey. 2008. *Citizen Employers: Business Communities and Labor in Cincinnati and San Francisco, 1870–1916*. Ithaca, N.Y.: Cornell University Press.

Hinshaw, John. 2002. *Steel and Steelworkers: Race and Class Struggle in Twentieth-Century Pittsburgh*. Albany: State University of New York Press.

Hitchcock, Frederick L. 1924. *History of the 13th Regiment, National Guard of Pennsylvania*. Scranton, Pa.: International Textbook Press.

Irons, Jenny. 2006. "Who Rules the Social Control of Protest? Variability in the State–Countermovement Relationship." *Mobilization* 11: 165–80.

Isaac, Larry. 2002. "To Counter 'The Very Devil' and More: The Making of Independent Capitalist Militia in the Gilded Age." *American Journal of Sociology* 108: 353–405.

Isaac, Larry, and Lars Christiansen. 2002. "How the Civil Rights Movement Revitalized Labor Militancy." *American Sociological Review* 67: 722–46.

Isaac, Larry, and Daniel Harrison. 2006. "Corporate Warriors: The State and Changing Forms of Private Armed Force in America." *Current Perspectives in Social Theory* 24: 149–84.

Isaac, Larry, Daniel Harrison, and Paul Lipold. 2008. "Class Conflict in Capitalist Society: Foundations and Comparative-Historical Patterns." In *Encyclopedia of Violence, Peace, and Conflict*, 2nd ed., edited by Lester Kurtz, 275–95. Oxford: Academic Press.

Johnson, Bruce C. 1976. "Taking Care of Labor: The Police in American Politics." *Theory and Society* 3: 89–117.

Kaufman, Jason. 2001. "'Americans and their guns': Civilian Military Organizations and the Destabilization of American National Security." *Studies in American Political Development* 15: 88–102.

Leonard, Henry B. 1979. "Ethnic Cleavage and Industrial Conflict in Late 19th Century America: The Cleveland Rolling Mill Company Strikes of 1882 and 1885." *Labor History* 20: 524–48.

Lipold, Paul, and Larry Isaac. 2009. "Striking Deaths: Lethal Contestation and the 'Exceptional' Character of the American Labor Movement, 1870–1970." *International Review of Social History* 54 (August): 167–205.

Lo, Clarence Y. H. 1982. "Countermovements and Conservative Movements in the Contemporary U.S." *Annual Review of Sociology* 8: 107–34.

Loveman, Mara. 2005. "The Modern State and the Primitive Accumulation of Symbolic Power." *American Journal of Sociology* 110: 1651–83.

Luders, Joseph. 2003. "Countermovements, the State, and the Intensity of Racial Contention in the American South." In *States, Parties, and Social Movements,* edited by Jack A. Goldstone, 27–44. New York: Cambridge University Press.

Mahon, John K. 1983. *History of the Militia and the National Guard.* New York: Macmillan.

Martin, Edward Winslow [James Dabney McCabe]. 1877 [1971]. *The History of the Great Riots.* New York: Augustus M. Kelley.

McCammon, Holly J. 1993. "Government by Injunction: The U.S. Judiciary and Strike Action in the Late 19th and Early 20th Centuries." *Work and Occupations* 20: 174–204.

———. 1994. "Disorganizing and Reorganizing Conflict: Outcomes of the State's Legal Regulation of the Strike since the Wagner Act." *Social Forces* 72: 1011–49.

McCammon, Holly J., and Karen E. Campbell. 2002. "Allies on the Road to Victory: Coalition Formation between Suffragists and the Women's Christian Temperance Union." *Mobilization* 7: 231–51.

Meyer, David S., and Suzanne Staggenborg. 1996. "Movements, Countermovements, and the Structure of Political Opportunity." *American Journal of Sociology* 101: 1628–60.

Montgomery, David. 1993. *Citizen/Worker.* Cambridge: Cambridge University Press.

Mottl, Tahi. 1980. "The Analysis of Countermovements." *Social Problems* 27: 620–35.

Obach, Brian K. 2004. *Labor and the Environmental Movement: The Quest for Common Ground.* Cambridge, Mass.: MIT Press.

Pereira, Anthony W. 2003. "Armed Forces, Coercive Monopolies, and Changing Patterns of State Formation and Violence." In *Irregular Armed Forces and Their Role in Politics and State Formation,* edited by Diane E. Davis and Anthony W. Pereira, 387–407. Cambridge: Cambridge University Press.

Prechel, Harland. 1990. "Steel and State: Industry Politics and Business Policy Formation." *American Sociological Review* 55: 648–68.

Reinders, Robert. 1977. "Militia and Public Order in Nineteenth Century America." *Journal of American Studies* 11: 81–101.

Report of the Adjutant-General of the State of Indiana to the Governor, Two Years Ending December 31, 1878. 1879. Indianapolis: Indianapolis Journal Company, State Printers.

Rohlinger, Deana A. 2006. "Friends and Foes: Media, Politics, and Tactics in the Abortion War." *Social Problems* 53: 537–61.

Rose, Fred. 2000. *Coalitions across the Class Divide: Lessons from the Labor, Peace, and Environmental Movements.* Ithaca, N.Y.: Cornell University Press.

Sewell, William H., Jr. 2001. "Space in Contentious Politics." In *Silence and Voice in the Study of Contentious Politics,* edited by Ronald R. Aminzade, Jack A. Goldstone, Doug McAdam, Elizabeth J. Perry, William H. Sewell Jr., Sidney Tarrow, and Charles Tilly, 51–88. Cambridge: Cambridge University Press.

Silver, Beverly. 2003. *Forces of Labor: Workers' Movements and Globalization since 1870.* Cambridge: Cambridge University Press.

Singer, P. W. 2003. *Corporate Warriors: The Rise of the Privatized Military Industry.* Ithaca, N.Y.: Cornell University Press.

Skowronek, Stephen. 1982. *Building a New American State: The Expansion of National Administrative Capacities, 1877–1920.* Cambridge: Cambridge University Press.

Smith, Robert M. 2003. *From Blackjacks to Briefcases: A History of Commercialized Strikebreaking and Unionbusting in the United States.* Athens: Ohio University Press.

Stearns, Linda Brewster, and Paul D. Almeida. 2004. "The Formation of State Actor–Social Movement Coalitions and Favorable Policy Outcomes." *Social Problems* 51: 478–504.

Stowell, David O. 1999. *Streets, Railroads, and the Great Strike of 1877.* Chicago: University of Chicago Press.

Turnbaugh, Roy. 1979. "Ethnicity, Civic Pride, and Commitment: The Evolution of the Chicago Militia." *Journal of the Illinois State Historical Society* 72: 111–22.

Uviller, H. Richard, and William G. Merkel. 2002. *The Militia and the Right to Arms.* Durham, N.C.: Duke University Press.

Van Dyke, Nella. 2003. "Crossing Movement Boundaries: Factors That Facilitate Coalition Protest by American College Students, 1930–1990." *Social Problems* 50: 226–50.

Van Dyke, Nella, and Sarah A. Soule. 2002. "Structural Social Change and the Mobilizing Effect of Threat: Explaining Levels of Patriot and Militia Mobilizing in the United States." *Social Problems* 49: 497–520.

Van Tassel, David D., and John J. Grabowski, eds. 1996. *The Dictionary of Cleveland Biography.* Bloomington: Indiana University Press.

Voss, Kim. 1993. *The Making of American Exceptionalism: The Knights of Labor and Class Formation in the Nineteenth Century.* Ithaca, N.Y.: Cornell University Press.

Vourlojianis, George N. 2002. *The Cleveland Grays: An Urban Military Company, 1837–1919.* Kent, Ohio: Kent State University Press.

Walker, Samuel. 1979. "Varieties of Workingclass Experience: The Workingmen of Scranton, Pennsylvania, 1855–1885." In *American Workingclass Culture,* edited by Milton Cantor, 361–76. Westport, Conn.: Greenwood Press.

Weber, Max. 1947. *The Theory of Social and Economic Organization.* Translated by
   A. M. Henderson and Talcott Parsons. New York: Free Press.

Wolfson, Mark. 2001. *The Fight against Big Tobacco: The Movement, the State, and
   the Public's Health.* New York: Aldine De Gruyter.

Zack, Lisabeth. 2003. "The *Police Municipale* and the Formation of the French State."
   In *Irregular Armed Forces and Their Role in Politics and State Formation,* edited
   by Diane E. Davis and Anthony W. Pereira, 281–302. Cambridge: Cambridge
   University Press.

Zald, Mayer N., and Bert Useem. 1987. "Movement and Countermovement Interaction: Mobilization Tactics and State Involvement." In *Social Movements in an
   Organizational Society,* edited by Mayer N. Zald and John D. McCarthy, 247–
   72. New Brunswick, N.J.: Transaction.

3

Interstate Dynamics and Transnational Social Movement Coalitions: A Comparison of Northeast and Southeast Asia

Dawn Wiest

State leaders around the world have embraced regionalism as a desirable model for organizing and managing interstate relations. Because social movements develop within a context of institutionalized power relations, the reorganization of interstate relations through regionalism has important implications for transnational mobilization.[1] Building and maintaining transnational coalitions is a difficult process. Cultural heterogeneity, distance, and diverse national political systems impose obstacles, and politicized divisions between countries also complicate efforts to organize transnationally. With the increasing power of international institutions over national economic and social policy, however, activists separated by national boundaries have found common ground. Further, interstate organizations such as the Council of Europe along with social movement initiatives such as the World Social Forum have facilitated transnationalism by creating spaces for networking, agenda building, and information exchange among activists from different countries.[2]

In this chapter, I analyze the relationship between regionalism and mobilization by examining geographic patterns of participation in transnational social movement coalitions within Northeast and Southeast Asia.[3] With its emphasis on institutionalized power relations, the political process framework leads to the expectation that institutional differences at the regional level results in distinct patterns of transnational mobilization. Although Northeast Asia has a weakly developed regional infrastructure for coordinating relations among nation-states, state leaders in Southeast Asia have a long and moderately successful history of regional cooperation. Moreover, the Association of Southeast Asian Nations (ASEAN) retooled its mandate in response to the environmental and financial crises of the late 1990s and moved toward a participatory framework of governance. In contrast, because there have been few institutional mechanisms in place for promoting regional political and economic cooperation in Northeast Asia, transnational collaboration among activists in the subregion has been much more limited. Countries within Northeast and Southeast Asia also vary on factors that are theoretically important for understanding cross-national differences in transnational social movement participation: economic resources, national political conditions, and international state ties. Variation on these factors will help illuminate the relative impact of national-level and regional-level factors on patterns of participation in transnational coalitions.

This chapter is organized into three sections. I first situate my research in the literatures on social movement coalitions, transnational social movements, and international organization. To set the context for an analysis of transnational civil society relations within the two subregions, I follow the first section with a discussion of interstate relations in Northeast and Southeast Asia. I then present a comparative analysis of the structure of relations formed through participation in social movement coalitions that linked activists across national borders in the year 2000.

Shifting Conditions for Transnational Coalition Formation

Cross-group cooperation in social movements ranges from loosely organized and temporary to highly formal and long-lived. Coalitional forms fall in the middle of this analytic scale, featuring more routine communication and resource sharing than most networks but less formalization and centralization than individual organizations or federations (Smith and Bandy 2005). Coalitions are significant to the work of social movements because they are engines of tactical innovation (Clemens 1997; Murphy 2005) and identity transformation (Baldez 2006; DiazVeizades and Chang 1996); they also are often key players in coordinating protests and other collective actions (Meyer and Corrigall-Brown 2005; Van Dyke 2003).

The resource mobilization perspective suggests that competition for resources, elite attention, and membership makes cooperation among social movement groups the exception rather than the norm. Because they involve cross-national coordination, transnational coalitions add complexity to the already difficult task of building interorganizational alliances. Impediments to transnational coalition building reside not only in competition among groups, but also in national differences in politics, culture, resources, and institutional access, as well as in patterns of interstate conflict, which influence activist decisions about collaboration, framing, and tactics (Cortright and Pagnucco 1997; Fox 2000; Hathaway and Meyer 1993; Wallerstein 1990).

But national factors that limited the formation and scope of transnational coalitions in the past have been altered by globalization and by the increasing authority of organizations and treaties created to address the challenges of globalization. As a response to globalization, regionalism creates an important political and economic relational context that shapes possibilities for transnational activism. Consider a few specific ways in which regionalism may alter national-level impediments to building transnational coalitions. Four major obstacles have been identified in the literature: (1) cultural and political diversity; (2) distance; (3) economic barriers to the easy flow of people, goods, and information; and (4) varying political contexts (Smith and Bandy 2005, 8). As regional integration proceeds, and as regional institutions exert more influence into domestic realms (potentially or in fact), activists have strong incentive to work through differences that may have forestalled cross-national collaboration in the past. This process has been documented in studies of transnationalism in various regional contexts, including North America (see, e.g., Bandy 2004; Kay 2005) and the European Union (e.g., Cullen 2005; Imig and Tarrow 2001). In these contexts, activists formed regionally based, transnational social movement organizations, coalitions, and networks mobilized around a range of issues in response to the increasing power and authority of regional institutions (see also Wiest and Smith 2006, 2007). Regionalism also facilitates the flow of people, goods, and information across borders, further enhancing possibilities for transnational coalition building (e.g., Guarnizo and Smith 1998; but see Watts 2003).

The fourth obstacle—variation in political contexts—may present the toughest challenge to cross-border collaboration because national polities shape opportunities not only for domestic movements acting locally or nationally, but also for those seeking transnational affiliation. In authoritarian state contexts, the obstacles to mobilization are immense (e.g., Schock 2008). At the same time, state antagonism may provide the greatest impetus for transnational collaboration as activists seek allies in the international arena (Keck and Sikkink 1998; but see Wiest 2007). State connections to the world polity embolden and, in some cases legitimate activist efforts to influence home governments.[4] Such ties can make state leaders vulnerable to international pressure by opening access for domestic movements to important international allies and resources (Brysk 1993; Schock 1999, 2008). As conduits of support and tactical innovation, transnational social movement coalitions are themselves integral features of the international opportunity context (Keck and Sikkink 1998; Khagram 2004; Smith, Chatfield, and Pagnucco 1997; Tarrow 1994; Tsutsui 2004).

Following the political process perspective on social movements, institutional changes at the international level alter the context in which movements mobilize, facilitating or hindering efforts to build transnational alliances (Keck and Sikkink 1998; Smith 1995; Tarrow 2005). As international institutions exert more influence in domestic and global political arenas, their relevance as targets of contention and arenas for securing resources and allies increases. Certainly, the institutional structure of the international system is only one of a set of factors that shape prospects for movement transnationalism. Activist agency can produce idiosyncratic forms of transnational participation (Bob 2002), and international civil society events such as the World Social Forum can facilitate cross-national and cross-movement collaboration (Smith et al. 2007). However, transnational activism is rooted in social structure. The rise in and formalization of transnational activity that characterize our contemporary era would not have been possible without policies and other institutional mechanisms to sustain and legitimize consistent transborder interaction and exchange (Fligstein and Stone Sweet 2002; Tarrow 2005).

In the following section, I discuss interstate relations within the subregions of Northeast and Southeast Asia. I focus on forces that have inhibited the formation of regional organizations in Northeast Asia and those that have altered the substance and scope of regionalism in Southeast Asia. I then turn to an analysis of geographic patterns of coparticipation in transnational, civil society coalitions.

The Context of Interstate Relations: Northeast and Southeast Asia in Comparison

Northeast Asia

Since the end of World War II, the economies of Northeast Asia have become highly interdependent. Yet unlike many other world regions with high levels of economic interdependency among nation-states, state leaders in Northeast Asia have been unsuccessful in developing an organizational infrastructure to bolster economic development and promote political cooperation within the region. Northeast Asia's organizational gap is especially problematic in light of the region's geopolitical volatility and vulnerability to financial crises—concerns that arguably would be better addressed through multilateral cooperation (Calder and Fukuyama 2008). This is not to say, however, that no regional architecture exists in Northeast Asia. Since the Korean War and up until the late 1990s, the security and economic interests of the United States played a paramount role in shaping regional relations. With the rising threat of communist China in the early 1950s, the United States successfully pressured Asian state leaders to adopt a bilateralist over a multilateralist approach to security and trade.[5] The result was a hub-and-spoke system of politico-economic relations with the United States at its center, and shallow integration among countries of the region. This system endured through the cold war; the United States viewed the bilateralist arrangement and the "continued estrangement of Asian states from one another" as the best guarantee of regional security (Calder and Fukuyama 2008, 9).

Over the past decades, Northeast Asian state leaders initiated discussions about regionalism on several occasions, but factors unique to the region have precluded cooperation around key issues. First, bilateral commitments and tensions have interfered with the process of region building. Japan's security and trade ties to the United States have made it reluctant to pursue regionalism; since the Korean War, the United States has consistently viewed Northeast Asian regionalism as antithetical to its own interests (Peng 2000; Rozman 2004; but see Krauss 2003). Other bilateral relationships within the region have also forestalled regionalism. In the mid-1990s, for instance, South Korea was more invested in the possibility of reunification with the north than it was in building multilateral relationships within the region (Rozman 2004). Further, while South Korea has strong economic ties with Japan, into the 1990s, it was hesitant to forge other ties with that nation (Rozman 2004).

Nationalism has further exacerbated bilateral tensions, hampering regionalism (Akaha 1999; Rozman 2004; Scalpino 1999). Democratization in South Korea and national interests in China helped foment anti-Japan protests in those two countries. As South Korea democratized through the 1990s, "mass movements drew the Korean public more openly into parading their loathing of Japan's occupation" (Rozman 2004, 355). Further, anti-Japanese nationalism in Russia contributed to the blockage of proposals for regional and bilateral economic cooperation in the mid-1990s (Rozman 1999). Japanese nationalism has also been on the rise over recent decades, at times turning public opinion against closer ties with its immediate neighbors (Calder 2003; Scalpino 1999; Stubbs 2002).

Political heterogeneity has also been cited as an obstacle to regional cooperation. Although Japan and South Korea have democratic capitalist systems, China features a one-party authoritarian capitalist system, and the communist state of North Korea is governed by a one-man dictatorship. Further, Taiwan lacks diplomatic recognition as an independent state, a situation that further complicates regional relations (Jie 2001). Such political diversity has made it difficult to build a regional organization that would hasten functional integration (Peng 2000). In addition, formal economic cooperation has been hindered by uneven development. For example, in the late 1990s, the per-capita GDP of Japan was seventy times higher than that of China (Peng 2000). However, since the financial crisis of 1997–98, orientations within Northeast Asia have shifted more decisively toward global and regional multilateralism (Calder and Fukuyama 2008; Krauss 2003; Park 2005). Although the causes of the crisis that affected many East Asian economies are disputed, there is little doubt that the volatility of global financial flows exacerbated preexisting vulnerabilities. Shortly after the signal event in July 1997—the collapse of the Thai baht—the crisis spread to other Southeast Asian economies as well as to Japan and South Korea. In South Korea, for instance, the won lost 60 percent of its value in six months, while unemployment rose fourfold and poverty tripled. It was widely thought that existing institutions—ASEAN, the Asia-Pacific Economic Cooperation, and the International Monetary Fund—mishandled the crisis, causing labor market turmoil and social upheaval. Because of these failures, the crisis was a strong impetus for establishing a regional organization that could manage difficulties associated with financial and economic globalization while building on the region's distinct form of capitalism, its history, and its cultural traditions. At present, it appears that cooperation among countries of Northeast Asia will be nurtured within the context of ASEAN. The first meeting of ASEAN Plus Three in 1997 included the participation of the ten ASEAN member states plus China, South Korea, and Japan. Since then, it has progressed from an informal gathering to an institutionalized forum. Many ASEAN Plus Three–affiliated agencies, including young leaders, labor ministers, and working groups, have been established in a few short years, potentially making ASEAN Plus Three a "major regional and international player" (Stubbs 2002, 455). In 2000, ASEAN Plus Three ministers agreed to create a bilateral currency swap network, the Chiangmai Agreement, to prevent future currency crises (Calder and Fukuyama 2008). The achievements within the ASEAN Plus Three forum represent a significant departure from United States–dominated regionalism in Northeast Asia and toward a multilateralist framework that can hasten cooperation around security and social policy and spark the development of regional civil society.

Southeast Asia

Although governments of Southeast Asia had initiated several forms of regional cooperation before 1967, it was the threat of communism that catalyzed the formation of ASEAN (Hussey 1991). Southeast Asian leaders were concerned that outside powers, especially the United States, would use the communist threat to manipulate politics within the region. With the Bangkok Declaration of 1967, ASEAN was established to promote cooperation around regional peace and stability, mutual respect for national sovereignty, economic development, and social and cultural progress (Hussey 1991; Solidum 2003). The five original member states—Indonesia, Malaysia, the Philippines, Singapore, and Thailand—were joined by Brunei Darussalam in 1984, Vietnam in 1995, Laos and Myanmar in 1997, and Cambodia in 1999.

For nearly a decade after its founding, however, ASEAN remained more of a symbolic institution than one that could advance the goals of the governments that founded it (Hussey 1991). The region was embroiled in religious and ethnic conflict, nationalism remained a contentious issue, and the small states' fear of domination by the larger regional powers impeded regional unity (Poon-Kim 1977). At the same time, the informality that characterized the early years of dialogue and agenda setting promoted an atmosphere of trust that laid the foundation for a more concrete and effective unity once communists took power in Vietnam, Laos, and Cambodia in the mid-1970s. The Treaty of Amity and Cooperation and the Declaration of Concord, signed by member states in 1976, formalized the determination to cooperate and respond collectively to outside threats and internal conflict (Poon-Kim 1977). Further, in 1977, a significant step was taken toward regional economic cooperation when governments signed the ASEAN Preferential Trading Arrangement.

Although scholars point to Northeast Asia's incompatible mix of political systems in hindering regionalism there (e.g., Peng 2000), Southeast Asia features the most eclectic mix of political regimes to come together under a single system of regional cooperation (Kivimaki 2001; Nesadurai 2003). This heterogeneity may have slowed regional economic integration and cooperation on other fronts (e.g., human rights and environment), but important progress was made on regional security and stability (Kivimaki 2001; Solidum 2003). Indeed, ASEAN has achieved an outcome that is often thought to be reserved for democratic countries: peaceful relations with neighbors, even though ASEAN's founding principle of noninterference in the domestic affairs of member states had insulated Southeast Asian states from democratization for decades (Acharya 2003). Nonetheless, democratic transitions have occurred—in the Philippines in 1986, Thailand in 1992, Cambodia in 1993, and Indonesia in 1998—and with them, ASEAN's "narrow elite-centered and sovereignty-bound framework" came under increasing attack from its own member states and civil society (Acharya 2003, 380; see also Ahmad and Ghosal 1999). The Thai government confronted ASEAN's founding principle of noninterference by openly criticizing human rights abuses in Burma (Acharya 2003). The principle was also challenged by the governments of Singapore and Malaysia when they reached out to the international community and to domestic NGOs for help in pressuring the Indonesian government to act more forcibly in constraining the activities of businesses responsible for the deadly pollution haze that engulfed the region in 1997 (Cotton 1999).

International pressures and incentives have also been integral to ASEAN's shift from elite-centered to participatory regionalism. Coinciding with a growing international trend linking investment decisions to perceptions of human security (e.g., Waldhorn 2002; but see Smith, Bolyard, and Ippolito 1999), ASEAN governments opened discussions on human rights, social development, and other non-trade-related issues to cast the region in a more favorable light (Acharya 2003). The region needed this boost because ASEAN governments were severely criticized for their handling of the financial and environmental crises. Charges of stagnation and irrelevance came from the international community and from citizens, threatening the legitimacy of ASEAN and its ability to secure the global trade and financial relationships it coveted (Chandra 2004).

The financial crisis sparked a resurgence of civil society in Southeast Asia. ASEAN-based social movements grew increasingly contentious in their condemnations of the regional organization's pursuit of economic globalization without social and environmental protections (Acharya 2003; Caballero-Anthony 2004). The region-based coalitions that emerged during the late 1990s were linked to wider Asian and global networks and participated in parallel meetings during sessions of ASEAN and the Asia-Pacific Economic Cooperation (Acharya 2003). Since the crisis and the concomitant opening of fissures in ASEAN's elite governance structure, human rights and sustainable development activism in Southeast Asia has been increasingly pursued at the regional level (Acharya 2003; Caballero-Anthony 2004).

How have interstate dynamics within the two subregions affected civil society relations across national borders? Structural changes at the international level alter the institutional context in which movements mobilize. Regional structures are integral components of the overall international opportunity context, and as such, they present both opportunities for and obstacles to transnational mobilization. Where the regional context is conducive, transnational association is more readily achieved. Without an institutional framework for activism, transnational association is more limited. To examine my main proposition, I turn to a comparative analysis of coparticipation in transnational social movement coalitions across the countries of Northeast and Southeast Asia.

Geopolitical Structuring of Transnational Ties

Data

Data on transnational social movement coalitions were collected from the 2000 semiannual *Yearbook of International Organizations,* commissioned since 1953 by the United Nations and published by the Union of International Associations. Each volume features profiles of both international NGOs and intergovernmental organizations (IGOs), and includes information on organizational founding, aims, activities, organizational structure, relations with other international organizations, and countries with participation. The coalitions that I selected for analysis had participation from at least three countries and were active in Northeast Asia, Southeast Asia, or both. Although a small number (fifteen) of these coalitions were organized exclusively within Asia, most had membership from at least two world regions.

To ensure as much as possible that the data included only coalitions, I excluded networks of individuals and federated organizations from analysis (i.e., international labor unions and federated organizations such as Greenpeace). Participation in the groups I analyze below consisted of autonomous organizations only or of organizations and individuals. I identified coalitions associated with social movements by the goals and activities listed in the *Yearbook.* Coalitions that were mobilized around explicit social and/or political change goals (e.g., human rights, economic justice, or environmental protection) and that used nonviolent tactics (e.g., protest, lobbying states and/or international institutions, issue awareness campaigns) were chosen for analysis.

Methodology

I used network analysis to uncover the structure of relations formed through patterns of participation in transnational social movement coalitions. To create a matrix for analysis, I converted a two-mode affiliation network of countries and coalitions into a one-mode network of countries linked through shared participation in movement coalitions. In the matrix, each cell contained the total number of coalitions in which organizations from two countries shared participation. I converted the raw counts into a binary strong tie matrix, with 1 indicating that a strong tie was present between a pair of countries and 0 indicating its absence. When a country participated in 75 percent or more of the same coalitions as a second country, the pair of countries was coded as 1, indicating the presence of a strong tie, and below this threshold, a country pair was coded as 0 to indicate the absence of a strong tie.

In graph theoretic terms, the resulting matrix is a directed graph, or digraph G_d (N, L), with a set of nodes, $N = \{n_1, n_2, \ldots, n_b\}$, representing countries in the network and a set of arcs, $L = \{l_1, l_2, \ldots, l_g\}$, directed between pairs of countries (Wasserman and Faust 1994). Each arc is an ordered pair of nodes (countries), $l_k = <n_i, n_j>$, with the arc $<n_i, n_j>$ directed from n_i to n_j. Directionality is conceptualized here as consistent coparticipation. For instance, if there is participation from any Japanese organizations in 75 percent or more of coalitions with South Korean membership, the existence of the arc $<n_{South\ Korea}, n_{Japan}>$ is indicated by 1 in the matrix. That the reverse is not necessarily true gives the graph its directionality. If there is participation from South Korean civil society in less than 75 percent of coalitions with Japanese membership, then arc $<n_{Japan}, n_{South\ Korea}>$ does not exist and is indicated by 0 in the matrix.

I extracted the network visualizations presented in the analysis from the global network formed through shared participation in transnational social movement coalitions.[6] The global network is a scale-free network whose degree distribution (i.e., the number of ties each node has to or from another) approximates a power law (Barabási and Albert 1999). That is, the network is characterized by a relatively small number of hubs with strong ties to $n - 1$ nodes (all nodes but itself), and a large number of nodes with a small number of strong ties (in this network, the hubs and nodes are countries). The scale-free quality of the global network has important implications for understanding the geographic dimension of transnational social movement coalition formation. First, network formation is a dynamic process: the geographic paths upon which communication and information consistently flow have evolved over time through the continuous addition of new nodes and the rewiring of edges between nodes (e.g., changes in relations among countries). Second, the nodes that enter a network do not connect to others randomly. Rather, the properties of the nodes that are already in the network determine the placement of the edge that links the new node to the network. The scale-free model proposed by Barabási and Albert (1999) shows that the probability of a new node linking to existing node i depends on the degree k_i of node i: new nodes connect to the network by linking to nodes that already have a high number of connections.

To understand a social network as that formed through cross-national participation in transnational social movement coalitions, other nodal properties along with conditions external to the network must be taken into consideration. Axelrod's (1997) model for the dissemination of culture provides one precedent for analyzing the evolving structure of a network in terms of nondegree nodal properties. Individuals in the Axelrod model are described by a vector Q of cultural characteristics that are quantified and take on n

integer values. As the number of individuals with the same cultural traits in the neighborhood increases, so too does the probability that neighbors will interact (Axelrod 1997). As this number increases, the system undergoes an ideal type transition from a disordered phase—a culturally fragmented network—to an ordered phase—a culturally polarized network (Grabowski and Kosiński 2006). However, I do not expect the structure of relations under consideration here to depend solely on nodal homogeneity measured by country-level characteristics such as political system, economy, and state ties to the international system. Rather, as discussed, characteristics of the neighborhood (that is, the regional geopolitical environment) are expected to influence how activists are linked transnationally through shared participation in transnational social movement coalitions.

I used NetDraw (Analytic Technologies, Lexington, Ky.) to generate the network diagrams and a spring-embedding algorithm to arrange nodes by geodesic distance. Geodesic distance expresses the number of ties in the shortest path between a pair of nodes (i.e., countries). Nodes with the smallest path lengths to one another and with similar ties to other nodes in the network are situated close to one another in the diagrams.

In the following discussion of economic and political differences among countries, I draw on data collected from a variety of sources. I use GDP per capita to measure and compare economic resources across countries. These data were collected from the World Bank's *Human Development Indicators Data Bank,* which reports the value of a country's economy in U.S. dollars. The structure of a country's political system is used as a proxy measure here for citizen rights and access to political decision making. These data were collected from the CIA's *World Factbook,* an annual census of economic, political, and demographic conditions for all countries of the world. Finally, data on state participation in IGOs were collected from the *Yearbook of International Organizations.* The data include simple counts of the number of IGOs in which a state participates. The IGOs counted are multilateral (as opposed to bilateral) and include both global (e.g., the United Nations Conference on Trade and Development) and regional (e.g., the Council of Europe) bodies.

Analysis

Before turning to the network analysis, I first discuss how transnational social movement coalition participation varied with state-level factors in the year 2000. Table 3.1 provides country-level information on GDP per capita, political system, multilateral organizational membership, and the number of transnational social movement coalitions that had membership in each

Table 3.1. National-Level Characteristics for the Year 2000

Country	GDP per Capita (US$)	Political System	No. of Intergovernmental Organizations	No. of Transnational Social Movement Coalitions
Northeast Asia				
China	949	Communist state	50	53
Hong Kong	24,810	Limited democracy	11	61
Japan	37,409	Constitutional monarchy with parliamentary democracy	63	124
South Korea	10,885	Democratic republic	52	69
Mongolia	395	Mixed parliamentary/presidential democracy	26	26
North Korea	914	Communist state/one-man dictatorship	17	11
Taiwan	14,519	Multiparty democracy	11	49
Southeast Asia				
Brunei	17,600	Constitutional sultanate	NA	11
Cambodia	287	Multiparty democracy under a constitutional monarchy	24	27
Indonesia	800	Democratic republic	54	85
Laos	329	Communist state	22	17
Malaysia	3,927	Constitutional monarchy	51	73
Myanmar	NA	Military junta	25	21
Philippines	1,003	Democratic republic	46	105
Singapore	22,768	Parliamentary republic	33	50
Thailand	1,998	Constitutional monarchy	52	89
Vietnam	397	Communist state	36	39

Sources: Yearbook of International Organizations; World Bank Human Development Indicators Data Bank; CIA World Factbook; the New Zealand Ministry of Foreign Affairs and Trade (http://www.mfat.govt.nz); and the Government of Taiwan (http://investintaiwan.nat.gov.tw). NA, not applicable.

country. State-level factors varied widely in each of the subregions. Turning first to economic resources, in Northeast Asia, Japan's GDP per capita was more than three times higher than that of South Korea, whereas Mongolia and North Korea had the lowest in the subregion. In Southeast Asia, Singapore had the highest GDP per capita, followed by Brunei, and Cambodia and Laos had the lowest average income in the subregion. Additionally, a higher proportion of countries in Southeast Asia than in Northeast Asia had very low GDP per capita; 60 percent compared to 25 percent, respectively, had a GDP per capita of less than $1,000.

As Table 3.1 indicates, high GDP corresponds with high transnational social movement participation in Northeast Asia but not in Southeast Asia. The average number of transnational social movement coalitions in the richest countries of Northeast Asia is seventy-six compared to thirty for the poorest countries. In contrast, while the richest countries of Southeast Asia average fifty-six transnational social movement coalitions, the average for countries with the lowest GDP per capita was fifty-four. Brunei had the second richest economy in Southeast Asia but the lowest participation in transnational social movement coalitions ($n = 11$), whereas the Philippines, having a much lower GDP per capita than Singapore, Brunei, Malaysia, and Thailand, had the highest number of active transnational social movement coalitions in Southeast Asia in 2000.

As discussed above, there was also variability in governance structures across the two subregions. The communist states of China and North Korea in Northeast Asia and Vietnam and Laos in Southeast Asia, the military-ruled state of Myanmar, and the restrictive Sultanate of Brunei existed side by side with democratic (or democratizing) states such as Japan, South Korea, the Philippines, and Thailand. Although not considered fully authoritarian, the governments of Malaysia and Singapore in Southeast Asia retained strict control over political expression and association into 2000. Underscoring the relationship between democratization and participation in transnational civil society (see, e.g., Smith and Wiest 2005), the democratic countries of both subregions had the highest number of transnational social movement coalitions active within their borders in the year 2000. With intact democracies before 2000, Japan, South Korea, and Taiwan in the north and the Philippines, Thailand, and Indonesia in the south averaged the highest participation in transnational social movement coalitions. These countries averaged eighty (Northeast Asia) and ninety-three (Southeast Asia) coalitions, compared to thirty-seven (Northeast Asia) and thirty-four (Southeast Asia) for other countries.

State participation in IGOs also influences opportunities for citizen participation in transnational social movement coalitions (e.g., Reimann 2002; Smith and Wiest 2005; Tarrow 2005). As discussed above, such ties provide channels of access to important international resources such as political allies that are engaged in multilateral processes and international events that facilitate cross-national communication and collaboration. In both Northeast and Southeast Asia, countries with more ties to the intergovernmental realm also tended to have the highest participation in transnational social movement coalitions. On average, these countries had participation in eighty-two (Northeast Asia) and eighty-four (Southeast Asian) coalitions. Among the countries with low IGO participation, the average number of transnational social movement coalitions was twenty-six for Southeast Asia and thirty-seven for Northeast Asia.

The relationship between state ties to the international system and transnational social movement coalition participation in the absence of a full democracy is apparent for China, Malaysia, and Vietnam. In these countries, transnational social movement participation was relatively high despite national restrictions on political expression and association. Conversely, where state participation in multilateral organizations was low, transnational social movement coalition participation was also low.

Because regionalism provides a shared institutional context for activism, it is expected to reduce barriers to transnational affiliation even in the presence of heterogeneous political systems, disparate economic resources, and variability in state ties to the international system. To assess this proposition, I first turn to an analysis of ties across the countries of Northeast Asia, where interstate regional cooperation was weak in 2000. Figure 3.1 illustrates the network visualization of relations across civil societies. Japan is the hub of this network, bridging relations between all other pairs of countries. As the network visualization suggests, the regional context was not conducive to broader collaboration across the civil societies as measured by shared participation in transnational social movement coalitions. All countries were linked through Japan, and no other pair of countries had direct, strong ties to each other in the year 2000. Resource and information exchange via transnational social movement coalition participation was centered on Japan, which had the highest participation in Northeast Asia. Japan's centrality in this web of exchange was conditioned by its long-standing democracy, wealth, and level of internationalization, all of which facilitated the development of robust NGOs and social movement sectors with ties to international society (Reimann 2002; Shirasu and Sim-Yee 1999).

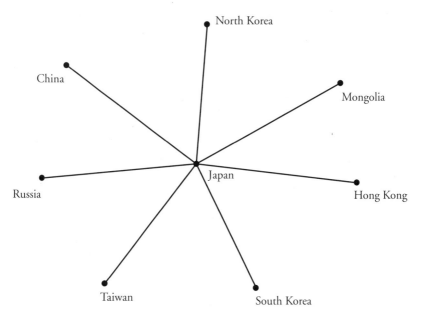

Figure 3.1. Network structure of transnational ties across Northeast Asia, 2000.

So far, the findings hint at the importance of regional-level factors in shaping the network's structure. Although the Internet has dramatically changed the landscape of social movement participation and activity, it has not eradicated all political boundaries between peoples separated by national borders. In 2000, Northeast Asia had no regional infrastructure that would ease the flow of people, resources, and information across the borders of its member states. Although the ending of the cold war brought with it a slight loosening of restrictions on these flows, divergent political and economic orientations within the region continued to hinder cross-border exchange in the year 2000 (Shirasu and Sim-Yee 1999).

At the same time, the findings underscore the significance of transnational social movement coalitions for bridging differences that could hinder collaboration across civil societies. With its imperial history and strong ties to the United States, Japan has been one source of division within the region. Yet the evidence here suggests that Japanese civil society plays an important role in linking other Northeast Asian civil societies to transnational civil society. Indeed, since the 1990s, Japanese NGOs have led efforts to foster cooperative linkages throughout the region (Shirasu and Sim-Yee 1999).[7]

How does the structure of relations across Southeast Asia compare to Northeast Asia? In Southeast Asia, countries were as diverse in their political and economic orientations as they were in Northeast Asia. But a shared institutional context at the regional level facilitated cross-national exchange across civil societies, and the structure of relations formed through coparticipation in transnational social movement coalitions reflected regional level opportunities for cross-national collaboration. The large integrated cluster shown in Figure 3.2 includes the oldest members of ASEAN. The democratic countries—the Philippines, Indonesia, and Thailand—are joined in this cluster by Singapore, Brunei, and Malaysia, which are countries with firm restrictions on freedom of expression and political association. A crucial difference between the structure of relations across Southeast Asian compared to Northeast Asia is that civil societies in the larger cluster of interconnection were directly connected to one another rather than indirectly tied through a central hub. Brunei, for example, had very low participation in transnational social movement coalitions, but its pattern of participation expressed regional proclivity. Of the eleven coalitions in which activists in Brunei participated, activists in Malaysia, Indonesia, and Thailand participated in ten of them, and activists in the Philippines and Singapore participated in eight.[8] That all countries in this cluster were directly tied to one another suggests that resource exchange and patterns of cross-national

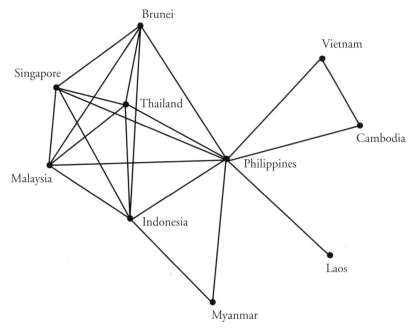

Figure 3.2. Network structure of transnational ties across Southeast Asia, 2000.

collaboration could occur along multiple paths. Resources were exchanged from Brunei to Singapore and Malaysia, or from Thailand to the Philippines to Vietnam and Cambodia. The patterns of ties in Northeast Asia are anything but conducive to multiple pathways of exchange because all sites were connected through only one regional hub.

A shared opportunity context at the regional level fostered the formation of multiple paths of exchange and collaboration among activists in Southeast Asia. But historically, the elite-centered regionalism of ASEAN precluded nongovernmental participation in political processes, thus forestalling the development of a regionwide civil society. The threatening conditions engendered by financial and environmental crises in the late 1990s changed this and catalyzed the formation of activist communities that crossed national boundaries. Social movement scholars have documented the role of threat in sparking movement mobilization (e.g., Almeida 2003; Tarrow 1996; Tilly 1978; Van Dyke and Soule 2002) and facilitating cross-movement coalition building (e.g., McCammon and Campbell 2002; Staggenborg 1986; Van Dyke 2003). In Southeast Asia, it was the intersection of a facilitative institutional context with the shared threat of the financial and environmental crises that strengthened activist ties across countries and led to the emergence of a regionwide civil society. As government leaders in Thailand, Singapore, and Malaysia blatantly violated the norm of noninterference that had been the cornerstone of ASEAN regionalism since its founding, they legitimated outside interference in matters formerly reserved to the leaders of individual nation-states (Cotton 1999).

A brief comparison of relations across Southeast Asian civil societies from 1980 to 2000 will further clarify the changing structure of transnationalism in relation to the evolution of ASEAN regionalism. As Figure 3.3 shows, in 1980, Southeast Asian participation in transnational social movement coalitions occurred in two distinct clusters. The Philippines, Singapore, and Thailand had direct, strong ties to each other. The other two ASEAN countries in 1980—Malaysia and Indonesia—formed part of a distinct cluster but had no direct, strong ties between them. In 1980, the regional context was not conducive to cross-national collaboration among Southeast Asian activists. The elite-centered regionalism of ASEAN was still very much intact, and the organization had not yet made any gains in cooperation beyond security and economy by 1980. Also, the other countries with which Malaysian and Indonesian activists shared consistent participation in transnational social movement coalitions were part of the Indochine peninsula, a distinct political and cultural bloc. The countries in this cluster (Laos, Vietnam, Burma, and Cambodia) were not yet part of ASEAN in 1980.[9] Although Indonesia was not

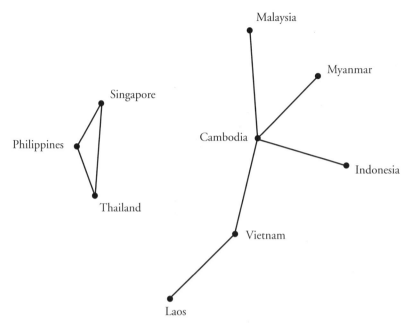

Figure 3.3. Network structure of transnational ties across Southeast Asia, 1980.

geographically part of the Indochine peninsula, the security of the peninsula was vital to its economic interests. In the early 1980s, it played a prominent diplomatic role in ending the Vietnam–Cambodian conflict, elevating its own national interests above ASEAN's regional policy of noninterference. Further, national interest had made Indonesia reluctant to integrate its own economy with ASEAN and to support the regional security instrument, the 1976 Treaty of Amity and Cooperation. The structure of relations across the civil societies of Southeast Asia in 1980 reflected these political divisions and alignments, as well as the then-fragmentary nature of ASEAN regionalism.

As democratization fueled social movements at the national level in the Philippines, Thailand, and Indonesia, and as the elite-centered, state-protective regionalism of ASEAN broke down with the financial and environmental crises of 1997–98, the conditions for the emergence of Southeast Asian civil society ripened. Increased interconnection among Southeast Asian countries in the year 2000 through shared participation in transnational social movement coalitions both reflected and supported these shifts.

Conclusions, Limitations, and Directions for Future Research

I have argued that geopolitical relationships affect the dynamics of transnational coalition formation. As one avenue through which relations among nation-states are altered, regionalism creates an institutional context that may help activists overcome obstacles to transnational collaboration. As described above, transnational coalition formation is an arduous process. Activists not only contend with the challenges of interorganizational cooperation and coordination when seeking transnational collaboration, but they also face differences in politics, culture, resources, and institutional access, as well as limitations imposed by geographical distance. The economic and political diversity of ASEAN member states theoretically undermines cooperation among states and across civil societies. Nevertheless, by the year 2000, the pattern expressed through the network analysis indicates strong ties across multiple pairs of countries. Conversely, in Northeast Asia, transnational activism has been constrained by bipolar divisions, differences in national polities and economic circumstances, and variation in state ties to the international system. In the year 2000, Japan was at the center of the regional civil society network, playing a crucial role in bridging relations between national social movement groups and transnational civil society. I argue that the hub-and-spoke pattern of relations across Northeast Asian civil society reflected a weakly developed institutional infrastructure for facilitating civil society relations across nation-states.

Rather than suggesting that geopolitical relations play a primary causal role in shaping opportunities and constraints for transnational activism, this research highlights the interplay of transnational- and national-level forces. The East Asian crises sparked demand for more effective regional governance. Acting against the traditions of Southeast Asian regionalism, democratizing ASEAN member states played a key role in opening the institution to the influence of a variety of external actors, including civil society organizations. Thus, on the one hand, the slight opening of ASEAN that has occurred over the past decade was promoted from below by its democratic member states and citizen activists seeking to influence the operational dynamics of the institution. On the other hand, over the course of the decade that it shifted its mandate in response to these pressures, ASEAN reestablished its institutional legitimacy and provided a crucial impetus to the further development of Southeast Asian civil society. In recent years, these networks and coalitions have used their growing legitimacy to press for a variety of changes. In 2007, ASEAN leaders adopted a new charter that establishes the institution as a legal entity and a rules-based organization. This change is significant because since its creation in 1967, ASEAN's founding principle of noninterference in the affairs of member states stood in the way of a more bureaucratized structure with legal power over the activities of members. The charter also provides for a human rights body and a multilateral dispute-settlement mechanism—changes that came about through a ten-year effort on the part of Southeast Asian civil society networks and coalitions.

Even as civil society organizations have increased their presence in regional forums, however, their inclusion in key negotiations and policy development remains limited. Consultation with civil society organizations on the content of the charter was minimal, and it remains unlikely that ASEAN will develop mechanisms to enforce adherence to international human rights law in the immediate future. The key here is that the institution has provided a focal point for activism and an impetus for strengthening civil society ties across countries. Continued civil society pressure on ASEAN member states may eventually culminate in the adoption of human rights enforcement mechanisms, which in turn may catalyze important political and social changes in recalcitrant member states such as Myanmar.

What insights into social movement coalitions and transnationalism can be drawn from the analysis of Southeast and Northeast Asia presented in this chapter? The findings underscore the multilayered array of forces that operate to shape social movement transnationalism and the geographic contours of coalition formation. On the one hand, globalizing technologies such as the Internet along with international civil society events such as the World Social Forum provide spaces where activists from distinct national backgrounds and experiences can work to overcome differences and learn from one another. These spaces have aided the diffusion of social movement frames, strategies, and tactics, creating possibilities for the formation of new transnational coalitions. But on the other hand, political and economic divisions between countries, along with state limits on citizen association, expression, and political participation, hinder transnational collaboration in social movement coalitions. For the life of a coalition, consistent communication and resource sharing among constituent organizations are vital to success. Thus, drawing from the resource mobilization perspective on social movements, we should expect that transnational coalitions will form along tested geographic pathways to ensure as much as possible the reliable exchange of information and other resources as well as access to relevant elites. ASEAN regionalism serves as an important mechanism through which pathways into the countries of Southeast Asia are created and reinforced; transnational coalitions and networks are built on the routine exchanges among Southeast Asian societies facilitated by regionalism. This is not to say that novel forms of transnational collaboration do not arise. This research examined strong ties, or consistent patterns of collaboration in transnational coalitions, and these patterns rely to an important degree on institutionalized channels of interchange across nation-states.

I would like to address three limitations of the research presented in this chapter and offer suggestions for future studies. First, because the data analyzed above capture transnational coalitions with membership in three or more countries, binational coalitions are overlooked. Recent research on transnational activism involving South Korean and Chinese activists reveal growing ties between civil societies in those two countries (Futrell 2008). Future research should focus on the ways in which activists from countries separated by political, economic, and/or cultural divisions work to overcome differences to form transnational coalitions. Second, although the analysis of Southeast Asia suggests a relationship between regionalism and geographic patterns of participation in transnational movement coalitions, a more direct way to examine this question would be to consider the extent to which activists seek alliances with ASEAN elites and participate in multiactor networks and coalitions. ASEAN regionalism may have sparked more widespread collaboration among Southeast Asian activists, but how central is that institution to the strategic repertoire and mobilization goals of activists? Is increased transnational affiliation simply a by-product of Southeast Asian countries opening to one another via regionalism? Above, I offered a few examples of how activists have worked to change ASEAN, but this may represent only a small subset of Southeast Asian activism. A third limitation is that this research cannot explain how activists from authoritarian states such as Myanmar and North Korea link to transnational coalitions, nor does it shed light on the nature of their participation. Questions such as these call for research that focuses on the dynamics of transnational social movement coalitions.

The research presented here suggests that regionalism alters the opportunity context faced by activists in authoritarian states, legitimizing forms of transnational affiliation that may provide a foundation for building movement coalitions. Our understanding of social movements would benefit greatly from a more direct exploration of whether and how coalitions develop from other social ties formed across national borders.

Notes

This material is based on work supported by the National Science Foundation (grant 03-24735). Comments from Holly McCammon, Nella Van Dyke, Noel Parker, and Jackie Smith are gratefully acknowledged. An earlier version of this paper was presented at the 2007 International Studies Association Annual Meeting in Chicago, Ill.

1. In this chapter, I use the concept of regionalism to refer to geographically specified interstate relations involving the routinization of exchange across state borders, the creation of region-level policies, and the creation of institutions charged with implementing policy and managing intraregional and external relations (see,

e.g., Falk 1995; Grugel 2006). In this view, regionalism is considered a "project of governance which aims to refashion the norms and the networks that underpin policy-making and the ways in which authority and legitimacy are exercised in bounded but post-sovereign spaces" (Grugel 2006, 209).

2. The World Social Forum is a semiannual gathering of social movement activists, NGOs, and left-leaning scholars and political leaders from around the world. The first forum took place in Porto Alegre, Brazil, in 2001 as a counterevent to the World Economic Forum, an international gathering of political and economic elites held yearly in Davos, Switzerland.

3. Geographically, Northeast Asia includes the following countries: People's Republic of China, Japan, South Korea, North Korea, and Taiwan. Patterns of economic and security relations lead some scholars (e.g., Rozman 2004) to also include the Russian far east and Mongolia as part of Northeast Asia. Southeast Asia includes Thailand, Malaysia, the Philippines, Singapore, Brunei, Myanmar, Cambodia, Indonesia, Vietnam, and Laos.

4. International connections may also imperil domestic movements. When movements adapt their goals and tactics to attract international support, they may grow isolated from other national movements (Bob 2002). Further, new tactics aimed at attracting international allies may also draw state repression (Bob 2002, 402).

5. Before China fell to communist rule, the United States supported the Pacific Pact, which outlined a multilateralist approach to regional security. However, under time pressure after China's intervention in the Korean War, the United States pressed for the San Francisco agreement, a bilateral approach to regional security that was eventually adopted. This agreement tied countries of the region to the United States through security pacts and preferential trade arrangements. It gave the United States the right to post military bases in allied countries (see Calder and Fukuyama 2008).

6. I used UCINET (Borgatti, Everett, and Freeman 2002) and NetDraw software (Borgatti 2002) to generate the visualizations.

7. South Korean NGOs have also worked to establish collaborative relations with NGOs in countries throughout the region (see, e.g., Jung 1999).

8. Coalitions in which these countries shared participation included World Women in Defense of the Environment, Clean Up the World, and the Asian Society for Environmental Protection.

9. Brunei was also not part of ASEAN at the time.

Works Cited

Acharya, Amitav. 2003. "Democratization and the Prospects for Participatory Regionalism in Southeast Asia." *Third World Quarterly* 24: 375–90.

Ahmad, Zakaria Haji, and Baladas Ghoshal. 1999. "The Political Future of ASEAN after the Asian Crisis." *International Affairs* 75: 759–78.

Akaha, Tsuneo. 1999. "Nationalism vs. Regionalism in Northeast Asia." In *Politics and Economics in Northeast Asia: Nationalism and Regionalism in Contention,* edited by T. Akaha, 367–82. New York: St. Martin's Press.

Almeida, Paul. 2003. "Opportunity Organizations and Threat-Induced Contention: Protest Waves in Authoritarian Settings." *American Journal of Sociology* 109: 345–400.

Axelrod, Robert. 1997. "The Dissemination of Culture: A Model with Local Convergence and Global Polarization." *Journal of Conflict Resolution* 41: 203–26.

Baldez, Lisa. 2006. *Why Women Protest: Women's Movements in Chile.* Cambridge: Cambridge University Press.

Bandy, Joe. 2004. "Paradoxes of Transnational Civil Societies under Neoliberalism: The Coalition for Justice in the Maquiladoras." *Social Problems* 51: 410–31.

Barabási, Albert-László, and Réka Albert. 1999. "The Emergence of Scaling in Random Networks." *Science* 286: 509–12.

Bob, Clifford. 2002. "Political Process Theory and Transnational Movements: Dialectics of Protest among Nigeria's Ogoni Minority." *Social Problems* 49: 395–415.

Borgatti, S. P. 2002. *NetDraw: Graph Visualization Software.* Harvard, Mass.: Analytic Technologies.

Borgatti, S. P., M. G. Everett, and L. C. Freeman. 2002. *Ucinet for Windows: Software for Social Network Analysis.* Harvard, Mass.: Analytic Technologies.

Brysk, Alison. 1993. "From Above and Below: Social Movements, the International System, and Human Rights in Argentina." *Comparative Political Studies* 26: 259–85.

Caballero-Anthony, Mely. 2004. "Non-State Regional Governance Mechanism for Economic Security: The Case of the ASEAN Peoples' Assembly." *Pacific Review* 17: 567–85.

Calder, Kent E. 2003. "Japan as a Post-Reactive State?" *Orbis* 47: 605–16.

Calder, Kent E., and Francis Fukuyama. 2008. *East Asian Multilateralism: Prospects for Regional Stability.* Baltimore: Johns Hopkins University Press.

Chandra, Alexandra. 2004. "Indonesia's Non-State Actors in ASEAN: A New Regionalism Agenda for Southeast Asia?" *Contemporary Southeast Asia* 26: 155–74.

Clemens, Elizabeth. 1997. *The People's Lobby: Organizational Innovation and the Rise of Interest Group Politics in the United States, 1890–1925.* Chicago: University of Chicago Press.

Cortright, David, and Ron Pagnucco. 1997. "Limits to Transnationalism: The 1980s Freeze Campaign." In *Transnational Social Movements and Global Politics: Solidarity beyond the State,* edited by Jackie Smith, Charles Chatfield, and Ron Pagnucco. Syracuse, N.Y.: Syracuse University Press.

Cotton, James. 1999. "The 'Haze' over Southeast Asia: Challenging the ASEAN Mode of Regional Engagement." *Pacific Affairs* 72: 331–51.

Cullen, Pauline. 2005. "Conflict and Cooperation within the Platform of European Social NGOs." In *Coalitions across Borders: Transnational Protest and the Neoliberal Order,* edited by Joe Bandy and Jackie Smith, 71–94. Lanham, Md.: Rowman & Littlefield.

DiazVeizades, Jeannette, and Edward T. Chang. 1996. "Building Cross-Cultural Coalitions: A Case-Study of the Black–Korean Alliance and the Latino–Black Roundtable." *Ethnic and Racial Studies* 19: 680–700.

Falk, Richard. 1995. "Regionalism and World Order after the Cold War." *Australian Journal of International Affairs* 49:1–15.

Fligstein, Neil, and Alec Stone Sweet. 2002. "Constructing Polities and Markets: An Institutionalist Account of European Integration." *American Journal of Sociology* 107: 1206–43.

Fox, Jonathan. 2000. "Assessing Binational Civil Society Coalitions: Lessons from the Mexico–U.S. Experience." Working Paper 26. Chicano/Latino Research Center, University of California, Santa Cruz.

Futrell, W. Chad. 2008. "Shallow Roots: Transnational Environmental Civil Society in Northeast Asia." Paper presented at the 103rd Annual Meeting of the American Sociological Association, Boston, Mass., August 4.

Grabowski, A., and R. A. Kosiński. 2006. "Evolution of a Social Network: The Role of Cultural Diversity." *Physical Review* E-73 (016135): 1–7.

Grugel, Jean. 2006. "Regionalist Governance and Transnational Collective Action in Latin America." *Economy and Society* 35: 209–31.

Guarnizo, Luis Edualdo, and Michael Peter Smith. 1998. *Transnationalism from Below.* New Brunswick, N.J.: Transaction.

Hathaway, Will, and David S. Meyer. 1993. "Competition and Cooperation in Social Movement Coalitions: Lobbying for Peace in the 1980s." *Berkeley Journal of Sociology* 38: 156–83.

Hussey, Antonia. 1991. "Regional Development and Cooperation through ASEAN." *Geographical Review* 18: 87–98.

Imig, Doug, and Sidney Tarrow. 2001. "Studying Contention in an Emerging Polity." In *Contentious Europeans: Protest and Politics in an Emerging Polity,* edited by D. Imig and S. Tarrow, 3–26. Lanham, Md.: Rowman & Littlefield.

Jie, Chen. 2001. "Burgeoning transnationalism of Taiwan's Social Movement NGOs." *Journal of Contemporary China* 10: 613–44.

Jung, Ku-Hyun. 1999. "Nongovernmental Initiatives in Korea for Northeast Asian Cooperation." In *Politics and Economics in Northeast Asia: Nationalism and Regionalism in Contention,* edited by T. Akaha, 347–66. New York: St. Martin's Press.

Kay, Tamara. 2005. "Labor Transnationalism and Global Governance: The Impact of NAFTA on Transnational Labor Relationships in North America." *American Journal of Sociology* 111: 715–56.

Keck, Margaret, and Kathryn Sikkink. 1998. *Activists beyond Borders: Advocacy Networks in International Politics.* Ithaca, N.Y.: Cornell University Press.

Khagram, Sanjeev. 2004. *Dams and Development: Transnational Struggles for Water and Power.* Ithaca, N.Y.: Cornell University Press.

Kivimaki, Timo. 2001. "The Long Peace of ASEAN." *Journal of Peace Research* 38: 5–25.

Krauss, Ellis S. 2003. "The U.S., Japan, and Trade Liberalization: From Bilateralism to Regional Multilateralism to Regionalism." *Pacific Review* 16: 307–29.

McCammon, Holly J., and Karen E. Campbell. 2002. "Allies on the Road to Victory: Coalition Formation between the Suffragists and the Woman's Christian Temperance Union." *Mobilization* 7: 231–51.

Meyer, David S., and Catherine Corrigall-Brown. 2005. "Coalitions and Political Context: U.S. Movements against Wars in Iraq." *Mobilization* 10: 327–45.

Murphy, Gillian. 2005. "Coalitions and the Development of the Global Environmental Movement: A Double-Edged Sword." *Mobilization* 10: 235–51.

Nesadurai, Helen S. 2003. "Attempting Developmental Regionalism through AFTA: The Domestic Sources of Regional Governance." *Third World Quarterly* 24: 235–53.

Park, Bae-Gyoon. 2005. "Spatially Selective Liberalization and Graduated Sovereignty: Politics of Neo-Liberalism and 'Special Economic Zones' in South Korea." *Political Geography* 24: 850–73.

Peng, Dajin. 2000. "The Changing Nature of East Asia as an Economic Region." *Pacific Affairs* 73: 171–91.

Poon-Kim, Shee. 1977. "A Decade of ASEAN, 1967–1977." *Asian Survey* 17: 753–70.

Reimann, Kim D. 2002. "Building Networks from the Outside In: Japanese NGOs and the Kyoto Climate Change Conference." In *Globalization and Resistance: Transnational Dimensions of Social Movements,* edited by Jackie Smith and Hank Johnston, 173–87. Lanham, Md.: Rowman & Littlefield.

Rozman, Gilbert. 2004. *Northeast Asia's Stunted Regionalism: Bilateral Distrust in the Shadow of Globalization.* Cambridge: Cambridge University Press.

Scalpino, Robert. 1999. "Northeast Asia at a Historical Turning Point." In *Politics and Economics in Northeast Asia: Nationalism and Regionalism in Contention,* edited by T. Akaha, xi–xxii. New York: St. Martin's Press.

Schock, Kurt. 1999. "People Power and Political Opportunities: Social Movement Mobilization and Outcomes in the Philippines and Burma." *Social Problems* 46: 355–75.

———. 2008. *Unarmed Insurrections: People Power Movements in Nondemocracies.* Minneapolis: University of Minnesota Press.

Shirasu, Takashi, and Lau Sim-Yee. 1999. "Nongovernmental Initiatives in Japan for

Regional Cooperation." In *Politics and Economics in Northeast Asia: Nationalism and Regionalism in Contention,* edited by T. Akaha, 329–46. New York: St. Martin's Press.

Smith, Jackie. 1995. "Transnational Political Processes and the Human Rights Movement." *Research in Social Movements, Conflicts, and Change* 18: 185–219.

Smith, Jackie, and Joe Bandy. 2005. "Introduction: Cooperation and Conflict in Transnational Protest." In *Coalitions across Borders: Transnational Protest and the Neoliberal Order,* edited by Joe Bandy and Jackie Smith, 1–17. Lanham, Md.: Rowman & Littlefield.

Smith, Jackie, and Dawn Wiest. 2005. "The Uneven Geography of Global Civil Society: National and Global Influences on Transnational Association." *Social Forces* 84: 621–51.

Smith, Jackie, Charles Chatfield, and Ron Pagnucco. 1997. *Transnational Social Movements and Global Politics: Solidarity beyond the State.* Syracuse, N.Y.: Syracuse University Press.

Smith, Jackie, Melissa Bolyard, and Anna Ippolito. 1999. "Human Rights and the Global Economy: A Response to Meyer." *Human Rights Quarterly* 21: 207–19.

Smith, Jackie, Marina Karides, Dorval Brunelle, Christopher Chase-Dunn, Donatella della Porta, Rosalba Icaza Garza, Jeffrey S. Juris, Lorenzo Mosca, Ellen Reese, Peter Smith, and Rolando Vazquez. 2007. *Global Democracy and the World Social Forums.* Boulder, Colo.: Paradigm.

Solidum, Estrella D. 2003. *The Politics of ASEAN: An Introduction to Southeast Asian Regionalism.* New York: Eastern Universities Press.

Staggenborg, Suzanne. 1986. "Coalition Work in the Pro-Choice Movement: Organizational and Environmental Opportunities and Obstacles." *Social Problems* 33: 374–90.

Stubbs, Richard. 2002. "ASEAN Plus Three: Emerging East Asian Regionalism?" *Asia Survey* 42: 440–55.

Tarrow, Sidney. 1994. *Power in Movement.* New York: Cambridge University Press.

———. 1996. "States and Opportunities: The Political Structuring of Social Movements." In *Comparative Perspectives on Social Movements: Political Opportunities, Mobilizing Structures, and Cultural Framings,* edited by Doug McAdam, John D. McCarthy, and Mayer N. Zald, 41–62. Cambridge: Cambridge University Press.

———. 2005. *The New Transnational Activism.* Cambridge: Cambridge University Press.

Tilly, Charles. 1978. *From Mobilization to Revolution.* Reading, Mass.: Addison-Wesley.

Tsutsui, Kiyoteru. 2004. "Global Civil Society and Ethnic Social Movements in the Contemporary World." *Sociological Forum* 19: 63–87.

Union of International Associations. 2000. *Yearbook of International Organizations.* 37th ed. Munich: K. G. Sauer.

Van Dyke, Nella. 2003. "Crossing Movement Boundaries: Factors That Facilitate Coalition Protest by American College Students, 1930–1990." *Social Problems*. 50: 226–50.

Van Dyke, Nella, and Sarah Soule. 2002. "Structural Social Change and the Mobilizing Effect of Threat: Explaining Levels of Patriot and Militia Organizing in the United States." *Social Problems* 49: 497–520.

Waldhorn, Steven A. 2002. "On the Wrong Track." *Social Policy* 32: 3–5.

Wallerstein, Immanuel. 1990. "Antisystemic Movements: History and Dilemmas." In *Transforming the Revolution,* edited by Samir Amin, Giovanni Arrighi, Andre Gunter Frank, and Immanuel Wallerstein, 13–54. New York: Monthly Review Press.

Wasserman, Stanley, and Katherine Faust. 1994. *Social Network Analysis: Methods and Applications.* Cambridge: Cambridge University Press.

Watts, Julie. 2003. "Mexico–U.S. Migration and Labor Unions: Obstacles to Building Cross-Border Solidarity." Working Paper 79. Center for Comparative Immigration Studies, University of California, San Diego, http://escholarship.org/uc/item/7267b8n4. Accessed April 14, 2010.

Wiest, Dawn. 2007. "A Story of Two Transnationalisms: Global Salafi Jihad and Human Rights Mobilization in the Middle East and North Africa." *Mobilization: An International Journal* 12: 137–60.

Wiest, Dawn, and Jackie Smith. 2006. "Regional Institutional Contexts and Patterns of Transnational Social Movement Organization." *Korea Observer* 37: 93–127.

———. 2007. "Explaining Participation in Regional, Transnational Social Movement Organizations." *International Journal of Comparative Sociology.* 48: 137–66.

II
Movement Ideology and Coalition Formation

4

Approaching Merger: The Converging Public Policy Agendas of the AFL and CIO, 1938–1955

Daniel B. Cornfield and Holly J. McCammon

Now, more than fifty years after its formation, the American Federation of Labor and Congress of Industrial Organizations (AFL-CIO) continues to play an important role in shaping public policy. The labor federation has promoted its broad public policy agenda on social welfare, labor law, employment policy, international trade, public education, and other public policies in federal and state legislatures (Brady 2007; Cornfield and Fletcher 1998; Frege and Kelly 2004). At the time of the AFL-CIO merger, observers noted that pursuing a comprehensive legislative agenda was one goal of the merger. Among the AFL-CIO legislative objectives were improvements in Social Security, unemployment insurance and worker's compensation benefits and coverage, alleviation of chronic unemployment in distressed areas, and repeal of state right-to-work labor laws (Bloch 1956). Referring to the broad legislative goals of the newly merged federation, the U.S. Bureau of Labor Statistics reported in the *Monthly Labor Review* that "both federations subscribed to these objectives before the merger, as evidenced in the wide-ranging resolutions introduced at their conventions during recent years . . . and their activities in connection with legislative matters. Thus, the merger was expected to concentrate, rather than to disperse, efforts in support of favorable legislation" (Bloch 1956, 147; *Industrial and Labor Relations Review* 1956).

The AFL-CIO merger in December 1955 followed a period of increased convergence in the public policy goals of the two rival labor federations. This was acknowledged at the founding AFL-CIO convention. Referring to a public policy subcommittee of the AFL-CIO Unity Committee, Resolutions Committee cochair Matthew Woll noted at the founding AFL-CIO convention that this Committee particularly studied the resolutions and policies adopted at the 1954 Conventions of the two organizations. The Committee discovered that on virtually all major issues, the two organizations had adopted policies which were in all respects either identical or very similar. . . . The resolutions which have been approved by the Resolutions Committee for submission to this [AFL-CIO] Convention reflect to the maximum possible extent the viewpoints previously adopted by the AFL and CIO. (*Proceedings of the First Constitutional Convention* 1955, 34)

In fact, the two federations had already begun to cooperate in their legislative and political activities before their 1953 No-Raiding Pact, which became effective January 1, 1954.[1] In arguing for CIO ratification of the No-Raiding Pact on the floor of the 1953 CIO convention, CIO leader John Brophy noted that the CIO and AFL had "achieved a large measure of working unity. A substantial degree of cooperation in legislative and political work has come into being between the two federations in recent years" (*Proceedings of the Fifteenth Constitutional Convention* 1953, 365).

Social movement scholars argue that a critical ingredient necessary for coalition formation is ideological congruence between movement organizations (Maney 2000; McCammon and Campbell 2002). For coordinated action to occur, groups must have a certain degree of overlapping interests, goals, and core beliefs. Barkan (1986), in his study of the civil rights movement, argues that groups with pronounced disagreements over policy goals will rarely come together and work jointly to achieve social change. Van Dyke's (2003, 237) study of college student protest reveals that movement organizations with broad agendas—that is, multi-issue groups with wide-reaching goals—are more likely to form partnerships and stage protest events with other activist organizations, largely because the breadth of their agenda provides a "broad, multi-issue ideology" that can more easily accommodate the goals of other groups. McCammon and Campbell (2002) find that the when the arguments of the woman suffragists became more in line with those of the Woman's Christian Temperance Union—that is, when the suffragists began utilizing more traditional conceptualizations of women's role as they voiced their demands for voting rights—then a coalition between the suffragists and the Woman's Christian Temperance Union occurred.

We argue that a close examination of the policy goals of the AFL and CIO in the years just before their merger reveals a growing convergence in the ideological orientations of the two labor organizations. The evidence strongly suggests that this growing ideological convergence in the early 1950s helped pave the way for the groups' merger in 1955. In the years before the

1950s, conflicts between the AFL and CIO over organizational philosophy, union jurisdictions, membership recruitment, and public policy goals, as well as personality conflicts among labor leaders, led to several abortive merger efforts (Seidman 1956). But the increased convergence in policy goals of the two federations during the early 1950s lifted one crucial obstacle to the eventual merger (Zieger 1995, 359–60). Like Van Dyke (2003) and McCammon and Campbell (2002), we find that a shift in the ideological orientation of one of the groups that entailed a broadening in the AFL's policy agenda and its widening embrace of the emerging New Deal welfare state (Cornfield and Fletcher 1998) set the stage for the organizational merger.[2]

Although a handful of scholars have investigated the role of ideological alignment between groups entering into partnerships (in addition to those mentioned above, see Lichterman 1995; Obach 2004), few have used quantitative measures to assess ideological convergence. In the following discussion, we trace the history of the convergence in AFL and CIO public policy goals through a close examination of enacted policy resolutions in different policy domains at the annual AFL and CIO conventions from 1938 to 1954. We use two measures, the index of dissimilarity and a dispersion index, to illustrate quantitatively the convergence in the policy platforms of the two federations over this historical period. Our findings reveal a policy convergence between the two groups, suggesting growing ideological congruence. Our results also show, similar to claims made by Van Dyke (2003), that a broadening in the policy agenda of the AFL was instrumental in allowing the merger to happen.[3]

Convergence of AFL and CIO Public Policy Goals

In the mid-1930s, a dissident group within the American Federation of Labor made up of leaders from the United Mine Workers, Amalgamated Clothing Workers, the International Typographical Union, and other smaller unions within the AFL began a process that would result in severed ties with the AFL (Cornfield 2006, 2007; Zieger 1986). The dissidents criticized the AFL's lack of aggressive organizing among industrial workers. They also maintained that the new inclusive CIO model of industrial unionism, in which all production workers of a single industry, regardless of occupation and skill level, belonged to one union, was more effective than the older exclusionary occupational AFL craft unionism of skilled workers for organizing the new lower-skill factory workforce in mass-production manufacturing (Cornfield 2007). The AFL, founded in 1886, had throughout its history focused its organizing on highly skilled craft workers in construction, manufacturing, and transportation, excluding less skilled mass production workers from its

ranks. After two years of insurgency within the AFL with the dissidents trying to convince the leadership to take a more inclusive approach, in 1938, the
Congress of Industrial Organizations held a separate convention, adopting
a new constitution and finalizing its break with the AFL. Thus began a period
of rivalry between the AFL and the newly formed CIO that lasted until the
years leading up to the organizational merger in 1955.

But as the data presented here will show, AFL and CIO legislative goals
increasingly converged during this period of tension between the two labor
federations. This trend is evident in the changing range of public policy resolutions passed by the delegates to the annual conventions of each federation (Bloch 1956, 147), shown in Table 4.1. Table 4.1 contains, for both the
AFL and the CIO, the annual percentage distribution of all public policy resolutions passed at their respective conventions across nineteen policy domains.
The nineteen policy domains exhaust the areas of public policy that were of
interest to the AFL and the CIO. The data series begin in 1938, the year of
the founding CIO convention, and end in 1954, the year of the last pre-
merger convention at which each federation passed public policy resolutions.
Data are not available for 1945 because neither federation convened that year.
The source of the data in Table 4.1 is the annual convention *Proceedings* of
each federation.[4]

Increasing convergence in public policy goals is indicated by the trend
in the annual index of dissimilarity shown at the bottom of Table 4.1. For
each year, this index measures the degree of dissimilarity between the AFL
and CIO percentage distributions of resolutions across policy domains. The
index of dissimilarity is constructed as the percentage of policy resolutions
(for either the AFL or CIO) that would have to be reassigned to a different
policy domain category in order for the two federations to achieve identical
percentage distributions of resolutions across the nineteen policy domain
categories.[5] The formula for the dissimilarity index (DI) is

$$DI = \tfrac{1}{2}(\sum_{i=1,}^{19} | P_{\mathrm{AFL}i} - P_{\mathrm{CIO}i} |)$$

where i is one of nineteen policy domains. $P_{\mathrm{AFL}i}$ is the percentage of AFL resolutions, and $P_{\mathrm{CIO}i}$ is the percentage of CIO resolutions, both accounted for
by the ith policy domain. Thus for 1938, for the social welfare policy domain
(or $i = 1$), $P_{\mathrm{AFL}1} = 2.1$ and $P_{\mathrm{CIO}1} = 8.2$. The index of dissimilarity for 1938 is
62.70. Once computed, the index ranges from 0, indicating no dissimilar-
ity, to 100, which indicates complete dissimilarity. In 1938, then, just under
63 percent of the policy resolutions would have to be reassigned to different
policy domain categories in order for the two federations to have identical

Table 4.1. Percentage Distribution of Public Policy Resolutions Passed at CIO and AFL Conventions by Policy Domain and Federation, 1938–54

Policy Domain	1938 CIO	1938 AFL	1939 CIO	1939 AFL	1940 CIO	1940 AFL	1941 CIO	1941 AFL
Social welfare	8.2	2.1	12.5	2.5	17.4	8.8	5.3	1.6
Civil rights	4.1	2.1	7.5	2.5	6.5	0	3.5	3.3
Civil liberties	16.3	4.2	12.5	0	17.4	2.9	22.8	1.6
Tax policy	0	0	2.5	0	2.2	0	1.8	1.6
Education and training	0	2.1	2.5	2.5	2.2	5.9	1.8	4.9
Price, wage, and inflation control	0	0	2.5	0	2.2	0	3.5	1.6
Health policy	2	2.1	5	2.5	4.3	4.4	1.8	1.6
Regulation of employment conditions								
Private sector	4.1	18.8	5	15	4.3	10.3	10.5	16.4
Public sector	2	33.3	5	27.5	4.3	35.3	7	19.7
Other social legislation	0	0	0	0	0	0	0	1.6
Immigration policy	0	0	0	2.5	0	0	0	0
International trade	0	2.1	0	17.5	0	0	0	1.6
Employment stimulation	10.2	0	5	0	4.3	1.5	5.3	1.6
Industrial policy	4.1	2.1	10	0	2.2	10.3	3.5	11.5
Labor law	26.5	14.6	7.5	7.5	19.6	5.9	15.8	9.8
Employment stabilization	0	2.1	2.5	2.5	0	1.5	3.5	6.6
Limits on labor supply	2	12.5	2.5	12.5	0	5.9	1.8	4.9
Defense and foreign policy	4.1	2.1	2.5	0	4.3	4.4	8.8	6.6
Other	16.2	0	15	5	8.7	2.9	3.5	3.2
Total[a]	99.8	100.2	100	100	99.9	100	100.2	99.7
N	49	48	40	40	46	68	57	61
Index of dissimilarity	62.70		62.50		56.35		40.95	
Dispersion index: CIO	5.39		3.52		4.56		4.01	
Dispersion index: AFL	6.11		5.65		4.8		4.12	

distributions of resolutions across the nineteen policy domains. This suggests a sizable divergence in policy positions for the two federations in the late 1930s.

The public policy agendas of the two federations, however, converged increasingly after World War II. The index of dissimilarity tended to be smaller after 1944. In six of the seven years of the earlier 1938–44 subperiod, the index of dissimilarity exceeded the overall median index value of 56.3; in seven of the nine years of the later 1946–54 subperiod, the index was smaller than the median. Before 1946, the index varied between 40.95 in 1941 and 80.25 in 1943; later, it varied between 42.85 in 1946 and 65.55 in 1951. The

Table 4.1. (continued)

Policy Domain	1942 CIO	1942 AFL	1943 CIO	1943 AFL	1944 CIO	1944 AFL	1946 CIO	1946 AFL
Social welfare	0	2.2	7.1	2.7	12.5	5.6	6.3	0
Civil rights	10	0	7.1	0	4.2	5.6	3.1	5.8
Civil liberties	10	2.2	3.6	0	12.5	0	12.5	2.9
Tax policy	0	4.4	3.6	0	4.2	1.4	3.1	2.9
Education and training	5	13.3	0	10.8	0	0	6.3	4.3
Price, wage and inflation control	5	2.2	17.9	2.7	8.3	5.6	3.1	1.4
Health policy	0	2.2	0	2.7	4.2	1.4	3.1	4.3
Regulation of employment conditions								
Private sector	5	17.8	3.6	27	0	18.1	6.3	14.5
Public sector	0	37.8	0	27	0	23.6	0	20.3
Other social legislation	0	0	3.6	2.7	0	0	3.1	4.3
Immigration policy	0	0	3.6	0	0	4.2	0	0
International trade	0	0	0	0	0	0	0	1.4
Employment stimulation	10	0	3.6	0	0	0	3.1	0
Industrial policy	0	2.2	7.1	2.7	12.5	6.9	12.5	15.9
Labor law	10	4.4	17.9	2.7	20.8	9.7	15.6	8.7
Employment stabilization	0	4.4	3.6	0	0	8.3	3.1	2.9
Limits on labor supply	0	2.2	0	10.8	0	5.6	0	4.3
Defense and foreign policy	35	2.2	17.9	2.7	12.5	2.8	6.3	2.9
Other	10	2.2	0	5.4	8.3	1.4	12.5	2.9
Total[a]	100	99.7	100.2	99.9	100	100.2	100	99.7
N	20	45	28	37	24	72	32	69
Index of dissimilarity	76.65		80.25		61.10		42.85	
Dispersion index: CIO	5.62		4.56		5.32		3.81	
Dispersion index: AFL	5.61		5.76		4.37		4.11	

index reached its zenith during World War II, when it was 76.65 and 80.25 in 1942 and 1943, respectively. The index declined after the war and stabilized at a relatively low level, varying between 43.85 percent and 45.95 percent, during the last three years of the data series, just before the AFL-CIO merger.

The public policy goals of the two federations became more similar with the deceleration of the union membership growth rate after World War II. This deceleration in growth helps us understand why the policy agendas of the two groups converged after the war. The drop in the index of dissimilarity between the 1938–44 and 1946–54 subperiods corresponds approximately to the trend in the percentage unionized of nonagricultural U.S. employment.

Table 4.1. *(continued)*

Policy Domain	1947 CIO	1947 AFL	1948 CIO	1948 AFL	1949 CIO	1949 AFL	1950 CIO	1950 AFL
Social welfare	14.8	12.2	10.3	2	12.9	5.5	6.1	5
Civil rights	11.1	2.4	3.4	5.9	0	9.1	0	10
Civil liberties	3.7	2.4	0	9.8	6.5	1.8	6.1	2.5
Tax policy	3.7	1.2	3.4	2	3.2	0	3	0
Education and training	3.7	2.4	6.9	7.8	3.2	3.6	3	7.5
Price, wage and inflation control	3.7	0	6.9	0	0	0	0	0
Health policy	0	1.2	0	0	0	0	6.1	2.5
Regulation of employment conditions								
Private sector	7.4	15.9	6.9	21.6	3.2	27.3	3	12.5
Public sector	0	32.9	0	9.8	0	12.7	0	2.5
Other social legislation	3.7	4.9	3.4	9.8	16.2	5.5	12.2	0
Immigration policy	0	0	0	5.9	0	0	0	5
International trade	0	0	0	0	0	1.8	0	10
Employment stimulation	3.7	1.2	0	0	3.2	0	6.1	0
Industrial policy	7.4	13.4	20.7	9.8	9.7	5.5	18.2	5
Labor law	11.1	1.2	10.3	2	9.7	9.1	12.1	5
Employment stabilization	0	0	0	2	0	1.8	0	2.5
Limits on labor supply	3.7	2.4	3.4	5.9	0	3.6	0	2.5
Defense and foreign policy	11.1	1.2	6.9	0	9.7	3.6	3	15
Other	11.1	4.9	17.2	5.9	22.5	9.1	21.2	12.5
Total[a]	99.9	99.8	99.7	100.2	100	100	100.1	100
N	27	82	29	51	31	55	33	40
Index of dissimilarity	51.05		56.25		55.30		61.05	
Dispersion index: CIO	3.92		4.65		5.3		4.84	
Dispersion index: AFL	5.63		4.16		4.39		3.78	

During the 1938–45 period, when the AFL and CIO competed fiercely with each other in union organizing and when wartime labor policies expanded union memberships, the percentage unionized jumped from 27.5 percent in 1938 to its all-time high of 35.5 percent in 1945 (U.S. Bureau of Labor Statistics 1979, 507). Between 1946 and 1955, when unions had organized "most workers in readily organizable industries and occupations" and the Taft-Hartley Act of 1947 constrained unionization efforts, the percentage unionized stabilized and varied between 31.5 percent and 34.7 percent (U.S. Bureau of Labor Statistics 1958, 7). Thus, as conditions for competition to organize additional workers began to wane between the two labor organizations after

Table 4.1. *(continued)*

Policy Domain	1951 CIO	1951 AFL	1952 CIO	1952 AFL	1953 CIO	1953 AFL	1954 CIO	1954 AFL
Social welfare	0	5.9	6.9	6.3	6.9	10.9	9.1	5.6
Civil rights	0	2	0	2.1	0	4.7	0	3.7
Civil liberties	7.1	0	6.9	0	10.3	1.6	6.1	3.7
Tax policy	3.6	2	3.4	2.1	6.9	0	3	0
Education and training	0	11.8	0	4.2	0	4.7	3	3.7
Price, wage and inflation control	7.1	11.8	3.4	2.1	0	0	0	0
Health policy	7.1	2	6.9	2.1	6.9	1.6	3	1.9
Regulation of employment conditions								
Private sector	0	9.8	3.4	10.4	0	10.9	3	11.1
Public sector	0	21.6	0	18.8	3.4	15.6	0	14.8
Other social legislation	0	3.9	0	0	3.4	0	0	1.9
Immigration policy	0	2	6.9	2.1	3.4	3.1	3	0
International trade	0	0	0	4.2	0	0	0	3.7
Employment stimulation	3.6	2	3.4	4.2	3.4	0	3	0
Industrial policy	25	7.8	10.3	8.3	20.7	17.2	18.2	7.4
Labor law	14.3	3.9	10.3	4.2	6.9	3.1	9.1	9.3
Employment stabilization	0	0	0	4.2	3.4	4.7	3	1.9
Limits on labor supply	0	2	0	0	0	4.7	0	5.6
Defense and foreign policy	14.3	3.9	20.7	6.3	10.3	6.3	15.2	13
Other	17.9	7.9	17.2	18.8	13.7	11	21.2	13.1
Total[a]	100	100.3	99.7	100.4	99.6	100.1	99.9	100.4
N	28	51	29	48	29	64	33	54
Index of dissimilarity	65.55		45.95		43.85		44.05	
Dispersion index: CIO	5.89		4.65		4.28		4.99	
Dispersion index: AFL	4.17		3.91		4.24		3.96	

Source: Proceedings of the 1938–54 AFL and CIO Conventions.

[a] Totals may not sum to 100.0% due to rounding.

the war and Taft-Hartley (Seidman 1956), the need for ideological distinction began to recede as well. Also, new leadership in the AFL with the election of George Meany to the presidency in 1952 brought new efforts in that organization to expand social welfare legislation, bringing the AFL in line with the CIO in this policy arena (Cornfield and Fletcher 1998; Zieger 1986, 159).

Before 1946, the two federations differed most in their emphases on four of the nineteen policy domains: civil liberties, regulation of private-sector employment conditions, regulation of public-sector employment conditions, and labor law. One can examine a decomposition of the index of dissimilarity for these four policy domains to establish the percentage of the value of the index of dissimilarity that is attributable to the four policy domains. For a single policy domain, this percentage is the percentage of the total index value that is attributable to half of the absolute value of the difference between the two federations in the percentage of resolutions each federation passed in the policy domain, which can be represented as

percentage of DI attributable to policy domain

$i = 100 \times [½(|\ P_{AFLi} - P_{CIOi}\ |)/(DI)]$.

The decomposition value for any one domain can then be added to that of other domains to establish the percentage attributable to a subgroup of policy domains.

The decomposition of the index of dissimilarity (derived from Table 4.1) indicates that the two federations placed distinctly different emphases on civil liberties, regulation of private-sector employment conditions, regulation of public-sector employment conditions, and labor law policy domains. For each of the years 1938, 1940, 1941, and 1944, most of the index of dissimilarity—53.4 percent to 57.9 percent—was attributable to federation differences in emphasis of these four policy domains. In the other three years of the 1938–44 subperiod, the four policy domains accounted for 36.0 percent to 43.1 percent of the annual indexes of dissimilarity.

As the public policy agendas of the federations became more similar in the 1946–54 subperiod, the two federations differed less in their emphases of these four policy domains. A decomposition of the index of dissimilarity (again derived from Table 4.1) indicates that for the last seven of the nine years of the 1946–54 subperiod, no more than 42.2 percent of the index of dissimilarity was attributable to the four policy domains. By 1954, the percentage of the index of dissimilarity that was attributable to the four policy domains had dropped to 28.9 percent. By the early 1950s, the policy emphases of the AFL and CIO were substantially more similar than they had been before and during World War II.

Changes in the Public Policy Goals of the AFL and the CIO

The growing convergence in the public policy goals of the two federations resulted mainly from a broadening of the range of public policy domains of interest to the AFL. At the time of the AFL-CIO merger, observers such as labor economist Edwin Witte (1956, 412) reported that the CIO, more than the AFL, had emphasized the importance of public policy for labor. The greater emphasis of the CIO on public policy, according to labor relations expert Joel

Seidman (1956, 357), derived from the lower skill levels of CIO union members who, compared to skilled AFL craftsmen, "were more dependent upon government legislation to supplement the gains possible through collective bargaining" and were concerned with a broader array of national public policies. But, again, with reduced rivalry for members between the unions following World War II and the passage of the Taft-Hartley Act and with new leadership in the AFL, the AFL began to broaden its policy goals, producing greater similarity in the policy stances of the two labor organizations.

The broadening of the AFL policy agenda constituted an ideological shift from voluntarism toward the CIO's social democratic embrace of the New Deal welfare state. According to Cornfield and Fletcher's (1998) analysis of changes in AFL convention resolutions over the complete AFL history (1881–1955), the AFL originally adopted a voluntarist philosophy, calling for public policy that legitimized trade unionism and protected trade unions as private actors engaged in wealth redistribution via collective bargaining. Over the ensuing three-quarters of a century, the AFL increasingly supported a social democratic approach that entailed state redistributive intervention and enactment of social welfare legislation for all workers, unionized and nonunionized alike. Cornfield and Fletcher (1998) attribute the AFL ideological shift to dynamics in the multiorganizational field of the AFL. Specifically, they argue that the AFL increasingly enlisted the state as a third-party ally as increases in industrial productivity reduced employer dependence on unions for labor supply and the growth of the welfare state increased the political opportunity for labor alignments with the state.

We use a measure of the dispersion of resolutions across the nineteen policy domains (for one federation in one year) to assess the range of policy domains of interest to the federations. The formula for this annual dispersion index for one federation is

$$\text{annual federation dispersion index} = 1/19 \left(\sum_{i=1}^{19} | P_i - 5.26 | \right)$$

where i indicates one of nineteen policy domains, P_i is the percentage of overall federation policy resolutions accounted for by the ith policy domain, and $5.26 = 1/19$.[6] For each federation and year, once computed, the index measures the degree of dispersion of the resolutions across the nineteen policy domains. The larger the index, the more concentrated the resolutions are in a smaller range of policy domains. A dispersion index of 0, indicating the widest possible dispersion of resolutions across policy domains, signifies that each of the nineteen policy domains accounted for the same percentage of all resolutions—that is, 5.26 percent (or 1 of 19)—passed at the annual federation convention. Were 100 percent of the resolutions passed in only one policy domain, the dispersion index would be 10.0. Thus, the dispersion index ranges from 0 to 10.

The trend in the AFL and CIO dispersion indexes in Table 4.1 indicates that it was the broadening of AFL public policy goals, more than changes in the breadth of CIO public policy goals, that resulted in greater convergence in AFL and CIO public policy goals. Before 1946, the CIO convention tended to pass resolutions in a broader range of policy domains than had the AFL convention (i.e., the dispersion index is smaller for the CIO in these earlier years). In five of the seven years of the 1938–44 subperiod, the AFL dispersion index exceeded the CIO index. The average annual CIO index was 4.72 in the 1938–44 subperiod, virtually identical to its later 1946–54 subperiod average value of 4.70. The average annual AFL index, in contrast, was 5.20 in the earlier 1938–44 subperiod and declined by 18.1 percent to 4.26 in the 1946–54 subperiod, indicating a broadening of the AFL policy agenda in these later years.[7]

The impact of the broadening of the AFL public policy agenda is also discernible in the shifts by the federations in their emphases of the four policy domains on which they had differed (Table 4.1). In the earlier 1938–44 subperiod, two of the four policy domains—the regulation of private- and public-sector employment conditions—dominated the AFL public policy agenda. Resolutions on the regulation of private sector employment conditions dealt with improvements in the benefits and coverage in such laws as the Fair Labor Standards Act and prevailing wage laws. Resolutions on the regulation of public employment conditions called for improvements in a wide range of government employee employment and working conditions, including pay, benefits, work schedules, grievance procedures, and seniority and civil service systems.[8] On average, these two policy domains alone accounted for 46.8 percent of all resolutions passed at each annual AFL convention, but only 7.3 percent of those at the annual CIO convention, during the 1938–44 subperiod.

For the CIO, in contrast, the two policy domains that dominated its public policy agenda in the earlier 1938–44 subperiod—civil liberties and labor law—accounted for an annual average of 30.5 percent of its convention resolutions during this subperiod. (At the annual AFL conventions during the 1938–44 subperiod, these policy domains, on average, accounted for only 9.4 percent of all resolutions.) Resolutions on civil liberties addressed such issues as imprisonment of labor activists, civil liberties for civilian defense workers, and privacy protections. Among the issues addressed by labor law resolutions were the strengthening and extension of rights to unionize, opposition to antilabor state labor laws, requests for government intervention in specific labor–management conflicts, and wartime labor policies.[9] The AFL, then, focused more intently on its top two policy areas (which accounted for 46.8 percent of all resolutions passed at each annual AFL convention) than did the CIO during these earlier years. The AFL thus possessed the more narrow policy agenda of the two labor organizations during this period.

During the later 1946–54 subperiod, the average annual percentage of resolutions accounted for by the two policy domains that had previously dominated the AFL public policy agenda dropped to 31.4 percent, revealing that the organization broadened its policy outlook. The average annual percentage of resolutions in the two policy domains that had previously dominated the CIO public policy agenda declined to 17.6 percent during the 1946–54 subperiod. Unlike the AFL public policy agenda, however, the CIO public policy agenda did not broaden during the later subperiod. The decline in the shares of CIO convention resolutions in the civil liberties and labor law policy domains was largely offset by the increase in the share of resolutions in the industrial policy domain during the 1946–54 subperiod. (The annual average percentage of CIO convention resolutions in the industrial policy domain increased from 5.6 percent in the 1938–44 subperiod to 15.9 percent in the 1946–54 subperiod.) The overall dispersion of CIO resolutions, then, across policy domains remained stable over the two subperiods compared to that of the AFL.

The results from the dispersion indexes thus suggest that the policy agenda of the AFL in the years just after World War II and just before the merger broadened to include policy domains given little attention by that federation in earlier years. This broadening introduced greater overlap between the policy interests of the AFL and CIO and the increasing overlap in interests provided a social democratic ideological foundation on which the merger of the two organizations could be based.

The Founding AFL-CIO Convention

The founding convention of the AFL-CIO in 1955 enacted public policy resolutions in a wide range of policy domains (Bloch 1956). The percentage distribution of these resolutions across the nineteen policy domains is shown in Table 4.2. The wide breadth of the policy domains addressed by the convention is indicated by the low dispersion index of 3.99. This dispersion index is smaller than those of either the AFL or the CIO in thirteen of the previous sixteen years in which the two groups held separate conventions (see Table 4.1).

Despite the larger membership of the AFL, the public policy agenda of the founding AFL-CIO convention bore the imprint of the CIO more than it did the AFL. This is shown by the indexes of dissimilarity in Table 4.2, which compare the percentage distribution of resolutions at the founding AFL-CIO convention with that of the 1954 CIO convention and with that of the 1954 AFL convention. Comparing the 1955 AFL-CIO convention and the 1954 CIO convention yields a low index of dissimilarity of 25.25. The index of dissimilarity between the 1955 AFL-CIO and 1954 AFL conventions, on the other hand, is 44.70, which approximates the indexes of

Table 4.2. Percentage Distribution of Policy Resolutions by Policy Domain, First AFL-CIO Convention, 1955

Policy Domain	%
Social welfare	12.9
Civil rights	0
Civil liberties	6.5
Tax policy	3.2
Education and training	0
Price, wage, and inflation control	0
Health policy	6.5
Regulation of employment conditions	
Private sector	3.2
Public sector	3.2
Other social legislation	6.5
Immigration policy	6.5
International trade	0
Employment stimulation	6.5
Industrial policy	16.1
Labor law	9.7
Employment stabilization	0
Limits on labor supply	0
Defense and foreign policy	9.7
Other	9.7
Total[a]	100.2
N	31
Dispersion index	3.99
Index of dissimilarity between the AFL-CIO and:	
CIO, 1954	25.25
AFL, 1954	44.7

Source: Proceedings of the First Constitutional Convention of the American Federation of Labor and Congress of Industrial Organizations (New York, December 5–8, 1955). For indexes of dissimilarity, see Table 4.1.

[a] Totals do not sum to 100.0% as a result of rounding.

dissimilarity between the AFL and the CIO in the three years before the merger (Table 4.1). The percentage distribution of resolutions at the 1955 AFL-CIO convention also resembled that of the 1954 CIO convention, especially in its emphasis on the social welfare, industrial policy, and labor law policy domains, which composed 38.7 percent of the resolutions passed at the AFL-CIO convention. The 1955 AFL-CIO resolutions also deviated from those of the 1954 AFL convention in their deemphasis of regulating private- and public-sector employment conditions. These policy domains formed 6.4 percent of the resolutions passed at the founding AFL-CIO convention (Table 4.2), 25.9 percent of those at the final AFL convention, and only 3.0 percent of those at the final CIO convention (Table 4.1). These similarities between the 1955 AFL-CIO and 1954 CIO conventions belie statements made by some contemporary witnesses of the merger. Michael Quill, president of the Transport Workers Union, remarked that the union merger represented "the tragic liquidation of the CIO" and that it meant the end of CIO ideals (Zieger 1995, 4). The results provided here, however, reveal a different story: the CIO's policy goals and ideological framework lived on in the AFL-CIO.

Having developed a comprehensive public policy agenda, the newly merged federation commenced its mission to "spearhead the fight for legislation beneficial to all wage earners" (Meany 1956, 350), organized and unorganized workers alike, and to "bring economic and social justice and freedom to all" workers (Reuther 1956). The delegates to the founding AFL-CIO convention, led by labor balladeer Joe Glazer, sang these words of "All Together" (*Proceedings of the First Constitutional Convention* 1955, 122), composed in honor of the merger:

> . . . "What's good for America," we're proud to note,
> "Is good for labor," and this you may quote.
> So ring those bells and get out the vote
> To build our country strong.
> All together, all together, we are stronger
> Every way, AFL-CIO
> We will build together, work together for
> A better day, AFL and CIO.

Conclusion

As a number of scholars have argued (Maney 2000; McCammon and Campbell 2002), ideological convergence is a critical ingredient in the formation of social movement partnerships. Our results suggest that a convergence between the AFL and CIO in the public policy domains the two federations chose to emphasize at their annual conventions played a role in producing the formal merger of the groups in 1955. Our measures of policy dissimilarity show that in the years just before the merger, the two groups became substantially more similar in their annual policy resolutions. In addition, our policy dispersion measures show that it was a broadening in the AFL's policy orientation that particularly explains the growing similarity between the two labor organizations. In the years just before the merger, the AFL widened its policy scope, focusing less heavily on a narrow range of policy domains and instead giving serious treatment to a more expansive array of policies, including social welfare policies. This made the AFL more similar to the CIO in its publicly stated ideological orientation. We argue that this crucial development made the 1955 merger of the two labor organizations possible.

Our evidence of the historic importance of ideological similarity as a precursor to a formal alliance between these two labor organizations may shed light on more contemporary developments in the U.S. labor movement and beyond, to global alliances among laboring groups. In the United States, Change to Win's recent split with the AFL-CIO represents another dissident group parting ways with a major labor federation (Cornfield 2006; Milkman 2006). But just as importantly, Change to Win is also a labor coalition of seven unions representing six million unionized workers.[10] Their coalescence in opposition to the AFL-CIO was in part possible because the various constituencies that came together, although representing workers from a diverse set of industries, occupations, and ethnic and racial groups, shared a common belief that economic restructuring in the U.S. economy and the increasing globalization of the marketplace have fundamentally changed the terrain on which workers organize themselves and struggle for reasonable wages, benefits, and working conditions (Cornfield 2006, 2007). Change to Win argues that U.S. workers need "to build a new movement of working people equipped to meet the challenges of the global economy and restore the American Dream" (Change to Win 2010). The formation of Change to Win might be said to mark the beginning of a new period of stepped-up social movement unionism and coalition building in the United States that Turner (2003, 24) tells us is "necessary for the revitalization of labor movements." The importance of shared interests in the historic case of the CIO and AFL merger in the 1950s, then, helps us understand the critical role of shared beliefs not only in drawing together the Change to Win coalition but in reestablishing a powerful presence for the American labor movement in the U.S. economy and polity.

On a broader scale, the lesson of the AFL-CIO merger helps us see that a fundamental step in forging transnational networks and organizations among labor groups across the global north and south lies in establishing forums in which potential allies from a rich variety of backgrounds can confer, realize, and articulate common difficulties and goals. As Waterman (2005, 142) points out, the World Social Forums provide critical spaces where activists, including labor activists, from diverse cultural perspectives can come together to "talk across differences" and, at least to a degree, hone shared understandings of their plights. Other scholars (Anner and Evans 2004; Carty 2004; Garwood 2005) also assert the importance of opportunities for shared dialogue across national borders to foster global coalitions among laboring groups.

From this brief account of the AFL-CIO merger, social movement scholars will find evidence suggesting that ideological congruence plays an important role in facilitating the formation of social movement organizational partnerships. Just as Van Dyke (2003) indicates in her research on joint protests among college student movement organizations, we also find that organizations with a broader ideological outlook are more likely to form alliances. Similar to McCammon and Campbell's (2002) investigation of suffragists, we find that the ideological orientation of one group can shift, producing a greater alignment of organizational ideologies and allowing an alliance to form. In the early years we examined here, when the AFL had a more narrow policy agenda, the merger did not occur. Once the AFL's policy platform shifted and broadened, the formal partnership came into existence. The broader ideological orientation provides a greater chance of overlapping interests and goals for movement organizations. This may, in fact, provide a lesson that will serve labor unions well in the global north and south desirous of overcoming the barriers that separate workers in these regions. Organized workers in both arenas will have to broaden and refine their perspectives in order to build organizational unity in an international labor movement.

Notes

An earlier version of this paper was presented at the World Meeting of Labor Studies and Sociology of Work, University of Puerto Rico, Mayagüez, February 1996. We are grateful to Larry Griffin, Nella Van Dyke, and Bill Fletcher for helpful comments on an earlier draft and to the Vanderbilt University Research Council and the National Science Foundation for supporting the research. The authors bear sole responsibility for the contents of the article.

1. A no-raiding pact is an agreement between unions stipulating that if one union holds bargaining rights in a workplace, the other will not attempt takeover of the bargaining unit by campaigning among unionized workers for a new certification election (Krislov 1954).

2. Other conditions also contributed to the merger. Seidman (1956) and Zieger (1986, 1995) point to the importance of leadership changes. Barbash (1976) argues that the hostilities directed toward labor by the Eisenhower administration was a main factor propelling the merger. On other political conditions facilitating the merger, see Witte (1956). On the conditions surrounding more recent union mergers and coalitions, see Cornfield (1991a, 1991b, 2006), Sverke, Chaison, and Sjoberg (2004), Turner and Cornfield (2007), and Williamson (1995).

3. A merger is at one end of a continuum of types of coalition work (Cook 1977, 73–74; Zald and Ash 1966, 335) and among activist groups is in fact a rare occurrence (Wilson 1973). Mergers are largely permanent and highly formalized forms of cooperation between groups, as opposed to the ad hoc and loosely coordinated coalition work that occurs at the other end of the alliance continuum.

4. The lead author (D.B.C.) assigned the resolutions to each of the nineteen policy-domain categories in Table 4.1.

5. The index of dissimilarity is commonly used as a measure of racial residential or gender or racial occupational segregation (Jacobs 1993; Lieberson and Carter 1982).

6. This dispersion measure is the mean difference between the observed percentage of a federation's resolutions in a policy domain and the percentage of resolutions in a policy domain that would obtain if all resolutions were distributed equally across all nineteen policy domains. The latter percentage is 5.26 percent, or 1 of 19 of all 19 policy domains.

7. In 1948 and later years, the dispersion index for the CIO is greater than that for the AFL, indicating that due to the broadening of the AFL agenda, in these later years, the CIO agenda was more concentrated than the AFL agenda. The CIO public policy goals did not change substantially between the earlier 1938–44 subperiod and the later 1946–54 subperiod. Thus, changes in the AFL, not changes in the CIO, resulted in the convergence of organizational ideologies.

8. For descriptions of resolutions on the regulation of private- and public-sector employment conditions, see the *Proceedings* of the 1938–44 AFL conventions.

9. For descriptions of resolutions on civil liberties and labor law, see the *Proceedings* of the 1938–44 CIO conventions.

10. The Change to Win coalition exited the AFL-CIO in 2005 and comprises the International Brotherhood of Teamsters, Laborers' International Union of North America, Service Employees International Union, United Brotherhood of Carpenters and Joiners of America, United Farm Workers of America, United Food and Commercial Workers International Union, and UNITE HERE (the last a merger between the Union of Needletrades, Industrial, and Textile Employees and the Hotel Employees and Restaurant Employees International Union).

Works Cited

Anner, Mark, and Peter Evans. 2004. "Building Bridges across a Double Divide: Alliances between U.S. and Latin American Labour and NGOs." *Development in Practice* 14: 34–47.

Barbash, Jack. 1976. "The Labor Movement after World War II." *Monthly Labor Review* 99: 34–37.

Barkan, Steven E. 1986. "Interorganizational Conflict in the Southern Civil Rights Movement." *Sociological Inquiry* 56: 190–209.

Bloch, Joseph. 1956. "Founding Convention of the AFL-CIO." *Monthly Labor Review* 79: 147–48.

Brady, David. 2007. "Institutional, Economic, or Solidaristic? Assessing Explanations for Unionization across Affluent Democracies." *Work and Occupations* 34: 67–101.

Carty, Victoria. 2004. "Transnational Labor Mobilizing in Two Mexican Maquiladoras." *Mobilization* 9: 295–310.

Change to Win. 2010. http://www.changetowin.org/about-us.html. Accessed April 7, 2010.

Cook, Karen S. 1977. "Exchange and Power in Networks of Interorganizational Relations." *Sociological Quarterly* 18: 62–82.

Cornfield, Daniel B. 1991a. "The Attitude of Employee Association Members toward Union Mergers: The Effect of Socioeconomic Status." *Industrial and Labor Relations Review* 44: 334–48.

———. 1991b. "The U.S. Labor Movement: Its Development and Impact on Social Inequality and Politics." *Annual Review of Sociology* 17: 27–49.

———. 2006. "Immigration, Economic Restructuring, and Labor Ruptures: From the Amalgamated to Change to Win." *WorkingUSA* 9: 215–23.

———. 2007. "Conclusion: Seeking Solidarity . . . Why, and with Whom?" In *Labor in the New Urban Battlegrounds: Local Solidarity in a Global Economy,* edited by Lowell Turner and Daniel B. Cornfield, 235–51. Ithaca, N.Y.: Cornell University Press.

Cornfield, Daniel B., and Bill Fletcher. 1998. "Institutional Constraints on Social Movement 'Frame Extension': Shifts in the Legislative Agenda of the American Federation of Labor, 1881–1955." *Social Forces* 76: 1305–21.

Frege, Carola, and John Kelly, eds. 2004. *Varieties of Unionism: Strategies for Union Revitalization in a Globalizing Economy.* Oxford: Oxford University Press.

Garwood, Shae. 2005. "Politics at Work: Transnational Advocacy Networks and the Global Garment Industry." *Gender and Development* 13: 21–33.

Industrial and Labor Relations Review. 1956. "The AFL-CIO Merger." *Industrial and Labor Relations Review* 9: 347–457.

Jacobs, Jerry A. 1993. "Theoretical and Measurement Issues in the Study of Sex

Segregation in the Workplace: Research Note." *European Sociological Review* 9: 325–30.

Krislov, Joseph. 1954. "Raiding among the 'Legitimate' Unions." *Industrial and Labor Relations Review* 8: 19–29.

Lichterman, Paul. 1995. "Piecing Together Multicultural Community: Cultural Differences in Community Building among Grass-Roots Environmentalists." *Social Problems* 42: 513–34.

Lieberson, Stanley, and Donna Kay Carter. 1982. "Temporal Changes and Urban Differences in Residential Segregation: A Reconsideration." *American Journal of Sociology* 88: 296–310.

Maney, Gregory M. 2000. "Transnational Mobilization and Civil Rights in Northern Ireland." *Social Problems* 47: 153–79.

McCammon, Holly J., and Karen E. Campbell. 2002. "Allies on the Road to Victory: Coalition Formation between the Suffragists and the Woman's Christian Temperance Union." *Mobilization* 7: 231–51.

Meany, George. 1956. "Merger and the National Welfare." *Industrial and Labor Relations Review* 9: 349–51.

Milkman, Ruth. 2006. "Divided We Stand." *New Labor Forum* 15: 38–46.

Obach, Brian K. 2004. *Labor and the Environmental Movement: The Quest for Common Ground.* Cambridge, Mass.: MIT Press.

Proceedings of the Fifteenth Constitutional Convention of the Congress of Industrial Organizations. 1953. Cleveland, Ohio, November 16–20.

Proceedings of the First Constitutional Convention of the American Federation of Labor and Congress of Industrial Organizations. 1955. New York, December 5–8.

Reuther, Walter. 1956. "Labor's New Unity." *Industrial and Labor Relations Review* 9: 352.

Seidman, Joel. 1956. "Efforts toward Merger, 1935–1955." *Industrial and Labor Relations Review* 9: 353–70.

Sverke, Magnus, Gary N. Chaison, and Anders Sjoberg. 2004. "Do Union Mergers Affect the Members? Short- and Long-Term Effects on Attitudes and Behaviour." *Economic and Industrial Democracy* 25: 103–24.

Turner, Lowell. 2003. "Reviving the Labor Movement: A Comparative Perspective." In *Research in the Sociology of Work: Labor Revitalization: Global Perspective and New Initiatives,* edited by Daniel B. Cornfield and Holly J. McCammon, 23–58. Oxford: Elsevier.

Turner, Lowell, and Daniel B. Cornfield, eds. 2007. *Labor in the New Urban Battlegrounds: Local Solidarity in a Global Economy.* Ithaca, N.Y.: Cornell University Press.

U.S. Bureau of Labor Statistics. 1958. *A Guide to Labor–Management Relations in the United States.* Bulletin 1225. Washington, D.C.: Government Printing Office.

———. 1979. *Handbook of Labor Statistics 1978.* Bulletin 2000. Washington, D.C.: Government Printing Office.

Van Dyke, Nella. 2003. "Crossing Movement Boundaries: Factors That Facilitate Coalition Protest by American College Students, 1930–1990." *Social Problems* 50: 226–50.

Waterman, Peter. 2005. "Talking across Difference in an Interconnected World of Labor." In *Coalitions across Borders: Transnational Protest and the Neoliberal Order,* edited by Joe Bandy and Jackie Smith, 141–61. Lanham, Md.: Rowman & Littlefield.

Williamson, Lisa. 1995. "Union Mergers: 1985–94 Update." *Monthly Labor Review* 118: 18–25.

Wilson, James Q. 1973. *Political Organizations.* New York: Basic Books.

Witte, Edwin. 1956. "The New Federation and Political Action." *Industrial and Labor Relations Review* 9: 406–18.

Zald, Mayer N., and Roberta Ash. 1966. "Social Movement Organizations: Growth, Decay and Change." *Social Forces* 44: 327–40.

Zieger, Robert H. 1986. *American Workers, American Unions, 1920–1985.* Baltimore: Johns Hopkins University Press.

———. 1995. *The CIO, 1935–1955.* Chapel Hill: University of North Carolina Press.

5

"Organizing One's Own" as Good Politics: Second Wave Feminists and the Meaning of Coalition

Benita Roth

In the following, I argue that shared ideas about the proper way to organize militated against U.S. feminists forming coalitions across racial/ethnic lines in the 1960s and 1970s, the period commonly referred to as the second wave of feminist protest. Feminist mobilizations in the United States during that period were part of a heightened cycle of social protest (Tarrow 1994). I use the plural in discussing second wave feminist organizing because that organizing was characterized by multiple origins and resulted in organizationally distinct movements (B. Roth 2004). Most literature on the second wave has emphasized the twin social bases from which (white) feminist organizing emerged: the network of professional women who organized what was generally known as liberal feminism and the decentralized and reticulate network of radical political women involved in movements for social change who formed women's liberation groups on the left (Buechler 1990; Ferree and Hess 2000; Freeman 1975). Of late, more attention has been paid to the feminist organizing of working-class women (Cobble 2004; S. Roth 2003) and to activism by feminist women of color working autonomously within oppositional racial/ethnic communities (García 1997; Harris 1999; Naples 1991, 1998; B. Roth 2004; Ruiz 1998; Springer 2005; Townsend Gilkes 1994).

Given the proliferation of organizationally distinct feminisms in the second wave, we might ask about their different political agendas. Did these multiple feminist movements work on different issues? Despite differences in political community and in political style, when it came to women's issues, feminists on the left had much in common with liberal feminists, such as those working in the National Organization for Women (NOW). On the other hand, black and Chicana feminists tended to characterize white feminists, including women's liberationists on the left, as being insufficiently attentive to economic survival issues, overly focused on narrowly construed "personal" political issues of the body and body image, and cavalier about the key role of family in the lives of women of color (Baca Zinn 1975; Cherot 1970; B. Roth 2004; Springer 2005). Yet in retrospect, it is striking how many elements of a political agenda feminists shared across the spectrum. White women's liberation, black feminism, and Chicana feminist second wave movements were all characterized by multi-issue political platforms calling for radical economic change and for the radical overhaul of male/female relationships. Most feminist groups, and especially those on the left, practiced what has become known as consciousness raising—that is, the use of small group discussion to theorize how the personal is political (Hanisch 1970; see also Hanisch 2006). All feminists in racial/ethnic groups on the left wanted access to abortion, with feminists of color being additionally concerned with government intervention into their ability to reproduce (i.e., sterilization programs, intrusive welfare policies). All feminists on the left called for state-funded, accessible child care; all called for freedom from sexual violence and domestic abuse; all wanted greater educational opportunities for women; all demanded greater employment opportunities for women, even as they argued for the dismantling of an unfair capitalist state. And of course, many of these agenda items were shared by liberal feminists. I do not wish to minimize the differences between feminist movements in terms of their social bases or disparate elements of ideology; these existed. But feminists' political agendas overlapped enough to prompt the question of why there was so little joint organizing among feminists located in different racial/ethnic movements until at least ten years after the emergence of feminisms on the left.

In order to explain this failed coalition, I argue that second wave feminists' ideology about what constitutes good politics militated against coalition formation even in the face of shared goals. Coalition formation among black, Chicana, and white feminists on the left was discouraged in part because feminists in all three racial/ethnic communities shared what I have called an ethos of organizing one's own (B. Roth 2004) that shaped their ideas about how to organize as authentic radicals. This cultural factor, a consensual ethos that linked organizational form with concerns about authenticity, shaped feminist efforts and led to the deprioritizing of coalition. To make the case for the importance of organizing one's own as an explanation for the dearth of coalition activity, I first briefly review the sociological literature on conditions that foster or militate against coalition formation in movements, arguing that the factors emphasized by scholars do not explain the dynamics of second wave feminist protest. Next, I consider how the ethos of organizing one's own became important to feminists and the left; I consider especially how it became linked to a particular kind of organizational form, that of the small, racially homogeneous group. In the conclusion, I return to the broader question of how the meaning of coalition for activists should be considered in thinking about factors that facilitate or constrain coalition, as activists' ideas about coalition may be tied to identity in a consequential manner.[1]

Factors that Facilitate Coalition Formation

In exploring coalition formation, scholars have chiefly focused on understanding what conditions make coalitions possible; coalition formation is potentially a strategy that makes extrainstitutional challengers more powerful vis-à-vis institutions, and thus coalitions can be causally significant factors in explaining social change (Van Dyke 2003). Activists also regard coalitions in a favorable light; they tend to see the "desirability of formal alliances between relatively compatible political organizations" (Hathaway and Meyer 1997, 63). Conditions that facilitate coalitions can be grouped into those external to social movement organizations and factors internal to them. The external factors facilitating coalition have been conceptualized as general conditions of environmental opportunities and environmental threats, where the environment consists of the relationships present between institutions of authority (most commonly the state) and social movement organizations, and relationships among social movement organizations themselves (Ferree and Roth 1998; Hathaway and Meyer 1997; McCammon and Campbell 2002; Staggenborg 1986; Van Dyke 2003). Internally, among the factors that incline individual social movement organizations toward coalition are formalized leadership structures (Staggenborg 1986), the presence of well-networked "bridge" leaders (Bandy and Smith 2004; Ferree and Roth 1998; Robnett 1997; Rose 2000; Shaffer 2000), or ideology congruent with that of other groups (Kleidman and Rochon 1997; McCammon and Campbell 2002; Staggenborg 1986; Zald and Ash 1966).

At a macro level, environmental conditions in the political field that can facilitate coalitions have been characterized as political opportunities: increases in government funding; splits in elites; contingent events that threaten impending legislation; and repressive government action. There is some ambiguity as to how one defines opportunity or threat, but there is increasing evidence that threat matters more than opportunity in providing an impetus for coalition formation (Hathaway and Meyer 1997; McCammon and Campbell 2002). In the face of threat, coalition formation is opportunistic, in the technical sense of the word, because social movement organizations can bolster strength through alliances. For example, in their study of late nineteenth- and early twentieth-century coalitions between the woman's suffrage and temperance movements, McCammon and Campbell (2002) found that it was external political threats to, and not opportunities for, enacting the goals of the movements that affected the tendency of social movement organizations from one movement to form coalitions with organizations from the other. The threats to the movements took the specific forms of political defeats in institutional politics, "changing social circumstances" (e.g., an increase in the number of saloons), and the existence of countermovements (McCammon and Campbell 2002, 232). These authors also found that political opportunities were not conducive to coalition formation, insofar as organizations were more able to accomplish goals in the face of opportunities. In her study of twentieth-century protest behavior among U.S. college students, Van Dyke (2003) found that threat was also important to coalition formation across issue-based movement boundaries. Van Dyke distinguished levels of environmental threat as having differential impacts on coalition formation: "local threats inspire[d] within-movement coalition events, while larger threats that affect[ed] multiple constituencies or broadly defined identities inspire[d] cross-movement coalition formation" (2003, 226). Van Dyke's schema of levels of environmental threat is further echoed by Borland's work (this volume) on coalition formation between feminist and nonfeminist (class-based, popular) women's groups in Argentina during a time of societywide economic crisis, the collapse of the Argentinean economy in the 2001 as a result of neoliberal restructuring. The questions of role and the level of crisis addressed by Borland are directly relevant to the case of second wave racial/ethnic feminisms, as is Van Dyke's finding that a commitment to multi-issue politics inspired coalition formation and more coalition events.

Of course, activists' reactions to environmental threats (or opportunities) are not automatic; they make decisions from within social movement organizations—organizations that they seek to maintain. This point was emphasized in Staggenborg's (1986) examination of U.S. pro-choice movement politics. Staggenborg noted that movement organizations had different senses of how important their organizational survival was:

> Movement organizations that are less concerned with organizational maintenance might join coalitions to take full advantage of environmental opportunities or, alternatively, to fight against environmental threats. On the other hand, organizations that are more preoccupied with organizational maintenance might also form coalitions when such cooperation allows them to conserve resources and engage in a broader range of strategies and tactics

than would otherwise be possible. Thus, movement organizations with different resources and maintenance needs might *all* have the same interests in forming coalitions under certain environmental conditions, but for different reasons. (Staggenborg 1986, 380)

Thus, even while environmental threats (and opportunities) beckoned, within individual social movement organizations, the costs and benefits of joining coalitions were weighed. Activists generally understand the trade-off in terms of transferring their energy from maintaining individual organizations to maintaining the coalition, as Staggenborg (1986) notes (see also Balser 1997). Moreover, once a coalition is actually created, tensions may arise among member organizations with different amounts of resources, different political emphases, and different styles of organization. Such tensions are costly in terms of time and energy.

External environmental factors, whether threats or opportunities, cannot will coalitions into being; decisions have to be made by social movement participants in particular organizational settings. One factor that makes coalitions more possible among groups is having compatible ideologies (Kleidman and Rochon 1997; McCammon and Campbell 2002; Staggenborg 1986; Zald and Ash 1966). If groups have similar visions of social change and/or similar political ends, one area of difference that could threaten working together is eliminated. In forming coalitions, organizations may even engage in practices to make ideology more congruent; Kleidman and Rochon (1997, 51) suggest that "goal selection" was essential to the formation of coalitions in the 1980s nuclear freeze movement, as constituent organizations agreed on "least-common denominator goals that all members could live with."

Another internal organizational factor that studies have found significant for the facilitation of coalitions is the existence of individuals whose network connections straddled movement organizations or movements themselves (Bandy and Smith 2004; Ferree and Roth 1998; Robnett 1997; Shaffer 2000). Following Robnett (1997), a bridge leader was someone who could move among different social movement organizations and grassroots constituencies. In his work on links between working-class and middle-class movements, Rose (2000) emphasized that these individuals moved not just between social movement organizations and unorganized constituencies, but also among different movements in one locale. Rose found that bridge-building activists tended to be older and experienced in both movement and local electoral politics; they had additionally mastered various styles of communication and were able to adjust their discourse to the appropriate (class) setting.

In general, then, scholars have posited that coalitions are more likely form in response to environmental opportunities, but especially to environmental threats; that they are facilitated by the existence of multi-issue movements; that they are easier when groups share political ideologies and/or styles; and that they can be aided by the intentional efforts of bridge-building individuals. How well do these factors explain the failure of coalitional efforts on the part of feminists situated in different racial/ethnic communities in the 1960s and 1970s? The explanatory power of these previously considered factors is decidedly mixed. Regarding environmental factors, it is hard to actually assess how much threat (or opportunity) feminist movements faced. Repressive government measures were directed against the left, but most government efforts were directed against racial liberation movements or the antiwar left. On the other hand, emerging feminists situated within already existing left movement groups faced a continual series of localized crises (see Freeman 1973, 1975), as other members of the oppositional communities within which feminists were situated were against autonomous feminist organizing. These internal threats were spurs to autonomous feminist organizing, but they were also factors that militated against coalition formation, at least on the part of feminist women of color who countered the backlash against their emerging movement by asserting their independence from white feminists (B. Roth 2004). Although emerging second wave feminists were in the process of cementing activist identities as feminists, competition existed for their energies, and alternative avenues existed for their activism. As in Borland's analysis of the competing pulls on coalition efforts among women's groups in Argentina exercised by existing organizational ties, crises spurred increased activism by women already embedded in organizations but did not result in the overcoming of all existing barriers to unity.

As to multi-issue politics, all three feminist movements in the U.S. postwar period—black, Chicana, and white—were decidedly multi-issue; indeed, it was the umbrella agendas of these movements that provided the potential overlap, the political common ground among feminists working in different racial/ethnic communities. Black, Chicana, and white feminist movements on the left also shared much in the way of political style and vocabulary. Neither overlapping political agendas nor congruent political styles were enough to spur sustained efforts at coalition. Last, there were potential bridge leaders on the ground during the mid- to late 1960s and 1970s; one thinks immediately of white women's liberationists such as Pam Allen; black feminists such as Pat Robinson of the Black Women's Liberation Group of Mount Vernon/ New Rochelle, New York Mount Vernon, or the founders of the National Black Feminist Organization who had connections with *Ms.* magazine; or even someone like Chicana feminist Anna Nieto-Gómez, who, if not eager to cross over, at least attempted to go to NOW meetings in the 1970s (B. Roth 2004). Yet the presence of these women and others did not result in large-scale coalition efforts; even the National Black Feminist Organization founders saw the need for another NOW type of organization specifically oriented around the needs of black women (B. Roth 2004; Springer 2005).

I suggest that we need to look further into the meaning of coalition to understand why emerging second wave feminists on the left were (perhaps uniquely) dismissive of coalition formation. This would mean attempting to understand the historical and contemporaneous role that specific cultural meanings about coalition had in localized settings. Zald and Ash (1966, 335) speculated that one key obstacle to coalition formation could be ideology, what they called "the unlikelihood of shared perspectives." But what would happen if shared ideology discourages coalition? Although it is clear that history, ideology, and cultural investments influence how, or whether, coalition efforts are made across organizational lines (see Guenther, this volume), I have found little analysis in the literature on coalition formation as to how it is that what actors think about coalition as such can matter. I believe that the meaning of coalition can matter, especially if the meaning of coalition is tied to what activists think about what constitutes good politics. In considering coalitions, it is probably the case that activists define good politics as a combination of good strategy and workable identity; that is, there are extra-rational reasons behind political decisions made by challengers regarding not just the necessity but also the ideological value of coalition formation. In the next section, I argue that in the 1960s and 1970s, feminists emerging from racial/ethnic oppositional communities shared an ethos of organizing one's own that influenced their choices regarding an authentically radical way to organize. This shared consensus about what kinds of organizing was good politics was based on the necessity of maintaining difference, and thus coalitions were seen as suspect.

Second Wave Feminisms and the Ethos of Organizing One's Own

During the 1960s and 1970s, an ethos of organizing one's own existed in the left social movement sector that specified a link between forms of organizing and radical activist authenticity (B. Roth 2004, chap. 5). This consensually held ethos helped shape emerging feminist views about the possibilities for cross-racial/ethnic coalition formation as they consolidated their movement groups. Second wave feminist activists coming out of the black, Chicana/o, and white left deprioritized coalition efforts across racial/ethnic lines in favor of organizing their own, with "their own" defined as fellow (female) members of their racial/ethnic community. The disparagement of coalition formation was not the result of strategic decision making, but resulted from activists holding to a set of ideological directives about how to do politics the right way. Instead of working together on shared political goals, feminist women in different racial/ethnic communities invested in forms of organization that highlighted the perceived necessity of maintaining difference in organizing.[2]

I call organizing one's own an ethos because I wish to denote a characteristic spirit of second wave left political communities, including feminist ones. The word *ethos* is closely tied to the word *ethic,* and it thus carries with it a moral imperative to do things in a particular way. The ethos of organizing one's own constituted a generalized, consensual, and specific instruction as to how to organize as authentic leftists. As movements proliferated, it directed/justified the way that leftists organized. As such, the ethos of organizing one's own did not belong to the family of collective action frames— that is, "action-oriented sets of beliefs and meanings that inspire and legitimate the activities and campaigns of social movement organizations" (Benford and Snow 2000, 614). Nor was it an elaborated "system of meaning," as might be expected of a full-blown ideology (Oliver and Johnston 2000, 43). The ethos was a value judgment that resulted in a directive about how to be radicals, and activists invoking it did not actually establish what the politics of the groups organizing on their own should be so much as how the groups should be formed.

In examining the history of second wave feminist emergences on the left, it is particularly striking just how intertwined the matters of organizational form and feminist politics were. As Clemens (1996, 205) has noted, organizational form can dictate politics; she has argued that "organizational form appears as a movement frame which both informs collective identity and orients groups toward other actors and institutions." Forms of organization may be expressive of collective identity; having chosen particular forms, groups are then further shaped by organizing in those forms, as they become "both a statement of collective identity and a set of a goals and values" (206). Adopted forms may or may not articulate well with larger systems of political opportunities, but this question of how successful a form will ultimately be may be secondary to emerging groups. Clemens correctly emphasized that the "answers to the pragmatic question of 'How do we organize?' reverberate inward to the shaping of collective identity and outward to link movements to institutions or opportunity structures" (209). I will only add that asking "how do we organize?" in itself does not presuppose that activists in any particular case are more concerned with collective identity than strategy (or vice versa); that is a researchable question.

In the case of second wave racial/ethnic feminisms, the adoption of common organizational forms for the most part—small groups based on consciousness raising—was based on the organizing of one's own ethos. These small groups were focused, especially in the mid- to late 1960s, on internal education. Part of that internal education was about how to be feminist and radical at the same time because many fellow activists in mixed-gender groups saw feminism as a "bourgeois" diversion (Weinfeld 1970, 1). Thus, agreement among feminists in different racial/ethnic communities about a common organizational form itself diminished opportunities for cross/racial ethnic alliances, but intentionally so. Even when second wave feminists wished to go beyond the small group form, they kept the ethos of organizing one's own. For example, when a small group of black feminists in New York City announced the existence of the National Black Feminist Organization in 1974, the hierarchical chapter structure they envisioned, which was based to some extent on the structure of NOW, was meant to give black women a voice apart from white feminist organizations (B. Roth 2004, chap. 3; Springer 2005).

Feminists adhered to the ethos of organizing one's own and to the small group form of organization that most clearly embodied the ethos because they came out of left social milieus where the ethos had become common wisdom. Within a cycle of social protest, ideas may be current that are irresistible to activists, whether or not they are well suited to their ultimate intentions. This phenomenon of irresistibility has been broached theoretically in the recognition of the existence of master frames that emerge early in cycles of protest and then take wider hold (Snow and Benford 1992). Beginning in the 1960s, the ethos of organizing one's own came to dominate leftist politics, and as groups on the left proliferated, the ethos had the effect of shaping everyone's—white, black, and Chicano; male and female—ideas about what constituted authentic, radical political protest. Feminists did not abandon the ethos as they organized; organizing as women in order to address the left's shortcomings as to gender politics rather bolstered the ethos because it was just one more living demonstration of its wisdom.

In retrospect, the idea of organizing around one's own oppression has been commonly seen as emanating from a series of events in the black movement, especially the decision by the Student Non-Violent Coordinating Committee to kick out white activists and ask them to go into their own communities to address racism there (Carson 1981; Evans 1979; Stoper 1989). Student Non-Violent Coordinating Committee members' actions, the result of the influx of white volunteers into the organization in the wake of Freedom Summer, were (and still are) seen as sanctioning the New Left idea that the most authentic, and therefore most radical, forms of activism involved fighting one's own oppression (Echols 1992). The Student Non-Violent Coordinating Committee's actions were important to white activists both because of the ties individual activists had to the organization and because of the committee's role as a vanguard model for activism (see Evans 1979, 173–74). But the ethos of organizing one's own was not simply the result of growing black militancy, or even of attempts by white activists to make the best of a bad situation. Rather, the ethos was clearly part and parcel of the organization Students for a Democratic Society. This society started in the early 1960s as the student arm of a left-wing group, the League for Industrial Democracy. Disputes between younger organizers and League for Industrial Democracy elders led to efforts to organize a new and separate student-led movement (Gitlin 1987). By June 1962, Tom Hayden and other student activists meeting in Michigan drafted "The Port Huron Statement," which was subtitled "An Agenda for a Generation." Students were the focus of the call represented by the statement, as they fought against racial injustice, for the breaking of stalemated cold war politics, and against the anti-intellectual, business-as-usual atmosphere of college life. In the light of Students for a Democratic Society's student-oriented efforts, those of the free speech movement at Berkeley (Evans 1979), and the growing student vanguard in the civil rights movement, the expulsion of white volunteers from the Student Non-Violent Coordinating Committee became an affirmation of a growing consensus about how authentic radicalism was accomplished, rather than its first moment.

The ethos of organizing one's own predated and helped shape the decisions made by feminists in each racial/ethnic movement about how to organize. But although the ethos was consensually held across different racial/ethnic oppositional communities, its meaning had different shadings for feminists in different racial/ethnic communities. For white women's liberationists emerging primarily from the New Left, the ethos helped justify the idea that they, even though white and largely middle class, were oppressed and needed to work on their own oppression (B. Roth 2004, chap. 2). One example of this was the fact that although white women's liberationists took racial oppression seriously, some white feminists made decisions early on not to complicate their organizing with the politics of race, so as to have a freer hand to work on their own oppression. Echols (1989, 369–77) reproduced part of a transcript from the Sandy Springs, Maryland, conference in 1968 where white feminists discussed the pros and cons of making contacts with radical black women. Disagreement about the wisdom of such a move centered directly on the matter of keeping the politics of women's liberation focused—that is, making sure that politics were being done the right way. Echoing earlier concerns about feminist organizing, certain women present voiced concerns that black women would derail the women's liberation agenda with a critique of racist and classist politics. Echols reported that in the end, the group at Sandy Springs decided to contact Kathleen Cleaver regarding a future conference on black women's and white women's liberation, a conference that never materialized.[3]

As noted above, by the mid-1960s, the ethos of organizing one's own was dominant and had emanated from multiple sources (Students for a Democratic Society ideology, Student Non-Violent Coordinating Committee actions, a civil rights movement that needed white people less, etc.). Among emerging white women's liberationists, feminism was seen as the answer to the need for self-determination on the part of women. In one widely circulated position paper jointly published with Judith Brown, Beverly Jones (1968, 2), a white feminist from Gainesville, Florida, argued that it was an accepted truth that "people don't get radicalized . . . fighting other peoples' battles." Other statements of the ethos of organizing one's own by emerging white feminists included those by Robin Morgan (1968); by an unsigned activist meeting with radical women in Chicago in 1968 (Radical Women, Chicago 1968); by members of Berkeley Women's Liberation in 1969 (Berkeley Women's Liberation 1969); by the authors of the unsigned articles "Why Liberation?" and "SDS [Students for a Democratic Society] on Women's Lib," published in San Francisco's *Daily Gater* on December 10, 1969; by Carol McEldowney (1969a, 1969b), in letters describing her experiences with the mixed-gender left; and by Weinfeld (1970). Although not all white feminists in the late 1960s agreed with organizing one's own, even those who questioned the ethos understood its use. Pam Allen, a civil rights movement activist and an early white women's liberationist, noted that it was probably "a relief" for white middle-class women to discover that they were oppressed (1968, 1–2) and that it was okay to organize around that oppression. Another white women's liberationist, Betsy Stone, went so far as to argue that only those who had unsophisticated understandings of radical politics would expect women of different races/ethnicities to work together in the same organizations (B. Stone 1970, 9).

The ethos of organizing one's own had direct influence on the way African American and Chicana feminists organized in the second wave. In contrast to views that read the autonomous feminist organizing of women of color as only a reaction to demonstrably present racism on the part of white feminism (davenport 1981; Moraga and Anzaldúa 1981; Redd 1983; Spelman 1982), it seems clear that feminists of color were committed to organizing their own. For black feminists, the ethos justified the need to organize autonomous women's groups that would be linked to the black movement but would focus on women's issues. The black feminist "vanguard center" ideology posited that black women existed at the bottom of an intersection of hierarchies of race, gender, and class and thus were the ones best positioned to lead a movement that would liberate all those dominated (B. Roth 2004, chap. 3; see also Beal 1970). Their work on their own issues, working from the bottom up, thus represented not black feminist selfishness but vanguardism, a move toward the development of a politics that had wide-scale liberating potential.

For Chicana feminists who began forming feminist organizations in 1969, the ethos of organizing one's own was so firmly in place that organizing with Anglo women or black women was not part of their initial discussions (B. Roth 2004, chap. 4). Instead, the major portion of Chicana feminist debate about autonomous organizing involved how Chicana feminists should relate to the rest of the Chicano movement. The idea that Anglo feminism was basically irrelevant to Chicana feminist organizing, that Chicana feminism flowed from the internal and inevitable logic of developments within the Chicano movement, was a theme that helped Chicanas fight male activist challenges, and it was strategic in its overstatement. However, the idea of joining up with Anglo women was not so much rejected as simply not seen as a real option; coalitions were not on the slate of possible strategic options.

Thus, organizing one's own as an ethos transcended racial/ethnic boundaries. To the extent that all feminists—white, black, and Chicana—were faced with making either/or choices about how to organize (i.e., stay within mixed-gender organizations or leave them and form new ones), organizing one's own confirmed the wisdom of working within groups that had race and class homogeneity. The growing consensus regarding the ethos of organizing one's own as an example of elective affinity between an ideological imperative and the proliferating movements and movement groups in the 1960s or an ideological imperative that made possible the proliferation itself led to a consensual separation of emerging feminisms along racial/ethnic lines. This separation was deemed legitimate and fitting by feminists in all three racial/ethnic communities, leading to a consensus whereby feminists agreed among themselves that it was impossible for them to organize across lines of race and ethnicity. When feminists did talk to each other across color lines, they frequently found common ground on just how impossible it would be for them to work closely together. Instead, separate movements in some sort of vaguely defined but definitely future alliance were more often the preferred vision.

For example, even black feminists who were sympathetic to white women's liberation and liberal feminism remained firmly enmeshed in the ethos of organizing one's own. When longtime black community labor organizer Dorothy

Pittman was interviewed for *Mademoiselle* magazine by veteran journalist Mary Cantwell, Pittman told Cantwell that black people had moved past the point of wanting whites to help them with their problems: "We'd rather do it ourselves, thank you" (Cantwell 1971, 221). According to Pittman, the political moment required the necessary separation of women into different racial/ ethnic groups doing separate political work on community issues. In an exchange printed in June 1970 in the *Christian Century,* two black activists, Joan Brown and Helen Fannings, and one white activist, Peggy Way, shared their ideas about the possibilities for black and white women's feminist activism. Way recounted that early on in the decade,

> probably more of us than would admit it were working for blacks rather than with blacks, though we didn't realize that until things became blacker and blacker, and what were we left with? . . . So I think that some of us in women's liberation are seeking a reification of who we are out of loss of the identity we thought we were developing in the movement. (M. Stone 1970, 1)

The sin, as Way seemed to see it, was not working on one's own oppression, which caused white women activists to lose their way. White feminism thus represented was the path back to the proper ground of authentic activism. Joan Brown approved of this move by white women, although for somewhat different reasons: "I hope that white women are really trying to understand their own oppression, because if this country could ever unlock the riddle of why women, particularly white women are treated the way they are. . . . That understanding might lead to other possibilities" (1). Both women continued to agree that each group of women—white and black—had to work separately. Way stated, "I think more people now are realizing that the black woman has a thing she has to do. It's not our thing" (2). And Brown once again concurred that white feminist issues are beyond the consideration of black women: "As a black woman I don't even feel that [white feminism] is my problem or my responsibility. Under the circumstances, I wouldn't be a part of a women's lib movement for anything in the world" (6). Here, Helen Fannings, the second black activist at the discussion, supported Brown: "That is your problem, Peggy. We just don't have time for it" (6).

As the examples above show, in the 1960s and 1970s, brakes were put on coalition formation by feminists across racial/ethnic lines by activist notions of good politics. Despite elements of an overlapping feminist agenda, coalition formation was not prioritized. Indeed, as feminists organized in different racial/ethnic oppositional communities, coalition was deemed to be inauthentic and unwise strategy; cross-racial feminist organizing was seen as simultaneously impossible, and if possible, dangerous to the cause.

Conclusion: The Variable Meanings of Coalition

In the 1960s and early 1970s, feminist activists emerging from movements on the left believed that organizing one's own represented the way toward authentically radical and thus effective politics. The ethos of organizing one's own may have also represented a way of managing competing demands on their time and loyalty as activists, but subscribing to it was not, I argue, primarily a matter of strategy; subscription was a matter of belief, of wisdom received from previous experiences on the left. Focusing on organizing one's own meant that efforts toward coalition were at the very least downplayed, and at the most held to be politically suspect. The failure of emerging feminists to form coalitions across racial/ethnic divides was due to extrarational calculations—that is to say, ideas about the truly authentic way to organize as radical women. Therefore, the case of emerging feminisms in the United States' second wave challenges scholarly views of coalition formation that rely solely on a delineation of structurally facilitative environmental conditions and/or resources. Ideological factors can impede coalition formation and may do so in ways that go beyond the lack of similarity in political agendas or political styles (see Guenther, this volume). I suggest that when we think about how coalitions happen, we look at understanding how the meaning of coalition fits into activists' views of what makes for good politics. This consideration of activists' consensual ideas about good politics would move the study of coalition formation closer to a constructionist approach that has room for the consideration of ideational factors alongside the consideration of structural factors.

Although the question needs more historical and, when possible, ethnographic exploration, I would suggest that activist decisions about coalition efforts are never the result of cost/benefit calculations alone. The more than decade-old social constructionist turn in social movement theory (Morris and Mueller 1992) has provided more room for acknowledging that strategic opportunities need to be perceived as useful in order for actors to take them. I would go further and suggest that coalition efforts need to be perceived as good politics in order to be made. For activists, good politics is not only what is potentially most effective; good politics is a matter of what actions are most congruent with established meanings in activist communities around identities and ethics. Following this view, I would argue that at times, coalitions represent not just challenges to organizational maintenance, a dynamic recognized by scholars; coalitions represent challenges to activists' identities. Those identities are constructed on several levels of salience, including that of the organization (Gamson 1992). In the current historical moment, for example, it seems to be possible to intentionally construct coalitions on the specific basis of maintaining certain forms of grassroots identities, as in the establishment of world forums as well as U.S.-based social forums (see Juris 2008). However, the possibility for the incorporation of activists separated by inequalities within one coalitional rubric is variable; as Borland (this volume) shows, in the Argentinean case, class loyalties among women were not universally overcome in organizing against a universal economic crisis.

Finally, I wish to be clear that I do not recommend jettisoning our understandings of structural conditions, external or internal, that facilitate coalition in favor of a renewed and exclusive focus on culture. Rather, I suggest that we look further into the meaning of a coalition, and conversely at the meaning of autonomy for social movement actors in particular historical (or current) circumstances. We need to consider the meaning of coalition for situated groups of social movement actors in order to understand how or whether that meaning may have influenced decisions that participants made.

Notes

1. A word about methodology: I used second wave grassroots journals, underground publications, and mainstream newspapers as primary sources for this chapter, in addition to eleven interviews/oral histories (nine of which I conducted myself). A few secondary sources were also consulted. Taylor and Whittier (1992, 105–6) defined primary materials as "books, periodicals and narratives by community members," as well as "newsletters, position papers and other documents from . . . organizations." Other primary materials included were flyers (and other such ephemera), personal correspondence, material disseminated by two news services, the Liberation News Service and the Underground Press Service, and material published by small left-wing presses (e.g., Pathfinder Press and the New England Free Press). Within the oppositional social movement sector of the 1960s and 1970s, feminist groups used their publications to communicate ideas through the reprinting of articles from one movement journal to the next. Underground newspapers and magazines should thus be seen as organizations in themselves that both disseminated information and articulated discontent (Rosen 1974). My exploration of these materials has not been strictly representative of the movements, but I have taken pains to look at materials from different parts of the country and from different organizations; given the informality of membership (Baxandall 2001) in the reticulate, decentralized, and fluid left social movement sector in the 1960s and 1970s, constructing a universe to randomly sample from would itself be suspect.

2. An emphasis on difference as such need not discourage coalition formation; it is activists' interpretation of the organizational needs of difference that helps or hinders coalition formation. See Juris (2008).

3. Buechler (1990, 134) has argued that white women's liberationists had "unconsciousness" regarding race matters as a result of their relatively privileged position, and therefore they neglected organizing around race. However, white feminists' well-documented experiences (see Evans 1979) in the civil rights movement belie the idea they were not conscious of racial issues and instead suggest that racial politics were at the heart of white women's feminist emergence. As noted by Echols, the unconscious neglect of racial issues by white feminists was at least sometimes conscious and strategic.

Works Cited

Allen, Pam. 1968. "Memo to My White Sisters in Our Struggle to Realize Our Full Humanity." Draft of position paper sent in letter from Pat Robinson to Joan Jordan (Vilma Sanchez), April 21. Joan Jordan Papers, State Historical Society, Madison, Wis.

Baca Zinn, Maxine. 1975. "Political Familialism: Toward Sex Role Equality in Chicano Families." *Aztlán* 6: 13–26.

Balser, Deborah B. 1997. "The Impact of Environmental Factors on Factionalism and Schism in Social Movement Organizations." *Social Forces* 76: 199–228.

Bandy, Joe, and Jackie Smith, eds. 2004. *Coalitions across Borders: Transnational Protest and the Neoliberal Order.* Lanham, Md.: Rowman & Littlefield.

Baxandall, Ros. 2001. "Re-visioning the Women's Liberation Movement's Narrative: Early Second Wave African American Feminists." *Feminist Studies* 27: 1: 225–45

Beal, Frances. 1970. "Double Jeopardy: To Be Black and Female." In *The Black Woman: An Anthology,* edited by Toni Cade (Bambara), 109–22. New York: New American Library.

Benford, Robert D., and David Snow. 2000. "Framing Processes and Social Movements: An Overview and Assessment." *Annual Review of Sociology* 26: 611–39.

Berkeley Women's Liberation. 1969. "Why the Women's Liberation Movement Must Be Autonomous." Unpublished position paper from Berkeley Women's Liberation Conference, August 15–17. Schlesinger Library, Harvard University, Cambridge, Mass.

Buechler, Steven M. 1990. *Women's Movements in the United States: Woman Suffrage, Equal Rights and Beyond.* New Brunswick, N.J.: Rutgers University Press.

Cantwell, Mary. 1971. "'I can't call you my sister yet': A Black Woman Looks at Women's Lib." *Mademoiselle,* May.

Carson, Clayborne. 1981. *In Struggle: SNCC and the Black Awakening of the 1960s.* Cambridge, Mass.: Harvard University Press.

Cherot, Lorna. 1970. "I Am What I Am." *Liberation News Service* 294 (October 29): 16.

Clemens, Elizabeth S. 1996. "Organizational Form as Frame: Collective Identity and Political Strategy in the American Labor Movement." In *Comparative Perspectives on Social Movements: Political Opportunities, Mobilizing Structures, and Cultural Framings,* edited by Doug McAdam, John D. McCarthy, and Mayer N. Zald, 205–26. Cambridge: Cambridge University Press.

Cobble, Dorothy Sue. 2004. *The Other Women's Movement: Workplace Justice and Social Rights in Modern America.* Princeton, N.J.: Princeton University Press.

davenport, doris. 1981. "The Pathology of Racism: A Conversation with Third World Women." In *This Bridge Called My Back: Writings by Radical Women of Color,* edited by Cherríe Moraga and Gloria Anzaldúa, 85–90. Watertown, Mass.: Persephone Press.

Echols, Alice. 1989. *Daring to Be Bad: Radical Feminism in America, 1967–1975.* Minneapolis: University of Minnesota Press.

———. 1992. "'We gotta get out of this place': Notes toward a Remapping of the Sixties." *Socialist Review* 22: 9–33.

Evans, Sara. 1979. *Personal Politics: The Roots of Women's Liberation in the Civil Rights Movement and the New Left.* New York: Vintage Books.

Ferree, Myra Marx, and Beth B. Hess. 2000. *Controversy and Coalition: The New Feminist Movement across Four Decades of Change.* 3rd ed. New York: Routledge.

Ferree, Myra Marx, and Silke Roth. 1998. "Gender, Class, and the Interaction between Social Movements: A Strike of West Berlin Day Care Workers." *Gender and Society* 12: 626–48.

Freeman, Jo. 1973. "The Origins of the Women's Liberation Movement." *American Journal of Sociology* 78: 792–811.

———. 1975. *The Politics of Women's Liberation.* New York: Longman.

Gamson, William A. 1992. "The Social Psychology of Collective Action." In *Frontiers in Social Movement Theory,* edited by Aldon D. Morris and Carol McClurg Mueller, 53–76. New Haven, Conn.: Yale University Press.

García, Alma. 1997. *Chicana Feminist Thought: The Basic Historical Writings.* New York: Routledge.

Gitlin, Todd. 1987. *The Sixties: Years of Hope, Days of Rage.* Toronto: Bantam Books.

Hanisch, Carol. 1970. "The Personal Is Political." In *Notes from the Second Year: Women's Liberation.* New York: Shulamith Firestone and Anne Koedt (self-published).

———. 2006. New introduction to "The Personal Is Political." In *Women and Social Movements in the United States, 1600–2000: The Second Wave and Beyond.* http://scholar.alexanderstreet.com.

Harris, Duchess. 1999. "'All of who I am in the same place': The Combahee River Collective." *Womanist Theory and Research* 2: 1. http://www.uga.edu/womanist/harris3.1.htm.

Hathaway, Will, and David S. Meyer. 1997. "Competition and Cooperation in Movement Coalitions: Lobbying for Peace in the 1980s." In *Coalitions and Political*

Movements: The Lessons of the Nuclear Freeze, edited by Thomas R. Rochon and David S. Meyer, 61–79. Boulder, Colo.: Lynne Reinner.

Jones, Beverly, and Judith Brown. 1968. "Toward a Female Liberation Movement." Pamphlet published by authors. Women's Liberation Ephemera Files, Special Collections, Northwestern University, Evanston, Ill.

Juris, Jeffrey S. 2008. "Spaces of Intentionality: Race, Class, and Horizontality at the United States Social Forum." *Mobilization* 13: 353–72.

Kleidman, Robert, and Thomas R. Rochon. 1997. "Dilemmas of Organization in Peace Campaigns." In *Coalitions and Political Movements: The Lessons of the Nuclear Freeze,* edited by Thomas R. Rochon and David S. Meyer, 47–80. Boulder, Colo.: Lynne Reinner.

McCammon, Holly J., and Karen E. Campbell. 2002. "Allies on the Road to Victory: Coalition Formation between the Suffragists and the Woman's Christian Temperance Union." *Mobilization* 7: 231–51.

McEldowney, Carol. 1969a. Letter (July/August). Carol McEldowney Papers. State Historical Society, Madison, Wis.

———. 1969b. Letter/position paper draft. (October 1). Carol McEldowney Papers. State Historical Society, Madison, Wis.

Moraga, Cherríe, and Gloria Anzaldúa. 1979. "Introduction." In *This Bridge Called My Back: Writings by Radical Women of Color,* edited by Cherríe Moraga and Gloria Anzaldúa, xxiii–xxxv. Watertown, Mass.: Persephone Press.

Morgan, Robin. 1968. "The Oldest Front: On Freedom for Women" *Liberation* 8: 34–37.

Morris, Aldon D., and Carol McClurg Mueller, eds. 1992. *Frontiers in Social Movement Theory.* New Haven, Conn.: Yale University Press.

Naples, Nancy. 1991. "Just What Needed to be Done: The Political Practice of Women Community Workers in Low-Income Neighborhoods." *Gender and Society* 5: 478–94.

———, ed. 1998. *Community Activism and Feminist Politics: Organizing Across Race, Class, and Gender.* Philadelphia: Temple University Press.

Oliver, Pamela E., and Hank Johnston. 2000. "What a Good Idea! Ideologies and Frames in Social Movement Research." *Mobilization* 4: 37–53.

Radical Women, Chicago. 1968. "Meeting of Radical Women, Chicago, March 24–25, 1968." Report. Women's Liberation Ephemera Files, Special Collections, Northwestern University, Chicago, Ill.

Redd, Spring. 1983. "Something Latino Was Up with Us." In *Home Girls: A Black Feminist Anthology,* edited by Barbara Smith, 52–59. New York: Kitchen Table/ Women of Color Press.

Robnett, Belinda. 1997. *How Long? How Long? African-American Women in the Struggle for Civil Rights.* Oxford: Oxford University Press.

Rose, Fred. 2000. *Coalitions across the Class Divide: Lessons from the Labor, Peace, and Environmental Movements.* New York: Cornell University Press.

Rosen, Gerald. 1974. "The Development of the Chicano Movement in Los Angeles from 1967 to 1969." *Aztlán* 4: 155–83.

Roth, Benita. 2004. *Separate Roads to Feminism: Black, Chicana, and White Feminist Movements in America's Second Wave.* New York: Cambridge University Press.

Roth, Silke. 2003. *Building Movement Bridges: The Coalition of Labor Union Women.* Contributions to Sociology Series. Westport, Conn.: Praeger.

Ruiz, Vicki L. 1998. *From Out of the Shadows: Mexican Women in Twentieth Century America.* New York: Oxford University Press.

Shaffer, Martin B. 2000. "Coalition Work among Environmental Groups: Who Participates?" *Research in Social Movements, Conflicts, and Change* 22: 111–26.

Snow, David A., and Robert D. Benford. 1992. "Master Frames and Cycles of Protest." In *Frontiers in Social Movement Theory,* edited by Aldon D. Morris and Carol McClurg Mueller, 133–55. New Haven, Conn.: Yale University Press.

Spelman, Elizabeth V. 1982. "Theories of Race and Gender/The Erasure of Black Women." *Quest: A Feminist Quarterly* 5: 36–62.

Springer, Kimberly. 2005. *Living for the Revolution: Black Feminist Organizations, 1968–1980.* Durham, N.C.: Duke University Press.

Staggenborg, Suzanne. 1986. "Coalition Work in the Pro-choice Movement: Organizational and Environmental Opportunities and Obstacles." *Social Problems* 33: 374–90.

Stone, Betsy. 1970. "Sisterhood Is Powerful." Pamphlet reprinted from *The Militant* (October 23). New York: Pathfinder Press.

Stone, Michael. 1970. "Liberation Struggle Generates Tension on Race, Sex Issues." Reprint of article from *The Christian Century* (June 10). Social Action Files, State Historical Society, Madison, Wis.

Stoper, Emily. 1989. *The Student Nonviolent Coordinating Committee: The Growth of Radicalism in a Civil Rights Organization.* New York: Carlson.

Tarrow, Sidney. 1994. *Power in Movement: Social Movements, Collective Action and Politics.* Cambridge: Cambridge University Press.

Taylor, Verta, and Nancy Whittier. 1992. "Collective Identity in Social Movement Communities: Lesbian Feminist Mobilization." In *Frontiers in Social Movement Theory,* edited by Aldon D. Morris and Carol McClurg Mueller, 104–29. New Haven, Conn.: Yale University Press.

Townsend Gilkes, Cheryl. 1994. "'If it wasn't for the women . . .': African American Women, Community Work and Social Change." In *Women of Color in U.S. Society,* edited by Maxine Baca Zinn and Bonnie Thorton Dill, 229–46. Philadelphia: Temple University Press.

Van Dyke, Nella. 2003. "Crossing Movement Boundaries: Factors That Facilitate

Coalition Protest by American College Students, 1930–1990." *Social Problems* 50: 226–50.

Weinfeld, Martha. 1970. "Women's Liberation Advances the Movement." Unpublished position paper (December 15) for Wednesday Night New Course Group, Berkeley Women's Liberation. Women's Liberation Ephemera Files, Special Collections, Northwestern University, Chicago, Ill.

Zald, Mayer N., and Roberta Ash. 1966. "Social Movement Organizations: Growth, Decay and Change." *Social Forces* 44: 327–41.

6

The Strength of Weak Coalitions: Transregional Feminist Coalitions in Eastern Germany

Katja M. Guenther

During the collapse of state socialism in East Germany in 1989 and the subsequent unification of East and West Germany in 1990, women in East Germany mobilized first to bring feminist concerns into discussions of a reformed socialism and, when the dissolution of the German Democratic Republic (GDR, or East Germany) became inevitable, to preserve some of the gender equity policies of the GDR in the unified Germany. Yet by late 1990, women's social movement activity in eastern Germany was increasingly scarce at the national level. The primary organization representing eastern German women, the Independent Women's Association (Unabhängiger Frauenverband), was falling apart, and many activists stopped participating in the association in favor of activism within the established political parties or with local women's organizations in their immediate communities (Ferree 1994; Hampele 1993). In fact, since the conclusion of this brief period of national-level mobilization by eastern German feminists in 1989–90, feminist organizing in eastern Germany has focused on the local level. Not only is there no national feminist movement in eastern Germany, but feminist organizations within eastern Germany have limited contact with each other and only rarely work together as part of cooperative endeavors.

Yet these local women's movements also do not operate in isolation. Rather, they often look to partners and influences outside of eastern Germany, engaging in transregional coalition work. In the immediate unification period, when local women's groups in eastern Germany were just starting to form, established feminist activists and feminist organizations from outside eastern Germany began heading to East Germany in the hopes of supporting their formerly socialist sisters. Offering everything from ideological resources to pragmatic know-how, these relationships were at times complicated by differing understandings of gender, feminism, civic participation, and the state. Nevertheless, coalition work with outside partners has become one of the enduring features of local women's movements in eastern Germany since 1989.

Examining the coalition work of the local women's movements in two medium-sized cities in eastern Germany, Erfurt and Rostock, illuminates the mechanisms through which these movements came to establish ties to feminist activists and movements outside of eastern Germany. Drawing on in-depth, semistructured interviews with sixty-three feminist activists and policy makers, as well as on participant observation and archival data, I find that the emergence of these coalitions depended both on the accessibility of possible coalition partners to each other, the presence of historic patterns of regionalization, and ideological alignment.

My analysis of coalition activity in Erfurt and Rostock, which challenges understandings of coalition formation as the outgrowth of rational, calculated interests, demonstrates that preexisting affinities and ideological congruence play a major role in coalition formation. In these two cases, regional alliances predating unification oriented coalition activity during and after unification. Specifically, linkages between Erfurt and West Germany before unification, coupled with the city's vision of itself as western German, helped forge coalitions between feminists from western Germany and activists with the new women's organizations that sprang up in Erfurt in the wake of unification. On the other hand, Rostock's Baltic identity and orientation toward Scandinavia, especially Sweden, contributed to identification with Swedish models of gender policy and provided the groundwork for coalition building between feminists in Rostock and Sweden.

As the experiences of women's organizations in Erfurt and Rostock reveal, coalition partnerships can be critical formative experiences for emerging social movement organizations, even when coalitions are relatively weak. In fact, weak coalitions in Rostock and Erfurt have had strong effects. Before turning to the two cases, I contextualize coalition activity in the two cities by providing a brief review of the unification process and feminist activism during unification, as well as of extant conceptualizations of coalition activity. I then analyze coalition activity in Erfurt and Rostock, examining the formation and function of regional coalitions involving the feminist movements in these two cities.

Feminism in Eastern Germany

German unification brought with it massive social transformations, including in gender relations. Socialist East Germany placed a strong policy emphasis on assisting women in combining paid labor with parenting. Policy programs benefiting women and aimed at helping women balance work and family were dismantled during the unification process. In their stead, West German social policy, which reflects a significantly more traditional view of women and their status in family and society than East German social policy, came into effect in the new eastern German states. Among tangible losses for eastern German women were year-long maternity leaves, access to abortion on demand, state-funded child care, and various positive action programs in education and employment (Einhorn 1992; Nickel 1993). Although the GDR was not a fully egalitarian state—especially insofar as women were expected to work full time and be primarily responsible for family life—women experienced significant setbacks as a consequence of unification.

The Independent Women's Association and western German feminist organizations were unsuccessful in their efforts to advance feminist concerns as part of the unification process (Kamenitsa 1998; Young 1999). Except for abortion, which became the single most contentious issue of German unification (Funk 1993; Maleck-Lewy 1995; Maleck-Lewy and Ferree 2000), women's issues were largely marginalized, as were women's voices, during the unification process. Many feminist activists in eastern Germany seemed to give up on the national state as a meaningful target for social movement activity. After repeated setbacks in the national arena in 1989–90, feminist activists in eastern Germany largely followed one of two paths: either they joined the major political parties and sought to advance women's interests through these parties, or they founded or joined localized women's organizations that generally provide services to women and organize politically around feminist issues at the local level. In spite of interactions with feminists from other cities and regions within Germany through the Independent Women's Association, few of these connections survived the dissolution of the Independent Women's Association.[1] Instead, the eastern German women's movement metamorphosed into many localized women's movements.

The development of coalitions across local women's movements within eastern Germany has been hampered by several structural and ideological factors. First, experiences during the socialist era varied across regions within East Germany, as do more recent responses to unification. These differences in turn feed into distinctive feminist ideologies, goals, and strategies, which inhibit solidarity and coalition building (Guenther 2010). Second, because Germany is a federal state that affords regional states and municipalities a relatively high degree of autonomy in matters of social policy, activists working in different settings have had significantly different experiences since unification. Feminists in Rostock, for example, encounter a state that is largely open to the claims and demands made by the women's movement there, whereas activists in Erfurt struggle with a local state that is resistant to addressing issues of social inequality. Activists across regions thus do not see themselves as sharing the same experiences or fighting the same kinds of battles. Third, the availability of other coalition partners within the feminist social movement field steered local women's movements away from each other and toward outside partners. Albeit presumably unintentionally, transregional coalition partners inhibited coalition work between localized women's movements in eastern Germany.

Why Weak Coalitions?

According to David S. Meyer and Nancy Whittier (1994, 290), "Coalitions are structuring mechanisms that bring a broad spectrum of otherwise distinct organizations into contact, spreading interpretive frames, organizational structures, political analysis, and tactics." Much of the extant scholarship on social movement coalitions has focused on the development of coalitions, with particular emphasis on the conditions under which coalitions form and survive (e.g., McCammon and Campbell 2002; Obach 2004; Rose 2000; Staggenborg 1986; Van Dyke 2003). In general, political threats and opportunities catalyze both within-movement and cross-movement coalitions, which have the greatest longevity when those threats appear sustained, resources are bountiful, and either ideologies or identities overlap or resonate in some way.

Coalition activity between local feminist movements in eastern Germany and their coalition partners mostly follows these patterns. Unification wrought both crisis and opportunity for feminists in eastern Germany. New challenges facing women, and new possibilities for social movement activity, initially gave rise to efforts at organizing a mass German women's movement involving women from both West and East Germany. The failure of this effort, coupled with the strength of municipal and regional governance and identities, facilitated the development of local women's movements with transregional coalition partners.

Alliances between feminists in Erfurt and those in western Germany, and between feminists in Rostock and those in Sweden, have two important features. First, these coalitions are the outcome of patterns of influence far broader than shared interests or a common enemy. Specifically, although rational models of coalition building take as a starting point that organizations will engage in mutual support and cooperation when their interests align (Hojnacki 1997), culture and social relationships influence perceptions of interests and of potential allies and strategies (Rose 2000). Consequently, coalition formation may take place even in cases where shared interests are quite loose or where targets differ, if other social conditions exist that render coalition activity purposeful. The coalitions in Rostock and Erfurt emerge less out of shared strategic interests than out of historical ties and shared ideological foundations.

Second, in both cities, coalitions are relatively weak. Weak coalitions involve groups that share broad ideologies, but that are not necessarily deeply invested in the same strategic interests and that may, as in the case of the coalitions under analysis here, develop more out of an interest in solidarity than in concrete outcomes for either coalition partner. Weak coalitions may also lack a sense of collective identity or have only partially overlapping identities and interests, and thus they may develop as an alternative to strong coalitions in conditions that are not conducive to deep integration between coalition partners. Whereas formalized organizational ties and overlapping organizations—possibly including shared umbrella organizations—characterize strong coalitions, there are few continuous formal ties between organizations involved in weak coalitions. Umbrella organizations that include organizational members from different segments of the coalitions and bridge organizations that involve members from both coalition partners are notably absent. Still, even coalitions that appear informal and disorganized can be successful and can have important effects. In the two cases under consideration here, it appears that weak coalitions are also the only viable coalition form. Highly integrated strong coalition activity would likely fail.

Their weak coalition partnerships, coupled with the transregional character of the coalitions in Rostock and Erfurt, may, on the face of it, look like transnational advocacy networks. However, in spite of some similarities with transnational advocacy networks, activity between feminists in Erfurt and those in western Germany and between feminists in Rostock and those in Sweden, is more typical of social movement coalition activity than transnational advocacy networks. These networks involve individuals and groups, including both institutional and noninstitutional actors, who are networked transnationally around a shared concern, such as environmental degradation or human rights (Keck and Sikkink 1998; Stillerman 2003; Zippel 2004). Actors within transnational advocacy networks are "bound together by shared values, a common discourse, and dense exchanges of information" (Keck and Sikkink 1998, 2). Although transnational advocacy networks are characterized by at least some, if not a preponderance of, elite activity, social actors involved in the alliances in Rostock and Erfurt are largely nonelite, everyday actors, especially on the eastern German side of the coalition. Transnational advocacy networks also include a far greater variety of organizations and institutions—churches, media outlets, government sectors—than is evident in the alliances under consideration. Finally, the networks routinely focus on supranational or international targets and/or audiences, whereas targets in Rostock and Erfurt remain solidly localized. Given the parameters of extant terminology, I view coalitions in Rostock and Erfurt as weak coalitions and as analytically distinct from transnational advocacy networks.

Building across the Border: Erfurt and Western German Feminism

In early December 1989, the fledgling women's movement in Erfurt was briefly catapulted into the public limelight. Working on a tip from colleagues in Berlin, members of Women for Change, a newly formed group of women in Erfurt committed to integrating women's demands and needs into the political, social, and economic changes accompanying the collapse of state socialism, organized the storming of the local barracks of the East German secret police, commonly known as the Stasi. Emboldened by the action in Erfurt, dissident and feminist groups in other cities in eastern Germany followed suit. These protests were the final symbolic defeat of the ruling party of the GDR in Erfurt and elsewhere. In the days, weeks, months, and even years after the occupation of the Stasi barracks, the public hailed Women for Change and its leaders for catalyzing significant changes in Erfurt and across the GDR. The city government recognized Women for Change's key role in democratization by granting the organization full control over the Stasi building. In June 1990, the Stasi headquarters in Erfurt became the first official municipal women's center in East Germany.

Given its high-profile activities, Women for Change attracted attention from women in West Germany as well. Feminists in the West heard about the activities of women in Erfurt through the news coverage of unfolding events in the East, and they saw an opportunity to help these women and, ideally, to work together for a more egalitarian Germany should unification be realized. West German women joined ride shares and arrived in Erfurt in late 1989 and early 1990 to provide logistical and emotional support to the emerging women's movement in Erfurt. Their arrival and continued presence in the city was facilitated by Erfurt's closeness to the former East–West border and by its solid transportation infrastructure, which came to include high-speed rail access a few years after unification. Western German feminists brought feminist texts and brochures from their own organizations, transmitting their ideologies both through written materials and direct personal contact. In a place where women were largely accustomed to thinking of men as their collaborators in the socialist project, women from West Germany brought surprising new concepts with them, such as patriarchy and oppression.

These concepts were not unfamiliar to all activists in Erfurt, however. Through work with the disarmament movement, a key leader of Women for Change was familiar with West German feminism, and she shared her knowledge with other women in Erfurt, opening their eyes to the possible ramifications of unification for women. One member of Women for Change recalls hearing about how women in West Germany rarely worked outside of the home from an activist who had been exposed to the West through her participation in an anti–nuclear arms group: "She warned us that we, too, could be victims of unemployment like that [faced by women in West Germany]. She said, 'We must do something. . . . ' So the call to all women was: get organized, get involved."

Although only a handful of activists had any experience with West Germans—and even though such experience was often second or third hand—these activists became coalition brokers of a sorts (Obach 2004), translating the issues and problems facing women in West Germany for neophyte activists in East Germany. Threats of a retreat to the domestic sphere inspired many women to agitate for change during the tumultuous autumn of 1989 and into 1990. Their work was often facilitated by local churches, which offered activists one of few spaces in the GDR where groups could meet free from state surveillance.

In fact, in addition to individuals serving as conduits of information about the West, before and during unification, churches sheltered dissident activities and less political self-help groups for women, both of which became venues for ideological transmission from the West. Helbing's story is typical of those of women who were first exposed to Western feminist thought through church-based women's groups. Beginning in the late 1980s, Helbing joined a self-help group focused on women's physical and spiritual well-being. She was in her early twenties at the time, and struggling with her identity as a lesbian and with her desire to work as an artist, which was complicated by censorship in the GDR. As a photographer with access to a darkroom, she agreed to take on a risky job for the women's group: Because the copying of documents was illegal in the GDR and copying devices were almost impossible to come by, she would photograph feminist books from the West page by page, and make copies of the pages as photographs for group members to read.

Through her involvement with this group, Helbing was exposed to West German and Western feminist thought, including feminist theology. The Boston Women's Health Collective's *Our Bodies, Ourselves* (1979) and writings by West German feminist author and cultural critic Alice Schwarzer (1975, 1984, 1985) provided the fuel for discussions about patriarchy, gender inequality, oppression, women's health, violence against women, sexuality, and women's work, and helped Helbing to start looking at the world from what she calls a "woman's viewpoint." She adopted a new vocabulary centered on patriarchy, women's oppression, and women's autonomy.

Her participation with this group before and during the collapse of the GDR laid the foundation for her future political action, as it did for many women like her. In January 1990, Helbing was part of a group of women from both sides of the border that founded an autonomous women's center in Erfurt with a focus on the issue of violence against women. Helbing and her eastern German colleagues expressed extreme gratitude to their western German collaborators, who offered assistance in establishing nonprofit status and in training women to work with survivors of violence. As one eastern German staff member at the women's center notes, "Without them, we would not have known what to do."

Later, in the mid-1990s, western German feminists also played a key role in helping to found an ecological and feminist housing collective located on a former farm some thirty kilometers outside of the city. This project mostly involved women who were or had been active with the autonomous women's center. Again, western German women played a critical role in offering practical advice. Yet their ideological messages were as, if not more, important in working with women in Erfurt. Women involved with these two autonomous organizations adopted the radical, separatist feminist ideology common in the autonomous women's movement in western Germany. This ideology emphasizes separatism from men, a discourse of oppression and patriarchy, and a need for women and women's organizations to become autonomous from men and from male institutions such as the state. Some feminist activists in Erfurt first encountered such ideological messages through groups before unification. Ideological transmission and reinforcement continued after unification as western German feminists continued their involvement in Erfurt, teaching women there about their brand of feminism.

Conservative women's groups, most notably the women's association of Germany's largest right-leaning political party, the Women's Union of the Christian Democratic Union (CDU-FU), also worked to enlist new members in Erfurt. Unlike women involved with radical feminist organizations, these feminist activists focus on helping women balance work and family and on cooperating with men and the state to increase women's status in society. They adopt a more maternal feminism that stresses women's differences from men as nurturers, and they advocate women's increased political participation on the grounds that women will bring compassion and civility into the public sphere.

Early encounters between eastern and western German women through the CDU and CDU-FU were occasionally problematic for women in Erfurt because of divergent expectations of work, family, and political involvement. Maria, a feminist state policy maker active in the CDU-FU, recalls her first impressions of—and concerns about—women from the West:

> In the beginning, when I joined the Women's Union [CDU-FU], and went to our first meeting together at the national level and saw the ladies from the old German states—those were still very well-situated ladies who I met then, often housewives, one kid, politics as a hobby. With us, it was still different. At that age, you'd have at least two kids, or more. Women of my age had more than just one child! Here [in the former East] it's just a given that you have multiple children and are still involved. Mrs. Rita Süssmuth, she also said something—she was the nationwide President [of the CDU-FU] for years. We had an event that dealt with the theme of employment, political engagement, and family. And Mrs. Süssmuth says there, "Well, fine, if you have two kids, maybe you can still do this [political career], but with three kids, it's just not possible. It just can't be done." To which I said, "Frau Süssmuth, if that's the case, then I have to stand up now and get my bag and drive home again because I am single and have three children and *here I am.*"

In this conversation, Maria identifies differences in attitudes toward family and work life as the primary difference between women from East and West Germany involved with the CDU-FU. Although women from the East generally had several children and long careers working outside of the home, women from the West more often had only one child or no children, had not worked outside of the home or worked only on a part-time basis, and considered politics a recreational activity. Mrs. Süssmuth's comments came as an affront to Maria, who was building a successful political career while acting as a single mother to three children.

Instead of responding to such incidents and attitudes by shunning women from the West, Maria and others who had similar experiences tried to integrate their experiences as working parents into the platform and practices of the CDU-FU and its parent organization. Not only did their simple presence among elected officials open the eyes of western German feminists to the possibility of combining elected office and parenthood, but they urged the CDU-FU to become friendlier toward mothering women by making free or low-cost child care available at major events and by better integrating work–family issues into the organization's political agenda. Maria and her peers in the CDU-FU in Erfurt, seeing no way to avoid working with these women other than defecting from the CDU, pushed western German members to reevaluate their existing expectations of women and work. They accomplished this through their subtle but consistent insistence on attention to issues salient for eastern German women, but without open discussions about the different experiences of eastern and western German women. Rather, coalition work functioned as a type of contact zone through which eastern and western German feminists had the opportunity to work together without necessarily explicitly addressing their different experiences and subjectivities.

By 2003, Maria and other members of the CDU-FU in Erfurt believed that this effort had been largely successful. They no longer felt singled out as either easterners or as working mothers, they believed that their dual roles as mothers and political leaders were appreciated, and they noticed that women from western Germany had adjusted their expectations of work and family in their own lives as well. The tremendous success of CDU-FU women in eastern Germany as governors, state representatives, and most recently as chancellor has served to bolster the participation of eastern German women and to substantiate the CDU's claims that it supports women.

In addition to the CDU-FU, politically unaffiliated conservative women's organizations came into contact with western German women through religious institutions. Church missions operate both shelters for battered women in Erfurt. The Order of the Good Shepherd, based in Munich (western Germany), founded and manages one of the shelters. The nuns of the order promote women's right to live free from violence and support efforts to improve women's status in the family and their chances in the labor market. The eighty-year-old nun who leads the mission in Erfurt is also a public figure in the city who works closely with eastern German activists. Along with a smattering of other western German women, the nuns advocate and propagate maternalist feminism, which has become the guiding feminist ideology of several organizations in Erfurt, including the tremendously successful Center for Women and Families, which, as its name indicates, centers women squarely within the family.

With such high levels of contact between Erfurt and the West, Erfurt has been influenced by western German values and norms, both in the women's movement and elsewhere. Sometimes these influences benefit feminists and feminist issues, even in the absence of formal coalition work. For example, one of the unintended outcomes of the shelter movement in West Germany in the 1970s and 1980s had been to entrench violence against women as a significant and legitimate social problem there. Because West German television and radio signals permeated the GDR, most East Germans were familiar with the issue of battering before unification, and especially with the feminist positioning of battering as a social problem. After the collapse of state socialism, many communities in eastern Germany sought to catch up with western Germany. Feminist organizers in cities such as Erfurt were able to mobilize support for battered women's shelters among policy makers and the public by stressing that such shelters were a necessary part of catching up. Similarly, feminist organizations have succeeded in securing state funding, and in radical feminist organizations, in reconciling the receipt of state funds with their own belief in autonomy from the state by asserting that their presence is an important part of catching up with the West. Even radical feminists who advocate independence seek to strengthen their position by reminding local policy makers and potential funders that their brand of radical feminism is relatively typical in the West, and that organizations such as theirs are a critical part of civil society, thereby warranting financial support from the state.

Still, the effects of coalition work between women in Erfurt and those in western Germany have not been unilaterally positive. In fact, ideological conflicts between conservative and radical feminisms in western Germany have been transposed to Erfurt, where the women's movement has suffered from infighting, struggles over resources, and power plays. Even when of the same general mind on a specific issue—such as violence against women—radical and conservative feminists are rarely able to work together successfully. Oftentimes, activists in these two camps disagree on the root causes of problems facing women or otherwise interpret issues differently. For example, although radical feminists see domestic violence as an expression of male dominance and a patriarchal social structure, conservative feminists offer a more gender-neutral analysis of domestic violence that focuses on how violence is endemic throughout the society (and especially in the media) and on how spousal abuse reflects broader social and familial strain wrought by the erosion of nuclear families and economic uncertainty. Conflict over issues such as abortion and equal rights for lesbians and gays also overpowers shared interests. The only major coalition of women's organizations within Erfurt, the State Women's Council, has suffered from infighting across different feminist groups, and many organizations in Erfurt have dropped out of this political lobbying organization altogether because of interorganizational disagreements.

Although these conflicts may well have emerged even in the absence of western German coalition partners, continued ideological reinforcement from western feminists seems to aggravate conflict. Western German coalition partners are well aware of disagreements in Erfurt and often contribute to continued conflict and polarization. For example, according to an active feminist, when members of one radical feminist organization considered a partnership around a specific issue with more conservative feminists, their western German coalition partners admonished them for "hopping into bed with the enemy." The partnership was quickly dissolved.

In sum, the postsocialist women's movement in Erfurt has been characterized by the strong influence of two strands of western German feminism. Working with western German feminist coalition partners has helped maintain ideological divisions within the local women's movement in Erfurt. At the same time, western German feminists offered material assistance, logistical know-how, and symbolic resources, including ideologies, discourses, and frames. Although on occasion interactions between eastern and western German feminists have been tense, activists from both sides of the former border seem to cooperate successfully in this city. This success is supported by the weakness of the coalition, which does not require the integration of western and eastern German feminists as coworkers or close colleagues.

Building across the Baltic: Rostock and Swedish Feminism

Although feminists in Erfurt joined in coalition with feminists from western Germany, coalition activity in Rostock is oriented toward Sweden rather than toward western Germany. A few early efforts on the part of western German feminists to work with feminists in Rostock had mixed results. Unlike activists in Erfurt, respondents in Rostock reported strong ideological and personal conflicts with western German women. In encounters with western German feminists, they felt exoticized and sometimes ridiculed for their status as easterners, who occupy a low status in Germany. Reports of experiences with western German feminists and western German feminist organizations were often laced with hostility. Respondents recounted how western Germans treated them like "apes escaped from the ape house" and as "stupid" and "inferior."

One of few cooperative efforts between western German feminists and activists in Rostock was in the founding of the Women's Technical Center, which offers technical and computer training and job placement to women and men in Rostock. After unification, women from the Women's Technical Center in Hamburg (western Germany) decided to fund the founding of a sister organization in Rostock. One of the original staff members in Rostock, Katrin, recalls:

> The Women's Technical Center in Hamburg was looking for women to help build a center like the one there [in Hamburg]. I heard about it, and I looked at the center in Hamburg, and thought, "Maybe this is some militant feminist troop—who knows? Who knows?" But then I saw that it's

really based on, and built around, the fact that women and men have different access to technology. And our women in particular had no experience with technology; while they studied in technical fields quite often,
computer technology had no role because it just wasn't there [in the GDR].
And so I thought this would be a wonderful task, creating something like
this.

Here, Katrin initially feared that women involved in Hamburg would be
militant feminists; instead, Katrin was pleasantly surprised to find that their
goals and objectives made perfect sense to her in their emphasis on providing women with equal access to technology. With a doctorate in biological
sciences herself, and having spent her working life up until unification at a
government research institute, Katrin was well aware of how dated technology, and especially computer technology, was in the GDR. The mission of
the work of enhancing women's technological skills appealed to her, especially
when she realized her western German benefactors were not a "militant feminist troop."

The Women's Technical Center has turned out to be wildly popular.
Classes in computer technology fill quickly, and the center has continuously
expanded since its inception. It is now widely viewed as one of the most successful women's organizations not only in Rostock, but in the entire state of
Mecklenburg-Vorpommern. However, the scope of coalition work between
the two technical centers was short lived. After the Women's Technical Center in Hamburg helped select and train the director and one technology
instructor, the center in Rostock was entirely independent from its mother
organization in Hamburg. Long-term staff members report that their contact with the center in Hamburg faded quickly, in part because the center in
Hamburg was experiencing its own financial and personnel problems. While
the Women's Technical Center in Rostock continues to thrive, the one in
Hamburg closed its doors in the late 1990s.

Katrin's comments about her first encounters with women from Hamburg highlight preconceived notions many eastern German women had about
western German feminists and indicate that activists in Rostock found certain
aspects of western German feminism, most especially ideology, unappealing.
Unlike some women in Eruft, who were exposed to western German feminists
before unification through their dissident activity based in religious institutions, women in Rostock only learned about the West through state-
controlled means. Channels of transmission present in Erfurt, namely large
and active churches, were absent in Rostock, and the city, which is positioned
in Germany's most rural and underdeveloped state, was notoriously slow to

wake up to the protest movement against the ruling party of East Germany, the Socialist Unity Party. Activists in Rostock had only extremely limited contact with western German feminists or feminist ideas before unification, primarily through what little feminist information was transmitted via radio or television. Schooled in the GDR to believe that feminism was bourgeois and anti-socialist, many women in Rostock avoided identification as feminist during unification and were skeptical about the salience of western German feminism for their own lives. Unlike their counterparts in Erfurt, who were exposed to western German feminist ideologies even before unification and who live in a region that strives to be as western as possible, activists in Rostock had little exposure to western German feminism either before or after unification; they inhabit a city that is more skeptical about western ideas and influences. Even a few positive encounters, such as those among the women involved with the Women's Technical Center, could not outweigh the litany of complaints women in Rostock voiced about western German feminists, particularly among early members of the Independent Women's Association who tried to work with western German feminists during unification (Ferree 1995; Young 1999). Separated for forty years and living with radically different systems of governance, socialization, and economics, women from Rostock often found little in common with their counterparts from western Germany. Rather than embracing the radical western feminist ideology dominant in the autonomous women's movement in western Germany, activists in Rostock subscribed to a feminist ideology more reminiscent of the gender ideology of the GDR in its emphasis both on cooperation between women and men and on economic issues as the engine behind unequal gender relations (Guenther 2006).

Although they shunned western German feminist ideologies, activists in Rostock were not closed to all outside partners. Instead, feminists in Rostock engaged in coalition work with Swedish feminists. Activists and political leaders in Rostock repeatedly invoked their efforts at following the Swedish model of high levels of state support for working parents, implicitly or explicitly critiquing the German federal state's approach to gender relations and inequality. One feminist policy maker, for example, notes that Swedish social policies "simply make more sense" in Rostock than those set forth by the federal German government, a sentiment other respondents widely echoed.

Respondents explained their initial openness to Sweden as the consequence of historic connections between Rostock and Sweden, pointing out Rostock's centuries-old ties to Sweden and other Scandinavian nations and noting that even during the GDR, Sweden, a neutral country, maintained relations with East Germany. These feelings of goodwill continued in Rostock after unification. Daily ferry service between Rostock and various Scandinavian nations ensures a regular flow of people across borders. Two major western German cities, Berlin and Hamburg, are fewer than 350 kilometers from Rostock, but Rostock has no airport, high-speed rail service, or, until a decade after unification, direct access to the Autobahn, Germany's famed highway system. In effect, Sweden seems as accessible as western Germany.

Local identity in Rostock continues to center on the city's Baltic identity. This involves both celebrating the city's Baltic heritage and welcoming guests from the Baltic region. Rostock's annual Hansesail, a sailing regatta instituted after unification that in recent years has attracted up to one million visitors, is a perennial favorite among Swedes, Danes, and Finns, who are also frequent vacationers in the city's beach district. Workers in the hospitality industry in Rostock routinely learn to speak basic Swedish and Danish, and Scandinavian nations are common destinations for outmigrating young people and vacationers from Rostock. The women's center in Rostock offers only two foreign-language courses: German as a second language and Swedish.

Given Rostock's historic orientation toward the Baltic and its more recent infrastructure bias, Sweden was a natural place to look for assistance and support after 1989. Already during the collapse of socialism, Swedish feminists reached out to the fledgling women's movement in Rostock. With its emphasis on cooperation between the sexes and the issue of balancing work and family, Swedish feminism resonated with feminist activists in Rostock as they also focused on women's employment, state interventions to increase women's chances in the labor market, and cooperation between women and men to combat gender inequality. Women's organizations in Rostock and Sweden coordinated trips between the two countries so that activists and feminist policy makers could meet one another and learn about challenges and successes on both sides of the Baltic.

Not only did the Swedish influence support and reinforce the feminist emphasis in Rostock on women's employment issues and cooperation with men and the state, but Swedish feminists and feminist organizations have also provided resources for concrete legislative and praxis changes. This has been most evident in the adoption of gender mainstreaming in Rostock (Guenther 2008). Gender mainstreaming, a policy concept emanating from the European Union and widely adopted in Sweden, requires that all policy proposals be examined for a disparate impact on women and men before acceptance and implementation. As a broader agenda, gender mainstreaming seeks to reduce differences between women and men by challenging gendered expectations of political, social, and economic behavior (Schmidt 2005; Stratigaki 2005; Woodward 2003). With support from Swedish feminists, women's organizations in Rostock have widely integrated gender mainstreaming into their work. As Uschi, the director of an organization that focuses on training others on how to implement gender mainstreaming, recalls:

> We organized many educational trips to Sweden. We also took many politicians with us so that they could just see what the situation there was like and truly experience the spirit of it [gender mainstreaming], and we did a lot of publicizing about Swedish equality politics and gender mainstreaming.

Impressed by the level to which gender mainstreaming is integrated into daily life in Sweden, Uschi, along with colleagues at other women's organizations, made it a priority to encourage direct experiences with gender mainstreaming by bringing activists and politicians from Rostock to Sweden. They also hosted Swedish feminists in Rostock, where they conducted workshops on gender policies in Sweden. Through these exchanges, feminists in Rostock learned more about the successes of Swedish feminists in promoting gender egalitarianism. Numerous activists from both sides of the Baltic came to serve as bridges between Rostock and its northern neighbor. In keeping with the weak coalition, these interactions focused on practical and strategic concerns rather than on developing consensus, shared identities, or complete ideological cohesion.

Building on this momentum, in 2001, Rostock became the first city in Germany to pass a municipal gender mainstreaming initiative. Gender mainstreaming advocates on both sides of the Baltic hailed this as a major victory. Through the transfer of knowledge about gender mainstreaming from Sweden to Rostock, feminists and municipal policy makers acquired enough knowledge and practical advice to implement gender mainstreaming within the city.

Swedish feminism has thus been the paramount feminist influence in Rostock. Because of their physical and psychological isolation from western Germany, ties northward were attractive for feminists in Rostock because they build on a history of cooperation and friendship within the Baltic region and on shared ideas about gender relations. Although one women's organization in Rostock was founded through coalition work with a western German women's organization, overall, western German feminism had little appeal. Barriers to coalition formation with western German feminists included both ideological and political differences, as well as Rostock's historic and contemporary isolation from western Germany. An alliance with Swedish feminists, on the other hard, was made possible and enhanced by a shared history of past cooperation, common principles of gender relations, and infrastructure that rendered

Sweden accessible to activists in Rostock. Still, this remains a weak coalition. In the absence of a shared history, state, or culture, these feminists do not necessarily identify closely with one another. They collaborate in the interests of solidarity and support without the goal of understanding one another.

Conclusion

In both Erfurt and Rostock, coalitions are relatively weak insofar as they are largely informal and noninstitutionalized, and they are often built at the individual, rather than the organizational, level. The weakness of these coalitions is a condition for their success. Weak coalitions do not require full recognition and discussion of identities, ideologies, and goals, and they permit only limited challenges to group boundaries. The closer collaboration and tighter communication and understanding necessary for strong coalitions would likely yield conflict and highlight difference (see Borland, this volume, for a discussion of some of the key challenges facing feminist coalitions). Low levels of integration permit the coalitions to thrive in coalition environments in which differences are rarely explicitly acknowledged or discussed. This also comes at a cost: the coalitions do not provide an extensive contact zone through which feminists from different regions could talk and debate, as well as share problems, issues, and experiences (Juris 2008; Santos 2006).

Participation in weak coalitions influences the chances at social movement success within the home space of local movements, sometimes in ways that coalition partners have not intended. For example, many of the ideological rifts within the western German women's movement were transmitted to, and even amplified in, Erfurt during and after unification. These rifts led to extensive conflict within the women's movement in Erfurt, reducing the movement's external legitimacy and inhibiting efforts at securing state support for feminist organizations and issues. On the other hand, in Rostock, collaboration with Swedish feminists has strengthened the legitimacy of the women's movement in the eyes of the local state, which looks favorably on policy ideas emanating from Scandinavia and has increased state support for feminist goals.

Although the outcomes of coalition work have been somewhat different in Erfurt and Rostock, the two cases still share several common features that warrant mention because they problematize some of the assumptions present in extant analyses of coalitions and broaden knowledge about coalitions. First, in regard to coalition development, geopolitical and historical patterns played a significant role. The seeds of coalition work were planted well before unification and greatly depended on the geopolitical positioning of the two cities. Both coalitions grew out of regional identities that predated the collapse of state socialism and that reflect historic patterns of regionalization.

In Erfurt, affinities for western German forms of feminism emerged through the dissident movement and Erfurt's long-standing seat in Germany's conservative south. In Rostock, ties to Sweden during the socialist era were grounded in a regional Baltic identity and feelings of goodwill and were not specifically feminist. This is not to suggest that movements crossing state borders necessarily require some context of previous cooperation to develop and flourish, but rather to encourage future consideration of the role of broader structural and historical patterns in facilitating or retarding coalition formation and sustainability.

Second, and also relevant for understanding coalition formation, successful coalition building in these two cases was dependent on positive—or at least neutral—informal experiences preceding formal coalition contact and during initial coalition contact. In Erfurt, western Germany, and by association western German feminism, was viewed positively before, during, and after unification. Although many feminists in Rostock characterized western German feminists as uppity, militant, man-hating, and rude, feminists in Erfurt saw these women as generous, helpful, and supportive. These negative perceptions of western German feminism inhibited coalition building between feminists in Rostock and western German feminists. In contrast, positive encounters with Swedes, as well as a positive perception of Sweden overall, were critical in supporting early coalition activity between feminists in Rostock and Sweden.

Third, these coalitions challenge rational models of coalition formation that posit that coalitions are primarily born out of alignments of strategic interests. These two coalitions are unidirectional, following a one-way model in which the outside coalition partners support the work of local organizations in eastern Germany with little to gain for themselves other than a sense of feminist solidarity. The outside senior partner participates in ideological transmission, the legitimation of the work of the eastern German women's movement, and logistical support, but receives nothing tangible, or even anything obviously strategic, in return, at least in the short term.[2] This suggests that successful coalitions need not involve mutual or tangible benefits when other benefits—such as reinforced regional identities or a sense of feminist solidarity—render coalition labor purposeful. Benita Roth (this volume) demonstrates how coalition decisions are based in part on social movement organizations' understandings of what constitutes good politics. In the case of the western German and Swedish feminist organizations that engaged in solidarity-based coalition work with the women's movements in Erfurt and Rostock, respectively, supporting fledgling feminist movements is part of their understanding of good politics.

Fourth, the experiences of the coalition partners in this analysis speak to broader questions within the literature on social movements about if and how social movements are developing transnationally and shifting their targets away from domestic politics. Although both of these coalitions involve transregional partnerships that cross current or past national borders, neither coalition is focused on transnational issues. Social movement scholarship has examined transnational activism and its global targets, such as international governmental organizations (e.g., Stillerman 2003; Tarrow 2005; Wapner 2003). Yet social movement activity in Rostock and Erfurt, including that involving coalition partners, has focused exclusively on the local level, seeking to catalyze policy change at the levels of the municipality or local state. This suggests that future scholarship on international coalitions should look not only for coalitions that are obviously operating at the transnational level in terms of targets, but also for those that operate across borders but that still have localized targets. This readjustment may also reveal arenas in which women and other marginalized peoples are especially likely to be active.

Finally, both coalitions, in spite of their weakness, have been quite durable. This requires a rethinking of extant ideas about coalition longevity as durability is often viewed as correlating with a shift to formalization and "paper" coalitions (Tarrow 2005). In Rostock and Erfurt, coalitions with outside partners have survived close to two decades and became largely institutionalized aspects of the local feminist movements in these two cities. This is true even though both coalitions remain highly informal. These weak transregional coalitions find their strength in ideological congruence and regional identities that have contributed to their formation and durability through almost twenty years of postsocialist change.

Notes

1. Although the Independent Women's Association was not officially disbanded until 1996, it was essentially defunct by early 1991.

2. An exception would be the CDU-FU, as the CDU has a stake in attracting votes and popular support to build the party's strength in eastern Germany. Although none of the respondents specifically addressed this issue, a longer-term goal for all coalition partners could also be the development of a broader German and/or transregional, or even pan-European, feminist movement.

Works Cited

Boston Women's Health Collective. 1979. *Our Bodies, Ourselves.* New York: Simon & Schuster.

Einhorn, Barbara. 1992. "German Democratic Republic: Emancipated Women or

Hardworking Mothers?" In *Superwoman and the Double Burden,* edited by Chris Corrin, 125–54. Toronto: Second Story Press.

Ferree, Myra Marx. 1994. "'The time of chaos was the best': Feminist Mobilization and Demobilization in East Germany." *Gender and Society* 8: 597–623.

———. 1995. "Patriarchies and Feminisms: Two Women's Movements in Post-Unification Germany." *Social Politics* 2: 10–24.

Funk, Nanette. 1993. "Abortion and German Unification." In *Gender Politics and Post-Communism: Reflections from Eastern Europe and the Former Soviet Union.* edited by Nanette Funk and Magda Mueller, 194–200. New York: Routledge.

Guenther, Katja M. 2006. "'A bastion of sanity in a crazy world': A Local Feminist Movement and the Reconstitution of Scale, Space, and Place in an Eastern German City." *Social Politics* 13: 551–75.

———. 2008. "Understanding Policy Diffusion across Feminist Social Movements: The Case of Gender Mainstreaming." *Politics and Gender* 4: 1–27.

———. 2010. *Making Their Place: Feminism after Socialism in Eastern Germany.* Stanford: Stanford University Press.

Hampele, Anne. 1993. "The Organized Women's Movement in the Collapse of the GDR: The Independent Women's Organization (UFV)." In *Gender Politics and Post-Communism: Reflections from Eastern Europe and the Former Soviet Union,* edited by Nanette Funk and Magda Mueller, 180–93. London: Routledge.

Hojnacki, Marie. 1997. "Interest Groups' Decisions to Join Alliances or Go It Alone." *American Journal of Political Science* 41: 61–87.

Juris, Jeffrey S. 2008. "Spaces of Intentionality: Race, Class, and Horizontality at the United States Social Forum." *Mobilization* 3: 353–72

Kamenitsa, Lynn. 1998. "The Complexity of Decline: Explaining the Marginalization of the East German Women's Movement." *Mobilization* 3: 245–63.

Keck, Margaret, and Kathryn Sikkink. 1998. *Activists beyond Borders: Advocacy Networks in International Politics.* Ithaca, N.Y.: Cornell University Press.

Maleck-Lewy, Eva. 1995. "Between Self-Determination and State Supervision: Women and the Abortion Law in Post-Unification Germany." *Social Politics* 2: 62–75.

Maleck-Lewy, Eva, and Myra Marx Ferree. 2000. "Talking about Women and Wombs: The Discourse of Abortion and Reproductive Rights in the GDR during and after the Wende." In *Reproducing Gender: Politics, Publics, and Everyday Life after Socialism,* edited by Susan Gal and Gail Kligman, 92–117. Princeton, N.J.: Princeton University Press.

McCammon, Holly J., and Karen E. Campbell. 2002. "Allies on the Road to Victory: Coalition Formation between the Suffragists and the Woman's Christian Temperance Union." *Mobilization* 7: 231–51.

Meyer, David S., and Nancy Whittier. 1994. "Social Movement Spillover." *Social Problems* 41: 227–98.

Nickel, Hildegard Maria. 1993. "Women in the German Democratic Republic and in the New Federal States: Looking Backward and Forward (Five Theses)." In *Gender Politics and Post-Communism: Reflections from Eastern Europe and the Former Soviet Union,* edited by Nanette Funk and Magda Mueller, 138–50. New York: Routledge.

Obach, Brian K. 2004. *Labor and the Environmental Movement.* Cambridge, Mass.: MIT Press.

Rose, Fred. 2000. *Coalitions across the Class Divide: Lessons from the Labor, Peace, and Environmental Movements.* Ithaca, N.Y.: Cornell University Press.

Santos, Boaventura de Sousa. 2006. *The Rise of the Global Left.* London: Zed Books.

Schmidt, Verena. 2005. *Gender Mainstreaming—An Innovation in Europe?* Opladen, Germany: Barbara Budrich.

Schwarzer, Alice. 1975. *Der kleine Unterschied und seine großen Folgen.* Frankfurt am Main: Fischer Verlag.

———. 1984. *Das Emma-Buch.* Munich: DTV.

———. 1985. *Lohn Liebe, Zum Wert der Frauenarbeit.* Frankfurt am Main: Suhrkamp Taschenbuch.

Staggenborg, Suzanne. 1986. "Coalition Work in the Pro-Choice Movement: Organizational and Environmental Opportunities and Obstacles." *Social Problems* 33: 374–90.

Stillerman, Joel. 2003. "Transnational Activist Networks and the Emergence of Labor Internationalism in the NAFTA Countries." *Social Science History* 27: 577–601.

Stratigaki, Maria. 2005. "Gender Mainstreaming vs. Positive Action." *European Journal of Women's Studies* 12: 165–86.

Tarrow, Sidney. 2005. *The New Transnational Activism.* Cambridge: Cambridge University Press.

Van Dyke, Nella. 2003. "Crossing Movement Boundaries: Factors That Facilitate Coalition Protest by American College Students, 1930–1990." *Social Problems* 50: 226–50.

Wapner, Paul. 2003. "Transnational Environmental Activism." In *The Social Movements Reader: Cases and Concepts,* edited by James Goodwin and James M. Jasper, 202–9. Malden, Mass.: Blackwell.

Woodward, Alison. 2003. "European Gender Mainstreaming: Promises and Pitfalls of Transformative Policy." *Review of Policy Research* 20: 65–88.

Young, Brigitte. 1999. *Triumph of the Fatherland: German Unification and the Marginalization of Women.* Ann Arbor: University of Michigan Press.

Zippel, Kathrin. 2004. "Transnational Advocacy Networks and Policy Cycles in the European Union: The Case of Sexual Harassment." *Social Politics* 11: 57–85.

III
Broad Political Influences
on Social Movement Coalitions

7
Organizing across Ethnic Boundaries in the Post–Civil Rights Era: Asian American Panethnic Coalitions

Dina G. Okamoto

Thousands of Asian Americans rallied outside of New York's city hall in May 1996 to protest city councilwoman Julia Harrison, who had been quoted in a *New York Times* article published on March 31 about the growing Asian population in Queens. Harrison had spoken at length about the immigrants in her district, describing Asians as criminals, rude merchants, and illegal aliens. She blamed them for inflated housing prices, increased levels of crime, and the depressed wages of native-born workers (Toy 1996). Despite the fact that most of the Asian immigrants in Harrison's district were Chinese, more than forty social, political, and religious organizations representing different Asian ethnic groups formed the Asian American Alliance after the *New York Times* article was published. The Asian American Alliance was central in organizing a visible and well-attended rally where a diverse set of participants, including garment workers from Chinatown and Korean American business owners from Queens, gathered at city hall to denounce the councilwoman for her insensitive comments. The New York Chinatown Senior Citizens Center, Korean-American Association of Mid-Queens, and a host of other Asian ethnic community-based organizations were part of the alliance. They successfully gained the attention of political elites and the press, and eventually received a public apology from the councilwoman. Cross-ethnic coalition events such as this one demonstrate that organizations with different interests, goals, and histories can effectively coordinate their efforts for a common cause.

In this chapter, I investigate the conditions that encourage groups to form organizational alliances across ethnic boundaries. I draw on theoretical frameworks from the social movements and race/ethnicity literatures to build a theoretical model of coalition formation among ethnic groups in the United States. Specifically, I focus on factors in the external environment that lead groups to form shared interests and examine how different structural conditions heighten ethnic and racial boundaries and affect social action.

Past Research on Interracial Coalitions

Research on interracial coalitions has primarily focused on biracial political coalitions (see Eisinger 1976; Meier and Stewart 1991; Regalado 1995; Sonenshein 1989, 1993). These studies tend to explore how political coalitions develop in major cities and aid in the election of minority candidates to mayoral and city council positions. For example, Browning, Marshall, and Tabb (1984) discovered that African Americans in ten Northern California cities made significant gains within the political system when they garnered the support of white liberals, and at times Latinos. Another set of studies focuses on panethnic or multiracial coalitions in the form of new organizations that deal with community, civic, or advocacy issues (see Espiritu 1992; Padilla 1985; Vo 2004). In an in-depth study of racial politics in Los Angeles, Saito (1998) examined how interracial coalitions among Asian Americans and Latinos evolved around the issues of redistricting and anti-immigrant legislation during the 1980s and 1990s. He found that shared interests, similar histories of discrimination, and benefits from organizational scale created by coalitions contributed to the formation of organizations such as the Coalition for Harmony in Monterey Park, a multiracial coalition established to fight a local English-only resolution.

Although this research has helped us understand how groups can combine their efforts for greater chances of success in reaching their goals, little research focuses on organizational coalitions present at collective action events. Study of such cross-ethnic coalitions is important because short-term organizational alliances not only provide the foundation for formal coalitions, but they also foster networks between different ethnic communities. When two or more organizations that serve different ethnic populations work together to sponsor, coordinate, and support collective action events such as a political protest or cultural celebration, it represents the extent to which groups are able to broaden their ethnic boundaries to take on other groups' interests as their own in a public arena. These organizational coalitions also show how ethnic groups collaborate and share the collective goods generated from a larger project.

In this chapter, I focus on the cross-ethnic coalition efforts of Asian Americans in the post–civil rights era. The Asian American case is particularly useful for studying coalitions because the different ethnic groups that compose the racial category of Asian did not initially share any larger goals or movement activity and had different histories and identities. In addition, past antagonistic histories of Asian countries and the negative images and stereotypes brought from the different homelands to the United States shape intergroup relations and can often hinder cooperation among the various Asian ethnic groups.

In the next section, I provide some historical background on the patterns of organizational formation within the Asian American community, which has set the stage for the formation of cross-ethnic coalitions.

Coalition Formation in the Asian American Movement

Historically, Asian ethnic groups residing in the United States created their own separate organizations based on kin, province, prefecture, and dialect (Chan 1991). In response to growing dominant group hostility directed at the different ethnic communities in the mid-1800s and continuing into the 1900s, ethnic leaders formed organizations that were based on national identity instead of clan and kin. Chinese, Japanese, Korean, and Filipino groups, among others, formed ethnic-specific organizations that primarily met the needs of ethnic communities, but also created networks of community ties and strengthened cultural values and ethnic identities (see Daniels 1988; Kwong 1996). Ethnic organizations instituted a framework for group members to express their collective interests, and also reinforced the spatial segregation of the different ethnic communities who had come to view themselves as having little in common (Chan 1991).

During the early 1970s, there was a shift in organizing within the Asian American community. The failure of the Vietnam War and the success of the civil rights movement politicized Asian American college students, most of whom were of Chinese, Japanese, and Korean descent (Espiritu 1992; Omatsu 1994; Wei 1993). Finding that their experiences within the United States were more similar than different, these students forged a new movement and began to create a shared culture and history for all Asian Americans.

Organizations to support the new movement formed, characterized by broad mission statements about the inclusion of all Asian ethnic communities and by panethnic names to reflect their constituency and membership. Pan-Asian organizations such as the Asian Pacific American Labor Alliance and the Organization of Pan Asian American Women lobbied against discriminatory immigration legislation, brought media attention to racial profiling, and pursued employment issues that relate to Asians, while providing a context for the development of networks and relationships across ethnic boundaries. These organizations also facilitated the construction and dissemination of an Asian American history and culture (Kibria 1997).

Faced with heightened levels of anti-Asian violence and sentiment in the 1980s resulting from international economic competition, the Asian American movement experienced a new burst of organizing (Espiritu 1992; Lien 2001). Asian ethnic communities began to organize collectively and construct shared interests in the face of new threats. Organizing along a panethnic boundary was also recognized by the state through official racial classification systems and the distribution of resources (Espiritu 1992; Vo 2004), and by the mid-1980s, panethnicity was well established as an organizing principle for building a community among groups with different ethnic origins. In such an environment, ethnic organizations were encouraged to take on broader pan-Asian issues. Some ethnic organizations adapted to the new organizational environment by maintaining their ethnic interests and forming cross-ethnic coalitions, a short-term expression of political and social support for other ethnic groups and for the broader Asian American community.

One of the first formal cross-ethnic organizational coalitions formed in 1973 in San Diego. The Union of Pan Asian Communities was made up of seven existing ethnic organizations, including the Council of Pilipino American Organizations, Chinese Social Service Center, and Chamorro Nation (Vo 2001). Other cross-ethnic coalitions followed, such as the Asian American Voters Coalition, which was composed of local and national organizations representing Chinese, Filipino, Korean, Japanese, South Asian, and Vietnamese communities. In addition, less formal cross-ethnic coalitions appeared at protests, demonstrations, and festivals, where ethnic organizations representing different ethnic groups worked collectively to organize, sponsor, and support an ethnic or panethnic claim. These coalitions signified the extent to which ethnic-specific organizations took on the issues of other ethnic groups or of the larger panethnic community, and they laid the foundation for the possibility of formal coalition building. It is of particular interest, then, to understand the conditions that encourage *coalition events*, or collective action events where ethnic organizations coordinate their efforts in support of an ethnic or panethnic cause.

Theoretical Framework: The Role of Threat, Competition, and Segregation in the Creation of Shared Interests

Social movements and race/ethnicity scholars have suggested that coalitions are less likely to form between groups with different collective identities (Diaz-Veizades and Chang 1996; Kriesberg 1998; Lichterman 1995; McCammon and Campbell 2002). These collective identities are often associated with differences in interests and ideologies, which can further divide groups from one another. Sonenshein (1993) argues that groups can potentially form a coalition if racial ideology is shared and if leaders can shape how group members perceive their own group interests and the interests of others. His study of political coalitions in Los Angeles confirmed this idea and illustrated that alliances forged between African Americans and whites were largely due to community and political leaders with shared philosophies. Similarly, Regalado (1995) discovered that two formal interracial coalitions in Los Angeles, the Black–Korean Alliance and Latino–Black Roundtable, ultimately failed because their members could not move beyond racial group loyalties. In this case, leadership was unable to shape respective group interests so that they were aligned, and the interracial coalitions ultimately dissolved.

The issue of collective identity is an interesting one for the Asian American community. Because the larger society views Asians as a racialized group, cultural and linguistic differences among Asian ethnic groups are often overlooked (Espiritu 1992; Omi and Winant 1994). In addition, the groups composing Asian America do not share similar immigration histories or historical relations with the United States, which often results in differences in identity and group formation (see Espiritu 2004). However, broader social forces may influence these groups to see themselves as sharing similar experiences and life chances. Below, I review the theoretical and empirical literature on the factors that encourage distinct ethnic groups to heighten their ethnic and racial boundaries, paying special attention to competition and segregation processes, and create hypotheses about the effects of boundary heightening on cross-ethnic coalitions.

External Threats

Research on social movements has demonstrated that coalitions are more likely to occur when a group or organization is faced with threats in the form of restrictive legislation or powerful countermovements (Hathaway and Meyer 1993; McCammon and Campbell 2002; Meyer and Staggenborg 1996; Staggenborg 1986). Threats to a particular movement, group, or organization provide incentives for members to overcome differences and seek out allies or coalition partners to achieve a larger collective goal (Gerhards and Rucht 1992; Van Dyke 2003). For example, McCammon and Campbell (2002) found that threats to the suffrage and temperance movements were central in understanding the coalitions formed between women's suffrage organizations and Woman's Christian Temperance Unions in a collective effort to win the vote for women. In a study of coalition protest among college students, Van Dyke (2003) discovered that local threats, such as the presence of counterdemonstrators at a previous event, contribute to the formation of within-movement coalitions, while threats at the federal level, such as a current

Republican administration, encourage cross-movement coalitions among student organizations.

Similarly, past research in the area of race and ethnicity has focused on the role of external threats in facilitating interracial coalitions and collective action across ethnic lines. In a study of an urban community in Los Angeles, Chung (2001) found that African Americans and Koreans were able to form an effective coalition organization to establish community policing programs despite distinct group understandings of why such programs were needed. Both racial groups perceived a common enemy—the law enforcement system that had failed to deal with crime and safety in their neighborhoods—and were compelled to work together to improve their community. Similarly, Espiritu's (1992) work on Asian American panethnicity suggested that a threat to the group, anti-Asian sentiment and violence during the 1980s, led to the formation of pan-Asian organizations. Despite their ethnic differences, group members were able to coordinate their interests to create new institutions that not only served the broader Asian American community and asserted a pan-Asian ideology, but also fought against negative images of Asians and anti-Asian attitudes (also see Okamoto 2006; Vo 2004).

In sum, the social movements and race/ethnicity literatures suggest that threats to groups, organizations, and movements encourage members to alter their strategies to achieve social justice and change by widening their collective base and finding new coalition partners. In short, when ethnic groups are faced with threats, cross-ethnic coalitions will be more likely.

Competition and Resources

Past research has also indicated that resources are important in understanding coalition formation. In fact, scholarship in this area suggests competing hypotheses regarding the effect of resource competition on coalition formation. Some social movements researchers argue that in an environment where funding is limited, resource-poor groups will seek out coalition partners who can provide them with access to additional funds, organizational capacity, and willing participants—all of which help to accomplish movement goals (McCammon and Campbell 2002). Thus, when resources are scarce, cross-ethnic coalitions will be more likely. However, other scholars claim that when funding is scarce, movement organizations compete with one another for resources, especially if these organizations are advancing similar causes (Zald and McCarthy 1980). Competition among groups increases tensions and hinders coalition formation. Therefore, when resources are scarce, cross-ethnic coalitions will be less likely.

Research in the race and ethnicity literature has supported the latter hypothesis: when resources are scarce, competition among ethnic groups leads to conflict, not coalition formation (Olzak 1992; Olzak, Shanahan, and McEneaney 1994, 1996). In fact, when ethnic or racial groups compete for resources, collective action in the form of protest will occur because both groups are attempting to exclude others from resources and opportunities to maintain or improve their standing in the social and economic hierarchy (Banton 1983; Barth 1969; Hannan 1979; Nielsen 1980; Olzak 1992; Park 1950). Competition theory posits that group boundaries will also be heightened when economic shifts, such as a breakdown in labor market segmentation, or demographic changes, such as the influx of new immigrants, increase contact between ethnic and racial groups, thus intensifying competition. Such changes can also lead groups to perceive that others are making relative gains in the economic and social arenas, which should increase intergroup competition. Thus, similar to the resource hypothesis, competition theory predicts that coalitions will form only under noncompetitive conditions when resources are plentiful.

However, an extension of competition theory provides for the possibility of cross-ethnic alliances to emerge under competitive conditions. I use a theory of panethnicity (Okamoto 2003) to argue that because group boundaries can be asserted at multiple levels (i.e., along ethnic or racial lines), we must pay attention to the boundary level at which competition is occurring to understand collective outcomes such as cross-ethnic coalitions among Asian Americans.

Recent research has documented a curious phenomenon among contemporary immigrant groups: the layering of ethnic identities that allows for the expansion and contraction of ethnic boundaries. Waters (1999) found that West Indian immigrants identified as black, acknowledging their similarities to native-born blacks in terms of their color and experiences. At other times, these new immigrants emphasized their ethnic dress, culture, and accent to distinguish themselves from blacks and resist racial categorization. Here, ethnic identities based on a panethnic boundary such as black can be shifted downward to be based on smaller ethnic identities such as Jamaican, Haitian, or Dominican. Conversely, ethnic identities based on national origin boundaries can shift upward to be based on a panethnic boundary. It is these different boundary levels that we must take into account to understand collective outcomes among new immigrant groups.

The ethnic identity options for groups of Asian descent are based on national origin (i.e., Chinese, Filipino, Korean, Indian) and the larger panethnic boundary of Asian American, but these two levels of identification are often complicated by differences in language, culture, religion, and immigration histories. Nevertheless, to understand when cross-ethnic coalitions will emerge, it is important to consider the conditions that activate these different group boundaries. When competition for resources such as economic gain, social status, or political power occurs between racial groups, this heightens racial boundaries and has implications for cross-ethnic coalition building. In this case, competition between Asians and other racial groups such as whites, Latinos, or blacks should encourage different Asian ethnic groups to generate shared interests and act collectively. Thus, when racial groups are in competition for scarce resources, racial boundaries are heightened, and coalitions between different Asian ethnic groups should be more likely. On the other hand, competition can also occur along ethnic lines. Under such conditions, ethnic groups constituting a racial category compete against one another for resources. Competition among ethnic groups should activate ethnic group boundaries, foster ethnic interests and networks, and deter any form of panethnicity. Thus, when Asian ethnic groups are in competition with one another, this increases the salience of ethnic boundaries, and cross-ethnic coalitions should be less likely. In short, competition can occur between and within racial groups and should have an effect on the emergence of cross-ethnic coalitions.

Segregation and the Creation of Intergroup Networks

Although external threats, the lack of resources, and intergroup competition may encourage groups to form coalitions across ethnic boundaries, an additional process could be at work. Theoretical work suggests that when racial groups are spatially segregated from other racial groups, the moderation of ethnic distinctions and the heightening of racial boundaries can be facilitated, leading to the possibility of cross-ethnic coalition formation (Blau 1977; Hechter 1999; Okamoto 2003). When racial and ethnic differences coincide with occupational and residential space, groups are more likely to generate shared interests. In addition, whether segregated by choice or discrimination, the spatial proximity of ethnic groups to one another may encourage social interaction, and this can generate new understandings and trust between groups. In turn, mutual understanding and the development of common interests increase the chances of a successful coalition. Scholars have found that segregation tends to foster intergroup networks and increase group solidarity. For example, Mettam and Williams (1998) discovered that segmented employment patterns that reflect the overrepresentation of Estonians in art, culture, and education created the basis for an Estonian nationalist identity and movement at the end of the Soviet era. In his work on the Basque country in northern Spain, Medrano (1994) found that ethnic occupational segregation heightened group boundaries in this region and led to voting patterns associated with these boundaries.

Like competition, we must specify the boundary level at which spatial segregation is occurring before we can understand how the structuring of groups affects cross-ethnic coalition formation. Spatial segregation along racial lines should heighten group boundaries, foster intergroup networks and relations, and increase solidarity within the group, resulting in cross-ethnic coalitions. Under such conditions, Asian ethnic groups will develop commonalities and shared interests, which should affect collective outcomes. Thus, when Asians as a group are spatially segregated from other racial groups, cross-ethnic coalitions will be more likely. Spatial segregation can also occur along ethnic lines. If Asian ethnic groups are segregated from one another, interethnic interaction should be less frequent, and shared interests across ethnic boundaries are unlikely to form. Ethnic group boundaries will be heightened under these conditions. Thus, when Asian ethnic groups are spatially segregated from one another, cross-ethnic coalitions will be less likely.

Data on Cross-Ethnic Organizational Coalitions

To test the hypotheses about the factors that influence cross-ethnic organizational coalitions, I use a data set of 393 collective action events involving Asian Americans in thirty metropolitan areas from 1970 to 1998.[1] Collective action events are defined as the public action of two or more persons that articulates an ethnic or racial grievance (Olzak 1992), which includes political protests and solidarity events that commemorate triumph over past discrimination. The event data come from newspaper articles published in the *Los Angeles Times, New York Times,* and *Chicago Tribune* during the entire period of interest. I used the generic descriptor strategy and searched under any relevant keyword in annual indexes from the three national newspapers to find candidate events. The events in the data set do not represent a complete enumeration of all collective action events but rather a sample of publicly visible events with ethnic and panethnic claims (see Okamoto 2003 for more on data collection).

The data on organizational alliances also come from newspaper reports from national newspapers. It would be ideal to use nonnewspaper sources such as formal newsletters or convention proceedings to gather information about the ethnic organizations that sponsor, organize, and support collective action events. Unfortunately, no such systematic data source exists. Although newspaper articles are not without bias in terms of which information is deemed important to print, most of the articles (71 percent) provided information on the organizations that sponsored, organized, or participated in the events.

A cross-ethnic coalition is a coordination of efforts between two or more organizations that serve different ethnic populations in the Asian American community.[2] Such a coalition will often emerge to pursue change regarding a particular issue (Chang 1995). A cross-ethnic coalition can also form when an organization serving a specific ethnic group coordinates its efforts of support, organization, and sponsorship with a panethnic organization. This signifies that the ethnic-specific organization is broadening its interests and supporting the larger Asian American community instead of only focusing on ethnic efforts. Ethnic organizations may view the strengthening of the pan-Asian community as directly related to their goals and interests. In contrast to a panethnic organization, there is no merging of identities in a cross-ethnic coalition. Ethnic organizations maintain their distinct ethnic identities, but they engage in a coalition to support another ethnic group's issues or to collaborate for a larger project that serves all Asian Americans.

Of the 393 events involving Asian Americans, about 70 percent were coded as ethnic—that is, where one ethnic group participated in an event and where an ethnic claim was presented. Many ethnic groups participated in the collective action events in the sample, but Chinese (34.4 percent), Japanese (15.4 percent), and Koreans (13.3 percent) were represented at higher levels than other groups, including Filipinos (4.2 percent) and Vietnamese (4.5 percent). A large percentage of the events (45.3 percent) were characterized as pro-rights, where ethnic group members publicly took up an issue or set of issues that was not in response to particular events. About one-fourth of the collective action events were grievances tied to previous events, where ethnic group members protested or brought claims against institutions or individuals for improper or discriminatory behavior. In terms of event form, cultural celebrations (31.4 percent) and demonstrations (13.9 percent) were the most dominant strategies used by Asian Americans to make their claims heard. Other strategies included marches, letter-writing campaigns, conferences, petitions, commemorations, and ceremonies. Finally, the total sample of events was evenly distributed in terms of event type (i.e., protest or solidarity).

Among the 279 events where organizational sponsors or organizers were reported, cross-ethnic coalitions were present at 36 (12.9 percent). Clearly, cross-ethnic coalitions do not occur with great frequency, but it is still of interest to understand the conditions that encourage different ethnic groups to take on another's claims or to collaborate for a larger panethnic project at a collective action event. Of the events where cross-ethnic organizational coalitions occurred, most were coded as pro-rights or antidiscrimination, and more than half were coded as panethnic. Consistent with the larger sample, East Asian groups were overrepresented, and half of the events were protests. In terms of the organizational coalitions themselves, most were characterized by an ethnic-specific organization coordinating its efforts to support and spon-sor an event with a panethnic organization. In addition, ethnic-specific orga-nizations serving Chinese, Japanese, and Korean Americans were the most predominant. However, Filipino, Indian, and Vietnamese ethnic-specific orga-nizations did participate in some cross-ethnic coalitions.

Measurement of Variables

Dependent Variable

The dependent variable is the duration between events with cross-ethnic organizational coalitions, or the rate of cross-ethnic organizational coalitions within thirty metropolitan areas with the largest Asian American populations. All collective action events involving Asian Americans are included in the sam-ple, but only those where different ethnic organizations either came together to organize or support an event or where an organization serving a specific ethnic group coordinated its efforts of support, organization, and sponsor-ship with a panethnic organization were coded as 1.

Independent Variables

The independent variables are measured at the metropolitan area level unless otherwise stated (Table 7.1). These variables represent social conditions that should affect cross-ethnic coalition formation among Asian Americans.

Threats

Threats to the group can lead to the formation of cross-ethnic coalitions, espe-cially because threats against Asians contribute to racialization, the process through which ethnic group members are viewed and treated as racial cate-gories instead of as distinctive groups that vary according to generation, eth-nicity, immigration history, culture, language, and religion.

Given that anti-Asian violence is one of the main consolidating forces for the Asian American community (Espiritu 1992), I use attacks against Asians as a measure of threat. Specifically, this variable captures the number of prior racially motivated attacks against Asian Americans in a given year across the nation. The data used to create this variable were taken from the *New York Times, Los Angeles Times,* and *Chicago Tribune.* I included all events that were reported as a racially motivated attack of an Asian person by a non-Asian person. This variable provides a leading indicator of the level of threat that Asians experience due to actual attacks.

I include a variable measuring Republican advantage at the state level. Such a political context is generally associated with the restriction instead of the expansion of racial and ethnic minority group rights. Republican advantage

Table 7.1. Means and Standard Deviations for Independent Variables

Independent Variable	Mean (Standard Deviation)
Resource and Competition Variables	
Economic Conditions	
Non-Asian in-migration rate	0.098 (0.080)
Percentage unemployed	0.066 (0.023)
Poverty rate	11.012 (2.76)
Resources	
Federal funding	5,265.170 (1,537.72)
Number of ethnic-specific organizations	20.560 (18.1)
Unemployment ratio	
Asian–white	0.948 (0.339)
Chinese–other Asian	1.197 (0.208)
Filipino–other Asian	1.045 (0.216)
Japanese–other Asian	0.597 (0.169)
Korean–other Asian	1.277 (0.265)
Threat and Segregation Variables	
External threats	
Number of attacks against Asians	1.262 (1.250)
Republican advantage	0.134 (0.342)
Occupational segregation	
Asian	0.556 (0.449)
Chinese	1.633 (0.400)
Filipino	1.669 (0.396)
Japanese	1.463 (0.351)
Korean	1.626 (0.354)
Residential segregation	
Asian	0.463 (0.050)
Chinese	0.575 (0.099)
Filipino	0.579 (0.097)
Japanese	0.608 (0.118)
Korean	0.582 (0.101)
Control Variables	
Population size (ln)	15.686 (0.562)
Percentage Asian	0.086 (0.092)
Heterogeneity index	0.802 (0.053)
Number of prior cross-ethnic coalitions	0.178 (0.661)
Panethnic event	0.150 (0.357)

Note: Descriptive statistics are unweighted; N = 319 for ethnic residential segregation variables; for all other independent variables, N = 393.

can constitute a threat to racial and ethnic minorities, leading groups to form coalitions in defense of their rights. If more Republicans than Democrats were represented in Congress for a particular state in the previous year, this variable was coded 1. Data from *Statistical Abstracts of the United States* were used to create this variable.

Resources

Some scholars argue that available resources in the larger environment hinder coalition formation. Under such conditions, groups do not need to seek out partners with which to work collectively to reach a common goal.

The availability of ethnic organizations in the local area is considered a vital resource for coalition building. Without these organizations, cross-ethnic alliances would not be possible. To capture the availability of ethnic organizations, I include a variable measuring the number of Asian ethnic organizations located in each metropolitan area in each year. This variable was constructed using a nonnewspaper source, the *Encyclopedia of Associations, National Organizations* (Gale Research 1970–98), a comprehensive listing of nonprofit membership organizations. Because this data source focuses on national organizations, it does not capture smaller, local organizations. In other words, this variable is biased in a downward fashion, potentially underestimating the density of ethnic organizations in geographic areas. However, given that large, established national organizations tend to organize, sponsor, and participate in collective action events reported by national newspapers, this measure is appropriate.

To capture additional resources in the environment available to organizations, I created a variable measuring the annual amount of federal grants to state and local governments. These funding figures are taken from the *Budget of the U.S. Government: Historical Tables,* presented in billions of dollars and measured at the national level. Because a fraction of these funds are funneled from state and local governments to nonprofit community-based organizations, I include this variable to measure the level of funding resources available per year.

Competition

The competition perspective suggests that economic shifts, such as a weakening economy, and demographic changes, such as influxes of racially and ethnically distinct others, will heighten group boundaries and intensify competition. In addition, when groups are objectively making gains relative to others, this should also activate group boundaries. Intergroup competition will then lead to collective action on the part of ethnic and racial groups in order to maintain their positions in the social and economic hierarchy and exclude others from access to resources. All of the competition variables were created from U.S. Census 5-Percent Public Use Microdata Sample (PUMS) and measured at the metropolitan level. Because PUMS data are only available in ten-year intervals, I used linear interpolation to fill in the values in between census years.

To measure competition between Asians and other racial groups, I created a variable capturing the influx of racially distinct others in a metropolitan area. These data were gleaned from a set of questions from the PUMS regarding a respondent's prior residence. If a respondent resided outside of the United States or in a different state or metropolitan area five years ago, the in-migration variable was coded 1. I then aggregated the number of non-Asian in-migrants and divided by the total metropolitan area population. According to competition theory, the entrance of racially distinct others in a metropolitan area should heighten racial boundaries and facilitate the formation of cross-ethnic coalitions.

To measure competition between Asian ethnic groups, I created a variable measuring the influx of ethnically distinct others within the Asian category. I constructed an in-migration variable for each Asian ethnic group. For example, the non-Chinese in-migration rate measures the percentage of Filipino, Japanese, Korean, South Asian, and Vietnamese in-migrants entering the metropolitan area. According to the theory, the entrance of ethnically distinct groups into the geographic area should heighten ethnic boundaries and contribute to a decline in cross-ethnic coalitions.

To measure the extent to which one group is making gains relative to another, I constructed unemployment ratios comparing Asians to whites and nonwhites, and specific Asian ethnic groups to all Asians. If Asians have a lower unemployment rate than whites, then the employment ratio would be as follows: $A_u / W_u = 5/10$, or 0.5. When the Asian–white unemployment ratio increases, this reflects a decrease in percentage white unemployed or an increase in percentage Asian unemployed. Either way, the relative degree of disparity between two groups has declined, and according to competition theory, Asians should feel threatened by the gains made by whites and interracial competition should erupt. Likewise, when relative gains are made by other Asian groups, specific Asian groups will compete for resources, diminishing the ability of groups to form an organizational coalition.

I include the overall unemployment rate and poverty rate to measure economic downturns in metropolitan areas. These variables also measure the extent to which a metropolitan area may be resource poor.

Segregation

Research suggests that it is the separation, not integration, of racial groups within occupational spaces that leads to higher levels of collective action. I constructed two variables to measure the level of spatial segregation between groups.[3]

The occupational segregation index (Charles 1992; Charles and Grusky 1995) measures the degree to which a racial group experiences occupational specialization. For the purposes of this research, when the value of the index increases, Asians experience high levels of occupational segregation relative to other racial groups. I also calculated an ethnic occupational segregation index that measures the level of occupational specialization each Asian ethnic group experiences relative to all other Asian ethnic groups. The main advantage of this index is that is it not influenced by the ethnic and racial composition of the labor force or the size of different occupational categories. These variables were constructed from PUMS data.

To measure residential segregation, I used the index of dissimilarity, D^*, which measures the level of residential segregation between Asians and whites (Massey and Denton 1987, 1992; Taeuber and Taeuber 1976). The index is a measure of evenness, defined as the proportion of minority group members that would have to move in order to achieve an even racial or ethnic distribution in a metropolitan area. To measure the levels of residential segregation between Asian ethnic groups, I calculated all pairwise combinations of Asian ethnic groups and then calculated the mean residential segregation index for each ethnic group.[4] U.S. Census Summary Tape Files were used to calculate segregation indexes aggregated from the census tract level. STF data are only available every ten years (i.e., 1980, 1990), so I used linear interpolation to fill in the values in between census years.

Control Variables

To measure the level of ethnic diversity within the Asian population in each metropolitan area, I constructed a heterogeneity index (Lieberson 1969). A score of 0 indicates that two randomly paired individuals in the geographic location share the same ethnic background. A score approaching 1 indicates that two randomly paired Asian individuals in the geographic area have different ethnic backgrounds, and therefore ethnic diversity is high. This measure is important because if several Asian ethnic groups reside in one area, where one group alone cannot mobilize successfully, a cross-ethnic organizational coalition may be more likely to occur. In addition, when one Asian ethnic group is dominant in size and there is less of a need to form a coalition across ethnic boundaries, cross-ethnic alliances should be less common.

I created a variable measuring the number of past cross-ethnic organizational alliances within each metropolitan area. Because the data set of collective action events has detailed information about the specific date of events, I am able to create a variable that varies over time within each metro area. This variable also controls for possible interdependence. Because repeating events are not independent of one another, it is necessary to include a control for this in the analysis.

Given that the sizes of the different metropolitan areas and the Asian population are likely to vary and could account for the rate of cross-ethnic coalitions, I include variables measuring total population size and the proportion of Asians in the metropolitan area.

I defined a collective action event as panethnic when it was clear that the public claim posed at the event was pan-Asian, where two or more Asian ethnic groups participated in a collective effort to represent an Asian American cause or celebration. These events were coded as 1. Conversely, ethnic collective action events were characterized by the representation of only one ethnic group and claims made by ethnic group members on the group's behalf. These events were coded as 0.

Analytic Strategy

To evaluate the effects of threats, resources, competition, and segregation, I use an event history model to predict the rate of cross-ethnic organizational coalitions.[5] This dynamic approach provides an understanding of the changing conditions that affect cross-ethnic coalitions, and it also evaluates how the sequence of events influences coalition formation. I use a fixed-effects partial likelihood model, a variant of the proportional hazards model, because it allows for repeatable events within geographic areas and time-varying covariates (Allison 1995). This model is represented in the following form:

$$\log h_{ij}(t) = \alpha_i(t) + \beta x_{ij}(t),$$

where $\alpha_i(t)$ is an unspecified function of time and $\beta x_{ij}(t)$ is an explanatory variable. The hazard rate, $h_{ij}(t)$, is defined as the instantaneous risk of having the event occur for the jth event for metropolitan area i at time t. If a coefficient is positively related to the dependent variable, then the independent variable of interest is interpreted as increasing the likelihood that an event will occur at any given moment; a negative coefficient suggests that this variable decreases the likelihood that the event will occur.

Results

Intergroup Dynamics

The results in Table 7.2 show the effects of threats, resources, and interracial competition and segregation variables on the rate of cross-ethnic organizational coalitions from 1970 to 1998. As suggested by competition theory, interracial competition may be the driving force behind coalition formation across ethnic lines. Two of the four estimates measuring competition are significant. Specifically, the effect of the in-migration rate is positive, indicating that an influx of racially distinct others increases the rate of cross-ethnic alliances on the part of Asians. Consistent with competition predictions, the racial boundary for Asians is heightened by the demographic shift, and cross-ethnic coalitions are formed to maintain or increase collective resources. The results in Table 7.2 also show that the estimate for the unemployment ratio

Table 7.2. Event History Analysis Estimating the Effect of Threat, Competition, and Segregation on the Rate of Cross-Ethnic Organizational Coalitions among Asian Americans, 1970–1998

Independent Variable	Estimate (Standard Error)	
Competition and resource variables		
Non-Asian in-migration rate	4.112*	(2.12)
Asian–white unemployment ratio	1.079	(10.6)
Poverty rate	0.853	(1.06)
Unemployment rate	−2.953†	(2.04)
Federal funding	0.001†	(0.000)
Density of ethnic organizations	0.023	(0.10)
Threat and segregation variables		
Attacks against Asians	0.418*	(0.25)
Republican advantage	−0.797	(1.62)
Asian occupational segregation	1.579	(1.83)
Asian residential segregation	1.123**	(0.52)
Control variables		
Ethnic heterogeneity	3.978	(15.2)
Percentage Asian	2.558**	(0.89)
Total population (logged)	4.127**	(1.64)
Panethnic event (=1)	2.371**	(0.49)
Prior cross-ethnic coalition	−3.395	(5.97)

Note: N = 393.
† p < .10;
* p < .05;
** p < .01 (one-tailed tests).

was not significant. When whites are making gains relative to Asians, this does not influence the formation of cross-ethnic coalitions.[6] In addition, it was hypothesized that worsening economic conditions should heighten racial competition and increase coalition building across ethnic lines. However, the estimate for poverty rate is nonsignificant and the estimate for the unemployment rate is negative and marginally significant, suggesting that poor economic conditions actually dampen the rate of cross-ethnic organizational activity.

In terms of resources, I find that the level of federal grants to state and local governments has a positive effect on cross-ethnic coalition formation. Even though the effect is not highly significant or large in magnitude, it suggests that when federal funds are plentiful, the rate of cross-ethnic activity is raised. This supports the idea that when resources are scarce, groups are likely to compete with one another and are much less likely to form coalitions. This result also helps us to rule out the hypothesis that groups will seek out coalition partners when resources are scarce. Surprisingly, the density of ethnic organizations, which serves as an important resource for organizing across ethnic lines, has no effect on coalition formation.

Turning to the threat and segregation variables, two of the estimates are significant and positive. Net of other variables, an increase in attacks against Asians raises the rate of panethnic organizing. In fact, an additional attack in a given year leads to a 50 percent increase in cross-ethnic organizational coalitions at collective action events involving Asian Americans. Interestingly, Republican advantage has no effect on the way in which Asians organize, suggesting that political shifts do not materialize into immediate threats that Asians must counter by forming coalitions across ethnic lines. Among the segregation variables, the estimate for residential segregation is positive and highly significant. When Asians as a group are residentially segregated from whites, this increases intragroup interaction and shared interests, leading ethnic groups to take on the issues and claims of others within the same racial category. A one-unit increase in residential segregation doubles the rate that a cross-ethnic organizational coalition will form.

Finally, it is worth noting that some of the control variables in Table 7.2 are significant. As expected, the size of the Asian population and the metropolitan area increase the frequency of cross-ethnic organizational coalitions. In addition, if a collective action event is panethnic, a higher rate of panethnic coalitions results. However, the number of prior cross-ethnic coalitions is not significant, nor is ethnic heterogeneity, suggesting that past panethnic activity and high levels of Asian ethnic diversity do not increase the rate of coalition formation across ethnic lines.

Intragroup Dynamics

The results in Table 7.3 test the hypotheses about the effects of interethnic competition and segregation on the rate of cross-ethnic organizational coalition formation. These analyses provide further understanding of the conditions that facilitate and discourage interethnic coalitions by including ethnic competition and segregation variables. Net of all other independent variables, these models include measures of occupational specialization, residential segregation, in-migration rates, and unemployment ratios specific to each Asian ethnic group (Chinese, Filipino, Japanese, Korean, Vietnamese, and Indian). The in-migration rate measures the influx of Asian ethnic outgroup members to metropolitan areas and tests whether this demographic shift has any effect on cross-ethnic coalition formation. For example, in model 1, the in-migration rate measures the percentage of non-Chinese Asians entering a metropolitan area. According to competition theory, the entrance of ethnically distinct others should heighten ethnic group boundaries and lead to interethnic competition for scarce resources. The estimate for this variable is not significant in model 1. However, the estimates for the in-migration variable are significant and negative for two of the six ethnic groups. In support of predictions, these results indicate that for Japanese and Vietnamese, the influx of ethnically distinct others leads to interethnic competition and depresses the rate of cross-ethnic organizational activity.

The results in Table 7.3 also show that another measure of competition— the extent to which relative resources are becoming equal between groups— does not have consistent effects across the ethnic groups. According to the theory, each ethnic group should feel threatened by the gains made by other Asians, resulting in interethnic competition and a decline in panethnic organizing. I find that this relationship only holds for Indians (model 5). For Chinese, when relative resources of other Asian ethnic groups are less unequal, this actually increases the rate of cross-ethnic coalitions, which is counter to predictions. For Filipinos, Japanese, Koreans, and Vietnamese, there is no significant effect of the unemployment ratio on cross-ethnic coalition participation in collective action events.

The effects of ethnic residential segregation are significant and negative across five of the six models. In particular, for Filipinos, Japanese, Koreans, Vietnamese, and Indians, an increase in residential segregation from other Asian ethnic groups discourages cross-ethnic organizational coalitions. This negative effect was predicted by the theory of panethnicity: as ethnic groups are spatially segregated from one another, ethnic boundaries are heightened, which discourages the development of interethnic networks, leading to a

Table 7.3. Event History Analysis Estimating the Effects of Ethnic-Specific Variables on the Rate of Cross-Ethnic Organizational Coalitions among Asian Americans, 1980–1998

Ethnic-Specific Independent Variables[a]	Model 1, Chinese	Model 2, Filipino	Model 3, Japanese	Model 4, Korean	Model 5, Asian Indian	Model 6, Vietnamese
In-migration rate	-2.067 (2.78)	2.056 (2.32)	-3.406† (2.52)	-1.441 (2.30)	-3.010 (4.40)	-6.607* (3.49)
Unemployment ratio	4.287† (3.05)	0.732 (2.21)	1.012 (1.30)	1.112 (1.41)	-0.860† (0.52)	-1.783 (1.52)
Residential segregation	-3.177 (3.64)	-6.573* (3.76)	-3.474* (2.01)	-5.617* (2.78)	-6.274** (2.73)	-4.834* (2.56)
Occupational segregation	2.874 (3.01)	0.823 (2.25)	-1.640 (0.639)	-2.402 (4.13)	-1.903 (6.39)	-2.781** (1.06)
-2 log likelihood	133.015	136.239	135.697	137.449	130.128	125.668

Note: N = 319 for Chinese, Filipino, Japanese, and Korean; N = 314 for Asian Indian and Vietnamese. Maximum likelihood estimates are shown here with standard errors in parentheses. Variables measuring Asian competition and segregation, resources, and threats in addition to control variables are included in the models above but not shown here.

[a] In model 1, the in-migration variable measures the percentage of non-Chinese Asian immigrants entering the metropolitan area in a given year. The unemployment ratio measures percent Chinese unemployed relative to all other Asian ethnic groups, and the segregation variables capture the extent to which Chinese are spatially segregated from all other Asian ethnic groups in a metropolitan area.

† p < .10;

* p < .05;

** p < .01 (one-tailed tests).

decline in the rate of panethnic organizing. For ethnic occupational segregation, only one estimate was significant. For the Vietnamese, being occupationally segregated from all other Asians contributes to a decline in cross-ethnic organizational coalitions.[7]

Discussion and Conclusion

Here I focus on the dynamics of cross-ethnic organizational coalitions, an understudied phenomena, and contribute to the social movements literature by examining how structural conditions heighten ethnic and racial boundaries and affect the formation of coalitions. Cross-ethnic coalitions are important because they often provide the strength in numbers needed to make racial minority claims visible in the public arena. These organizational coalitions also support particular social movements that are usually local, as demonstrated here, but they can also work toward building broader national or transnational movements surrounding issues such as the environment, social justice, or labor rights.

The results from the analyses indicated that threats, resources, segregation, and competition all play a role in facilitating cross-ethnic coalitions, but to varying degrees. First, segregation processes within and between groups were important in explaining the conditions that influence coalition formation. Specifically, the residential segregation of Asians from whites heightened group boundaries and increased the rate of cross-ethnic activity. At the ethnic level, when ethnic groups were spatially segregated from one another, the rate of coalition formation declined because ethnic groups were not proximate to one another and did not have the opportunity to generate new understandings and trust, or to recognize common interests.

The influx of distinct groups also played a role in understanding cross-ethnic coalitions. An increasing number of non-Asians entering local areas resulted in heightened panethnic group boundaries and raised the rate of cross-ethnic organizing, suggesting that a competition mechanism was at work. Similarly, an increase in ethnic outgroup members heightened ethnic boundaries for the Japanese and Vietnamese, and depressed the rate of cross-ethnic activity. Even though the Japanese are a well-established group in the United States, their numbers have been in significant decline because of the lack of immigration from Japan and the high numbers of the elderly in the community, and this may contribute to this group's response to the influx of others. The Japanese may be trying to maintain their cultural traditions and institutions, and heighten their group boundaries when others enter the local area. The situation of the Vietnamese is quite different: they are a relatively new group to settle in the United States as refugees and immigrants. Given their newness and their relative status within the Asian ethnic hierarchy, the Vietnamese may need to focus on their own group and again, heighten their group boundaries in the face of an influx of ethnic others.

It was predicted that racial boundaries would be heightened when economic conditions worsened, leading Asian Americans to compete with other racial groups by forming cross-ethnic alliances to maintain their economic and social position in the larger hierarchy. Instead, the results point to the idea (though the effect is weak) that when economic conditions are declining in local areas, cross-ethnic alliances will be less likely. Similarly, when federal funding, an important resource for organizations, is less readily available, ethnic groups are less likely to work together to accomplish movement goals. Taken together, these results support a resource mobilization perspective: when resources are scarce, ethnic groups tend to focus on their own issues and are unable to take on the issues of others, even those of panethnic organizations that may be able to advance the goals and objectives of ethnic-specific organizations.

Overall, the results presented here are consistent with past research on panethnic activity and coalition formation (see Diaz-Veizades and Chang 1996; Espiritu 1992; Okamoto 2003, 2006). One might have expected that competition for economic gain or political power would have been solely responsible for short-term organizational alliances. Nevertheless, threats and segregation had more consistent effects at both the racial and ethnic boundary levels, and are the main social forces that lead groups to generate shared interests.

The processes I elaborate on in this chapter help us understand contemporary ethnic and racial politics in the United States, but they also provide insights regarding broader coalitions and the development of transnational networks. For example, economic crises at national and international levels and the lack of available resources from public sources are likely to play important roles in discouraging diverse groups from building short-term organizational coalitions within and between countries. Future research should examine coalition formation among local, national, and international organizations that may be geographically dispersed but share membership in transnational movements. It will be important to identify and understand the broader social forces that generate the key processes discussed in this chapter for building coalitions, such as the development of overlapping networks, building mutual understanding and trust, and framing interests as common within the United States and across the world system.

Notes

1. The thirty metropolitan areas include Anaheim, California; Atlanta, Georgia; Baltimore, Maryland; Bergen-Passaic, New Jersey; Boston, Massachusetts; Chicago, Illinois; Dallas–Fort Worth, Texas; Denver, Colorado; Detroit, Michigan; Fresno, California; Honolulu, Hawaii; Houston, Texas; Los Angeles–Long Beach, California; Middlesex–Somerset–Hunterdon, New Jersey; Minneapolis, Minnesota; Nassau–Suffolk, New York; New York, New York; Newark, New Jersey; Philadelphia, Pennsylvania–New Jersey; Phoenix, Arizona; Portland, Oregon–Washington; Riverside–San Bernardino, California; Sacramento, California; San Diego, California; San Francisco–Oakland, California; San Jose, California; Seattle–Everett, Washington; Stockton, California; Vallejo–Fairfield–Napa, California; Washington, D.C., Maryland–Virginia.

2. It is important to note how a panethnic organization is different from a cross-ethnic organizational coalition. The former is a formal organization that serves and advocates for different ethnic groups in the Asian American community. Such an organization was formed for this distinct purpose and often provides a mission statement expressing its broad and diverse membership or constituency.

3. See Okamoto (2003) for equations used to calculate the segregation and ethnic heterogeneity indexes.

4. I also estimated models with each of the combinations of residential segregation between different Asian ethnic groups separately and found that the results are similar to models run with the means for each group.

5. To ensure that the overall results were robust, I estimated a discrete-time event history model using independent variables for each census year (1970, 1980, 1990) for each metropolitan area. I generally find the same results as the analysis using interpolated data.

6. I included the Asian/nonwhite unemployment ratio in the model, but it was not significant and it did not change the effects of the rest of the coefficients, so I do not include it in the final model.

7. The analysis in Table 7.3 does not capture the entire period of interest because data on specific Asian ethnic groups at the census tract level were not available in 1970. The models in Table 7.3 analyze data from 1980 to 1998. I estimated the same models without the ethnic residential segregation indexes and produce the same general results. Thirty-three of the thirty-six cross-ethnic alliances in the sample occurred between 1980 and 1998.

Works Cited

Allison, Paul D. 1995. *Survival Analysis Using the SAS System: A Practical Guide.* Cary, N.C.: SAS Institute.

Banton, Michael. 1983. *Racial and Ethnic Competition.* Cambridge: Cambridge University Press.

Barth, Fredrik. 1969. Introduction to *Ethnic Groups and Boundaries,* edited by F. Barth, 9–38. Boston: Little, Brown.

Blau, Peter M. 1977. "A Macrosociological Theory of Social Structure." *American Journal of Sociology* 83: 26–54.

Browning, Rufus P., Dale Rogers Marshall, and David H. Tabb. 1984. *Protest Is Not Enough: The Struggle of Blacks and Hispanics for Equality in Urban Politics.* Berkeley: University of California Press.

Budget of the United States Government: Historical Tables Fiscal Year 2005. "Table 12.2—Total Outlays for Grants to State and Local Governments, by Function and Fund Group: 1940–2009." http://www.gpoaccess.gov/usbudget/fy05/hist.html.

Chan, Sucheng. 1991. *Asian Americans: An Interpretive History.* Boston: Twayne.

Chang, Edward T. 1995. "The Impact of Civil Unrest on Community-Based Organizational Coalitions." In *Multiethnic Coalition Building in Los Angeles,* edited by Eui-Young Yu and Edward T. Chang, 117–33. Claremont, Calif.: Regina Books.

Charles, Maria. 1992. "Cross-National Variation in Occupational Sex Segregation." *American Sociological Review* 57: 483–503.

Charles, Maria, and David Grusky. 1995. "Modeling Cross-National Variability in Occupational Sex Segregation." *American Journal of Sociology* 100: 931–71.

Chung, Angie Y. 2001. "The Powers That Bind: A Case Study of the Collective Bases of Coalition Building in Post–Civil Unrest Los Angeles." *Urban Affairs Review* 37: 205–26.

Daniels, Roger. 1988. *Asian America: Chinese and Japanese in the United States since 1850.* Seattle: University of Washington Press.

Diaz-Veizades, Jeannette, and Edward T. Chang. 1996. "Building Cross-Cultural Coalitions: A Case-Study of the Black–Korean Alliance and the Latino–Black Roundtable." *Ethnic and Racial Studies* 19: 680–700.

Eisinger, Peter K. 1976. *Patterns of Interracial Politics.* New York: Academic Press.

Espiritu, Yen Le. 1992. *Asian American Panethnicity: Bridging Institutions and Identities.* Philadelphia: Temple University Press.

———. 2004. "Asian American Panethnicity: Contemporary National and Transnational Possibilities." In *Not Just Black and White: Historical and Contemporary Perspectives on Immigration, Race, and Ethnicity in the United States,* edited by Nancy Foner and George M. Frederickson, 217–36. New York: Russell Sage Foundation.

Gale Research. 1970–1998. *Encyclopedia of Associations.* Vol. 1, *National Organizations, 1970–1998.* Ed. 5–33. Detroit, Mich.: Gale Research Group.

Gerhards, Jurgen, and Dieter Rucht. 1992. "Mesomobilization: Organizing and

Framing in Two Protest Campaigns in West Germany." *American Journal of Sociology* 98: 555–95.

Hannan, Michael T. 1979. "The Dynamics of Ethnic Boundaries in Modern States." In *National Development and the World System,* edited by John W. Meyer and Michael T. Hannan, 253–75. Chicago: University of Chicago Press.

Hathaway, Will, and David S. Meyer. 1993. "Competition and Cooperation in Social Movement Coalitions: Lobbying for Peace in the 1980s." *Berkeley Journal of Sociology* 38: 156–83.

Hechter, Michael. 1999 [1975]. *Internal Colonialism: The Celtic Fringe in British National Development, 1536–1966.* New Brunswick, N.J.: Transaction Publishers.

Kibria, Nazli. 1997. "The Construction of 'Asian American': Reflections on Intermarriage and Ethnic Identity among Second Generation Chinese and Korean Americans." *Ethnic and Racial Studies* 20: 522–44.

Kriesberg, Louis. 1998. *Constructive Conflicts: From Escalation to Resolution.* Lanham, Md.: Rowman & Littlefield.

Kwong, Peter. 1996. *The New Chinatown.* New York: Hill and Wang.

Lichterman, Paul. 1995. "Piecing Together Multicultural Community: Cultural Differences in Community Building among Grassroots Environmentalists." *Social Problems* 42: 513–34.

Lieberson, Stanley. 1969. "Measuring Population Diversity." *American Sociological Review* 34: 850–62.

Lien, Pei-te. 2001. *The Making of Asian American through Political Participation.* Philadelphia: Temple University Press.

Massey, Douglas S., and Nancy A. Denton. 1987. "Trends in the Residential Segregation of Blacks, Hispanics, and Asians." *American Sociological Review* 52: 802–25.

———. 1992. "Residential Segregation of Asian-Origin Groups in U.S. Metropolitan Areas." *Sociology and Social Research* 76: 170–77.

McCammon, Holly J., and Karen E. Campbell. 2002. "Allies on the Road to Victory: Coalition Formation between the Suffragists and the Woman's Christian Temperance Union." *Mobilization* 7: 231–51.

Medrano, Diez. 1994. "The Effects of Ethnic Segregation and Ethnic Competition on Political Mobilization in the Basque Country, 1988." *American Sociological Review* 59: 873–89.

Meier, Kenneth J., and Joseph Stewart Jr. 1991. "Cooperation and Conflict in Multiracial School Districts." *Journal of Politics* 53: 1123–33.

Mettam, Colin W., and Stephen Wyn Williams. 1998. "Internal Colonialism and Cultural Divisions of Labour in the Soviet Republic of Estonia." *Nations and Nationalism* 4: 363–88.

Meyer, David, and Suzanne Staggenborg. 1996. "Movements, Countermovements, and the Structure of Political Opportunity." *American Journal of Sociology* 101: 1628–60.

Nielsen, François. 1980. "The Flemish Movement in Belgium after World War II: A Dynamic Analysis." *American Sociological Review* 45: 76–94.

Okamoto, Dina G. 2003. "Toward a Theory of Panethnicity: Explaining Collective Action among Asian Americans." *American Sociological Review* 68: 811–42.

———. 2006. "Institutional Panethnicity: Boundary Formation in Asian American Organizing." *Social Forces* 85: 1–27.

Olzak, Susan. 1992. *The Dynamics of Ethnic Competition and Conflict.* Stanford, Calif.: Stanford University Press.

Olzak, Susan, Suzanne Shanahan, and Elizabeth H. McEneaney. 1994. "School Desegregation, Interracial Exposure, and Antibusing Activity in Contemporary Urban America." *American Journal of Sociology* 100: 196–241.

———. 1996. "Poverty, Segregation, and Race Riots: 1960 to 1993." *American Sociological Review* 61: 590–613.

Omatsu, Glenn. 1994. "The 'Four Prisons' and the Movements of Liberation: Asian American Activism from the 1960s to the 1990s." In *The State of Asian America: Activism and Resistance in the 1990s,* edited by K. Aguilar-San Juan, 19–69. Boston: South End Press.

Omi, Michael, and Howard Winant. 1994. *Racial Formation in the United States: From the 1960s to 1990s.* New York: Routledge.

Padilla, Felix M. 1985. *Latino Ethnic Consciousness: The Case of Mexican Americans and Puerto Ricans in Chicago.* Notre Dame, Ind.: University of Notre Dame Press.

Park, Robert. 1950. *Race and Culture.* Glencoe, Ill.: Free Press.

Regalado, Jamie A. 1995. "Creating Multicultural Harmony? A Critical Perspective on Coalition-Building Efforts in Los Angeles." In *Multiethnic Coalition Building in Los Angeles,* edited by Eui-Young Yu and Edward T. Chang, 35–53. Claremont, Calif.: Regina Books.

Saito, Leland T. 1998. *Race and Politics: Asian Americans, Latinos, and Whites in a Los Angeles Suburb.* Chicago: University of Illinois Press.

Sonenshein, Raphael J. 1989. "The Dynamics of Bi-Racial Coalitions: Crossover Politics in Los Angeles." *Western Political Quarterly* 42: 333–53.

———. 1993. *Politics in Black and White: Race and Power in Los Angeles.* Princeton, N.J.: Princeton University Press.

Staggenborg, Suzanne. 1986. "Coalition Work in the Pro-Choice Movement: Organizational and Environmental Opportunities and Obstacles." *Social Problems* 33: 374–90.

Taeuber, Karl E., and Alma F. Taeuber. 1976. "A Practitioner's Perspective on the Index of Dissimilarity." *American Sociological Review* 41: 884–89.

Toy, Vivian S. 1996. "Councilwoman Apologizes for Comments about Asians." *New York Times,* May 3.

U.S. Bureau of the Census. 1970–98. *Statistical Abstracts of the United States.* Washington, D.C.: U.S. Bureau of the Census.

Van Dyke, Nella. 2003. "Crossing Movement Boundaries: Factors That Facilitate Coalition Protest by American College Students, 1930–1990." *Social Problems* 50: 226–50.

Vo, Linda Trinh. 2001. "The Politics of Social Services for a 'Model Minority.'" In *Asian and Latino Immigrants in a Restructuring Economy: The Metamorphosis of Southern California,* edited by Marta Lopez-Garza and David R. Diaz, 241–72. Stanford, Calif.: Stanford University Press.

———. 2004. *Mobilizing an Asian American Community.* Philadelphia: Temple University Press.

Waters, Mary. 1999. *Black Identities: West Indian Immigrant Dreams and American Realities.* Cambridge, Mass.: Harvard University Press.

Wei, William. 1993. *The Asian American Movement.* Philadelphia: Temple University Press.

Zald, Mayer N., and John D. McCarthy. 1980. "Social Movement Industries: Competition and Cooperation among Movement Organizations." *Research in Social Movements, Conflicts, and Change* 3: 1–20.

8

Social Movement Partyism:
Collective Action and Oppositional Political Parties

Paul Almeida

This chapter examines coalitions between oppositional political parties and social movements. I draw on evidence from recent trends in Latin American politics from Bolivia, Ecuador, El Salvador, Nicaragua, and Uruguay, emphasizing the forces driving oppositional political parties into alliances with social movements and how the alliances adopt extraparliamentary strategies of seeking political influence. In particular, the region's recent democratization and the ongoing economic threats associated with neoliberal policies forge the movement–party relationship. A sustained and potent coalition between a political party and social movements typically emerges when a majority of public opinion opposes economic liberalization policies and membership overlap occurs between oppositional political parties and social movement–type organizations.

With the third wave of democratization engulfing major portions of Latin America and the developing world between the late 1970s and early 2000s (Diamond 1999; Markoff 1996), the political context has been fundamentally altered for excluded social groups and the potential for political challenge from below (Almeida and Johnston 2006). Scholarly observers in the 1980s and 1990s viewed this initial democratization trend and "recomposition of state-popular sector links" (Chalmers, Martin, and Piester 1997, 554) as making political parties more central to political life while street politics and social movement activity would become less salient as political struggles moved into the formal political system. However, in the past fifteen years, with deepening democratization, Latin America exploded in a wave of protest, with political parties playing an increasingly active and unexpectedly contentious role.

In Colombia, the ascendancy of the Polo Democrático Alternativo oppositional political party eroded the dominance of the Conservative and Liberal parties in national and local politics after the 2006 parliamentary elections. The Polo Democrático Alternativo aligned with social movements on the streets against government plans to privatize social security, petroleum, and telecommunications. In Peru, a renovated nationalist party, Unión por el Perú, appeared on the political scene in 2005. It was backed by peasants and labor unions opposing a free trade agreement with the United States. The Unión por el Perú won in the first round of presidential voting (but lost in the second round) and took nearly 40 percent of oppositional seats in the national Congress (*El Comercio* 2006, 1). In Argentina, the small leftist political parties El Partido Obrero, El Partido Comunista Revolucionario, and the Partido Comunista sponsor part of the unemployed workers' movement (Alcañiz and Scheier 2007; Oviedo 2001), while in Costa Rica, legislative representatives of the Partido Acción Ciudadana oppositional political party actively participate in massive street demonstrations against free trade treaties (*Diario co Latino* 2007).

Many other cases of coalitions between social movements and oppositional political parties abound on the continent, such as La Causa Я in Venezuela and the Workers' Party in Brazil in the 1980s and 1990s. This chapter identifies the conditions that bring oppositional political parties and social movements together in a sustained coalition and the benefits that each group brings to such an alliance.

Democratization and Neoliberalism: Opportunities and Threats

Popular mobilization can be driven by opportunities (gaining new advantages), threats (losing existing benefits and resources), or a combination of the two (Tilly 1978; Van Dyke and Soule 2002). Recent theoretical and empirical work also predicts or demonstrates that opportunities and threats facilitate coalition formation between movement groups (Staggenborg 1986). Political and economic threats of unwanted public policies seem to be an especially powerful force pushing oppositional coalitions together (McCammon and Campbell 2002; Van Dyke 2003a), as are more generalized economic crises (Silver 2003). For the purposes of the present study, I define democratization as the central political opportunity shaping the social infrastructure (McCarthy 1987) in Latin America for popular contention and neoliberal policies as the core set of economic threats encouraging mobilization. Democratization and neoliberalism combined, or what Robinson (2006, 97) calls "market democracy," provide the political–economic setting in which social movement–oppositional political party coalitions come into existence.

Opportunities of Democratization

Democratization of entire countries or world regions creates systemwide opportunities for collective actors (Meyer and Minkoff 2004). Democratization efforts are critical to civil society because they generate at least three of the core political opportunities repeatedly found in the political process literature, namely institutional access, relaxation in state repression, and influential allies (McAdam 1996). Since the 1980s, Latin America has undergone its most extensive wave of democratization, replacing brutal military governments, bureaucratic authoritarian regimes, and personal dictatorships with systems of competitive multiparty elections (Mainwaring and Hagopian 2005). Tilly (1978, 167) notes that a competitive electoral system allows for the establishment of all kinds of civic associations. This is because episodes of political liberalization provide institutional access to more civil society organizations (Almeida 2008). Under such conditions, the state tolerates the existence of more groups and gives many of them legal recognition to operate inside its territorial boundaries (Yashar 2005). Hence, with democratization there is a rise in the number and variety of nongovernmental organizations (NGOs) that may be partially appropriated for collective action campaigns.

A relaxation in state repression makes it easier for oppositional groups to forge alliances and participate in joint action. For example, in a study of 281 austerity protest campaigns in Latin America between 1995 and 2001 (under democracy), it was found that over 40 percent of the campaigns involved at least two distinct challengers (Almeida 2007). Most important for the purposes of this study, the democratization process also encourages the emergence of influential allies aligned with popular movements.

Influential allies such as celebrities, lawyers, scientists, foundations, religious institutions, and transnational advocacy networks strengthen movement mobilization (Almeida and Stearns 1998; Bob 2005). Not overlooking the importance of these external groups, among the most crucial elite allies that state-oriented movements form bonds with are actors inside the state (Banaszak 2005; Goldstone 2003). State actors include municipal governments, the courts, governmental agencies, and political parties (Stearns and Almeida 2004). Among this list, the social movement–political party alliance appears to be especially potent in sustaining mass contention (Schwartz 2006), especially in contemporary Latin America. Regional democratization permitted the formation and expansion of a diversity of political parties, given the increasing credibility of the electoral process. The emerging political parties needed to secure a mass base in civil society to attain success at the ballot box. Threats of mounting austerity, neoliberal policy implementation, and global economic integration supplied incipient grievances that solidified the relationship of political parties with social movements.

Threats of Deepening Neoliberalism

Over the past thirty years, neoliberal economic policies have acted as one of the principal threats driving collective action in Latin America and the developing world (Almeida 2007; Walton and Seddon 1994). The origins of neoliberal policy making reside in the third world balance of payments crisis that erupted in the early 1980s, referred to as the debt crisis. Nearly all Latin American governments had taken on enormous foreign loans from northern banks in the 1970s. In the early 1980s, when interest rates began to fluctuate upward and third world export commodity prices plummeted, the governments in the region found themselves steeped in financial trouble. In order to "rescue" the indebted Latin American states, the International Monetary Fund, World Bank, and the Inter-American Development Bank stepped in and renegotiated the loans with individual countries. In exchange for debt relief, Latin American governments restructured their economies along free market lines. The negotiations resulted in formal agreements between international financial institutions and indebted states outlining specific economic reforms governments would undertake to reschedule past loan repayments, receive new lines of credit, and upgrade the country's financial risk rating (Walton and Seddon 1994).

By the mid-1980s, these structural adjustment agreements resulted in severe austerity measures throughout Latin America. The economic policies included cuts in public sector spending, employment, wages, and subsidies to education, health, food, and transportation. The measures also included currency devaluations, new sales taxes, and the selling off of government-run enterprises and factories. These actions led to a wave of antiausterity protests across the region in the 1980s (Walton and Shefner 1994). The popular sectors viewed the cutbacks as a threat to the hard-won economic and social benefits that had expanded in the previous period of state-led development (Eckstein and Wickham-Crowley 2003; Walton and Seddon 1994). However, democratization was just beginning to take off in Latin America (Almeida and Johnston 2006). In most countries, successive rounds of competitive elections had not yet occurred, allowing durable relationships to form between social movements and political parties. Autonomous political parties were just emerging (or reemerging) in the region, and social movements were making the transition from confronting authoritarian rule to the new political terrain of electoral politics.

In the 1990s, the foreign debt crisis remained unresolved; on average, Latin American countries tripled the level of debt owed since the beginning of the crisis in 1980. Governments in the region implemented a second generation of austerity measures and structural adjustment that combined many of the strategies of the first-generation reforms (especially subsidy cuts and public sector shrinkage) with the privatization of public services, utilities, and natural resources. Since the late 1990s, these second-generation reforms appear to have sparked an even larger wave of threat-induced protest across the continent (Almeida 2007; Auyero 2001; Green 2003; López Maya 1999; Shefner, Pasdirtz, and Blad 2006). This protest wave, though, arose in the context of deeper democratization and in many cases in conjunction with oppositional political parties.

Social Movement Partyism

With the rise of neoliberal democratization (the combination of free market reforms and competitive multiparty elections) in Latin America in the 1990s (Eckstein 2006; Robinson 2006), a new dynamic emerged whereby oppositional political parties are behaving as much like social movements as they are institutionalized political actors. I define this behavior as *social movement partyism*. Analogous to what labor scholars refer to as social movement unionism, whereby union militants rely on noninstitutional tactics and mobilize supporters beyond the labor organization's boundaries (Isaac and Christiansen 2002; Seidman 1994), political parties in several Latin American countries are mobilizing akin to a social movement. Oppositional parties increasingly use combative protests, organize outside strictly electoral campaigns, and mobilize groups beyond their own card-carrying party members. Two defining features of social movement partyism include (1) an electoral opposition political party taking up a social movement cause as its own by coalescing with a movement, and (2) the use of social movement–type strategies (e.g., disruptive actions and street demonstrations) to mobilize party members and other groups to achieve social movement goals.

The movement with which the political party allies is often composed of several coalitions of civic organizations and civil society groups. My analytical focus, however, centers on the coalition between the oppositional political party and the social movement campaign opposing a neoliberal policy. Social movement partyism more likely emerges in the multiparty parliamentary systems that predominate in contemporary Latin America.[1] Below, I discuss the mutual interests that drive oppositional political parties into a relationship with social movements.

How the Oppositional Political Party Benefits

Oppositional political parties (as opposed to dominant parties) are the candidates most likely to take on the social movement partyism form, especially over issues related to free market reforms. The party in power is the main booster of the neoliberal reforms and has less interest in launching a social movement–style campaign.[2] Nationalist, populist, and left-leaning oppositional political parties maintain an ideological affinity with civil society groups against neoliberal policies. By taking up the issue of neoliberal reform, an oppositional political party may be able to strengthen its position vis-à-vis the dominant party (Williams 2001), especially under conditions of public opposition to a particular liberalization measure (e.g., privatization, new sales tax, or free trade agreement) or an entire structural adjustment program involving a wide array of reforms. The oppositional party also builds a constituency in the near term by adopting issues with widespread appeal.

How the Social Movement Benefits

In order to sustain a nationwide campaign, social movements need allies with organizational resources across a wide geographical space. In the neoliberal age, few civil society associations sustain a national-level organizational reach. Trade unions are weakened by labor flexibility laws and global competition for reduced labor costs. In the rural sector, agricultural cooperatives become less potent as an organizational force with the privatization of communal lands and growing emphasis on individual and private ownership. Although these weakened traditional actors predominated in the social movement sector during the previous period of state-led development, in the neoliberal era, political parties remain one of the only nationally organized entities. Political parties can use their organizational structure to mobilize in the streets by calling on their supporters in multiple locales to participate in collective action campaigns. Political parties may also act inside the polity to push for the retraction of economic liberalization measures. These insider activities provide social movements with an incentive to join with political parties that can work on their behalf inside of parliament. Having an advocate inside the polity also raises success expectations for activists encouraging wider mobilizations (Klandermans 1997).

Public Opinion

The process of public opinion turning against neoliberal policies is often time dependent. Only if austerity policies and structural adjustment are viewed as threatening and making significant portions of the population worse off will public opinion turn against subsequent rounds of economic reforms. For example, one major finding of Walton and Ragin's (1990) study of more than fifty developing countries and the relationship between structural adjustment and popular discontent was that the more neoliberal policy agreements a country negotiated with the International Monetary Fund, the more widespread was the mass resistance to such measures. Therefore, oppositional political parties will likely be more successful taking up the cause of an antineoliberal social movement when large sectors of society are aware of and stand against such policies. Regional surveys of Latin America carried out by the Latin Barometer indicate that in the late 1990s and early 2000s the general public increasingly opposed privatization policies (McKenzie and Mookherjee 2003), providing an issue ripe for an oppositional political party to tackle. Oppositional political parties take advantage of this public discontent by adopting the cause of social movements combating economic liberalization.

Movement–Party Overlap in Membership

Overlapping membership in social movement organizations and political parties acts as a final dimension shaping the likelihood of social movement partyism. For example, Goldstone (2003, 3) notes, "Since the Republican movement in nineteenth-century France (Aminzade 1995), the same individuals have often been both social movement activists and political candidates." Scholars of Latin American politics refer to these multiple organizational affiliations as *doble militancia* (Luciak 2001, 188). Key individuals and leaders who participate in both oppositional political parties and nongovernmental organizations or social movements act as brokers bringing social movements into closer collaborations with electoral parties (Mische 2008). Such individuals promote the mutual interests of the party and movement in working together on economic policy issues. Such membership overlap promotes the coordination of meetings, protest campaigns, strategies, resource exchange (Diani 2004), and shared goals among movements and oppositional political parties. In the absence of such interpersonal ties, there would be much more distance between these two distinct types of organizational arrangements, making alliances costlier in terms of the time needed to build mutual trust.

Theoretical Summary

Democratization creates the potential for a social movement–party alliance by allowing an expanded civil society organizational infrastructure and granting legal recognition to oppositional political parties. The economic threats associated with neoliberal economic policies provide common interests that may bring parties and movements into an alliance. In such a partnership, social movements benefit from a party's national organizational reach and its ability to act inside the polity. Oppositional political parties aspire to establish a constituency on issues with widespread public opinion support that eventuates in greater electoral power in future elections. Social movement partyism builds particularly enduring coalitions when substantial organizational membership overlap exists between opposition parties and social movements. Such coalitions can sustain national-level campaigns that influence a state's policy-making trajectory. I next examine five cases of social movement partyism in Bolivia, Ecuador, El Salvador, Nicaragua and Uruguay.

Case Studies of Social Movement Partyism

Bolivia: The Gas Wars

In the late 1990s and early 2000s, social movements in Bolivia increasingly coalesced with oppositional political parties, especially the Movimiento Indígena Pachakuti and the Movement Toward Socialism. The rural farmer unions in the Confederación Sindical Única de Trabajadores Campesinos de Bolivia served as the mass support base of the Movimiento Indígena Pachakuti in the indigenous Aymara-dominated altiplano region in the provinces of La Paz. The Movement Toward Socialism originated in the coca farmers' movement *(los cocaleros)* in the Chapare region of Cochabamba and eventually united with urban and other rural movements against neoliberal policies (Postero 2007). The Movement Toward Socialism and Movimiento Indígena Pachakuti oppositional political parties formed in the late 1990s after changes in the nation's electoral laws (i.e., Ley de Participación Popular and the 1996 Electoral Law) allowed competitive elections at the municipal level and greater representation from the provinces in the national congress (Kohl and Farthing 2006). Hence the deepening democratization allowed systemwide opportunities for a greater variety of political parties (Stefanoni 2003, 60).

By the early 2000s, the Movement Toward Socialism and Movimiento Indígena Pachakuti secured political representation in 80 out of 314 municipal governments, and the Movement Toward Socialism grew to the largest oppositional political party, with deputies and senators in the Bolivian congress and senate. Between 2000 and 2005, both the Movement Toward Socialism and the Movimiento Indígena Pachakuti encouraged protests by their party members and supporters against water privatization and natural gas privatization. This led the parties to move beyond their base of Chapare *cocaleros* and altiplano peasants and to take up issues that affected the national population: the distribution of one of the country's most valuable resources, natural gas. In these same years, Bolivian scholars referred to the Movement Toward

Socialism as the antisystemic party because of its role in coordinating extra-parliamentary opposition (Assies and Salman 2003).

Although both oppositional parties (Movimiento Indígena Pachakuti and Movement Toward Socialism) originated from indigenous and rural social movements in the late 1990s (Van Cott 2005), the movement–party alliance manifested itself most forcefully nationally between 2003 and 2005 over the distribution of natural gas. Already in January 2003, the Movement Toward Socialism coordinated a multisectoral coalition with social movements called the Estado Mayor del Pueblo (People's High Command) in preparation for mass resistance against further neoliberal policy implementation, with natural gas nationalization high on the movement–party coalition's agenda. After the government violently repressed local protests and uprisings in February 2003 over the implementation of a new income tax (referred to as *febrero negro* in Bolivia), the Catholic Church, national government, and major political parties established a national dialogue, known as the *reencuentro nacional,* to establish a national agreement on several political issues threatening social peace. Included in the agenda of the national dialogue were issues about the distribution, taxation, and exportation of the country's natural gas deposits, which the neoliberal government partially privatized in the mid-1990s.

In early September 2003, the Movement Toward Socialism and Movimiento Indígena Pachakuti pulled out of talks when it became clear that the government of Gonzalo Sánchez de Lozada ignored their principal demands and planned to export natural gas deposits to wealthy countries in the global north. The government's refusal to change any of its neoliberal economic development strategies during the national dialogue also inflamed the opposition parties (*La Razón* 2003). In the early 2000s, the Movimiento Indígena Pachakuti was led by the Aymaran ruler Felipe Quispe, who served as both a member of parliament (until 2002) and general secretary of the Confederación Sindical Única de Trabajadores Campesinos de Bolivia (CSUTCB), the largest organization of indigenous peasants. Evo Morales acted as the principal leader of the Movement Toward Socialism and was an elected legislative representative in the national congress as well as the general secretary of the largest union of the Confederation of Coca Farmers (Seis Federaciones de Cocaleras del Trópico de Cochabamba). Hence, at the highest levels of leadership in the oppositional political parties, there was organizational overlap with some of the most militant social movement organizations in Bolivia. This made the social movement–party alliance much easier to accomplish.

By mid-September 2003, to show popular discontent with the government's natural gas policies, Quispe directed his organization to engage in roadblocks in La Paz and a hunger strike in El Alto while the Movement Toward

Socialism organized large street demonstrations and rallies in the major cities of the country. The dominant labor organization in the country, the Central Obrera Boliviana, began an open-ended general strike in late September with the participation of dozens of its individual union affiliates. The government brutally cracked down on the protests, especially the assertive tactic of highway roadblocks, killing an estimated seventy civilians. By mid-October, the crisis reached such explosive levels that President Sánchez de Lozada fled the country while 200,000 people congregated in La Paz to oppose his natural gas policies (Postero 2007). The sitting vice president, Carlos Mesa, assumed the presidency and convoked a national referendum on gas exports and natural gas nationalization in mid-2004—a key demand of the social movements and Movement Toward Socialism and Movimiento Indígena Pachakuti parties during the nationwide protests of September–October 2003. Over 80 percent voted in favor of nationalizing natural gas in the referendum. The strong showing of public support boosted the movement–party alliance in the next round of antineoliberal mobilization.

In May and June 2005, a second gas war erupted when interim president Carlos Mesa failed to tax transnational energy corporations to levels demanded by social movements and oppositional political parties. The national congress approved a new gas law on May 5, 2005, that only taxed transnational energy companies at 32 percent. The Movement Toward Socialism and social movement organizations demanded a tax of 50 percent and/or full nationalization of the strategic economic resource. On May 9, the Movement Toward Socialism political party convoked a meeting of the country's major oppositional movements in the eastern city of Santa Cruz. The civil society organizations present at the meeting included CSUTCB, Central Obrera Boliviana, Movimiento Sin Tierra (a movement of landless peasants), El Consejo Nacional de Ayllus y Markas del Qullasuyu (a national indigenous rights organization), and the Confederación Sindical de Colonizadores de Bolivia (a confederation of peasant settlers), as well as several other social movement organizations (*La Razón* 2005). The Movement Toward Socialism and the civic organizations agreed on a *pacto por la unidad* to mobilize nationwide against the new gas law. Movement Toward Socialism mayors, congresspersons, senators, and rank-and-file party members headed many of the demonstrations against the new natural gas legislation.

The protests eventuated in the fall of the Mesa government and the rescheduling of presidential and parliamentary elections for December 2005. At the very end of 2005, Movement Toward Socialism leader and coca farmer union general secretary Evo Morales was elected to the presidency with a higher percentage of votes than any president in recent Bolivian history. One of his first acts as president in early 2006 was to nationalize the nation's natural gas deposits and renegotiate existing contracts with foreign energy corporations.

Ecuador: Trade Liberalization

After passing most of the 1970s with a populist-oriented military regime, the Ecuadorian polity democratized in 1979. The political liberalization process deepened in 1984, when the national government abolished literacy restrictions for voting, greatly expanding suffrage rights for the indigenous peoples of the country (Yashar 2005). At the same time that the Ecuadorian polity was democratizing in the 1980s and 1990s, new neoliberal threats appeared on the political horizon that stimulated new rounds of mass organization throughout the nation, especially in the indigenous communities. In Ecuador, the movement of highland and Amazonian Indians united in the Confederación de Nacionalidades Indígenas del Ecuador (CONAIE) in 1986, representing a majority of the country's indigenous population (up to 30 percent of the national populace). CONAIE launched a nonviolent uprising in 1990 for indigenous rights (Zamosc 1994). In 1996, the indigenous movement along with a national coordinating council of social movements formed the Movimiento de Unidad Plurinacional Pachakutik–Nuevo País political party (known simply as Pachakutik). The oppositional party formed out of a successful campaign in 1995 to defeat a referendum on privatization of several public utilities and services (Collins 2004).

The 1995 referendum merged the interests of CONAIE with the secular left. The referendum was the culmination of over four years of intense activism by indigenous and labor groups against privatization and structural adjustment. A broad civil society coalition called the Coordinadora de los Movimientos Sociales formed in 1995 to mobilize the antiprivatization vote in the referendum. This coalition included the largest indigenous people's organizations in the country (e.g., CONAIE and la Confederación de Pueblos de Nacionalidad Kichwa del Ecuador [ECUANARI]) as well as public sector unions and student groups. The referendum also demonstrated that a sizable cross section of Ecuadorians had turned against many neoliberal policies by the mid-1990s. Indeed, over 60 percent of the public voted against privatization in the plebiscite (Guerrero Cazar and Ospina 2003). This impressive turnout signaled that public opinion stood against neoliberal policies and motivated indigenous and labor activists to form the Pachakutik electoral party that could align with the Coordinadora de los Movimientos Sociales (Guerrero Cazar and Ospina 2003). Many of the early leaders in the Pachakutik political party, including legislative representatives and mayors, enjoyed years of organizational experience in NGOs and social movements such as in CONAIE, ECUANARI, Coordinadora de los Movimientos Sociales, and La Confederación Nacional del Seguro Campesino (Lluco 2004). This dual affiliation by key individuals in political parties and social movement organizations facilitated the alliance of Pachakutik with organized civil society. The indigenous movement and its political arm (Pachakutik) mobilized simultaneously around indigenous rights issues and against the neoliberal threats associated with Ecuador's $13 billion foreign debt. In 1996, Pachakutik competed in municipal and parliamentary elections (Collins 2004). In 2000, it increased its local and regional political representation from the 1996 elections and moved from eleven to twenty-one mayors and from zero to five provincial-level councils (Larrea Maldonado 2004). Pachakutik used this new power inside the polity to support social movement claims on the streets and has remained in close alliance with the indigenous movement and other social sectors in the major nonviolent uprisings in 1997, 2000, 2001, and 2006 against neoliberal policies. It was precisely the neoliberal policies that made Pachakutik a national party centered on more than indigenous rights issues. In 2001, a national nonviolent uprising included the participation of Pachakutik mayors and governors (Larrea Maldonado 2004). During the 2001 mobilizations, Pachakutik assisted social movements in avoiding price hikes in basic consumer goods, transportation, and electricity and ensuring greater citizen participation in the formation of the nation's annual budget (Lluco 2004).

In March and April 2006, CONAIE and Pachakutik, along with an amalgamation of nongovernmental organizations (called Ecuador Decide), led a massive nationwide mobilization against a free trade agreement between the United States and Ecuador. The movement paralyzed the country with strategic roadblocks and mass marches. The movement achieved its goals, and the free trade negotiations were canceled. Pachakutik played an instrumental role over several years in supporting the protest movement that led to the national government's failure to sign a free trade agreement. Beginning in 2004, Pachakutik began educational and organizing drives against the trade liberalization measure as a continuation of an earlier struggle against the Free Trade Area of the Americas, a proposal for a regional free trade block.

The oppositional party endorsed the project of Ecuador Decide to collect one million signatures to force the government to hold a referendum on the free trade agreement before its implementation. Also in 2004, Pachakutik sponsored international conferences and street actions against the impending free trade agreement once its elected representatives in the national and Andean parliaments became aware that the Ecuadorian government had initiated closed-door negotiations over trade liberalization. In 2005, Pachakutik held several workshops in the provinces to educate its supporters about the potential social and economic consequences of the realization of a free trade accord. All of this preparatory work was critical when in March 2006 indigenous movements and other sectors launched the most successful social movement coalition against a free trade agreement in Latin America. During the nationwide protests, Pachakutik denounced repression and provided insider information on the status of the trade talks until the government decided to table the free trade agreement in April 2006.

El Salvador: Privatization of the Public Health System

In 1980, after experiencing five decades of military rule, El Salvador's oppositional movement, the Farabundo Martí Front for National Liberation (FMLN), formed through the unification of several clandestine revolutionary parties. Once state repression reached genocidal levels in the early 1980s, the FMLN transformed into a guerrilla army and battled the Salvadoran government in a prolonged civil war until early 1992 (Viterna 2006). After a United Nations–brokered peace agreement ended the civil war, the FMLN morphed once again into an electoral political party. By 1997, the FMLN firmly established itself as the largest oppositional political party in the country with impressive gains in municipal governments and legislative assembly seats.

In the early to mid-1990s, the FMLN focused on the transition from a revolutionary party to an institutionalized electoral political party. Labor union leaders and other party militants previously active in street politics placed greater emphasis on the electoral process. Other former radical political parties that had influence in social movements during the 1980s broke off from the FMLN in mid-1994 as a result of internal party disputes (Wood 2005). Hence, the movement–party linkage was relatively weak until the late 1990s. Given the disadvantage of social movements and opposition political parties in the early to mid-1990s, the neoliberal party in power, the National Republican Alliance Party (ARENA), after negotiating new state "modernization" loans from the World Bank and Inter-American Development Bank, launched a string of privatizations and economic reforms between 1995 and 1997. Social and labor movements fighting the privatization of telecommunications, pensions, and electrical power distribution failed to forge a strong enough bond with the FMLN in the mid-1990s. Each of these public entities transferred to private ownership after several unsuccessful protest campaigns.

During the late 1990s and early 2000s, from its new foothold in local and national government, the oppositional FMLN party turned to social movements on the streets to maintain its electoral strength. Between 1999 and 2003, the party aligned with the public health care unions in two massive and prolonged strikes to prevent the partial privatization of the medical system. In comparison to other social struggles in the post–civil war era, the alliance between party members and the health care movement was particularly potent. Public opinion stood against the government's plans to subcontract public health care and health insurance to the private sector, especially after witnessing prices rise with the privatization of telecommunications and electricity as well as the dollarization of the country's currency. According to national public opinion polls, 55 percent of the public opposed health care privatization in 1997 before the antiprivatization campaigns began, while 87 percent of the public was against health care privatization at the height of the second campaign in early 2003 (Almeida 2006). Both anti–health care privatization campaigns erupted in the months before the national parliamentary elections in 2000 and 2003.

Legislative leaders from the FMLN, such as Jorge Schafik Hándal and Humberto Centeno, met with striking doctors and workers and held press conferences publicly labeling the struggle against health care as a just cause. Inside parliament, FMLN representatives on the Health and Environment Commission introduced legislation that would legally prevent the outsourcing of public hospital services and units. The language for this legislation was originally drawn up by two public health care unions (El Sindicato de Trabajadores del Instituto Salvadoreño del Seguro Social and El Sindicato de Médicos del Instituto Salvadoreño del Seguro Social) and NGOs constituting the social movement. Because the FMLN lacked a parliamentary majority and the center–right parties (Christian Democrats and the Partido de Conciliación Nacional) vacillated in their support for the health care movement, parliamentary struggle by itself proved insufficient in preventing the privatization process. Consequently, the oppositional party redoubled its efforts by supporting the health campaign on the streets.

Mixing conventional protest with highly assertive actions, health care workers used two major tactics in their antiprivatization crusades—mass marches and roadblocks—and the FMLN played a pivotal role in both. The health care unions and their civil society allies, including students, NGO networks, and other labor unions, utilized the mass march as a central protest strategy in both rounds of contention. Many members of the mobilized civil society organizations also maintained an affiliation in the FMLN political party. The health care workers used symbolic capital by persuading participants in the marches to dress in white or paint themselves white to manifest solidarity with the medical profession. These organizing efforts resulted on several occasions in a meandering white river of bodies through the streets of downtown San Salvador. The mass street demonstrations immediately became known as *marchas blancas* (white marches) and are referenced as a high mark in mobilization by Salvadoran social movement activists. The *marchas blancas* ranged from 15,000 to 200,000 participants, making them the largest demonstrations in newly democratized El Salvador. In both antiprivatization campaigns, the *marchas blancas* also took place outside the capital in other major towns. Nearly all of the FMLN legislative representatives participated in the *marchas blancas,* and the FMLN used its weekly public gathering *(la tribuna abierta)* to encourage its over 80,000 party members to participate in the health care campaign and the *marchas blancas.*

The road blockade acted as the other major protest tactic in the antiprivatization mobilizations, especially in the 2002–3 strike. The mobilized defenders of public health care would hold national days of protest where they sat down en masse, blocking up to a dozen strategic highways and roads around the country. FMLN mayors and legislators demonstrated their support for such protests by participating in the blockades and protecting participants from police repression. The final outcomes of these campaigns included the suspension of the neoliberal government's public health privatization plans and the maintenance of the FMLN as the country's main oppositional party with relatively successful election results in the 2000 and 2003 municipal and legislative elections on the heels of the privatization protests (Almeida 2008). In the 2000s, the FMLN continues an alliance with social movements such as the Bloque Popular Social and the Movimiento Popular de Resistencia 12 de Octubre in battles against free trade and water privatization.

Nicaragua: Austerity, Price Hikes, and Privatization

Between 1990 and 2006, the Frente Sandinista de Liberación Nacional (FSLN) acted as the largest oppositional political party in Nicaragua. The FSLN, similar to the Farabundo Martí Front for National Liberation in El Salvador, originates from a clandestine revolutionary party in the 1970s that led an armed struggle against the dynastic dictatorship of the Somoza family. The FSLN overthrew the dictatorship in 1979 and headed a revolutionary government until 1990 when it was defeated in competitive presidential elections. Nonetheless, in the aftermath of electoral defeat, the FSLN remained the largest oppositional political party. Between 1990 and 2006, three successive governments ruling Nicaragua subscribed to neoliberal economic programs as the country suffered from a $10 billion external debt (Robinson 2003). Social movement organizations and civic associations created during the revolutionary period and after attempted on several occasions to coalesce with the FSLN party to fight the neoliberal policies of the postrevolutionary governments. Because the FSLN ruled during the 1980s, it maintained close relations with civic organizations that were once part of the party's formal structure. It had lower costs in implementing the social movement partyism strategy because an alliance was already in existence. Hence, in the postrevolutionary period (1990–2006), the FSLN formed movement–party alliances with several social sectors that served as the mass base during the revolutionary government (1979–90). These sectors included public schoolteachers in the Asociación Nacional de Educadores de Nicaragua, health care workers organized in the Federación de Trabajadores de la Salud, state sector employees, the national universities and student associations, and the neighborhood based associations in the Movimiento Comunal Nicaraguense. These groups immediately banded together in early 1990 after the first electoral defeat of the FSLN.

The new government of president Violeta Barrios de Chamorro (1990–96) began to enact austerity policies, and pro-Sandinista labor unions left over from the revolutionary period formed a coalition in April 1990 called the Frente Nacional de Trabajadores (FNT). This coalition drew its largest support from state-sector unions in government ministries, education, and health care, as well as farmers and agricultural laborers. The FNT sponsored massive general strikes in April, May, and July 1990 that forced the government to slow down the pace of austerity measures (Stahler-Sholk 1994). The individual affiliates of the FNT became more autonomous from the FSLN in their organizational decision making while continuing to maintain close ties. At times, the FSLN negotiated with the ruling government over workers' issues such as privatization, wage freezes, and layoffs in the public sector without the FNT's input. At other times the FSLN acted in concert with the Frente Nacional de Trabajadores, including the participation of thousands of party members along with workers in street protests. Throughout the 1990s and early 2000s, the FNT maintained its organizational structures and influence on the Nicaraguan polity. However, labor protest was largely defensive in these economically austere times. Tens of thousands of public sector workers lost their jobs between 1988 and the mid-1990s (O'Kane 1995). Other social sectors began to coordinate actions by the late 1990s and early 2000s, including university students and a variety of nongovernmental organizations and consumer protection–based groups.

From the mid-1990s to the early 2000s, the strongest movement–party alliance occurred between the FSLN and the university community. Beginning with the Chamorro government and enduring through the neoliberal administrations of Arnoldo Alemán (1997–2001) and Enrique Bolaños (2002–6), the national government continually underfunded the budget for higher education. This led to several massive street demonstrations between 1992 and 2004 in which scores of university students and police were injured (and at times killed). The FSLN sided with the students, workers, and administrators by actively participating in the street protests as well as voting for the complete budgetary allotment to universities in legislative debates inside the parliament (Almeida and Walker 2006). The FSLN also used the party newspaper, *La Barricada,* to inform the public about the university budget and the social movement trying to defend it. The outcomes of these incessant struggles (which broke out almost every year in this period) usually involved winning greater benefits for the university community, but not the full 6 percent of the national budget requested by the students.

Both the labor-based struggles of the early 1990s and the university protests of the late 1990s forged the movement–party relationship in Nicaragua in the neoliberal era. Nonetheless, these were mainly sector-specific struggles (largely state-sector workers on the defensive and the relatively narrow interests of the university community). Throughout the 1990s, the FSLN had fitful starts aligning with social movements on the streets, at times supporting mass mobilization and other times cooling it off as a consequence of a pact made between the FSLN's top leader, Daniel Ortega, and the Nicaraguan president, Arnoldo Alemán, in 1999. The FSLN political party called off a threatened general strike attempt in 1997 by its affiliated unions once it negotiated concessions from the national government. After the pact of 1999, there was a decrease in social movement activity.

The FSLN would need to align with larger civil society interests to strengthen the coalitions between the oppositional political party and social movements. Indeed, this seems to be the case for the early 2000s when the FSLN supported consumer issues affecting the mass of the impoverished population. In this decade, social movements became more active over several consumer issues, public health care, and a major teachers' strike. A powerful civic organization that emerged on the political scene in the late 1990s was the Red Nacional de Defensa a los Consumidores, led by two Frente Sandinista de Liberación Nacional office holders during the revolutionary period (Grigsby 2005), demonstrating movement–party overlaps in organizational affiliations. By the mid-2000s, the consumer-based movements played a pivotal role in the Nicaraguan social movement sector. For example, in 2006 alone, the Red Nacional de Defensa a los Consumidores along with Movimiento Comunal Nicaraguense, the Coordinadora Civil (a group of NGOs),

and the Unión Nacional de Asociaciónes de Consumidores y Usarios, convoked mass mobilizations in Managua, Ocotal, León, Bluefields, Bilwe, Jui-
galpa, Granada, Esteli, and Masaya against electricity price hikes (issued by
a recently privatized energy distributor and Spanish transnational corporation) and poor water services (Serra 2006).

At the same time, the FSLN began to increase its electoral fortunes at
the municipal level. The oppositional party won over the city government
in the capital Managua in 2001 and then over half of the country's 152
municipal governments, including fifteen of seventeen provincial capital cities,
in the elections of 2004. The newly elected FSLN mayors and city councils
aligned with consumer groups, students, and pro–FSLN bus driver cooperatives to oppose price hikes in public transportation in 2005, the most contentious episodes of collective action of the year (*La Prensa* 2005a, 2005b).
Finally, between 2005 and 2006, after major national strikes in the health
care and public education sectors (where labor leaders also serve as parliamentary representatives for the FSLN) as well as nationwide protests against
bus fare increases, the FSLN won back the presidency in the elections of
November 2006.

Uruguay: Water Privatization

From 1973 to 1985, a repressive military government dominated the Uruguayan polity and suppressed an active civil society (Loveman 1998). With
democratization, the traditional two political parties, Colorado and the Partido Nacional, returned to dominate the political landscape. However, a formerly outlawed socialist political party, the Frente Amplio (Broad Front Party)
allied with other political factions and transitioned once again into a legal
opposition party and won control of the capital, Montevideo, in 1990. The
Frente Amplio also continued to receive more votes for parliamentary and
presidential elections throughout the 1990s, becoming a major national oppositional political party. The leftist party also managed relationships with social
movements on the streets. Many of the neighborhood associations that
emerged after the economic crisis in 1999 had leaders also participating as
militants in the Frente Amplio (Falero 2003), a social dynamic that would
assist them in the construction of social movement partyism.

In 2003 and 2004, the Frente Amplio joined a massive national campaign against water privatization. The state's institution for water administration, Obras Sanitarias del Estado, created in 1952 during the epoch of
state-led development (Santos et al. 2006), seemed to be constantly under
threat of the neoliberal state disassembling its subdivisions and regional
branches and outsourcing them to transnational water and energy companies

under multidecade contracts. The Frente Amplio did not enter a formal alliance with the environmental groups and labor unions fighting water privatization until January 2003. At this time, it appeared clear that public opinion was turning against privatization when the social movement had already collected 100,000 signatures disapproving of the private outsourcing of state water and sanitation administration to multinational corporations (Valdomir 2006). The Frente Amplio oppositional party used its various factions (e.g., legislative, neighborhood, and youth chapters) in alliance with environmentalists and the state water workers' union the Federación de Funcionarios de Obras Sanitarias del Estado to launch mobilizations and petition drives to hold a popular referendum on state control of water administration. The referendum system in Uruguay provides a major institutional avenue for social movements to channel their grievances, unlike in most other Latin American countries. Frente Amplio legislative representatives released statements publicly supporting the referendum. Between late 2002 and late 2003, the campaign succeeded in gaining enough signatures to force a popular referendum on whether water administration should be exclusively the jurisdiction of the government or permitted to be outsourced to transnational firms. On the same day as presidential elections in October 2004, the population also voted on the water privatization referendum. The Frente Amplio won the presidency, and the water privatization efforts were defeated. During the 2004 election campaign, the Frente Amplio included the water privatization issue in its election platform and simultaneously handed out leaflets on the negative consequences of water privatization as it passed out propaganda on its party's slate of candidates for office.

The anti–water privatization campaign began at the regional level in the 1990s after the Uruguayan government began to outsource water administration to international corporations in Maldonado. In the late 1990s and early 2000s, more conflicts erupted in Corrientes, Colonia, and Montevideo as other experiments with water privatization and outsourcing were implemented and consumers claimed unfair price inflation and/or loss of access to water and sewer services. In 1999, the World Bank encouraged more contracting out of sewer and drinking water services to private sector firms. In 2002, the government signed a letter of intent with the International Monetary Fund in which greater participation of private water companies was one of the conditions of the structural adjustment agreement in order for Uruguay to receive a new loan (Santos et al. 2006). This particular act galvanized a wide variety of civil society organizations to form the Comisión Nacional en Defensa del Agua y de la Vida in October 2002—a coalition of environmentalists (Friends of the Earth–Uruguay), state water administration workers, chapters of the Frente Amplio oppositional political party, labor unions, university student associations, and several neighborhood and regional citizens' committees against water privatization (e.g., Liga de Fomento de Manatiales). Between late 2002 and October 2003, the Comisión Nacional en Defensa del Agua y de la Vida organized petition tables nationally to obtain the necessary number of signatures (10 percent of registered voters) to hold the referendum on public water administration. This commission sponsored a mass street march in Montevideo in October 2003 to hand over the petition with over 280,000 signatures to the national legislature.[3] The demonstrators carried hundreds of boxes full of signed petitions from the headquarters of the state water administration institute to the legislative palace.

Figure 8.1 provides information on the relationship between the campaign against water privatization in Uruguay and the electoral success of the Frente Amplio oppositional political party. The figure provides correlation coefficients for (1) the association between where the water distribution conflicts took place and the percentage of departmental votes for the Frente Amplio in the 2004 elections, and (2) the association between the level of departmental support for the water nationalization referendum and the percentage of votes achieved by the Frente Amplio in the presidential elections. Both covariates (social conflict over water privatization and departmental vote in favor of state control of water administration) are positively correlated with voting for the Frente Amplio's presidential candidate. Those departments that maintained social movement activity over water privatization and high voting participation rates in support of the referendum to uphold public control over water administration were positively associated with voting for

Water Privatization Variables	Departmental Vote for Frente Amplio (2004)
Reported conflict over water distribution in department, 1998–2002	0.69***
% votes for nationalization of water referendum in department	0.53*
N (No. of departments)	19

* p < .05;

*** p ≤ .001 (two-tailed tests).

Figure 8.1. Correlations of water distribution conflicts and votes for Uruguay's nationalization of water administration with percentage of departmental votes for Frente Amplio.

the political party that most supported the antiprivatization campaign and subsequently won the presidential elections: the Frente Amplio.

Conclusions

In contemporary Latin America, the social movement partyism coalition is forged by the combination of deepening democratization and economic liberalization. Oppositional political parties that take up the cause of a particular neoliberal measure and enter into coalitions with social movement campaigns expand their base of support. The finding that *economic* threats produced by neoliberalism support the marriage of parties with movements is consistent with other studies that find *political* threats as conducive to coalitional formation in social movements (McCammon and Campbell 2002; Staggenborg 1986; Van Dyke 2003a). The political party movement coalition more likely endures when a majority of public opinion also stands against the economic reforms such as in the cases of Bolivia, Ecuador, El Salvador, and Uruguay discussed above. In addition to favorable public opinion, the social movement partyism coalition is strengthened by preexisting organizational membership overlaps between social movements and oppositional political parties.

This chapter also asserts that for state-oriented movements, not all external allies are equal. Out of the universe of potential collaborators and coalitional partners potentially available to social movements, previous studies contend that actors inside the state appear more crucial to policy-oriented collective action (Banaszak 2005; Goldstone 2003; Stearns and Almeida 2004; Van Dyke 2003b). Oppositional political parties maintain a mass base of members and supporters (often at the national level) that can be used for social movement mobilization outside electoral campaigns, providing a unique resource to social movements. At the same time, oppositional political parties need social movements to build their electoral constituency.

In these five country cases, the most enduring forms of social movement partyism occurred once the oppositional political party achieved a moderate level of electoral success. The major social movement partyism campaigns in Bolivia, El Salvador, Nicaragua, and Uruguay all took place once the oppositional party in question ascended to the status of the second or third largest electoral force in the country. Stronger oppositional parties may provide a greater sense of hope for success among social movements that enter a coalition with the party. Strong parties appear able to stop unfavorable legislation inside the parliament, or at least stall it until more mass mobilization occurs. In addition, larger opposition parties have more members. The membership lists and organizational structure can be used to coordinate mass collective action beyond just voting.

More analytical weight should also be given to the idea of *doble militancia* in the construction of social movement partyism. Opposition party members who simultaneously participate in social movements as members and/or leaders of civic organizations (such as Evo Morales and Felipe Quispe in the peasant organizations of Bolivia and Luis Macas in the indigenous movement of Ecuador) likely provide the rudimentary network structure for launching a campaign led by a movement–party coalition. The degree of overlap existing between individuals/civic organizations and oppositional political parties may help determine the likelihood of a social movement partyism alliance emerging as well as its strength and endurance. One would also expect to observe a higher frequency of social movement partyism where long histories of movement–party overlap exist such as linkages forged in Nicaragua during the revolutionary period of the 1980s that were tapped decades later. Finally, a more explicitly comparative method would be useful in future studies that examine cases where the social movement partyism coalition both succeeds and fails in materializing.

Notes

1. The social movement–oppositional political party alliance is also more likely found in other historical and political contexts characterized by multiparty electoral systems such as Green parties in Western Europe (Maguire 1995) and labor parties in nineteenth-century France (Aminzade 1995)

2. An important caveat is the recent rise to power of leftist politicians and political parties in Bolivia, Ecuador, Honduras, Nicaragua, Paraguay, and Venezuela. Once in executive power, these leftist governments have encouraged mass demonstrations in support of their policies, such as holding constitutional assemblies.

3. The 280,000 signatures on the anti–water privatization petition represent over 8 percent of the entire Uruguayan population.

Works Cited

Alcañiz, Isabella, and Melissa Scheier. 2007. "New Social Movements with Old Party Politics: The MTL Piqueteros and the Communist Party in Argentina." *Latin American Perspectives* 34: 157–71.

Almeida, Paul D. 2006. "Social Movement Unionism, Social Movement Partyism, and Policy Outcomes: Health Care Privatization in El Salvador." In *Latin American Social Movements: Globalization, Democratization, and Transnational Networks*, edited by Hank Johnston and Paul Almeida, 57–76. Lanham, Md.: Rowman & Littlefield.

———. 2007. "Defensive Mobilization: Popular Movements against Economic Adjustment Policies in Latin America." *Latin American Perspectives* 34: 123–39.

————. 2008. *Waves of Protest: Popular Struggle in El Salvador, 1925–2005*. Minneapolis: University of Minnesota Press.

Almeida, Paul D., and Hank Johnston. 2006. "Neoliberal Globalization and Popular Movements in Latin America." In *Latin American Social Movements: Globalization, Democratization, and Transnational Networks*, edited by Hank Johnston and Paul Almeida, 3–18. Lanham, Md.: Rowman & Littlefield.

Almeida, Paul D., and Linda Brewster Stearns. 1998. "Political Opportunities and Local Grass-Roots Environmental Movements: The Case of Minamata." *Social Problems* 45: 37–60.

Almeida, Paul D., and Erica Walker. 2006. "The Pace of Neoliberal Globalization: A Comparison of Three Popular Movement Campaigns in Central America." *Social Justice* 33: 175–90.

Aminzade, Ronald. 1995. "Between Movement and Party: The Transformation of Mid-Nineteenth-Century French Republicanism." In *The Politics of Social Protest: Comparative Perspectives on States and Social Movements*, edited by J. Craig Jenkins and Bert Klandermans, 39–62. Minneapolis: University of Minnesota Press.

Assies, Willem, and Ton Salman. 2003. *Crisis in Bolivia: The Elections and Their Aftermath*. London: Institute of Latin American Studies.

Auyero, Javier. 2001. "Glocal Riots." *International Sociology* 16: 33–53.

Banaszak, Lee Ann. 2005. "Inside and Outside the State: Movement Insider Status, Tactics, and Public Policy Achievements." In *Routing the Opposition: Social Movements, Public Policy, and Democracy*, edited by David S. Meyer, Valerie Jenness, and Helen Ingram, 149–76. Minneapolis: University of Minnesota Press.

Bob, Clifford. 2005. *Marketing Rebellion: Insurgents, Media, and International Activism*. Cambridge: Cambridge University Press.

Chalmers, Douglas A., Scott B. Martin, and Kerianne Piester. 1997. "Associative Networks: New Structures of Representation for the Popular Sectors?" In *The New Politics of Inequality in Latin America: Rethinking Participation and Representation*, edited by Douglas Chalmers, Carlos M. Vilas, Katherine Hite, Scott B. Martin, Kerianne Piester, and Monique Segarra, 543–82. Oxford: Oxford University Press.

Collins, Jennifer. 2004. "Linking Movement and Electoral Politics: Ecuador's Indigenous Movement and the Rise of Pachakutik." In *Politics in the Andes: Identity, Conflict, Reform*, edited by Jo-Marie Burt and Philip Mauceri, 38–57. Pittsburgh: University of Pittsburgh Press.

Diamond, Larry. 1999. *Developing Democracy: Toward Consolidation*. Baltimore: Johns Hopkins University Press.

Diani, Mario. 2004. "Networks and Participation." In *The Blackwell Companion to Social Movements*, edited by David A. Snow, Sarah A. Soule, and Hanspeter Kriesi, 339–59. Oxford: Blackwell.

Diario Co Latino. 2007. "Masiva marcha contra el TLC en Costa Rica." February 27.

Eckstein, Susan E. 2006. "Urban Resistance to Neoliberal Democracy in Latin America." *Colombia Internacional* 63: 12–39.

Eckstein, Susan E., and Timothy P. Wickham-Crowley. 2003. "Struggles for Social Rights in Latin America: Claims in the Arenas of Subsistence, Labor, Gender, and Ethnicity." In *Struggles for Social Rights in Latin America*, edited by Susan Eckstein and Timothy Wickham-Crowley, 1–56. London: Routledge.

El Comercio. 2006. "Humala anuncia marchas contra la firma del TLC." June 8, 1.

Falero, Alfredo. 2003. "Sociedad civil y la construcción de una nueva subjetividad social en Uruguay: Condicionamientos, conflictos, desafíos." In *Movimientos sociales y conflicto en América Latina*, edited by José Seone, 41–54. Buenos Aires: CLACSO.

Goldstone, Jack. 2003. "Bridging Institutionalized and Noninstitutionalized Politics." In *States, Parties, and Social Movements*, edited by Jack A. Goldstone, 1–24. Cambridge: Cambridge University Press.

Green, Duncan. 2003. *Silent Revolution: The Rise and Crisis of Market Economics in Latin America*. 2nd ed. London: Latin American Bureau.

Grigsby, William. 2005. "¿Por qué hay tan poca movilización social?" *Revista Envío* 280 (July).

Guerrero Cazar, Fernando, and Pablo Ospina. 2003. *El Poder de la Comunidad: Ajuste estructural y movimiento indígena en los Andes ecuatorianos*. Buenos Aires: CLACSO.

Isaac, Larry, and Lars Christiansen. 2002. "How the Civil Rights Movement Revitalized Labor Militancy." *American Sociological Review* 67: 722–46.

Klandermans, Bert. 1997. *The Social Psychology of Protest*. Oxford: Blackwell.

Kohl, B., and L. Farthing. 2006. *Impasse in Bolivia: Neoliberal Hegemony and Popular Resistance*. London: Zed Books.

Larrea Maldonado, Anna María. 2004. "El Movimiento Indígena Ecuatoriano: Participación y resistencia." *Observatorio Social de América Latina* 13: 67–76.

Lluco, Miguel. 2004. "La Capitulación de un presidente y la ruptura de una alianza." In *Entre la utopía y el desencanto: Pachakutik en el gobierno de Gutiérrez*, edited by Augusto Berrera, 9–40. Quito: Editorial Planeta.

López Maya, Margarita. 1999. "La protesta popular venezolana entre 1989 y 1993 (en el umbral del neoliberalismo)." In *Lucha popular, democracia, neoliberalismo: Protesta popular en América Latina en los años de ajuste*, edited by Margarita L López Maya, 209–35. Caracas: Nueva Sociedad.

Loveman, Mara. 1998. "High-Risk Collective Action: Defending Human Rights in Chile, Uruguay, and Argentina." *American Journal of Sociology* 104: 477–525.

Luciak, Ilja A. 2001. *After the Revolution: Gender and Democracy in El Salvador, Nicaragua, and Guatemala*. Baltimore: Johns Hopkins University Press.

Maguire, Diarmuid. 1995. "Opposition Movements and Opposition Parties: Equal Partners or Dependent Relations in the Struggle for Power and Reform?" In *The Politics of Social Protest: Comparative Perspectives on States and Social Movements,* edited by J. Craig Jenkins and Bert Klandermans, 199–228. Minneapolis: University of Minnesota Press.

Mainwaring, Scott, and Frances Hagopian. 2005. "Introduction: The Third Wave of Democratization in Latin America." In *The Third Wave of Democratization in Latin America: Advances and Setbacks,* edited by Frances Hagopian and Scott Mainwaring, 1–13. Cambridge: Cambridge University Press.

Markoff, John. 1996. *Waves of Democracy: Social Movements and Political Change.* Newbury Park, Calif.: Pine Forge.

McAdam, Doug. 1996. "Conceptual Origins, Current Problems, Future Directions." In *Comparative Perspectives on Social Movements: Political Opportunities, Mobilizing Structures, and Cultural Framings,* edited by Doug McAdam, John D. McCarthy, and Mayer N. Zald, 23–40. Cambridge: Cambridge University Press.

McCammon, Holly J., and Karen E. Campbell. 2002. "Allies on the Road to Victory: Coalition Formation between the Suffragists and the Woman's Christian Temperance Union." *Mobilization* 7: 231–51.

McCarthy, John. 1987. "Pro-Life and Pro-Choice Mobilization: Infrastructure Deficits and New Technologies." In *Social Movements in an Organizational Society,* edited by Mayer N. Zald and John D. McCarthy, 49–66. New Brunswick: Transaction.

McKenzie, David, and Dilip Mookherjee. 2003. "The Distributive Impact of Privatization in Latin America: Evidence from Four Countries." Boston University Institute for Economic Development, Discussion Paper Series No. 128, Boston, Mass.

Meyer, David S., and Debra C. Minkoff. 2004. "Conceptualizing Political Opportunity." *Social Forces* 82: 1457–92.

Mische, Ann. 2008. *Partisan Publics: Communication and Contention across Brazilian Youth Activist Networks.* Princeton, N.J.: Princeton University Press.

O'Kane, Trish. 1995. "New Autonomy, New Struggle: Labor Unions in Nicaragua." In *The New Politics of Survival,* edited by Minor Sinclair, 183–207. New York: Monthly Review Press.

Oviedo, Luis. 2001. *Una historia del movimiento piquetero: De las primeras coordinadoras a las asambleas nacionales.* Buenos Aires: Ediciones Rumbos.

Postero, Nancy. 2007. *Now We Are Citizens: Indigenous Politics in Postmulticultural Bolivia.* Stanford, Calif.: Stanford University Press.

La Prensa (Nicaragua). 2005a. "Segovianos amenazan con protestas." April 26.

———. 2005b. "Diputados, alcaldes y concejales Sandinistas atizan protestas." April 27.

La Razón. 2003. "El MAS y el MIP se alistan para la 'guerra por el gas.'" September 3.

———. 2005. "Protestas se radicalizan desde hoy contra Mesa y el Congreso." May 16.

Robinson, William. 2003. *Transnational Conflicts: Central America, Social Change, and Globalization*. London: Verso.

———. 2006. "Promoting Polyarchy in Latin America: The Oxymoron of 'Market Democracy.'" In *Latin America after Neoliberalism*, edited by Eric Hershberg and Fred Rosen. 96–119. New York: New Press.

Santos, Carlos, Sebastián Valdomir, Verónica Iglesias, and Daniel Renfrew, eds. 2006. *Aguas en movimiento: La resistencia a la privatización del agua en Uruguay*. Montevideo: Ediciones de la Canilla.

Schwartz, Mildred A. 2006. *Party Movements in the United States and Canada*. Lanham, Md.: Rowman & Littlefield.

Seidman, Gay. 1994. *Manufacturing Militance: Workers' Movements in Brazil and South Africa, 1970–1985*. Berkeley: University of California Press.

Serra, Luis. 2006. "Las luchas sociales en Nicaragua en el contexto electoral." *Observatorio Social de América Latina* 20: 225–35.

Shefner, Jon, George Pasdirtz, and Cory Blad. 2006. "Austerity Protests and Immiserating Growth in Mexico and Argentina." In *Latin American Social Movements: Globalization, Democratization, and Transnational Networks*, edited by Hank Johnston and Paul Almeida, 19–42. Lanham, Md.: Rowman & Littlefield.

Silver, Beverly. 2003. *Forces of Labor: Workers' Movements and Globalization since 1870*. Cambridge: Cambridge University Press.

Stahler-Sholk, Richard. 1994. "El ajuste neoliberal y sus opciones: La respuesta del movimiento sindical nicaraguense." *Revista Mexicana de Sociología* 56: 59–88.

Staggenborg, Suzanne. 1986. "Coalition Work in the Pro-Choice Movement: Organizational and Environmental Opportunities and Obstacles." *Social Problems* 33: 374–90.

Stearns, Linda Brewster, and Paul D. Almeida. 2004. "The Formation of State Actor–Social Movement Coalitions and Favorable Policy Outcomes." *Social Problems* 51: 478–504.

Stefanoni, Pablo. 2003. "MAS-IPSP: La emergencia del nacionalismo plebeyo." *Observatorio Social de América Latina* 12: 57–68.

Tilly, Charles. 1978. *From Mobilization to Revolution*. New York: Addison Wesley.

Valdomir, Sebastián. 2006. "Rupturas y continuidades: El plebiscito del agua en la perspectiva de los procesos, 1989–2003." In *Aguas en movimiento: La resistencia a la privatización del agua en Uruguay*, edited by Carlos Santos, Sebastian Valdomir, Verónica Iglesias, and Daniel Renfrew, 155–86. Montevideo: Ediciones de la Canilla.

Van Cott, Donna Lee. 2005. *From Movements to Parties in Latin America: The Evolution of Ethnic Politics*. Cambridge: Cambridge University Press.

Van Dyke, Nella. 2003a. "Crossing Movement Boundaries: Factors That Facilitate Coalition Protest by American College Students, 1930–1990." *Social Problems* 50: 226–50.

———. 2003b. "Protest Cycles and Party Politics: The Effects of Elite Allies and Antagonists on Student Protest in the United States, 1930–1990." In *States, Parties, and Social Movements,* edited by Jack A. Goldstone, 226–45. Cambridge: Cambridge University Press.

Van Dyke, Nella, and Sarah Soule 2002. "Structural Social Change and the Mobilizing Effect of Threat: Explaining Levels of Patriot and Militia Organizing in the United States." *Social Problems* 49: 497–520.

Viterna, Jocelyn. 2006. "Pulled, Pushed, and Persuaded: Explaining Women's Mobilization into the Salvadoran Guerrilla Army." *American Journal of Sociology* 112: 1–45.

Walton, John, and Charles Ragin. 1990. "Global and National Sources of Political Protest: Third World Responses to the Debt Crisis." *American Sociological Review* 55: 876–90.

Walton, John, and David Seddon. 1994. "Food Riots Past and Present." In *Free Markets and Food Riots: The Politics of Global Adjustment,* edited by John Walton and David Seddon, 23–54. Oxford: Blackwell.

Walton, John, and Jonathan Shefner. 1994. "Latin America: Popular Protest and the State." In *Free Markets and Food Riots: The Politics of Global Adjustment,* edited by John Walton and David Seddon, 97–134. Oxford: Blackwell.

Williams, Heather. 2001. *Social Movements and Economic Transition: Markets and Distributive Conflict in Mexico.* Cambridge: Cambridge University Press.

Wood, Elisabeth Jean. 2005. "Challenges to Political Democracy in El Salvador." In *The Third Wave of Democratization in Latin America: Advances and Setbacks,* edited by Frances Haopian and Scott Mainwaring, 179–201. Cambridge: Cambridge University Press.

Yashar, Deborah. 2005. *Contesting Citizenship in Latin America: The Rise of Indigenous Movements and the Postliberal Challenge.* Cambridge: Cambridge University Press.

Zamosc, Leon. 1994. "Agrarian Protest and the Indian Movement in the Ecuadorian Highlands." *Latin American Research Review* 29: 37–68.

9
Political Opportunity and Social Movement Coalitions: The Role of Policy Segmentation and Nonprofit Tax Law

Brian Obach

Coalition formation is an increasingly important social movement strategy. The number of organizations engaging in coalition activity has risen markedly in recent decades, and evidence suggests that joining together with allies is important to movement success (Gamson 1990; Hula 1999; Van Dyke 2003). Whether or not social movement organizations (SMOs) engage in coalition strategies and with whom they ally are influenced by a number of factors. Coalition scholars have analyzed the impact of such variables as resource availability, the emergence of political threats, the types of movement organizations in a given environment, past SMO strategy, and shared identities.

Political opportunity theorists have long acknowledged the importance of allies for social movement mobilization and success, but the way in which exogenous factors influence coalition involvement has only been touched on. On those occasions when political opportunity theory has been utilized in relation to social movement coalitions, scholars typically focus on the strategic assessments of movement actors regarding the benefits and drawbacks of coalition membership within the context of a movement campaign. Such considerations tend to ignore the more stable political institutional framework within which movement coalitions form or fail to form. This type of state channeling has been found to be an important determinant of SMO behavior in a number of respects (McCarthy, Britt, and Wolfson 1991), although analyses of these mechanisms have not focused on movement coalition dynamics.

A more developed area of coalition study focuses on the organizational and interpersonal challenges of effective coalition action. Some have examined the way in which organizational cultures and identities inhibit coalition formation among certain types of organizations (Altemose and McCarty 2001; Barvosa-Carter 2001; Bystydzienski and Schacht 2001; Grossman 2001; Obach 2004; Rose 2000). Others have emphasized the importance of personal relationships among key movement actors for the establishment of coalitions (Brecher and Costello 1990; Bystydzienski and Schacht 2001; Loomis 1986; Sabatier 1988). Yet each of these factors must be considered in the context of the institutional environment within which movement organizations operate. To the extent that state institutions channel movement organizations and movement actors in different directions, they are influencing what types of coalitions are likely to form.

In this chapter, I utilize a political opportunity approach to analyze state policies in the United States to demonstrate that governing institutions channel some organizations toward coalition partnerships while inhibiting others. On the basis of research on coalition formation between labor unions and environmental organizations and on established findings regarding coalition behavior, I find that state structures foster some forms of interorganizational contact that facilitate coalition formation while hindering others. In particular, I focus on the way in which institutional barriers deter coalition development between organized labor and other movement sectors, thus inhibiting the formation of a broad working-class and middle-class movement alliance.

This analysis focuses primarily on policy-oriented professional movement organizations. Grassroots movements and informal organizations that do not have specific policy goals are in some ways less shaped by the state institutional mechanisms considered here. But most movement organizations do have at least some policy change goals (Gamson 1990), and most movement organizations that survive in the long term develop more formal and professional practices (McCarthy and Zald 1977; Staggenborg 1988). Here I analyze two institutional mechanisms that channel organizations of this type toward or away from coalition partnerships.

The first such mechanism is the general segmentation of policy arenas. Collaborative political efforts require a degree of trust and familiarity. Yet trust and familiarity are built through interaction, and thus important questions to consider are how and under what circumstances different movement organizations are brought together and how the state facilitates or discourages such contact. The creation of distinct policy domains is one means by which the state influences coalition activity. Although organizations within the same policy arena may be pushed together on the basis of the discrete state structures designed to address those defined policy areas, coalition formation among more diverse groups is inhibited by this policy segmentation. Thus, through the creation of separate and distinct policy apparatuses, the state insulates organizations from one another. The limited interaction between groups from different movements that results from this channeling hinders the development of familiarity and trust that is essential to meaningful collaborative efforts.

Electoral politics provide an opportunity for cross-movement coalition work, given shared interests in electing candidates broadly supportive of a range of movement causes. It is here that movement organizations could potentially reach beyond their issue domains and the associated policy structures to work with others of different movements who also stand to benefit through electoral action. However, a second institutional barrier inhibits this opportunity. That is, most SMOs are prohibited from participation in electoral politics by their nonprofit tax status. Organizations that are dependent on tax-deductible voluntary contributions or foundation funding are barred from participation in electoral politics. That affects virtually all of the middle-class-based professional movement organizations that have emerged since the 1960s, from civil rights groups to feminist organizations to environmentalists. Labor unions are not restricted in this way because of their funding mechanism and tax status. But the prohibition on electoral politics faced by most movement organizations effectively limits the extent to which labor, a movement that has served as one of the most important foundations for popular mobilization since industrialization, can work in conjunction with the movements that have gained prominence since the mid-twentieth century. Thus, state institutions have limited political opportunities for coalition formation in fundamental ways, including the imposition of significant barriers to the formation of a broad working-class and middle-class movement alliance. Beyond the limits states place on domestic movement alliance building, these findings also have implications for the way in which state channeling influences international movement coalition formation. In this chapter, I identify and analyze these and other state coalition channeling mechanisms.

Political Opportunity, Identity, and Social Movement Coalition Building

Many social movement scholars have utilized political opportunity as a basis for understanding social movement activity (McAdam 1982; Tarrow 1996; Tilly 1978). Yet political opportunity is less a unitary theory and more a basic recognition that exogenous features of the political environment influence collective action (McAdam 1996). Although most consider a variety of elements in the broader political environment as relevant to political opportunity, all consider state action to be of central importance to understanding a range of movement phenomena. David Meyer (2005) identifies a number of ways in which state institutions and policies shape how SMOs organize and pursue their goals, including the formation of coalitions. According to Meyer,

> State policy creates the conditions of coalition by producing identities and grievances through policy. . . . In some circumstances this is explicit; by mandating particular treatment and affording or restricting opportunities for participation, states create categories that can encourage the development of oppositional identities, based on racial, ethnic, sexual, or religious categories. (140)

He offers the example of how the passage of the Social Security Act of 1935 created a political constituency that subsequently mobilized to protect its newly shared interests (15). In essence, policy created (or at least significantly facilitated the creation of) a social movement among a population of senior citizens who previously had little in the way of concrete goals around which to organize. Defending and expanding Social Security benefits became that goal. Similarly, draft policy had a dramatic effect on the anti–Vietnam War movement. It mobilized a massive new constituency and dramatically altered the range of tactics available to the peace movement. State policy can also weaken a movement or channel movement participants into more conventional political activity. Decision makers can at times defuse movements or steer movement actors away from radical tactics by making limited policy concessions (Piven and Cloward 1977). Financial incentives are another means by which the state can lead movement groups to adopt different strategies that allow them to qualify for the funding that they believe will sustain their organization and advance the movement (Cress 1997; Jenkins and Eckert 1986; McCarthy, Britt, and Wolfson 1991).

In his breakdown of political opportunity approaches, Tarrow (1996, 42) would consider most of the above to be analyses of proximate opportunities, where movement actors respond to signals from "their immediate policy environment or from changes in their resources or capacities." This is in contrast to statist approaches to the examination of political opportunity structures, which focus on the way in which broader state institutions channel movement activity as a whole. For example, the size and use of the state's repressive capacity greatly shapes the extent and manner of all forms of mobilization. Other broad institutional arrangements, such as political party structures, also influence the form and strategies that movements adopt within a nation. For instance, the environmental movement in the United States takes a very different form from that in Germany, in part as a result of the proportional representation found in the German electoral system relative to the winner-take-all system found in the United States (McAdam, McCarthy, and Zald 1996).

Attention to coalition dynamics can be found primarily in the proximate branch of the political opportunity literature. Few have considered how broader state institutions shape coalition opportunities (Meyer 2004). Furthermore, with few exceptions, most consideration of coalitions focuses on the availability of elite allies, not horizontal cross-movement coalitions per se. One such exception can be found in Meyer and Corrigall-Brown's (2005) analysis of coalition participation in the U.S. antiwar movement. They conclude that

> the decision of social movement organizations to join a coalition is akin to the processes whereby individuals join social movements, involving an assessment of costs, benefits, and identity. As the political context changes, the costs and benefits are assessed differently and, for this reason, actively engaged coalitions are difficult to sustain over a long period as circumstances change. (327)

Although the proximate circumstances alluded to here can help explain coalition dynamics over the life course of an issue cycle, there are unexplored dimensions of coalition activity for which a statist approach would be useful. For example, the cost–benefit calculation described above is influenced by the level of familiarity between key movement actors within different organizations. The state influences the extent to which movement actors will develop that familiarity through the way it defines policy domains. If, for instance, environmental problems caused by a new housing development are considered to be an issue regulated by state law, then the policy apparatus designed to address it may bring together statewide environmental organizations and local community groups opposed to the project. Yet if the issue at hand is deemed to be local in nature and to be addressed by county or local officials, then state-based environmental organizations may not get involved, and contact with grassroots leaders does not occur. This has obvious direct implications for the development of a movement coalition between state and local organizations in this particular campaign, but it also has long-term consequences, given that the cost–benefit assessment of coalition involvement is greatly affected by the preexisting level of familiarity between movement actors. If movement actors are already familiar with one another, then the costs of coalition formation are much lower. The work associated with the building and maintenance of the coalition can be done without the additional effort associated with the careful negotiation and compromise necessary in agreements between strangers. By defining an environmental issue as a local matter to be addressed by local officials, the state is channeling grass-roots groups away from coalition partnership with broader-based organizations. In this way, the proximate circumstances that serve as the focus of coalition analysis, such as the cost–benefit calculations concerning coalition participation, are in fact greatly influenced by broader institutional factors.

In addition to the strategic calculations that movement actors undertake when considering coalition partnership, state institutions are also relevant to the identity issues that have served as the focus of coalition study. Much research on the barriers to social movement coalition formation centers on questions of identity and culture that divide movement participants and the organizations within which they work (Altemose and McCarty 2001; Barvosa-Carter 2001; Bystydzienski and Schacht 2001; Obach 2004). A shared identity has been recognized as a central component of movement participation generally (Friedman and McAdam 1992; Melucci 1994; Taylor and Whittier 1992). It is this identification with a cause or with a particular perspective or social position that fosters the solidarity necessary for collective action among individuals. Yet as participants come to identify with a particular movement or organization, to some extent they form boundaries that separate themselves from others (Bystydzienski and Schacht 2001; Gitlin 1993; McCammon and Campbell 2002; Taylor and Whittier 1992). Within distinct organizations, perspectives and practices develop that may not correspond to those of other groups. Participants in an organization, through routine internal communications as well as through broader discussions of goals, values, and strategies, reinforce a particular identity. Thus, when different groups come together in an attempt to address shared concerns, interpersonal barriers associated with each groups' identity and incompatible organizational practices can limit their ability to do so. This stands as a significant barrier to social movement coalition formation.

In seeking to understand the conditions under which movement coalitions can overcome these barriers, several analysts have emphasized the important role played by bridge builders or coalition brokers—that is, individuals who possess intimate knowledge of the different movements or organizations that are coming together or who hold a dual identity such that they have a rich understanding of the perspectives and cultures of two or more distinct groups (Grossman 2001; Hula 1999; Loomis 1986; Obach 2004; Rose 2000). These brokers are viewed as essential for their ability to foster the shared understandings that allow for cooperative activity. A number of case studies demonstrate the important role played by these actors. For example, Zoltan Grossman (2001) explains how these bridges were formed between a Native American rights group and a rural white outdoors organization, previously divided by race and culture, thus allowing them to work together to protect natural resources in northern Wisconsin. Similarly, Fred Rose (2000) emphasizes the role of bridge builders in overcoming cultural differences between movement actors divided by class. In his analysis of the military conversion movement in the post–cold war years, cooperation between peace activists and union workers in the defense industry was inhibited not so much by interests, but by class-based cultural barriers. Only those capable of bridging the class–culture divide were able to foster cooperation between these middle-class peace activists and blue-collar workers. In my work on labor–environmental movement coalitions, in virtually every instance of long-term intermovement cooperation between these two sectors, there could be found either a unionist with strong environmental commitments or an environmental advocate with a labor background who performed this coalition broker function (Obach 2004). These brokers played key roles in explaining or smoothing over organizational differences and generating shared understandings and trust between distinct movement actors.

The strategic assessments carried out by movement actors and issues of identity and culture are clearly important to understanding the process of social movement coalition formation. In addition, the presence or absence of coalition brokers can determine whether potential coalition partners will overcome cultural barriers or assign higher or lower costs to working with other movement groups. But these strategic calculations, identity formation, and development of coalition brokers are not divorced from the state. The state defines the scope of public policies and creates the policy apparatus that will serve as the focus of much movement activity. Strategic calculations are made and identity is shaped and reinforced in the context of that activity. To the extent that state policy separates organizations, it is influencing strategic calculations and defining and reinforcing different identities, all of which affects coalition propensities. This can be seen in some of the analyses of proximate influences on particular movement coalitions, but broader, more stable state institutional mechanisms must also be considered. It is this statist aspect of political opportunity that has gone largely unexplored in relation to movement coalition formation. Below I examine two such institutional mechanisms: state policy segmentation, and the tax laws that govern movement organizations.

State Policy Segmentation

In his analysis of bureaucracy, Max Weber (1946) revealed the way in which social functions are compartmentalized and organized into a series of rule-bound decision-making hierarchies in modern societies. This is true of both private organizations and public institutions. In the private sphere, this may mean that a corporation breaks down its business operations into separate units of marketing, distribution, and manufacturing. In government, this is manifest in the way that social policy is segmented into distinct spheres, each with its own departments and agencies. This is clearly evident within the U.S. federal government. The executive branch has fifteen separate agencies addressing policies ranging from agriculture to transportation, while the House and Senate have twenty and seventeen standing committees, respectively, each designed to address a similar range of defined policy areas. State governments have corresponding policy specialty areas. It is within these institutionally defined policy domains that movement organizations must operate in order to advance their goals. Movement leaders, staff members, and activists hold press conferences and protests outside of committee meetings and testify at public hearings. They lobby the elected officials and agency representatives associated with the relevant policy areas in order to shape policy according to their objectives. It is within these policy subsystems that movement actors from different organizations are provided with the opportunity to come into contact with one another (Jenkins-Smith 1991; Jenkins-Smith and Sabatier 1994; Sabatier 1988). For example, environmental movement participants are brought together as they engage with environmental agencies, committees, and legislators with appointments in the areas of environment and energy. This is in addition to several other venues, from fund-raisers to conferences to awards dinners, where movement actors within the same policy subsystem interact with one another, forming social bonds that are crucial determinants of coalition development (Grattet 2005). In essence, by defining policy domains and creating agencies designed to address these distinct domains, the state has essentially determined the community of movement organizations and personnel who will be brought into regular contact with one another. In this way, the state has created the opportunity for the interaction that allows for the familiarity and trust relationships that form the basis of coalition development. Analyses have confirmed that those most likely to work in coalition are those who are brought together within the same policy subsystem (Salisbury et al. 1987).

The ties formed through interaction within policy domains are further reinforced by the fact that personnel often shift positions or change organizations within a given subsystem. In some cases organizations even share personnel, as when "interlocking directorates" include mutual board members on two or more organizations or when different organizations hire the same consultants or researchers. These ties have been found to be central to the process of coalition formation. Kevin Hula (1999) specifies how these institutional

links facilitate coalition formation by solving information problems that must
be resolved when organizations are seeking coalition partners:

> These institutional links can provide effective conduits for the coordination
> of information exchange and group strategy, simplifying the intelligence-
> gathering efforts that would otherwise be required of organizations desiring
> to pursue collective strategies. If organizations are structurally or institu-
> tionally linked to one another, they do not face great challenges in "find-
> ing" one another (the first information problem of coordination), and there
> is a lower cost of discovering their preferences (the second information
> problem of coordination). (55)

In Hula's study, organizations report that these links, established through state-
defined policy subsystems, are important to their political strategy, including
coalition formation.

Just as the creation of discrete state policy realms fosters the creation of
networks among SMOs who then work together in coalition, these state-
defined policy spheres also serve to separate actors in different movements
from their counterparts, thus creating relatively little opportunity for interaction among actors in policy-distinct movements. This is true even when
the issues that different groups address may have considerable overlap. For
example, the Occupational Safety and Health Administration (OSHA), under
the federal Department of Labor, addresses issues associated with worker
health threats posed by toxic substances used in the workplace. Yet the health
consequences of those toxic substances *outside* of the workplace would primarily be the responsibility of a separate entity, the U.S. Environmental
Protection Agency. Thus, this policy segmentation creates separate and distinct realms in which activists from different movements operate. In my research on relations between labor unions and environmental organizations,
movement actors from these respective areas described few instances in which
they were brought together in the course of their daily routines (Obach 2004).
Without these opportunities for regular interaction, the costs associated with
coalition formation are much greater.

In those relatively rare instances when these actors are brought together,
unfamiliarity and suspicion inhibits the forging of common positions. This
is especially true given that, when issues do traverse policy domains, the
initial encounter between groups may occur after organizations have already
staked out a position on the relevant issue independently or within their own
issue community. Such was a case in Wisconsin in the early 1990s. Environmentalists devised a plan to reduce statewide toxic emissions to 1991 levels
by 1995. They worked with a legislator to develop the details of the proposal

even before members of the labor community in the state were made aware of it. Upon learning of the plan, labor leaders immediately spoke out in opposition, fearing that the limits would harm manufacturing industries in the state (Obach 1999). The measure was defeated when environmental advocates were unable to bring labor leaders on board. A similar case occurred in New York when environmentalists announced plans to reduce waste discharges into the Long Island Sound. Their first encounter with labor opposition occurred when union picketers staged a protest outside of a public hearing on the issue (Obach 2004). If these organizations had more interaction with one another through a shared policy subsystem, they probably could have devised a mutually beneficial policy and perhaps formed a coalition to advance it. In fact, in this instance, through a series of meetings and negotiations, these environmentalists and labor leaders in New York were able to come up with a mutually agreeable proposal. But this additional effort would not have been necessary in a context in which cross-movement interactions were more routine. In most cases, that effort is not made, and the initial divisions, such as those found in New York, would persist or grow.

Thus, state institutions play a major role in creating or limiting opportunities for coalition activity. The more proximate organizational issues or those rooted in identity or culture are clearly important, but the underlying institutional factors that influence organizational practices and identity formation must also be considered. This is especially true given that organizational and cultural differences can be overcome if representatives of different movement sectors can be brought together for sustained interaction. In instances where this is done, mutual understanding and compromise often result (Obach 2004). But it is difficult to overcome the differences that inhibit coalition formation without sustained interaction. Although that interaction can occur relatively easily among groups within the same policy sector, the separation of issue organizations caused by state policy segmentation creates significant barriers to other forms of coalition activity.

The addition of state institutional factors to the analysis of coalition processes does not diminish the importance of the role of coalition broker. Brokers are not only important for their ability to smooth cultural differences; they also often create the circumstances in which groups can be brought together despite structural obstacles. Again, unions and environmental organizations provide an example of this process. In the 1980s, national labor and environmental leaders created the OSHA–Environmental Network (later the Labor–Environmental Network) to foster collaborative efforts at the national and state levels (Obach 2004). They recognized that there was relevant issue overlap between them, but that because policies were devised in separate realms (OSHA and the U.S. Environmental Protection Agency, and the corresponding legislative bodies), additional intentional efforts would be needed to bring them together to devise common strategies, a task undertaken by coalition brokers.

This need also exists, but to a lesser degree, for different types of organizations within the same movement. Suzanne Staggenborg (1988) found that professional abortion rights organizations could easily collaborate and form coalitions with one another as a result of the structural compatibility of their work routines and their operation within a common policy subsystem. But alliances with grassroots organizations within the same movement were relatively rare. Such collaboration would likely require a coalition broker to persuade actors in both types of groups of the value of pooled effort. A professional movement staff member, for example, may need to be convinced by a coalition broker that it is worthwhile to meet in the evening at the house of a feminist collective member, rather than to expect the type of daytime office meeting they are accustomed to, but which will never take place with volunteer grassroots movement leaders. By providing a mutually trusted voice, coalition brokers reduce the cost of coalition formation between different types of organizations even within the same movement. They also help to resolve organizational and cultural differences that make coalition functioning difficult.

Structural barriers to coalition formation are not easily overcome, even when coalition brokers are present. This raises the important issue of resource availability. Several coalition scholars have emphasized the role that resources play in fostering or inhibiting coalition activity. Most studies indicate that resource availability helps to foster coalition activity primarily because it reduces competition among organizations dependent on common funding sources (Staggenborg 1986; Van Dyke 2003; Zald and McCarthy 1987). Yet the evidence is mixed when considering coalitions across movements. Nella Van Dyke (2003) found that resource availability had no effect on cross-movement coalition building among organizations on college campuses. But this may be due to the unique position of campus-based organizations, where, as a result of their proximity, information costs associated with learning about other organizations and logistical costs associated with meeting space, coordination among personnel, and so on are minimal. Among other movement organizations, the costs of forging cross-movement coalitions are likely to be higher, which requires resources to cover that cost.

All challenging groups face resource limitations. Organizational interests dictate that they must prioritize their core concerns, and that may not leave time or personnel available to make the additional effort necessary to forge ties with groups outside of their regular circle. The Wisconsin Labor–Environmental Network, a state affiliate of the national OSHA–Environmental Network, provides a prime example of this constraint (Obach 1999). Coalition brokers with ties to both the labor and environmental communities brought these two sets of actors together in the 1980s. Regular meetings provided movement leaders and activists with the opportunities to share concerns, forge bonds, and identify areas of common concern. Yet these were always viewed as extra efforts outside of the routine work of both sets of organizations. Even though personal bonds were formed and real gains were made through their collaborative efforts, the Wisconsin coalition atrophied when a key coalition broker retired from his staff position at one of the unions and an office used for coalition meetings was relocated and merged with another. No additional resources were dedicated to make sure that new staff could organize meetings or that space would be made available for people to conveniently come together.

This is one example of the way in which the availability of resources is important to cross-movement coalition building. Yet the resources necessary to engage in coalition activity are ultimately shaped by state-defined policy spheres, which can facilitate or inhibit routine interaction between movement organizations. Although maintaining ties among environmental organizations or among labor organizations is relatively easy given their routine interactions within the state policy subsystem, coalition work that traverses policy domains is costly—at times prohibitively so.

Tax Law and Coalition Channeling

A second way in which the state channels movement activity is through tax laws and laws governing political activity. According to McCarthy, Britt, and Wolfson, state regulations create "a *tangle of incentives* favoring certain standard forms of organization, tactical approaches and collective goals" (1991, 48). Tax law serves as an important state channeling mechanism for movement organizations. It is here that we once again see the role that resources, and the laws governing obtaining resources, influence coalition formation.

By and large, movement organizations obtain resources from two sources, foundation grants and individual contributions, both of which are significantly influenced by tax law (Walker 1983). Some organizations also receive funding from public sources, which has an additional channeling effect on a group's activity (Chaves, Stephens, and Galaskiewicz 2004; Fremont-Smith 2004; Marwell 2004; Powell 1987; Smith and Lipsky 1993).

For tax purposes, most SMOs define themselves as public charities, which are addressed in section 501(c)(3) of the Internal Revenue Code. This designation has significant resource ramifications for organizations because it not only provides the organization with tax-exempt status, but also allows donations to be tax deductible for the individual donor to the organization. This greatly enhances an organization's appeal for contributions from individual donors. It also makes them eligible for foundation grants, most of which are only available to charitable organizations (Jenkins 1989). Thus, SMO access to resources is crucially dependent on maintaining their tax status. But the opportunity to engage in many forms of political action is substantially limited for 501(c)(3) organizations, representing an important form of state channeling of movement activity.

The most significant channeling element of the Internal Revenue Code is the prohibition on political campaigning by this type of nonprofit movement organization. Such groups cannot "participate in, or intervene in (including the publishing or distributing of statements), any political campaign on behalf of any candidate for public office" (Kindell and Reilly 2002, 336). Given that movements very often have the state as their target, a prohibition on seeking to influence the election of those who are directly responsible for making state policy is a significant restriction. As if the ban on electoral politics was not enough, nonprofit organizations are also restricted in their lobbying activity. The Revenue Act of 1934 added language to existing charity regulations stating that "no substantial part" of a group's activity could include "propaganda" or "attempting to influence legislation" (McCarthy, Britt, and Wolfson 1991, 53). Thus, not only are these movement organizations banned from engaging in electoral activity to choose the state office holders who make policy, but they are also prohibited from engaging in any substantial lobbying activity designed to influence that policy.

Although some amount of political activity is allowable under these rules, there are some indications that the language of the regulations has a chilling effect on many organizations (Avner 2002; Raffa 2000). The ban on engagement in partisan political campaigning is fairly explicit, but limitations on advocacy on policy issues are decidedly unclear. There are two tests that the IRS uses as a basis for determining whether an organization is in compliance with lobbying limits. One is the substantial lobbying test. This traditional measure cites no specific rules or expenditure limits and leaves the determination open to a subjective assessment of whether an organization does more than insubstantial lobbying. The 1976 Lobby Law provided an alternative assessment mechanism that allows nonprofits to opt for a system of accounting for lobbying expenditures that must fall within specified limits (i.e., no more than 20 percent of expenditures for organizations with budgets less than $500,000). Organizations that opt to use this criterion for verifying their tax-exempt status are required to keep careful records on their various expenditures and to submit forms to the IRS demonstrating that they are within the legally defined limits.

Although careful accounting can allow an organization to avoid crossing legal boundaries, given the ambiguity of the rules and the importance of maintaining their tax status, many err on the side of caution and avoid activity that could place them in jeopardy (Avner 2002; Raffa 2000). Some guides for nonprofit organizations include statements that reinforce the danger associated with excessive lobbying. One guide states that "penalties are quite severe" if lobbying laws are violated (Avner 2002, 126). Another indicates that "actual boundaries can, at times, only be ascertained through an in-depth knowledge of the code sections, regulations, revenue rulings and case law" (Raffa 2000). Thomas Raffa (2000), a lawyer and consultant for nonprofit organizations, writes that many 501(c)(3) organizations significantly limit their political activities on the basis of their concerns about losing their tax-exempt status. Surveys of nonprofit executives also found widespread misconceptions, exaggerating the extent to which they were limited in their ability to engage in political activity (Berry 2005).

Although many nonprofit actors underestimate the extent to which they can legally engage in political activity, their caution is not unwarranted because some organizations have indeed lost their tax-exempt status and been subject to fines for violating IRS rules. The Sierra Club, the National Association for the Advancement of Colored People (NAACP), and the League of Women Voters have all lost their tax-exempt status at some point for political involvement that was deemed to cross the legal line (Jenkins 1989; McCarthy, Britt, and Wolfson 1991). In 2004, the NAACP was the target of an IRS investigation when its leader, Julian Bond, made statements critical of the Bush administration at the group's annual convention. Religious organizations have also come under IRS scrutiny for their political activity in recent years (Allen 2004).

Some issue-based nonprofit organizations get around the political limits imposed by IRS rules by creating separate sister organizations that establish themselves as "social welfare organizations" under section 501(c)(4) of the IRS tax code. This enables these entities to engage in unlimited lobbying activity. However, such organizations must ensure that their political actions are not intertwined directly with their main charitable counterpart. It is also the case that contributions to this type of organization are not tax deductible for the donors, and thus access to resources is greatly curtailed.

IRS regulations clearly impose extensive restrictions on the political activity of individual groups, but in doing so, they also limit opportunities for coalition involvement. Marie Hojnacki (1998) found that 501(c)(3) status diminished organizations' coalition participation. Obviously 501(c)(3) organizations are excluded from coalitions working directly on political campaigns. Given that elected officials are ultimately responsible for creating policy across a vast range of issue areas, electoral politics represents perhaps the greatest opportunity for movement organizations of diverse types to come together and work in coalition. Yet such participation is banned, thereby significantly limiting opportunities for an important type of coalition activity. This is especially important when we consider alliances between organized labor and other movement organizations (Kriesi 1996). Under the IRS tax code, labor unions are not classified as charitable organizations, and they are not restricted in their political activity in the same way as most other professional movement organizations. Unions are classified under the IRS Code as 501(c)(5) organizations, which renders them exempt from paying taxes, but unlike charitable organizations, contributions to labor unions are not tax deductible. In addition, unions are allowed to engage in unlimited lobbying, and more importantly, they are allowed to participate in political campaign activities (Reilly and Allen 2003).

For some labor organizations, lobbying and engaging in electoral politics are among their most important functions. This is true for labor federations that exist at the local, state, and national levels. Individual unions are primarily occupied with advancing the work-related interests of their own members through negotiation and bargaining with employers at the workplace. But union federations, those collections of unions from different employment sectors, coordinate on electoral strategy and to advance broad political goals.

In some cases, the goals adopted by organized labor extend beyond narrow work-related issues to include causes that are relevant to other movement sectors such as environmentalists, civil rights organizations, feminist groups, and senior citizens' associations, thus creating an opportunity for coalition activity. But despite the potential for movement coalitions involving union federations and issue-based groups, labor's extensive involvement in partisan activity can hinder movement coalition participation in at least two ways. First, those building movement coalitions around political issues may perceive labor entities as being too partisan and electorally focused. For a coalition composed primarily of nonpartisan nonprofit entities, partisan groups are not likely to be sought for involvement because their partisan orientation could violate the prohibition under which 501(c)(3) organizations must operate. Second, labor's focus on electoral politics creates a social network barrier between them and groups that cannot engage in such activity. Those crucial shared spaces that have been identified as necessary for the development of trust relationships are severely curtailed such that even when issues arise that would be relevant to a labor constituency, the bonds are not there to foster collective effort.

This may help to explain American labor's predominant business union orientation. Many labor scholars characterize U.S. unions as having a particularly narrow approach to politics and workplace advocacy (Dreiling 1998; Dreiling and Robertson 1998; Seidman 1994). At the workplace, unions tend to focus almost exclusively on wages, hours, and working conditions—the legally defined mandatory subjects of collective bargaining. In the political sphere, relative to the social union approach of their European counterparts, U.S. unions are more narrowly focused on directly work-related issues that are of particular interest to their members, as opposed to serving as a voice representing a broader swath of disadvantaged groups. This, in itself, can be attributed in part to state channeling mechanisms. By explicitly defining the mandatory subjects of collective bargaining, the state is orienting unions in ways that spill over into their political activity. Union leaders who are immersed in contract struggles focused on wages, hours, and working conditions are not likely to step into their political roles and abandon those concerns in favor of environmental protection, abortion rights, or gun control. Even federation leaders, who are free to pursue broader political objectives, have typically risen to power through individual unions where their perspective on labor's role was conditioned by the narrow concerns legally specified for collective bargaining. This is certainly not the only cause of U.S. labor's business union orientation. For example, some scholars point to the purging of class-oriented radicals during the cold war era as having had a constricting effect on labor's agenda (Zieger 1994). Yet although U.S. labor's conservatism can be explained on the basis of several factors, state channeling of certain movements away from coalition strategies should not be dismissed. Greater opportunity to interact with their nonpartisan, nonprofit counterparts would undoubtedly shape the way in which labor leaders approach political action and create more opportunities for coalition activity.

Cross-movement interaction has the effect of broadening organizational agendas and facilitating more encompassing approaches to social change (Obach 2004; Van Dyke 2003). But such interactions are relatively rare, in part as a result of the policy domain segregation described above, as well as the electoral campaign prohibition that limits opportunities for nonprofit issue groups to work in concert with organized labor. In this way, state institutions channel some organizations away from others, creating self-reinforcing distinctions, inhibiting the development of common understandings, and preventing the identification of shared concerns.

Conclusion

Coalition building is a central strategy used by SMOs and can be a key factor in social movement success. Thus, there is a growing body of research examining the conditions under which coalitions are likely to form. Political opportunity theorists have examined some of the proximate causes of coalition formation. Although several relevant variables have been identified, the enduring influence of state institutions on coalition development has been largely overlooked. Here I have analyzed the way in which state institutions in the United States create the opportunity for coalition participation among some while closing off this opportunity for others. Two factors in particular have been identified as important: state policy segmentation and tax laws.

Both of these mechanisms channel SMOs into or away from certain coalition partnerships. Policy segmentation provides extensive opportunity for coalition development among organizations within the policy subsystem. By defining policy spheres and creating the institutional mechanisms through which those policies will be addressed, the state is creating venues in which certain groups will be routinely brought together. At the same time, the state is cordoning off other policy matters, and in doing so, it limits the opportunity for cross-movement interaction. This is related to the well-established need for interaction among movement actors in order to develop the shared understandings and identities necessary for cooperative action. By creating discrete policy domains, the state is creating the political opportunity for coalition formation among some while closing off that opportunity for others.

Similarly, state tax policies and the associated restrictions on political activity channel organizations apart or together depending on their tax designation. The most crucial channeling mechanism is the prohibition on electoral political participation for organizations categorized under Internal Revenue Code section 501(c)(3) as public charities. By imposing this ban, the state greatly limits the opportunity for such groups to join in coalition with one another around electoral campaigns and greatly limits the opportunity for such groups to work with those categorized under sections of the code that allow for electoral engagement, such as labor unions.

By separating issue-based movement organizations from the labor movement in this way, the state is not only inhibiting certain coalition types, but by extension, it is also shaping the general political trajectory of the nation. This legal divide contributes to the segregation of class-based politics tied to organized labor from the issue-oriented movements that have grown in prominence since the mid-twentieth century. Although many factors differentiate the issues addressed by these relatively new movements from the concerns that have historically occupied American labor unions, the role of the state in limiting political opportunities for cross-movement coalition formation is an important consideration. State policies, by design or historical happenstance, greatly inhibit the formation of alliances of working-class and middle-class movement organizations represented by labor unions and issue-oriented new social movements, and this has significant implications for the overall trajectory of American politics.

In addition to the domestic movement coalition issues considered here, this work also raises questions about international movement coalition formation. As demonstrated here, national political institutions shape and constrain movement coalition propensities. Most movement organizations are based within individual countries, and their practices and abilities are thus shaped by the domestic policies that govern them. To the extent that these laws differ between nations, SMOs will adopt practices that may be incompatible with their counterparts elsewhere, thus undermining the prospects for international movement coalition formation.

Yet at the same time, international trade agreements and coordinating bodies such as the World Trade Organization are harmonizing the rules by which multinational corporations and other international economic entities operate. Thus, global cooperation among the powerful economic forces typically targeted by SMOs is growing, while the domestic rules that create incompatibilities among nationally based movement organizations remain. In an age of increasing globalization, especially in the economic sphere, this places popular movements at a grave disadvantage relative to their globally integrated and coordinated adversaries. The role of state channeling in social movement coalition formation is considerable and its implications broad, not just for the domestic U.S. case analyzed here, but for the overall development of movements internationally.

Works Cited

Allen, Mike. 2004. "NAACP Faces IRS Investigation." *Washington Post,* October 29, A08.

Altemose, J. Rick, and Dawn McCarty. 2001. "Organizing for Democracy through Faith-Based Institutions." In *Forging Radical Alliances across Difference,* edited by Jill Bystydzienski and Steven Schacht, 133–45. Lanham, Md.: Rowman & Littlefield.

Avner, Marcia. 2002. *The Lobbying and Advocacy Handbook for Nonprofit Organizations.* Saint Paul, Minn.: Amherst H. Wilder Foundation.

Barvosa-Carter, Edwina. 2001. "Multiple Identity and Coalition Building." In *Forging Radical Alliances across Difference,* edited by Jill Bystydzienski and Steven Schacht, 21–34. Lanham, Md.: Rowman & Littlefield.

Berry, Jeffrey M. 2005. *A Voice for Nonprofits.* Washington, D.C.: Brookings Institution.

Brecher, Jeremy, and Tim Costello. 1990. *Building Bridges: The Emerging Grassroots Coalition of Labor and Community.* New York: Monthly Review Press.

Bystydzienski, Jill, and Steven Schacht, eds. 2001. *Forging Radical Alliances across Difference.* Lanham, Md.: Rowman & Littlefield.

Chaves, Mark, Laura Stephens, and Joseph Galaskiewicz. 2004. "Does Government Funding Suppress Nonprofits' Political Activity?" *American Sociological Review* 69: 292–316.

Cress, Daniel. 1997. "Nonprofit Incorporation among Movements of the Poor: Pathways and Consequences for Homeless Social Movement Organizations." *Sociological Quarterly* 38: 343–60.

Dreiling, Michael. 1998. "From Margin to Center: Environmental Justice and Social Unionism as Sites for Intermovement Solidarity." *Race, Class, and Gender* 6: 51–69.

Dreiling, Michael, and Ian Robertson. 1998. "Union Responses to NAFTA in the U.S. and Canada: Exploring Intra- and International Variation." *Mobilization* 3: 163–84.

Fremont-Smith, Marion. 2004. *Governing Nonprofit Organizations.* Cambridge, Mass.: Harvard University Press.

Friedman, Debra, and Doug McAdam. 1992. "Collective Identities and Activism: Networks, Choices, and the Life of a Social Movement." In *Frontiers in Social Movement Theory,* edited by Aldon D. Morris and Carol Mueller, 156–73. New Haven, Conn.: Yale University Press.

Gamson, William. 1990. *The Strategy of Social Protest.* 2nd ed. Belmont, Calif.: Wadsworth.

Gitlin, Todd. 1993. "The Rise of 'Identity Politics': An Examination and Critique." *Dissent* 40: 172–77.

Grattet, Ryken. 2005. "The Policy Nexus: Professional Networks and the Formulation and Adoption of Workers' Compensation Reforms." In *Routing the Opposition: Social Movements, Public Policy and Democracy,* edited by David S. Meyer, Valerie Jenness, and Helen Ingram, 177–206. Minneapolis: University of Minnesota Press.

Grossman, Zoltan. 2001. "'Let's not create evilness for this river': Interethnic Environmental Alliances of Native Americans and Rural Whites in Northern Wisconsin." In *Forging Radical Alliances across Difference,* edited by Jill Bystydzienski and Steven Schacht, 146–59. Lanham, Md.: Rowman & Littlefield.

Hojnacki, Marie. 1998. "Organized Interests' Advocacy Behavior in Alliances." *Political Research Quarterly* 51: 437–59.

Hula, Kevin W. 1999. *Lobbying Together.* Washington, D.C.: Georgetown University Press.

Jenkins, J. Craig. 1989. "Social Movement Philanthropy and American Democracy." In *Philanthropic Giving: Studies in Varieties and Goals,* edited by Richard Magat, 292–314. New York: Oxford University Press.

Jenkins, J. Craig, and Craig Eckert. 1986. "Channeling Black Insurgency: Elite Patronage and Professional Social Movement Organizations in the Development of the Black Movement." *American Sociological Review* 51: 812–29.

Jenkins-Smith, Hank. 1991. "Explaining Change in Policy Subsystems: Analysis of Coalition Stability and Defection Over Time." *American Journal of Political Science* 35: 851–80.

Jenkins-Smith, Hank, and Paul Sabatier. 1994. "Evaluating the Advocacy Coalition Framework." *Journal of Public Policy* 14: 175–203.

Kindell, Judith, and John Francis Reilly. 2002. "Election Year Issues." http://www.irs.gov/pub/irs-tege/eotopici02.pdf. Accessed April 8, 2010.

Kriesi, Hanspeter. 1996. "The Organizational Structure of New Social Movements in a Political Context." In *Comparative Perspectives on Social Movements,* edited by Doug McAdam, John McCarthy, and Mayer Zald, 152–84. Cambridge: Cambridge University Press.

Loomis, Burdett. 1986. "Coalitions of Interests: Building Bridges in the Balkanized State." In *Interest Group Politics,* 2nd ed., edited by Allen Cigler and Burdett Loomis, 258–74. Washington, D.C.: CQ Press.

Marwell, Nicole P. 2004. "Privatizing the Welfare State: Nonprofit Community Based Organizations as Political Actors." *American Sociological Review* 69: 265–91.

McAdam, Doug. 1982. *Political Process and the Development of the Black Insurgency, 1930–1970.* Chicago: University of Chicago Press.

———. 1966. "Conceptual Origins, Current Problems, Future Directions." In *Comparative Perspectives on Social Movements,* edited by Doug McAdam, John McCarthy, and Mayer Zald, 23–40. Cambridge: Cambridge University Press.

McAdam, Doug, John McCarthy, and Mayer Zald, eds. 1996. *Comparative Perspectives on Social Movements.* Cambridge: Cambridge University Press.

McCammon, Holly J., and Karen E. Campbell. 2002. "Allies on the Road to Victory: Coalition Formation between the Suffragists and the Women's Christian Temperance Union." *Mobilization* 7: 231–51.

McCarthy, John D., and Mayer N. Zald. 1977. "Resource Mobilization and Social Movements: A Partial Theory." *American Journal of Sociology* 82: 1212–93.

McCarthy, John D., David Britt, and Mark Wolfson. 1991. "The Institutional Channeling of Social Movements by the State in the United States." *Research in Social Movements, Conflict and Change* 13: 45–76.

Melucci, Alberto. 1994. "A Strange Kind of Newness: What's 'New' in New Social Movements?" In *New Social Movements: From Ideology to Identity,* edited by

Enrique Laraña, Hank Johnston, and Joseph R. Gusfield, 101–30. Philadelphia: Temple University Press

Meyer, David. 2004. "Protest and Political Opportunities." *Annual Review of Sociology* 30: 125–45.

———. 2005. "Introduction: Social Movements and Public Policy." In *Routing the Opposition,* edited by David Meyer, Valerie Jenness, and Helen Ingram, 1–26. Minneapolis: University of Minnesota Press.

Meyer, David, and Catherine Corrigall-Brown. 2005. "Coalitions and Political Context: U.S. Movements against Wars in Iraq." *Mobilization* 10: 327–44.

Obach, Brian. 1999. "The Wisconsin Labor–Environmental Network: A Case Study of Coalition Formation among Organized Labor and the Environmental Movement." *Organization and Environment* 12: 45–74.

———. 2004. *Labor and the Environmental Movement: The Quest for Common Ground.* Cambridge, Mass.: MIT Press.

Piven, Frances Fox, and Richard Cloward. 1977. *Poor People's Movements.* New York: Pantheon.

Powell, Walter W. 1987. *The Nonprofit Sector: A Research Handbook.* New Haven, Conn.: Yale University Press.

Raffa, Thomas. 2000. "Advocacy and Lobbying without Fear: What Is Allowed within a 501(c)(3) Charitable Organization?" *Non-Profit Quarterly* 7, no. 2: 1–4. http://www.iknow.org/pdf/RAFFA_LOBBY_reprint1.pdf. Accessed April 8, 2010.

Reilly, John Francis, and Barbara A. Braig Allen. 2003. "Political Campaign and Lobbying Activities of IRC 501(c)(4), (c)(5), and (c)(6) Organizations." http://www.irs.gov/pub/irs-tege/eotopicl03.pdf. Accessed April 8, 2010.

Rose, Fred. 2000. *Coalitions across the Class Divide.* Ithaca, N.Y.: Cornell University Press.

Sabatier, Paul. 1988. "An Advocacy Coalition Framework of Policy Change and the Role of Policy Oriented Learning Therein." *Policy Sciences* 21: 129–68.

Salisbury, Robert H., John P. Heinz, Edward O. Laumann, and Robert L. Nelson. 1987. "Who Works with Whom? Interest Group Alliances and Opposition." *American Political Science Review* 81: 1217–34.

Seidman, Gay. 1994. *Manufacturing Militance.* Berkeley: University of California Press.

Smith, Steven, and Michael Lipsky. 1993. *Non-Profits for Hire: The Welfare State in the Age of Contracting.* Cambridge, Mass.: Harvard University Press.

Staggenborg, Suzanne. 1986. "Coalition Work in the Pro-Choice Movement: Organizational and Environmental Opportunities and Obstacles." *Social Problems* 33: 374–90.

———. 1988. "The Consequences of Professionalization and Formalization in the Pro-Choice Movement." *American Sociological Review* 53: 585–606.

Tarrow, Sidney. 1996. "States and Opportunities." In *Comparative Perspectives on*

Social Movements, edited by Doug McAdam, John McCarthy, and Mayer Zald, 41–61. Cambridge: Cambridge University Press.

Taylor, Verta, and Nancy Whittier. 1992. "Collective Identity in Social Movement Communities: Lesbian Feminist Mobilization." In *Frontiers in Social Movement Theory,* edited by Aldon Morris and Carol McClurg Mueller, 104–30. New Haven, Conn.: Yale University Press.

Tilly, Charles. 1978. *From Mobilization to Revolution.* Englewood Cliffs, N.J.: Prentice-Hall.

Van Dyke, Nella. 2003. "Crossing Movement Boundaries: Factors That Facilitate Coalition Protest by American College Students, 1930–1990." *Social Problems* 50: 226–50.

Walker, Jack L. 1983. "The Origins and Maintenance of Interest Groups in America." *American Political Science Review* 77: 390–406.

Weber, Max. 1946. "Bureaucracy." In *From Max Weber,* edited by H. H. Gerth and C. Wright Mills, 196–244. New York: Oxford University Press.

Zald, Mayer, and John D. McCarthy. 1987. *Social Movements in an Organizational Society.* New Brunswick, N.J.: Transaction.

Zieger, Robert H. 1994. *American Workers, American Unions.* Baltimore: Johns Hopkins University Press.

10
Sustained Interactions?
Social Movements and Coalitions in Local Settings

Mario Diani, Isobel Lindsay, and Derrick Purdue

In this chapter, we look at coalition activity in two British cities with very different political cultures and traditions: Bristol and Glasgow. However, we do so from a slightly different angle than other studies of the same topic; we take up some basic issues regarding the relationship between social movements and coalitions. We posit that coalition work among activists and their organizations can occur before the formation of a social movement, or at least before the entrance of these specific activists and their groups into the social movement. We argue that the shift from coalition interactions among organizations to their social movement participation is a shift more likely to occur in certain political contexts—specifically, as we develop in detail in this chapter, in local political cultures that are more radical and structured by deeper political and social cleavages.

We begin our discussion by distinguishing between coalition activity and social movement activity. We then turn to our analysis of two cities, Glasgow and Bristol. In Glasgow, we find that organizational involvement in sustained interactions in coalitions results in traits normally associated with social movements. But this is not the case in Bristol, where coalition activity does not translate into social movement activity. We account for these differences in light of different political opportunities in the two cities. In particular, we refer to two distinct political cultures: one, in Glasgow, is still quite polarized along class lines, and a neat distinction is retained between protest politics and pressure politics; the other, in Bristol, is characterized by moderation and convergence on the middle ground, by the pacification of class cleavage, and by nonconfrontational styles of issue representation.

Coalitions and Movements

Few would disagree with views of social movements as "coalition affairs, featuring sometimes loosely negotiated alliances among groups and individuals with different agendas . . . often comprised of multiple formal coalitions"
(Meyer and Corrigall-Brown 2005, 329). However, at the analytical level,
there are important differences that prevent us from treating social movements as mere aggregates of coalitions. In an early attempt to capture the
peculiarity of social movement processes, Diani (1992, 13) developed a view
of movements as networks "of informal interactions between a plurality of
individuals, groups, or associations engaged in a political or cultural conflict
on the basis of a shared collective identity."

Diani (1992; Diani and Bison 2004) also argues that although both
social movements and coalitions consist of dense interorganizational networks,
only the former display high levels of collective identity. Citizens' organizations do not necessarily need specific identity bonds to become involved in
dense collaborative exchanges with groups with similar concerns and to address
the same specific issues. Nor will they have necessarily elaborated one by the
time the specific actions and campaigns in which they were interested are
over. Joining forces to push forward a certain agenda may simply be driven
by an instrumental logic. If that is the case, specific coalition activities and
protest events will not be linked by actors into more encompassing narratives, which might assign them a broader meaning and make them part of a
sustained series of collective actions.

This view of coalitions is highly consistent with classic definitions of
this concept: "a group of players who are able to make binding agreements
to implement agreed strategies" (Hargreaves Heap et al. 1992, 95); "temporary, means oriented alliances among individuals or groups which differ in
goals . . . [with] little value consensus . . . [and] tacit neutrality on matters
which go beyond the immediate prerogatives" (Gamson 1961, 374); and an
"interacting group of individuals, deliberately constructed, independent of
the formal structure, lacking its own internal formal structure, consisting of
mutually perceived membership, issue oriented, focused on a goal or goals
external to the coalition, and requiring concerted member action" (Stevenson, Pearce, and Porter 1985, 261).

There are at least two elements shared by these approaches, although
they are most explicit in Gamson's passage: the definitions tell us that coalitions tend to focus on short-term objectives and that they abstain from explicit
expression of longer-term goals and broader values. These traits are clearly at
odds with dominant accounts of social movements that emphasize—if from

different angles—the role of longer-term values and identities, and a movement's capacity to weave together in broad narratives different campaigns and episodes of contention (e.g., Melucci 1989; Tilly 1994). Coalition work, on the other hand, is well reflected in how a community organizer from Bristol portrays the approach of his organization to mobilizing the local citizenry:

> We will encourage people to develop campaigns around specific things that has a short life. And when that campaign is finished then those people might lose interest. And different people next week might have another interest. And so we see our role as often times providing a meeting place, where people can meet to do those activities, or we or individual members might feel that is something they want to participate in. (Leader of a black and minority organization, Bristol)

Admittedly, some views of coalitions allow more space for the role of shared values and understandings. In particular, proponents of the concept of advocacy coalitions define them as "people from various governmental and private organizations who both (1) share a set of normative and causal beliefs and (2) engage in a nontrivial degree of co-ordinated activity over time" (Sabatier and Jenkins-Smith 1999, 120). This approach has often been applied to coalitions largely consisting of public interest groups, nongovernmental organizations, and social movement organizations (e.g., Ruzza 2004), and it has the advantage of recognizing the importance of shared beliefs and norms that brings it beyond the instrumentalism of many definitions of coalitions. At the same time, however, analyses of advocacy coalitions are mainly oriented to policy making rather than contention and mobilization.

In a social movement process, there will be more than networks of alliances and collaborations. Of course, organizations involved in a movement dynamic will share both material and symbolic resources in order to promote more effective campaigns, and they will be fairly closely linked to each other. But most important, they will also identify each other as part of a broader collective actor, whose goals and existence cannot be constrained within the boundaries of any specific protest event or campaign. The role of collective identity in linking organizations to each other will enable them to feel part of the same collective effort, even when specific campaigns or initiatives may be over, and to develop further joint actions on that basis.

To sum up, in order to capture the distinction between movements and coalitions, we need to recognize the role of the processes of meaning attribution that enable actors joining forces on one specific issue to locate their effort in a broader perspective. These may take different forms. They may consist of processes of cultural and identity production through which identifying symbols and shared understandings are produced and shared by activists and organizations. But they may also develop through the interactions that are created when the same organizations are mobilized in different campaigns, thus creating a connection between them and strengthening the sense of commonality between people and groups active in them.

This is the focus of our contribution. In what follows, we explore whether getting involved in numerous coalitions in the local sphere, and in the resulting interactions with other actors, actually increases actors' identification with social movements, or more broadly correlates with social movements' distinctive features.

Networks of Participatory Civic Organizations in Bristol and Glasgow

The data used in this chapter come from a broader project on networking by citizens' organizations in two British cities, Glasgow and Bristol (see also Baldassarri and Diani 2007, 745–50). We chose them as locations for our analysis because of the density and complexity of their associational life and because of their contrasting histories and civic cultures—Bristol, with its reputation for new social movement activity, and Glasgow, where so-called old left socialism continues to make its presence felt. Glasgow is an industrial city with shipbuilding as a major industry, a large working class, widespread endemic poverty, and a history of confrontational politics based on deep social cleavages. Obvious structural cleavages include the national polarization of Scotland against the central power of Britain, a religious sectarian divide between the dominant Protestantism of Scotland and a Catholic (Irish by origin) working class, and a history of class conflict and rent strikes (Budge et al. 2001). The Labour Party has strong historical roots in Glasgow and has been able to develop an "urban growth machine" (Logan and Molotch 1987) style of Labour politics. The main minority group in Glasgow, Pakistani Muslims, is well integrated into the Labour Party.

By contrast, Bristol is a southern English mercantile city set in a conservative rural region, with its wealth built on slavery, tobacco, chocolate, and aircraft production. Bristol is an affluent city with pockets of deprivation; it has high property values and a growing service sector, particularly on the northern fringe. The urban regime in Bristol has always been a little fragile, weakened by divisions between private and public sectors, within the public sector by competing authorities, and by a geographic north–south split in the city (Stewart, 1996, 2003). Bristol's civic culture has a mixed reputation. On the one hand, the city has been criticized for lacking a collaborative culture linking the public and private sectors and for a dearth of clear political leadership (Stewart, 1996, 2003). However, Bristol does have a stronger claim to well-developed networks within civil society, with more than a thousand groups in the Bristol and Bath area (Purdue et al. 1997).

The present study focuses on participatory organizations promoting advocacy and interest representation on a broad range of public issues. Organizations focusing on service delivery were not included unless they also engaged in at least some type of political pressure. In principle, it would have been desirable to map the whole set of organizations promoting collective action on public issues, whether on a service delivery– or a protest-oriented basis. However, resource limitations and the need to conduct costly face-to-face interviews, given the complexity of data collection on networks, forced us to concentrate on organizations active on a smaller set of issues. Between 2001 and 2002, data were collected for 124 organizations in Glasgow and 134 in Bristol, the main focuses of which were evenly distributed among issues of the environment, ethnicity and migration, community, and social exclusion, with a slight overrepresentation of environmental groups in Bristol and ethnic and migrant groups in Glasgow.[1]

Environmental issues included both classic conservation themes and urban ecology issues, promoted by both formal associations and grassroots groups. Ethnic and migration issues covered both a broad agenda on multiculturalism, equal opportunities, citizenship rights, and minority members' access to educational and welfare provisions, and a more specific agenda promoting migration-related—in particular, asylum-seekers'—interests, often involving the Pakistani, Indian, and Afro-Caribbean communities. Community issues included a whole range of themes related to the welfare of local communities and neighborhoods, from community development to the quality of service provision to local crime. Once again, they were acted on by a broad range of actors ranging from neighborhood associations to single-issue campaigns. Finally, social exclusion issues included all aspects of social inequality, from unemployment to education to poverty, addressed at the local, national, and global levels. These issues were taken up by a highly heterogeneous set of organizations, from voluntary associations focusing on capacity building in the community to direct-action groups.

These four main issues were chosen because they were distinctive enough to be the object of action by specific organizations, while at the same time they were amenable to attempts to merge them into broader and more encompassing agendas. Although nothing prevented the organizations we studied from acting mainly as independent organizations, it was possible for them to bridge their own issue priorities in broader agendas, similar to those promoted by large-scale coalitions and possibly social movements.

All the organizations that according to informants played a significant role at least at the city level were included. As for community organizations, rather than taking a small sample from across each city, efforts were concentrated on two areas, both relatively deprived. These were the Southside in Glasgow, an area with a massive historical presence of the working class, including neighborhoods such as Govan, Govanhill, Gorbals, and Pollokshields; and in Bristol, the area including the neighborhoods of Easton, Knowles, Withywood, and Hartcliffe, featuring a strong presence of ethnic minorities. If during the interviews other organizations not included in our original list were named as important allies by our respondents, they were noted; subjects from these organizations were interviewed after at least three references had been made. We have strong reasons to believe that with the exception of one ethnic organization in Bristol, all of the most central organizations in the two cities were contacted. Although many organizations were mentioned by respondents (over five hundred in both cities), none received more than three nominations. Only one interview was refused (by a Bristolian group that was central in the ethnic and migrants network but was going through a serious—if temporary—organizational crisis).

The organizations we interviewed differed on many characteristics. About one quarter of them had been established in the last five years, while a similar share had been in operation for over twenty years, with some of them dating back to the late nineteenth century. About one quarter focused on specific neighborhoods, while four in ten operated mainly at the city level. The rest combined local action with action at the national or transnational level. A proportion ranging from one third in Bristol to almost half in Glasgow had no formal membership, while about one in ten had a local membership exceeding a thousand. About one third had yearly budgets below £10,000 and could not count on any paid staff, not even on a part-time basis, while about one tenth had budgets exceeding £100,000 and more than twenty staff. Some (one in four) displayed very loose organizational forms, while others (one fifth in Bristol, one third in Glasgow) were highly formalized (Baldassarri and Diani 2007, 747).

Events and Coalitions in Local Civic Networks

In an immediate sense, by promoting or supporting a specific event, organizations become involved in a coalition. Joint involvement in public events creates opportunities for interactions that become sustained to the extent that the same organizations participate in several events over the years. Consistently with the Simmelian assumption that shared activities generate ties between the actors involved in them (Simmel 1955), we can investigate the shift from coalitions to movements by looking at how the interactions developed in one campaign are reproduced in another campaign. To this purpose, in both cities, we asked respondents to tell us about their organization's involvement in events (sometimes campaigns) that had taken place since the mid-1990s. Altogether, we looked at twenty-six events in Glasgow and seventeen in Bristol covering three phases in the two cities' recent history: the early 1990s (up to 1995), the late 1990s (1996–2000), and the early 2000s (Figure 10.1). The overall levels of involvement in events in the two cities were very similar (Figure 10.2).

These events were not necessarily protest driven or confrontational in nature. Many focused on influencing public opinion and/or policy makers through persuasion and good practice rather than threat. Some were even sponsored by the councils or other public agencies. Some events addressed ethnic and migrant issues, ranging from annual multicultural festivals largely symbolic in character to militant actions on specific instances of racial hatred or discrimination. Others shared what could be called an environmental justice frame, which linked urban ecology events, from opposition to local motorways, incinerators, or quarries, to the fight for social services in the local

Events[a]	Bristol	Glasgow
Before 1996	7	8
1996–2000	16	18
After 2000	8	18

[a] The sum of events exceeds 26 in Glasgow and 17 in Bristol because some events occur across more than one period (e.g., May Day marches, International Women's Day). More specifically, in Glasgow, four events span the late 1990s to early 2000s; two cover the entire 1990s. In Bristol, two events span the entire 1990s and two the late 1990s to early 2000s.

Figure 10.1. Distribution of events over time.

Events attended	Bristol (%) (N = 134)[a]	Glasgow (%) (N = 124)[a]
None	23	23
Up to 25 percent	61	55
25 percent to 50 percent	10	14
50 percent to 75 percent	6	5
More than 75 percent	0	3

[a] The figures in parentheses refer to the density of the entire network, including organizations established after 1996.

Figure 10.2. Percentage of events attended by civic organizations in the two cities (out of twenty-six in Glasgow and seventeen in Bristol).

communities or for better working conditions. Still others could be associated with global inequality, from Global Resistance actions to demonstrations to support asylum seekers, to campaigns targeting specific brands such as Nestlè (the Baby Milk Action Campaign in Bristol) or the Gap.

In both cities, the networks generated by these interactions display a cliquish structure that becomes less and less dense as the number of joint events required to posit the existence of a tie grows. They are also entirely connected, apart from a nonnegligible number of isolates (about one quarter; see Figure 10.2). In Glasgow, moving from very weak ties, where just one shared event out of twenty-six is required to posit a tie between two organizations, to strong ties, where two organizations share a link only if they have been involved in over one third of the local events, generates a much less connected network, as the density (Wasserman and Faust 1994, 101–3) drops from 0.38 to 0.005. Out of 124 organizations, 111 are isolates in the latter network. The remaining thirteen are connected in a core consisting of a single component. This approximates a so-called two clique, because all actors can be reached through one intermediate step. Conversely, when we relax the criteria for inclusion in the network and take weaker ties into account, this results in more organizations being added to the original core, rather than in the emergence of separate components disconnected from the rest of the network. For all the differences in the issues addressed in these events and for all the variation in their nature (all the way from confrontational grassroots protest events to routinized, council-backed public festivals), in Glaswegian civil society, there does not seem to be segmentation in the distribution of interactions between citizens' organizations. The same picture applies to Bristol, with network density dropping from 0.36 to 0.002 and 125 organizations out of 134 ending up isolates if involvement in at least one third of the events is taken as a threshold for the presence of a tie.

Local Peculiarities

Although civil society networks seem to display pretty similar structures across very different cities (also see Baldassarri and Diani 2007), one difference bears mentioning: the composition of the inner core in the two cities. In Glasgow, most organizations jointly involved in a high number of coalitions claim to identify with a social movement of some kind. These organizations include loose networks of groups promoting campaigns on globalization (Globalized Resistance), housing (Defend Council Housing), or local facilities such as public swimming pools (Milton), organizations close to new social movements such as Woman Aid or the Green Party, as well as old and new left organizations such as the Scottish Trade Unions or the Scottish Socialist Party.

In Bristol, in contrast, the inner core is evenly split between organizations identifying and not identifying with social movements. The core is also more homogeneous, with most organizations dealing with a development–health–environmental agenda, from Oxfam to the Soil Association via organizations fostering opportunities for ethnic minorities such as the Centre for Employment and Enterprise Development, or caring for the mentally ill such as Missing Link.

This suggests that the link between coalitions and social movements (and accordingly, the view of social movements as nested coalitions) might prove somehow problematic. It is thus worth exploring the relationship, if any, between the strength of interactions and organizations' characteristics. Do organizations defining themselves as part of social movements or displaying the traits usually associated with social movements also get more involved in public events (and thus in the sustained interactions or coalitions originating from them)? To address these issues, we ran separate regressions for the two cities on the percentage of events attended by the organizations. Independent variables (Table 10.1) include properties usually associated with social movements, such as identification with a movement and propensity to protest (see Diani 2005 for operationalizations). To allow for differences in local agendas in the two cities, we brought in as control variables levels of interest in five different macro issues: social exclusion, ethnicity and migration, housing, environmental, and globalization (again, see Diani 2005 for operationalizations). Finally, to check for the possibility that intensity of coalition work

Table 10.1. Mean Values of Variables in the Regression Equation, by City

Variable	Glasgow	Bristol	Total	p Value[a]
Percentage of public events attended	16.9	15.5	16.2	.524
Movement identification (0–1)	0.46	0.62	0.54	.010
Protest repertoire[b]	32	26	29	.067
Social exclusion issues[b]	50	40	45	.014
Ethnicity and migration issues[b]	41	25	33	.000
Housing issues[b]	47	26	36	.000
Environmental issues[b]	28	31	30	.465
Globalization issues[b]	23	22	22	.707
Degree of organizational formalization (0–9)	4.98	5.44	5.22	.086
Registered members	6,151	4,599	5,345	.804

[a] t-test.
[b] On a scale of 1 to 100 (see Diani 2005 for details).

and involvement in interactions is a function of organizational resources, we also include membership size and degree of organizational formalization. The two cities significantly differ in attention to social exclusion, ethnic groups and migrants and housing issues (attention is greater in Glasgow than in Bristol), and in the proportion of organizations identifying as part of social movements (greater in Bristol than in Glasgow).

The results provide an ambiguous answer to our question because the two cities turn out to differ substantially (Table 10.2). In Glasgow, the level of involvement in local events is certainly a function of interest in specific issues, particularly those related to ethnic minorities and migrants. Yet even controlling for these variables, high propensity to use protest tactics is also a significant predictor of the number of events in which organizations are involved, whereas the amount of resources controlled by organizations has no impact whatsoever. In Glasgow, frequent involvement in coalitions seems to co-occur with at least some of the traits normally associated with social movements.

In Bristol, in contrast, neither movement identities nor protest orientations predict involvement in events, nor does attention to any specific issue. The overall performance of the model is much poorer than in Glasgow (8 percent of adjusted variance explained for Bristol vs. 44 percent for Glasgow). The only variable that turns out to be significantly related to involvement in events for Bristol is a measure of the amount of organizational resources as reflected in membership levels: the more resources organizations can bank on, the more involved they tend to be in local events.

Table 10.2. Predicting Levels of Involvement in Public Events in Glasgow and Bristol

Variable	Glasgow		Bristol	
	Beta	p Value[a]	Beta	p Value[a]
Movement identification	0.101	.202	−0.101	.265
Protest repertoire	0.403	.000	−0.123	.252
Social exclusion issues	0.138	.217	0.07	.566
Ethnicity and migration issues	0.247	.013	0.026	.823
Housing issues	0.067	.476	−0.139	.180
Environmental issues	0.029	.749	−0.107	.418
Globalization issues	0.073	.446	0.181	.216
Degree of organizational formalization	−0.034	.671	0.134	.183
Registered members	−0.021	.771	0.239	.007
Adjusted R^2	0.434	.000	0.081	.023

[a] t-test.

We can explore further the differences between the two cities by look-ing at the evolution of patterns of interaction over time. To this purpose, we focus on organizations established before 1996, because they would have been, in principle, able to attend events in all three phases we consider. Eighty-two of these organizations were in Glasgow (66 percent) and 98 in Bristol (73 percent), a nonsignificant difference (p = .138). For both cities and for each phase, we assume the presence of a tie between two organizations if they had jointly attended or promoted at least one public event during that phase.

In Glasgow, we find the following. First, density in the networks of the longest established organizations grows from the early to the late 1990s but then falls in the early 2000s (Figure 10.3). Second, the density of the network based on events that occurred after 2000 increases substantially if we look at the totality of organizations surveyed. It is the organizations established since the mid-1990s that most contribute to recent overall levels of local mobilization. The pattern in Bristol is identical to Glasgow in the evolution of density scores, although density is higher than in Glasgow across all three phases; however, the density remains stable if we look at the whole popula-tion, suggesting no significant contribution by younger organizations.

In both cities, organizations that have been in existence since the early 1990s or earlier (sometimes much earlier) seem to display the same network patterns in relation to their involvement in public events, at least as far as the events we selected are concerned: interactions between them were less dense before 1996, grew later in the decade, and decreased again in the early 2000s. These findings suggest a relative demobilization in the last period covered by our research, or at least a reduction in the number of events attracting a mul-tiplicity of organizations, thus providing linkages between them. This pattern should not have been affected by differences in the number of events in the two cities, as the reduction in density is much more pronounced in Glasgow, where the number of events included in the list is the same as in the late 1990s. In Bristol, the number is actually halved (see Figures 10.1 and 10.3).

Time	Bristol	Glasgow
Before 1996	0.389	0.194
1996–2000	0.729	0.617
After 2000	0.545 (0.592)[a]	0.343 (0.875)[a]

[a] The figures in parentheses refer to the density of the entire network, including organizations established after 1996.

Figure 10.3. Density of networks based on joint activities (only organizations established before 1996; valued network).

We might relate this similar evolution in the two cities to the growing institutionalization of organizations that had been around for quite a while when we interviewed them. We might also wonder whether including in the network the most recently established (and thus the least institutionalized) organizations would alter the pattern. This turns out to be the case in Glasgow but not in Bristol. The strong rise of network density in the former (from 0.343 to 0.875) suggests a strong propensity of less-established organizations to engage in public events, consistent with views of collective action as the weapon of the excluded (or at least those who are not entirely included). In Bristol, however, differences are negligible (0.545 vs. 0.592), suggesting no real differences in patterns of participation across organizations with presumably different levels of access to institutions and consolidation. This is once again consistent with images of Glasgow as particularly conducive to social movement styles of collective action.

Political Culture, Political Cleavages, and Coalitions

According to our evidence, Glasgow and Bristol display important similarities: the propensity of citizens' organizations to get involved in coalition work is the same, and the structure of civil society generated by organizations' multiple involvements in events and the related coalitions is also very similar, resembling in both cases a clique the size of which increases as criteria for inclusion—for example, the number of jointly attended events required to posit a tie between two organizations—are relaxed.

Where the two cities differ, however, is in the relationship between levels of coalition involvement, and therefore of involvement in sustained interactions, and social movement activity. In Glasgow, there is a clear consistency between the two dynamics. High involvement in public events and thus in sustained interactions seems to strongly correlate with traits traditionally associated with social movements—in particular, protest (Table 10.2). Further, the density of the network based on joint involvement in the most recent events (those that took place in the early 2000s) grows strongly when we take new organizations into account (Figure 10.3). This is consistent with the expectation that new organizations, mobilizing on behalf of new agendas, will be more inclined to get involved in public action while more established ones will be less likely to do so.

In Bristol, however, the picture is very different. High involvement in public events does not correlate at all with any conventional social movement trait; involvement is much more evenly distributed across civil society than in Glasgow, and it seems to depend only on the resources organizations can invest in those activities, as measured by membership size (Table 10.2).

The density of the network based on joint involvement in the early 2000s events remains stable when we take the most recently established organizations into account (Figure 10.3), thus suggesting no particular inclination among new groups toward public mobilization.

In Glasgow, sustained involvement in coalitions may be plausibly associated with social movement activity, and the latter may be seen as the outcome of the recurrent interactions that take place when organizations get involved in multiple events. In Bristol, however, the connection between movements and coalitions is nowhere to be seen. It is still highly plausible that social movements would be "often comprised of multiple formal coalitions" (Meyer and Corrigall-Brown 2005, 329). However, at the very least, the relationship between coalitions and social movements appears to be heavily mediated by the local context.

But what traits of such context are we specifically referring to? Let us start from the basic distinction, dominant in early contributions to the political opportunity structure literature, between two key dimensions: citizens' channels of access to the political system, and the salience of traditional political cleavages (Kitschelt 1986; Tarrow 1994). In principle, the opening of access to the local political system might discourage citizens' organizations from engaging in public events—and particularly in public protest—because they might more comfortably pursue their own agendas through more conventional, less demanding channels. However, this does not seem to be a major factor here; Bristol and Glasgow have both experienced an increase in opportunities for formal institutional access, brought about by New Labour since the late 1990s, the trend toward professionalization of the voluntary sector, and its growing involvement in policy design and implementation, usually in partnerships with business and local government (Lowndes, Pratchett, and Stoker 2001; Taylor 2003).

Political culture and the salience of political cleavages seem more likely candidates to provide a reasonable explanation of our findings. Despite the conversion of Glasgow toward a more diversified and service-driven economy, the persisting levels of deprivation in some areas maintain a huge potential for collective action addressing social inequality and related issues. Of the three important historical sources of left activism in the city—the trade union movement, sections of the Labour Party, and the Communist Party—the unions have been by far the most active recently. Although the manual trade unions in shipbuilding and heavy engineering have now shrunk, there are elements of radicalism in sections of the public sector white-collar unions such as Unison and the Educational Institute of Scotland. More important, however, has been the role of the Scottish Trade

Union Congress. It was founded in 1896 and continues to have a significant left leadership role despite declining union membership. This was particularly important in the 1979–97 period of Conservative government, to which there was great hostility in Scotland. Its objectives were not just around employment and other economic issues, but also in the past thirty years on feminist, antiracist, and international issues, and it played an important role in the campaign for the establishment of a Scottish parliament. The left sections of the Labour Party were also significant in the past but are now more marginal in civic activism. As for the Communist Party, although it is no longer of much significance as an organization, there are still a number of individuals from this tradition who play a significant role in civic organizations and bring networking skills with them.

New organizations have continued some of the radical tradition in the city. These new political parties, the Scottish Socialist Party (SSP) and the Greens, still have many of the attributes of campaigning groups, and their networking role in campaigns and with community groups also emerged from our survey. The former was established in 1998 from left activists who had been in the Labour Party, the Scottish National Party, the Socialist Workers Party, and campaign groups, and Glasgow was its strongest base. The SSP built its reputation on poverty and local environmental issues but also antiwar and antiracism issues: "The SSP is more pragmatic. . . . They pick specific issues—they are outcome oriented—in that way they manage to build coalitions far more effectively" (Oxfam official). The Greens have also developed a broad agenda. "We have policies across the board—antiwar, antinuclear, antiroads, equal distribution of wealth, better public transport, better living conditions" (Green Party officeholder). One of the reasons these newer parties have been able to expand has been the proportionate electoral system for the Scottish parliament. This has given them representation, greater credibility, and resources. But they were able to take advantage of these electoral opportunities because they had a base of activism in local campaigns.

One recent element in radical politics in the city involves the Asian community. In general, the Glasgow Asian population has been largely conformist over the past thirty years, working largely through the establishment party in the city: Labour. Over the last few years, however, circumstances have changed. The deteriorating situation in Palestine and the Afghan and Iraqi wars created anger in the Muslim community. Local issues such as the closure of a swimming pool, problems around the settlement of refugees, and concern about a Home Office detention center for asylum seekers also intensified their discontent with the Labour leadership. This has been expressed in cooperation with the Justice Not War Coalition, the Scottish Campaign for Nuclear Disarmament, the Campaign to Welcome Refugees, and the Save Our Pool campaign. The outcome is that in the early 2000s, several hundred Glasgow Asians, many of them young and new to political activism, have taken part in campaigning activity working with various strands of radical groups in the city.

One should also remember the role of the center–periphery (Nationalist) cleavage. The Scottish National Party had grown rapidly in the late 1960s and 1970s, but it had declined in membership and grassroots activism in the 1980s and 1990s, although it was on the rise again in the 2000s after the disappointing performance of the Labour-dominated new Scottish government, established in 1997. Finally, the religious (Protestant vs. Catholic) cleavage, if largely unarticulated in political terms, also contributes to fostering a polarized political culture.

City politics in Bristol have also been dominated by Labour since the 1980s (at least until the May 2003 local elections), but the profile of the city is very different, with a history of swings between Labour and Tories in the context of an moderate political culture. For example, although Labour sympathizers amounted to about half the electorate in both cities at the beginning of the 2000s, the greater diversification of the political scene in Scotland resulted in Labour being the overwhelmingly dominant party in Glasgow, while the ratio of its sympathizers to Conservatives or Liberal Democrats in Bristol was much lower (Baldassarri and Diani 2007, 751–52). Most important, the left–right cleavage did not affect overall interorganizational relations within the civic sector in Bristol, while it did in Glasgow (Baldassarri and Diani 2007, 752).

In contrast to Glasgow, left-wing groups have never achieved organizational strength in Bristol despite a small, very active community of radical activists independent from any formal organization:

[In Bristol] there are groups that wouldn't think of going to the trade unions for support, they wouldn't assume that they would get support from the trade unions. . . . There is a weaker element in Bristol than you find in Glasgow. Groups tend to be more individualistic because you don't have that strong organized collective working class tradition that you've got in Glasgow. And that is a weakness for Bristol. (Activist, black and minority organization)

A distinctive trait of Bristol civic culture is what one of the activists interviewed for this project described as a "laid-back political culture"—that is, a style of politics in which radical polarization along major class divides comes second to the concerted attempts to mediate between multiple interests. A leader in the black and minority community compared the past and present:

> We had some very strong black, radical, Malcolm X–type activists. They are not there anymore. You have people like me who do it diplomatically. If I am going to put over my point, I don't need to stand in a line. I try and engage where it is important. Sitting around a table. . . . Some of my colleagues who have moved here and come to work here in Bristol find it really, really difficult because they are so used to the hustle and bustle and all the radical stuff going on in London, then they come to Bristol and it's all slowed down. . . . I don't know. It's just not in the make of the sector to protest. We're linked to debate and sit down for months on end if we have to. (Black and minority leader, Bristol)

This is quite a contrast to what a Scottish trade union official has to say on the same issue: "We [in Glasgow] are still prepared to get out on the streets in almost an old-fashioned way . . . so it's not all lobbying behind closed doors. . . . It's getting your message out to the people."

Even the impact of the new social movements in Bristol has mostly been at the cultural level, with a flourishing milieu of youth subcultures and alternative lifestyles addressing issues of health, alternative food, and body care (Purdue et al. 1997):

> I think in Bristol we do have something of a culture and tradition of seeking broader social change through things like cooperative, practical projects. . . . Bristol seems to have become a home for and naturally associated with quite a lot of that sort of activity which very much sees itself as being part of social change but working through practical demonstrations of possibilities or the small scale enterprises. . . . Trying to set up our own examples of good practice. (Friends of the Earth activist)

It is interesting that the differences in the salience of traditional cleavages and in the polarization of the local political scene do not translate into levels of involvement in coalition work. One might expect organizations in a more polarized city to be more prone to promote or support public events than organizations active in a more pacific situation. But this is not the case. Rather, the legacy of the Red Clyde tradition in Glasgow seems to affect which actors get attracted to sustained coalition work. In Glasgow, sustained participation in public events could still be largely perceived as the tool of those who lack the legitimacy and institutional access to pursue their interests through more routinized and less contentious means. More established organizations, enjoying easier access to policy making, might be tempted to refrain altogether from attending public events that might tarnish their image as reliable partners of institutions while adding little to their influence.

In contrast, in Bristol, home to a political culture driven by moderation and the propensity to negotiate with public authorities rather than twist their arms using more disruptive tactics, coalition work might take a different meaning. Far from being a "weapon of the weak" (Scott 1985), it might simply be one of the several tactical options open to citizens' organizations. As such, it might be adopted on the basis of ad hoc calculations, different for each specific issue and largely elite driven.

In these circumstances, even when groups participate in multiple events, they would still be unlikely to generate the kind of identification and long-term commitment that one usually associates with social movements.

Conclusion

The social movement literature has shown the role of political opportunities in shaping the overall intensity and features of collective action (e.g., Kriesi et al. 1995). Here, however, we have failed to extend this line of argument to explain the overall levels of citizen organizations' involvement in local coalitions. As we have seen, organizations participate in a fairly similar amount of public events, regardless of the political culture in which they are embedded. Despite stereotypical views of the two cities, it apparently matters little whether these events occur in supposedly contentious, protest-oriented Glasgow or in more laid-back, conciliatory, and mediation-oriented Bristol.

Where political culture matters, however, is in affecting which types of organizations get involved in public event coalitions. In a relatively mobilized political culture like Glasgow, the link between sustained coalition work and social movement activity is still quite strong. In Glasgow, less established organizations are more likely to engage in coalitions and thus in the sustained activities of social movements. In Bristol, however, such a connection is not there, suggesting a different dynamic. Strong movement identification in Bristol does not predict strong coalition involvement. Both fully established and newly established organizations are equally likely to participate in coalitions.

All this suggests a disentangling of the association between sustained coalition work and social movements. Nothing in our analysis challenges the view that social movements actually consist of sustained interactions that occur in the context of coalition work on broad sets of issues. It is indeed impossible to think of social movements in the absence of coalitions. However, the reverse does not apply. Coalition work does not necessarily translate into social movement activity. Coalition work rather represents a style of collective action that may well be adopted by actors who neither think of themselves as movement actors nor display the features conventionally associated with movements—most notably, the propensity to protest. The presence or absence of a strong link between coalitions and movements depends to a significant measure on the features of local political cultures and cleavages.

Notes

This chapter originates from the project "Networks of Civic Organisations in Britain," which we conducted at the University of Strathclyde in Glasgow and the University of West of England, Bristol, from June 2000 to September 2003. The study was part of the Democracy and Participation Program, funded by the Economic and Social Research Council (contract L215 25 2006). We thank program director Paul Whiteley and our collaborators in Glasgow and Bristol. We thank the late Chuck Tilly, Delia Baldassarri, Peter Bearman, Nella Van Dyke, and Holly McCammon for their comments.

1. The proportions in Bristol and Glasgow were as follows: environment (27 percent vs. 16 percent); ethnic minorities and migrants (19 percent vs. 28 percent); community issues (28 percent vs. 23 percent); social exclusion issues (25 percent vs. 33 percent). In order to identify our unit of analysis, we started from the directories of organizations generated by the umbrella organizations operating as service providers to the voluntary and community sector in the two cities, Glasgow Council for the Voluntary Sector and Bristol's Voluntary Organisations Standing Conference on Urban Regeneration (Voscur). We supplemented the information collected through those sources with data from a limited number of informants, representatives of the main umbrella organizations, related bodies such as the Bristol Racial Equality Council or the Glasgow Minority Network, or academics with specific research experience in the local scene.

Works Cited

Baldassarri, Delia, and Mario Diani. 2007. "The Integrative Power of Civic Networks." *American Journal of Sociology* 113: 735–80.

Budge, Ian, Ivor Crewe, David McKay, and Ken Newton. 2001. *The New British Politics.* Harlow: Pearson.

Diani, Mario. 1992. "The Concept of Social Movement." *Sociological Review* 40: 1–25.

———. 2005. "Cities in the World: Local Civil Society and Global Issues in Britain." In *Transnational Protest and Global Activism,* edited by Donatella Della Porta and Sidney Tarrow, 45–67. Lanham, Md.: Rowman & Littlefield.

Diani, Mario, and Ivano Bison. 2004. "Organizations, Coalitions, and Movements." *Theory and Society* 33: 281–309.

Gamson, William. 1961. "A Theory of Coalition Formation." *American Sociological Review* 26: 373–82.

Hargreaves Heap, Shaun, Martin Hollis, Bruce Lyons, Robert Sugden, and Albert Weale. 1992. *The Theory of Choice: A Critical Guide.* Cambridge, Mass.: Blackwell.

Kitschelt, Herbert. 1986. "Political Opportunity Structures and Political Protest: Anti-Nuclear Movements in Four Democracies." *British Journal of Political Science* 16: 57–85.

Kriesi, Hanspeter, Ruud Koopmans, Jan-Willem Duyvendak, and Marco Giugni. 1995. *New Social Movements in Western Europe.* Minneapolis: University of Minnesota Press.

Logan, J., and Harvey Molotch. 1987. *Urban Fortunes.* Berkley: University of California Press.

Lowndes, Vivien, Lawrence Pratchett, and Gerry Stoker. 2001. "Trends in Public Participation. Part II: Citizens' Perspectives." *Public Administration* 79: 445–56.

Melucci, Alberto. 1989. *Nomads of the Present.* London: Hutchinson Radius.

Meyer, David S., and Catherine Corrigall-Brown. 2005. "Coalitions and Political Context: U.S. Movements against War in Iraq." *Mobilization* 10: 327–44.

Purdue, Derrick, Jörg Dürrschmidt, Peter Jowers, and Richard O'Doherty. 1997. "DIY Culture and Extended Milieu: LETS, Veggie Boxes and Festivals." *Sociological Review* 45: 645–67.

Ruzza, Carlo. 2004. *Europe and Civil Society: Movement Coalitions and European Governance.* Manchester: Manchester University Press.

Sabatier, Paul A., and Hank C. Jenkins-Smith. 1999. "The Advocacy Coalition Framework: An Assessment." In *Theories of the Policy Process,* edited by Paul A. Sabatier, 117–66. Boulder, Colo.: Westview.

Scott, James C. 1985. *Weapons of the Weak.* New Haven, Conn.: Yale University Press.

Simmel, Georg. 1955 [1908]. *Conflict and the Web of Group Affiliations.* New York: Free Press.

Stevenson, William B., Lone J. Pearce, and Lyman W. Porter. 1985. "The Concept of 'Coalition' in Organization Theory and Research." *Academy of Management Review* 10: 256–68.

Stewart, Murray. 1996. "Too Little, Too Late: The Politics of Local Complacency." *Journal of Urban Affairs* 18: 119–37.

———. 2003. "Towards Collaborative Capacity." In *Urban Transformation and Urban Governance: Shaping the Competitive City of the Future,* edited by M. Boddy, 76–89. Bristol: Policy Press.

Tarrow, Sidney. 1994. *Power in Movement: Social Movements, Collective Action, and Politics.* Cambridge: Cambridge University Press.

Taylor, Marylin. 2003. *Public Policy in the Community.* Basingstoke: Palgrave Macmillan.

Tilly, Charles. 1994. "Social Movements as Historically Specific Clusters of Political Performances." *Berkeley Journal of Sociology* 38: 1–30.

Wasserman, Stanley, and Katherine Faust. 1994. *Social Network Analysis.* New York: Cambridge University Press.

IV
Coalitions and Combinations of Causal Factors

11

Crisis as a Catalyst for Cooperation? Women's Organizing in Buenos Aires

Elizabeth Borland

Women's movements in Argentina have long been divided along lines of class, sexual orientation, and other social cleavages. Yet in the wake of Argentina's 2001 political and economic crisis, there were attempts to overcome these barriers. By examining how activists did so, this project adds to a growing body of literature on the dynamics of social movement coalitions. The case of cooperation in the women's movement in Buenos Aires confirms the importance of external threats for the emergence of coalitions, particularly in the way a crisis can affect relationships between groups in the women's movement.

In this chapter, I outline the main cleavages within the women's movement in Argentina in 2001 and trace steps toward and away from collaboration, examining the process by which some barriers were breached and others were not. I chart how activists' perceptions of the crisis acted as a catalyst for overcoming social barriers and highlight how external conditions activated internal dynamics within the movement—recognition of common ideological perspectives, preexisting social network ties, and bridge building—that play a role in coalition formation. I find that some efforts at cooperation achieved more success than others: attempts between feminist organizations and activists to overcome cleavages based on sexual orientation, age, and organizational form were relatively successful, while endeavors to form coalitions between feminist and nonfeminist organizations never resulted in real collaboration.

After describing the context and methods for the research, I provide an overview of the women's movement in Argentina and outline the cleavages that existed in 2002 and 2003. I discuss why it seemed possible to form coalitions during this time and consider what went right and wrong in attempts at cooperation. This research contributes to literature on coalitions, to our understanding of how movements manage identity concerns, and to scholarship on women's movements by examining how barriers were navigated in an external context that facilitated convergence between modes of activism.

Shifting Context: Argentina's Crisis and Opportunities for Cooperation

Research on coalitions has differentiated between factors external and internal to movements (Staggenborg 1986), and both are relevant for this case. Meyer and Corrigall-Brown (2005, 328) argue that "the nature of movement coalitions can be best understood by focusing on the external circumstances under which coalitions develop." Drawing on their research on the recent U.S. antiwar movement, they theorize that groups cooperate when the potential benefits seem to outweigh the costs and when they "see their efforts on a particular set of issues and efforts as urgent and potentially efficacious" (332). This is why, they say, threats such as those observed in diverse movements by McCammon and Campbell (2002) and Van Dyke (2003) are likely to inspire coalition participation. As Almeida (2003) explains, threats close down political opportunities by making it seem like advances that have been made will be lost. He includes state-attributed economic problems as one type of threat, explaining that "when organized groups convincingly attribute to specific agents the responsibility for a decline in their economic conditions" (352), such as price increases and structural adjustment policies, they are more likely to resist collectively. As I show below, Argentina's crisis presented this type of threat to activists.

The crisis that emerged in 2001 created a new scene for social movements in Argentina, including women's movements, and opened doors for new forms of collaboration. On December 19, 2001, residents of Buenos Aires and other urban areas took to the streets to participate in a massive social protest marked by riots in some neighborhoods (Auyero 2007; Vezzetti 2002). The month before, the government erected barriers to limit bank account withdrawals in an attempt to reduce capital flight and to prevent a run on banks. This measure was immensely unpopular and contributed to the bitterness and cynicism that many had for politicians, particularly President Fernando De la Rúa. Protests called *cacerolazos* occurred throughout the nation as city dwellers banged on pots *(cacerolas)* and pans to express their dissatisfaction and to rally around the slogan "Que se vayan todos!" (They all must go!). This marked a turning point in Argentina's democracy. It precipitated the resignation of De la Rúa and was the climax of years of protests, most notably those by unemployed protesters called *piqueteros/as* (road barricaders) who had blocked major transport routes to demand employment and protest neoliberal policies during the 1990s (Auyero 2003; Giarracca and Teubal 2001).[1]

As the dust settled, Argentina struggled to make sense out of what had happened and to work collectively to address the economic crisis. People whose assets had been frozen organized protests outside of banks and state institutions. When the peso was depegged from the U.S. dollar in January 2002, the exchange rate plummeted and prices began to climb, disrupting everyday life and sending many Argentines into the streets to protest (Borland and Sutton 2007). Ovalles (2002) estimates a total of 2,014 *cacerolazos* throughout Argentina from December 2001 to March 2002. Metal barriers were erected around banks and government buildings, and riot police took up posts in the Plaza de Mayo (the central plaza of Buenos Aires) and in Congress, ready for protests (most of which were peaceful). Neighborhood assemblies organized citizens within urban neighborhoods to make demands on the government and began to channel efforts for social programs, such as soup kitchens, cooperative buying, and workshops (Briones and Mendoza 2003; Rossi 2005). Unemployment levels reached a high of 21.5 percent, and 49 percent of the population fell beneath the poverty line (INDEC n.d.), so *piqueteros/as* continued street protests, often joined by members of these assemblies. Journalists estimated that 12,766 street protests were staged during the eight-month period between January and August 2002 (Gallo 2002), and by March 2002, 272 assemblies were meeting regularly around Argentina (Fraga 2002).

Given the economic threats the crisis presented—and following Almeida's (2003) arguments that state-attributed economic problems constitute one form of threat that can inspire collective resistance—we might expect an increase in coalitions during this time. In fact, throughout these varied forms of collective action, many groups worked together in formal and informal coalitions (Di Marco et al. 2003; Rossi 2005). But for the women's movement, the crisis posed an additional threat: the possibility that claims about gender could become eclipsed by economic demands. Would gender-based issues be seen as a luxury in the face of rising poverty and unemployment? The crisis represented a kind of double threat to women's groups, making this case a good one for considering how decreasing opportunities affect movement interorganizational relations.

In particular, the case of the women's movement in Buenos Aires during this period draws attention to three internal factors that influenced coalition formation: bridge building, inclusive common ideology, and preexisting social ties. First, activists can serve as brokers (Bandy and Smith 2005) or bridge builders (Bystydzienski and Schacht 2001; Obach 2004) to foment and sustain coalition building between social movement organizations (SMOs), and some activists in Argentina acted in this capacity. Second, Rucht (2004) and Van Dyke (2003) find that groups with pluralistic ideological viewpoints are more likely to join coalitions, and scholars have noted how recent international phenomena, such as the World Social Forums (Alvarez, Faria, and Nobre 2003; Juris 2008) and the World March for Women (Conway 2008; Dufour and Giraud 2007), have recognized the need for coalitions and fostered inclusive ideology. For example, Juris (2008) argues that the World Social Forum creates space for dialogue and meeting between activists, emphasizing a culture that recognizes shared perspectives and actively confronts exclusion and inequality. Argentine activists have participated in these international endeavors, along with the Latin American and Caribbean feminist *encuentros* (meetings) that have similar norms and values (Alvarez, Faria, and Nobre 2003), so the movement has been influenced by this culture. Third, in addition to fostering pluralistic approaches for discourse, participation in these activities—as well as Argentine *Encuentros de Mujeres* (annual Women's Meetings) (Alonso and Díaz 2002) and local progressive organizing—means that many women activists in Buenos Aires had relationships that existed before the crisis, and prior social network ties can help SMOs participate in coalitions (Shaffer 2000). The presence of all three elements played a role in Argentina, particularly common ideology and prior social ties.

Specifically, I argue that perception of the crisis as a double threat for women in Argentina acted like an external catalyst to activate social network ties between individuals and organizations in the movement, internal conditions that could make collaboration possible. Although many individuals already knew one another, the context of the crisis made activists more eager to reach out and get beyond previous conflicts about ideological, strategic, and identity differences. Rather than emphasizing these differences, activists created a discursive space for collaboration by pointing to common ideology and shared understandings about how the crisis burdened women. By activating internal elements already present in the movement, the external crisis fostered attempts at cooperation, some of which were ultimately more successful than others.

Methods

The data for this study are derived from field research on the women's movement in Buenos Aires, the locus of political activism in Argentina. The research focused on women's SMOs active in Buenos Aires in the first twenty years of the democratic period (December 1983–June 2003) (Borland 2004b). For the analysis at hand, this includes groups in the reproductive rights movement; the lesbian movement; the movement against gender violence; and the housewives' movement, which demands consumer rights. As SMOs, they have social change goals and engage in protest or advocacy activities (Minkoff 1999).[2] In addition to observing and interviewing members of these groups, I also observed activities where members of these groups interacted with other activists from popular women's SMOs and other movements.[3]

The research combined these in-depth interviews with ethnographic observations conducted for fifteen months during December 2001 to July 2003. I performed sixty-eight tape-recorded semistructured interviews of activists who were in women's SMOs. I spent over four hundred hours doing observations in the field, attending over a hundred events, including street protests and rallies, panel discussions, open meetings, and formal and informal workshops that were part of the annual National Women's Meeting held in Salta, the Buenos Aires meeting of the World Social Forum, and annual feminist meetings. In general, my role in these events was as passive participant observer, attending the events and observing and listening, sometimes taking photos or using a small tape recorder, and usually writing notes in a small notepad. In street protest, I occasionally participated more actively, helping to hold banners or block traffic, and clapping or chanting. Shortly after attending field activities, I wrote detailed field notes.

For my analysis, I coded the data collected in the interviews and field notes on the basis of qualitative data reduction and interpretation methods (Coffey and Atkinson 1996; Marshall and Rossman 1995). Although some of my earlier research has focused on organizational factors contributing to coalition participation (Borland 2008), here I focus on a series of regular meetings attended by representatives of women's movement organizations and independent activists in which intermovement relations played out publicly, as well as the street protest events that were the planning objectives of these cooperative efforts. I pay particular attention to the discourse that activists used during these meetings as well as the backgrounds of meeting and protest participants—a changing group over the course of my fieldwork. In the sections that follow, I illustrate my arguments with material from interviews and field notes, using pseudonyms and obscuring the identities of subjects when necessary.

Women's Movements in Argentina: Cooperation and Division

Women have played an important role in social movements in Argentina and have been central in the fight against dictatorship (particularly the internationally known Mothers of the Plaza de Mayo) and in collective action in the subsequent democratic period (Borland 2004a; Borland 2006). The contemporary wave of the women's movement emerged in the early 1980s as the military government lost power and eventually ceded to democracy. When democracy was reestablished in 1983, feminists and other activists began to mobilize to support the Mothers, and to make claims about an array of gender issues. They formed a formal coalition called the Multisectoral de la Mujer (Women's Multisector Group), which was formed as an umbrella group to unite over forty women's groups and other progressive organizations, politicians, labor organizations, human rights activists, housewives, and individual feminists (Bellucci 1995; Flori 1988). The women in this coalition fought against *patria potestad* until 1985, when laws were changed so that parental authority rested equally on both parents (Flori 1988). Later campaigns also succeeded in reforming laws to improve access to birth control (1988) and to legalize divorce (1987).

Despite these gains, the coalition experience in the early democratic period was not altogether positive for feminists. According to the women who were involved, the Multisectorial de la Mujer and other efforts at collaboration in this period left feminists with a lingering bitter taste. Collaboration functioned well for three or four years, said one of the founding members, "but there was always [someone] trying to dominate it. . . . As other institutions opened in the democracy, women started to desert, and then only a few of us were left and some political party thought it would be easy to take it over. That was why we announced its end."[4] Feminists occasionally referenced these past difficulties in movement meetings, mentioning previous problems with joining with working-class groups that they thought had been co-opted by political parties.

The women's movement in Buenos Aires, although small, is marked by many social divisions and conflicts. The broadest and most overarching of these barriers is between feminists and nonfeminists; this cleavage parallels class divisions. Although feminists and nonfeminists in the women's movement have shared concerns about women's unequal opportunities and abuse, poor and working-class women in what are called popular women's groups (Chaneton 1995) have resisted being called feminists. Many prefer to call themselves "feminine" and often emphasize their maternal identities in organizing as women. These popular groups tend to be larger in size and are based in the outskirts of the city or in poor neighborhoods marked by marginalization and poverty. Some are affiliated with mixed-gender organizations or are women's subgroups of these organizations. For example, the group Mujeres de Pie (Women Standing Up), is part of the *piquetero/a* group Barrios de Pie

(Neighborhoods Standing Up). The largest of the popular women's groups organize as housewives (Fisher 2000).

In contrast, groups in the feminist movement challenge traditional gender roles and organize around issues they see as central to resisting patriarchy, such as the right to sexual and reproductive freedom. Although few in number, they have been able to make their claims about reproductive rights, mother's rights, and other equal rights issues heard on the national level, resulting in a wave of new women's initiatives (Navarro 2001). However, they have seldom made cross-class alliances on these issues with larger progressive movements.

In addition to class and ideological barriers, there are three significant cleavages among feminists: between women in formal nongovernmental organizations (NGOs) and women who call themselves *autónomas* (autonomous feminists who prefer a grassroots orientation with informal and usually horizontal organizations); between women who identify as lesbian feminists and those who do not; and even between women of different ages. In the following section, I describe the cleavages and how they operate in the movement.

Class: Popular Women's Groups and Feminism

As in other Latin American contexts (Alvarez 1990; Jacquette 1991),[5] poor and working-class women in the women's movement in Argentina generally see feminism as a middle-class notion, and sometimes as an imported foreign ideology. Countering these perceptions and raising consciousness about feminism across society are central concerns for feminists in Argentina, but they have made few inroads. Class divisions are hard to breach because they are reinforced by cultural markers such as language and dress, and because class shapes experiences such as educational background and neighborhood and other networks. Middle-class feminists who attempt to share their views with poorer women are likely to encounter problems because they speak in a way that is seen as "stuck up" *(concheta)* and unrealistic by women in popular groups.

Popular activists, in turn, often emphasize aspects of their identities as women that are not embraced by feminists. For example, in a breakfast meeting with over fifty women from many different organizations, an activist from Madres por la Vivienda (Mothers for Housing) stood up and made an impassioned plea for help. Mimicking the way the Mothers of the Plaza de Mayo wear headscarves, she wore a headscarf made from a blue and white Argentine flags, and she used nationalist language. She stated, "If I was alone and turned out on the street, I would not have a problem, but behind there are children and grandchildren." Her fight was not for herself (she claimed that she would not complain if she were homeless), but for her children. The feminist sitting next to me whispered her criticism of this woman and her speech ("What a clown!"), and suggested her nationalism and maternal emphasis was misguided. Middle-class feminists recognize that motherhood and child rearing are important for many women, but they challenge popular activists to recognize that these are not essential activities, and they call on women to make claims as individuals, not just in their roles as mothers and partners to men.

Sexual Orientation: *Lesbofobia*

Many lesbians in the women's movement in Buenos Aires have become increasingly vocal about what they term *lesbofobia* (fear of lesbians) and their invisibility in the movement and in society more generally. They challenge lesbian feminists who do not emphasize their sexual orientation, call on other lesbians to be more visible as lesbians, and question heterosexual activists who do not support lesbian demands as much as lesbians have supported claims not directly linked to sexual orientation. As Mariana, a young lesbian rights activist from a middle-class family, complained in an interview, "The feminists that I see, about 90 percent are *tortas* [slang for lesbians], but in reality they work for heterosexual women. They do not say that they are *tortas* and they do not do grassroots work and all that." At times, lesbian activists have drawn on Adrienne Rich's arguments about compulsory heterosexuality to take the stance that women who do not identify as lesbians are conforming to the norms of society and hiding their true sexual orientation.

For lesbian feminist activists, asserting their identity as lesbians is a political claim as well as an attempt to create a united community. Yet this assertion risks alienating others (mostly straight women and lesbian women who do not choose to strongly assert this identity), and it has contributed to conflict between lesbian and nonlesbian feminists. A long-term lesbian activist, Paulina, echoed this complaint in an interview: "Now all the urgency is on something else, and where are we going? Once again my lesbianism is left by the wayside."

Another related aspect of this cleavage is that some lesbians refuse to label themselves as women, drawing on theoretical arguments made by lesbian theorists (e.g., Monique Wittig). A minority of lesbian rights activists have asserted this position, challenging notions about sexuality and gender and raising debate among lesbians and within women's organizations. Although some of the activists who have rejected being labeled women have continued to attend women's movement events, most have preferred to work only with other lesbian activists or with queer groups, a tendency that parallels the trend to organize one's own group discussed in Roth's chapter in this volume. Others have joined progressive movements that have organized around more general issues.

Strategy and Organization: Women in NGOs vs. *Autónomas*

The divide between women in NGOs and *autónomas* is not a completely clear dichotomy in Buenos Aires, and it parallels a debate about "NGO-ification" that has marked the women's movement in Buenos Aires and elsewhere in the third world. The transformation or reclassification of SMOs into NGOs was a noted phenomenon in the 1980s and 1990s throughout Latin America (Frohmann and Valdés 1995). In part, this shift was related to the role played by NGOs in rebuilding democratic civil society, but it also had to do with neoliberal economic reforms that increasingly have relied on NGOs to outsource social programs. Increasingly, social change groups were divided between NGO-type SMOs and *autónomas*. In Buenos Aires, the NGO-type SMOs are organizationally different from autonomous groups in several ways. They are likely to have official status *(personería jurídica)* and are more formal and usually centralized groups with leaders and headquarters. They have often gotten grants from the Argentine government or agencies abroad to produce materials and provide services.

The debate is contentious and ideological: feminist *autónomas* tend to be more radical and less likely to negotiate or politically maneuver the way that lobbyists may. In addition to organizational and ideological differences, the debate is also related to professionalization (NGO members, if not employed by the SMO, are likely to have professional connections and benefits associated with their activism); class divisions (NGO activists are sometimes seen as bourgeois by other activists, even though both are middle class); and party politics (NGO members have been more likely to work with major parties, while autonomous women are generally either independent or work with small parties on the left). The debate also has to do with collective identity: the autonomous feminists see themselves as the real revolutionaries, the real feminists, and think the NGOs have watered down their goals in order to advance personal interests. The NGO feminists often resent these accusations and depict the *autónomas* as unrealistic. Mariela classifies herself as a "twenty-four-hour feminist," as opposed to the "nine to five" variety she disparages from NGOs. For her, this divide is also marked by physical and material/bodily choices (for example, not wearing makeup and heels, and allowing underarm and pubic hair to grow freely).

Age: Generational Differences

A final and prevalent cleavage in the women's movement arises from age differences among participants. Although generational divisions have been noted by feminists in other contexts (Medina Rosas and Wilson 2003), the age makeup of many movements in Argentina reflects a particular historical context: because many people were "disappeared" during the last military dictatorship (1976–83), a whole generation of activists is missing. In many movements, there are many participants who came of age before the dictatorship and who are now in their sixties and seventies, and then there is a growing new generation of activists who were young children during the dictatorship or not yet born and are now in their late teens, twenties, and thirties. There are fewer activists in between these generations because they disappeared or were silenced by the repression.

In the feminist movement, this age spread means that there are many instances where the "grandmothers" of the movement, who sometimes call themselves *históricas* (the historic ones)—pioneers of the early democratic period who were involved before and after the dictatorship—interact with the "granddaughters" of the movement who have only more recently learned about feminism. Many of these younger activists first encountered feminism after already being involved in other progressive movements, such as student activism at the University of Buenos Aires, or even through course material in women's studies. At best, they see the *históricas* as role models, women who had gained experience in many years of struggle. At worst, they view the older activists as inflexible, old-fashioned, and set in their ways. They say that it is hard to become integrated into the movement and report that they have to break their way in; at first, one feels like "a weirdo" *(un bicho raro),* as Ana, a young feminist, told me. The older activists welcome the new wave of interest in the women's movement, but they worry that young activists do not learn from the collective past and seem to feel a need to reinvent the wheel. Older activists also question some of the strategies favored by younger activists, such as painting graffiti or organizing rock concerts.

One persistent conflict between the *históricas* and younger activists has involved the participation of men. Although older feminists generally emphasize women-only spaces and have not involved men in feminist organizations and efforts, young women generally think that men can be feminists and an important component of the struggle. For example, a group of young feminists told me that they organized an open-air rock concert to support efforts for abortion legalization. Their top billing, a band called She-Devils, was a feminist group that called for legalization of abortion in one of their songs.

They seemed a perfect fit for the event. But their drummer was a man, and some older feminists called this into question. Although the She-Devils eventually went on to play, the young feminists felt like their considerable efforts to book the show were not supported, and the older feminists continued to challenge male involvement. Further, the young feminists did not collaborate with the older feminists in the subsequent year's Day for the Legalization of Abortion events.

These divisions—between women of different classes, generations, and sexual orientations, and from different types of organizations and ideologies—mark the landscape of the women's movement in Buenos Aires. The relationship between feminists and nonfeminist women activists was often discussed by the women I interviewed and observed, and conflicts among feminists were also readily acknowledged in movement activities. For instance, at the 2002 National Feminist Meeting, divisions were directly addressed: age, sexual orientation, and organizational type were recorded as "debates among feminists" in the meeting's final document. As one feminist academic at a public meeting suggested, "Feminism questions everything, you accept nothing, you have to question everything, and that also implies questioning our own practices constantly. . . . But how do we resolve the differences that we must resolve to act? And what differences can keep existing tranquilly and not impede the advance or growth of united effort?"

"We have to jump ahead": Attempts at Cooperation in Argentina's Crisis

During this time of massive crisis in Argentina, feminists involved in the protests knew they had to come together to make their gendered demands heard amid other claims. In my interviews and field notes, I coded the ways that activists labeled the crisis and explained this moment in time. These rhetorical statements were often used to justify and explain women's activism, and sometimes they provided a rallying cry to foster collaborative efforts. Many activists emphasized change. They spoke about the time as "a moment of change," as a "hinge," a "rupture," or an "opening." Some were optimistic, emphasizing the surge in activism and calling the moment an "advent," a "period of renaissance," and even a "catapult." But many were quick to express concern for the direction of this change, cataloging the many ways that the crisis brought problems for women.

There was a sense in this discourse that the feminists were involved in a competition for recognition of their claims, or as one feminist put it, "There is a fight for protagonism and space, women must insert themselves everywhere they can to work for change" (feminist from Buenos Aires at the National Women's Meeting). They pointed to how the social stress affected women in general in terms of deteriorating reproductive health, increasing domestic violence, and further aggravating unequal household division of labor, and they appealed for social change to address these problems. Activists also called on each other to redouble their efforts, so that women would not be left out of the rising protests and so that gender issues would be included in the demands being made. As one young feminist said at a public talk at the University of Buenos Aires in 2002, "We need to get women's things on the agenda, to build a bridge between the women's movement and other organizations and parts of society."

It was in this environment that women's movement activists were organizing. I heard a frustrated feminist at a workshop in the World Social Forum in Buenos Aires, an event attended by tens of thousands of people interested in social change in Argentina, state, "Women are here [in protest] like never before, but where are the feminists? And what are we going to do next?" The widespread protest and chorus of claims in society from many sectors made it a challenge for the small number of feminists to be heard. Some consistently carried large banners in lilac and wore lilac clothing, the international feminist color, to every protest they attended, proclaiming "Feminists Are Everywhere!"

The desire to make feminist voices heard sometimes meant taking attention-getting actions and making controversial claims. For example, at a feminist meeting on abortion activism, an SMO leader said, "In this moment when everyone is questioning everything, let's make sure they question the church too." In fact, there was a dramatic and unprecedented *escrache*[6] of the Cathedral of Buenos Aires by young feminists in the Plaza de Mayo at the end of the march for International Women's Day 2002, a march that culminated by joining a large rally (unrelated to Women's Day) with many different progressive SMOs in the Plaza. Among the graffiti were the words "Revolución en la casa en la plaza y en la cama" (Revolution in the home, in the plaza, and in the bed) and "Ni dios, ni amo, ni marido, ni partido" (Not god, not master, not husband, not party). This action was not coordinated with other groups, and in fact some older feminist organizations were concerned about the message it sent about feminism, including the local branch of the feminist group Católicas por el Derecho a Decidir (Catholics for a Free Choice), which was put in an awkward position by the *escrache*.

Despite this, the large turnout for the March 2002 International Women's Day events and the continued calls for dialogue to overcome difference are evidence of what Juris (2008) calls open space—a forum for diverse groups to share ideas and coordinate collaborative efforts. At a time when many movement groups were collaborating in Argentina, most notably in large *cacerolazos* and in preparation for the Argentine World Social Forum held in Buenos Aires in August 2002, there were more and more calls for women's groups to work together. Activists built on the zeitgeist of the moment and created new connections as they strengthened preexisting social ties.

The goal to work collaboratively led to a coalition between women's organizations coming together for International Women's Day in 2003. Like the German weak coalitions described in Guenther's chapter in this volume, the Buenos Aires women's coalition was an informal coalition. It never took on a name more than the generic "feminist meeting," but it was clearly an alliance of multiple SMOs and activists, with shared objectives and a final goal: to join forces for the celebration and commemoration of International Women's Day and to make claims together on this occasion. Women came together every few weeks, then every week, and then a few times a week as the date got closer, and they pooled funds to pay for their activities. They also met after International Women's Day to analyze what had transpired and to make plans for future activities, including a contingent for protests against the invasion of Iraq that were attended by many progressive activists in Buenos Aires. Thus, despite the temporal aspect of the groups' goal, it took on more permanence as an informal coalition.

The collaborative work was launched in late 2002, when a dozen feminists from various groups in Buenos Aires met in the mildewed basement of a women's bookstore to plan what they would do to mark the March 8, International Women's Day. They sat in a circle and started talking about whether or not to try to construct a feminist space for organizing in the continued protests that had marked Argentina for over a year. Most of these women had been involved in the large-scale protests that drew worldwide attention to Argentina's economic and political crisis; many had been feminist activists for years and had participated in national and international women's meetings. They knew one another, so preexisting social networks helped them come together and then reach out to others. Prior social ties also meant that women in the group shared experiences and some degree of trust—evidence that preexisting ties and spaces for dialogue helped make the coalition possible.

After agreeing to work together, the women debated about the claims to be made, particularly the contents of a shared document. There were many meetings to discuss the common elements for the document and other means of claims making for the march, including chants, signs, and the motto for the event that would head the document and be painted on a banner leading the march. In their e-mail calling for participation, the group convoked "feminist women, *piqueteras,* assembly women, from human rights, unions, from lesbian groups." In the end, though, mainly feminist women and lesbian feminists, but of different generations and from different types of organizations, joined Feminist Meeting and participated in the Women's Day march. Thus, the resulting coalition overcame some cleavages in the movement while demonstrating a failure to overcome others.

What Did Work: Steps toward Collaboration

Activists created room for increasing and deepening the already ongoing dialogue for cooperation by recognizing how divisions among women contribute to the lack of voice and action of feminists, and how these divisions were particularly problematic given the crisis and the need to organize. As the final document for the 2002 National Feminist Meeting put it, "The challenge is to think in common, to think of the future, to look for steps to unite us in a common feminist act *(hacer)* with feminist connection that each of us contributes to the group in diverse ways." The need to recognize and respect differences within the movement was a repeating theme in this document and in the cooperative efforts I witnessed in my fieldwork.

When I asked them about what was unique about contemporary organizing, many feminists pointed out the increasing number of young women working with the movement, noting that there was more cross-generational collaboration than in the past. Young feminists and *históricas* were present together in the Feminist Meeting group to plan events for International Women's Day 2003 and subsequent activism. Feminists from the missing generation—women in their thirties and forties—took on a bridge-building role by approaching younger women who seemed interested in feminism, and introducing young and old. In late 2002, the bridge leaders helped organize a standing-room-only event honoring a group of feminists active since the days of the dictatorship. The organizers emphasized the importance of recognition for the work of old and new feminists, and said that the movement needed to be united to show that feminism was relevant for people of all ages. The event created goodwill between generations; after the panel, a university student who called herself a novice feminist elicited applause when she spoke about how inspiring the *históricas* were to women of her generation. By organizing the panel during a time when so much activism was focused on the present, the bridge-building activists created a discursive space for reflection about the movement's past and future, fostering respect and dialogue between generations.

There was also movement toward collaboration between feminists from NGOs and *autónomas*. Feminists at meetings throughout 2002 and 2003 emphasized the need to connect these branches of the movement. At one meeting, an activist who had worked with various independent groups pointed out, "Autonomy is relative," stating that feminists want women to be paid for their work, and it seemed contrary to criticize women in NGOs who were paid for their work and activism. Although they did not regularly attend the Feminist Meeting group, the NGO feminists signed on to the final document and, during the 2002 and 2003 celebrations of International Women's Day, *autónomas* and women from NGOs could be found carrying banners together. A photograph of a mixed group even appeared in the newspaper article on the event that was published in the left-leaning mainstream newspaper *Página 12*.

One point of contention that was overcome sufficiently for collaboration, despite some lingering resentments, was regarding sexual orientation and the role of and recognition of lesbian women. The issues of lesbian invisibility and compulsory heterosexuality were often raised as major concerns within the group, particularly by lesbian activists. This point became one of the key *ejes* (axes) for the final document of the 2003 Women's Day group. In contrast to the second wave feminists described by Roth in her chapter in this volume, here there was ideological agreement that inclusivity and cooperation was beneficial; the problem was putting it into practice.

Lesbian activists continued to complain about their inclusion in the group, but their criticisms seemed to open rather than close dialogue. During the march for International Women's Day, a lesbian activist was holding the group's megaphone and leading chants about abortion rights and gender violence. When she began to sing out, "Soy lesbiana, yo soy lesbiana, porque me gusta, y me da la gana" (I'm lesbian, I am lesbian, because I like it, and I feel like it), many of the heterosexual women stopped chanting along. At a meeting after the event, lesbians called this an incident of *lesbofobia*. They complained about the lack of support and said they were hurt and angry that their claims were ignored. Nonetheless, it was a step forward because instead of leaving the group, the lesbian activists remained and demanded recognition. Other activists agreed that lesbian claims had not been sufficiently addressed in the movement, and there was a long discussion about what kind of new measures could be taken to open dialogue about *lesbofobia* within the movement.

Thus, the steps feminists took toward collaboration were both rhetorical and physical. Following the examples set by progressive and feminist activism in the World Social Forum, the World March for Women, and Latin American *encuentros,* activists confronted inequality and built on prior social networks to create this coalition. Their discourse emphasized inclusion, and the actual level of participation of women from different age groups, with different sexual orientations, and from both NGO activists and *autónomas* was a testament to these alliances. By working to recognize differences, to use inclusive language to identify activists in Feminist Meeting, and to incorporate feminists from distinct backgrounds and with different interests into the group and into the claims it made, the feminists were able to overcome some of the barriers that had plagued them in the past, even as others remained in place.

What Did Not Work: Steps Away from Coalition

Although the crisis fostered cooperation between feminists, it may have stood in the way of alliances between feminists and nonfeminists. As they discussed the possibility of working with other groups (neighborhood assemblies, *piqueteros/as,* other movements), activists in the Feminist Meeting group continually raised concerns about the preservation of feminist space. Recalling past experiences when people from political parties and unions co-opted women's movements or "took over the space" in the movement, feminists argued that they needed "to construct an agreement between ourselves first." Only after this "basic agreement" was reached, some said, would it be possible to make alliances with others. However, this type of agreement did not materialize fast enough to enable feminists to work with others.

This problem was compounded by the attitude that many feminists had about how to work with nonfeminists, and who would be in charge. At a meeting among women trying to plan an event for International Women's Day, Lorena (whose SMO works with poor women) said women from a *piquetero/a* group in a poor suburb were thinking about doing something on March 7 in the Plaza de Mayo, perhaps a rally with speakers. She said it would be good to organize something with the *piqueteras* because they already wanted to plan these events. Another woman suggested, "We should invite them to the march." Lorena said that it was not appropriate to invite them—implying that it was ridiculous for a group of fifty feminists to invite a massive movement of thousands to a march—and that the groups could actually plan together as a coalition. She explained, "[It's] just as you would not like it for others to say, 'Come on!'" There was a lack of understanding of the power dynamics involved in asking or inviting others to participate, versus true collaboration that might involve recognizing and addressing differences in power and privilege.[7]

Power dynamics also played out in the use of language. Women in popular groups who joined in a feminist protest for the legalization of abortion in 2002 asked why they couldn't *putear* (that is, call people *putas,* "whores," or *hijos de putas,* "sons of whores"). These are common curses, used far and wide to denigrate opponents, and they were often heard in protests targeting those in power. But feminists have long pointed out that to *putear* is to use sexist language, and they have questioned why maligning the mother of a politician is acceptable—or, for that matter, denigrating sex workers. Activists who wanted to *putear* were annoyed at being chastised by feminists for doing so during the protest—after all, it is a common turn of phrase, and for them, to *putear* is to stand up to the enemy. Like the East Germans in Rostock who Guenther (this volume) says felt ridiculed by West Germans, popular activists felt like middle-class Argentine feminists were patronizing them. The popular women thought they were being chastised for their manners (a classist critique); the feminists thought they were questioning the sexist assumptions behind the language and encouraging popular activists to be more enlightened. These critiques, and the misunderstandings that resulted, closed down the possibility of open debate on this issue, and the popular activists did not participate in later protests with feminists.

There was another language-related difficulty for Feminist Meeting: even when the feminists did determine the central *ejes* for their protest, they did not use accessible language to explain their points. Instead, they chose explanations that would be hard for others to understand, particularly those without advanced education. For example, in the final document produced for International Women's Day in 2003, feminists may have come up with a simple title and slogan—"For the Dignity, Pleasure, and Life of Women"—but they wrote four pages about the "economic and geopolitical interests of a State complicit with its allies" and how "the norm of heterosexuality is imposed and inherited by centuries of patriarchy." Even though they agreed that they needed to make a document that could reach a wide audience, feminists were unable to synthesize and communicate their ideas in an accessible way.

Furthermore, some issues were seen as touchy or unpalatable, particularly abortion. Religion and class get intertwined with abortion politics because in Buenos Aires, poor women activists were seen by feminists as more likely to be swayed by church doctrine on abortion. Early in the meetings held by feminists, several reproductive rights activists said they did not want to step backward by abandoning slogans against the church or for abortion rights, and they reminded the group that the year before, some young feminists had painted graffiti on the cathedral for International Women's Day. But Lorena, who had worked with *piqueteras* in the past, said that "from an ideological point of view, this makes it difficult to gather power"—the collective critique of the church would not be supported by the *piqueteras,* whose "religious sentiment goes against these practices." Although there were some activists from neighborhood assemblies, as well as *piqueteras* and other poor and working-class activists (such as the popular women who participated in the protest for the Day to Legalize Abortion mentioned earlier) who had taken a firm stance in support of reproductive rights, including abortion, feminists came to paint nonfeminist activists with the same brush, implying that compromise on abortion was impossible, and therefore alliances probably were too.

The tension between popular women's groups and feminists clearly can be seen in the few cases of feminists who worked with popular women. For example, there was a two-hour debate about how to sign the document produced by feminists in the women's movement for Women's Day in 2003. Groups and individuals had strong feelings about how to conclude the document. Should it say "We feminists"? "The women's movement" or "feminist movement"? At one point in the last meeting before the march and rally where the document would be read and distributed to passersby, one woman from a popular women's organization, who insisted on putting "women's movement" and not just "feminists," said she came representing her group, and that she personally was feminist, but that she identified herself more as part of the women's movement. People at the meeting trying to negotiate and build consensus said, "We are all feminists here," but clearly for her, being a representative of a popular women's group, a woman, and a member of the women's movement was important—more so than her identity as a feminist. This episode is similar to some of the conflicts around inequality and privilege discussed by Roth and Guenther in their chapters for this volume, and it illustrates the importance of labels for identity politics, perhaps in particular for those using labels such as "feminist," which have been often criticized and ridiculed.

Conclusions

For the women's movement in Buenos Aires, faced with economic crisis and the possibility of losing ground in its long-standing battle to address gender inequalities, external threats brought activists and groups together. But in addition, three related internal elements—bridge builders, prior social ties, and common ideology—were activated in this period. Feminist activists, in particular but not only those who acted as bridge builders between generations and other factions within the movement, created discursive spaces where differences could be recognized and respected, yet overcome for collective organizing. To do so, they emphasized inclusivity and common ideology, drawing on ties from their participation in transnational and national activist venues that embrace diversity and respect for difference, as well as their experiences in local protests. The external crisis acted like a catalyst, activating

these internal elements by making cooperative activism seem both more necessary and more feasible.

Activists who joined the Feminist Meeting were able to cooperate and
to bridge some boundaries that have long marked their movements, but the
cleavages between feminists and nonfeminists remained. This variation in
outcomes suggests that a channeling or selection process occurred, making
some boundaries more permeable than others. Crises alone do not create coalitions or other kinds of alliances. Activists seeking to cooperate must translate the crisis moment into fertile ground for a coalition, and this process is
fraught with difficulty. The persistence of enduring barriers to cooperation
is one of the key findings here.

The case is consistent with existing literature on the importance of political opportunities for coalitions, particularly external threats (McCammon
and Campbell 2002; Meyer and Corrigall-Brown 2005; Van Dyke 2003).
Activists must perceive these changes in the environment. As Brockett (1991,
255) argues, "Mobilization and action are mediated by perception," and these
perceptions must then become part of collective action framing. Croteau
and Hicks (2003) show that it takes a lot of framing and organizational work
to create a coalition, and this is true for the way activists handle threats as well.
When societies are marked by moments of crisis and disorder, the widespread
perception of this context can inspire people to participate in social movements, a factor that contributes to protest waves. It may also provoke changes
in alliances and can lead SMOs and activists to reassess their connections
with other groups and to redefine and renavigate these relationships. Bandy
and Smith (2005) state that coalitions need to balance personal interests and
group interests, and perceptions of changing political context can lead people and groups to reassess the costs and benefits of working cooperatively. In
Buenos Aires, this renegotiation can be seen in the repeated calls by feminists about the need to come together in the crisis, and the success of the
feminist meeting group to bridge cleavages on the bases of representation and
identity.

Yet the literature also notes that groups with common goals often fail to
successfully work together because of a failure to recognize their "common-
place" of similar goals and interests (Bystydzienski and Schacht 2001, 9),
a dynamic that is readily apparent in Roth's chapter in this volume, where
women of color prioritized the maintenance of difference. As Roth points
out, activists have to perceive cooperation itself as useful; it is not enough just
to perceive an external threat. Certainly, social boundaries can block the recognition of shared goals and can make cooperation seem untenable. For the
women's movement in Argentina, some identity barriers—those related to

representation and recognition—were able to be breached, while those related to resources were harder to overcome. Although inclusive solidarity has been called a necessary element for successful coalitions (Ferree and Roth 1998) and broad collective identity has the potential to attract more participants (Barvosa-Carter 2001), it may be hard to create inclusive solidarity with collective identities that bridge class during times of economic crisis. Given the economic nature of the external threat, the persistent cleavage between middle-class and popular sector women's groups may even have been heightened by Argentina's crisis. For example, middle-class feminist critiques of sexist language were seen as frivolous by popular sector activists who were mobilized first and foremost to address poverty and unemployment. The character of external threats (e.g., repression, economic problems, losing rights) may shape the type of alliance that is possible in coalitions and the social ties that are subsequently activated for collaboration between groups.

The case also points to the fact that coalitions are often complex gatherings of SMOs, and we can learn more subtle lessons about the organizational processes in coalitions by looking within already narrowly defined groups of organizations within coalitions. Here, lesbian rights organizations, for instance, were a subgroup within the Feminist Meeting group and had their own internal dynamics, such as whether or not to identify as women. We need to pay attention to the shifting nature of alliances, and the processes that mark boundary crossing within and between SMOs in a coalition and in coalition subgroups to help to explain why some alliances are more lasting than others.

This work also fits well with the literature on women's movements, particularly debates about practical versus strategic gender interests (Molyneux 1998). There has been widespread criticism of conceptualizing gender interests as either tied to practical or feminine concerns related to the division of labor, or to the transformation of the existing gender order—a feminist approach. Although this classification has been aptly criticized as too rigid and binary (Stephen 1997), and many movements have started by addressing practical interests and have later challenged patriarchal systems (e.g., Blondet 1995), in practice, the division between feminist and nonfeminist groups has remained important, at least in Argentina, where abortion has been a particularly difficult issue, given the power of the Catholic Church. The case suggests that the barriers that can exist between feminist and nonfeminist activists, particularly when reinforced by class divisions, are salient obstacles for cooperation.

Finally, the research raises questions about the longevity of collaborative alliances founded in the context of external threat. It may be hard to build more permanent coalitions based on crisis mobilization. Staggenborg (1986) found that when a crisis subsided, it marked an end for coalitions because ideological conflict proved more distracting to the group. Argentina's economy has improved since 2003 and the level of protest has subsided, but the women's movement has continued to express concerns about the effects of growing inequality as well as the still-high rates of poverty and underemployment for women. More research could examine how cooperation evolves as external threats change over time.

Notes

1. Note that the first large *piquetero/a* protests occurred in 1996 in the province of Neuquén, but the visibility and legitimacy of this form of mobilization increased in 2001.

2. I follow Minkoff's (1999) definition of SMOs, which includes both protest organizations and advocacy organizations. The former "use outsider methods of institutional challenge at least some of the time," whereas the latter use more "routine means like lobbying and litigation to influence policies and public opinion" (1667–68).

3. This decision—in part due to practical time constraints—is based on a distinction that is made in most women's movements in Latin America between popular groups and middle-class movements. The middle class has traditionally been very strong in Argentina and has been dominant in addressing gender issues. As a first world academic, I believe I had greater access to middle-class activists than I would have in more popular women's organizations.

4. I have translated this and all subsequent quotes originally in Spanish.

5. There are also divisions among women in popular women's groups along party lines, ideology, strategy, and support of church, but this is not the focus of my research.

6. Literally a scratch-out. This is a protest involving symbolic or actual denigration of a person or institution, often with chants and graffiti painting.

7. This dynamic is mentioned in Roth (this volume) and is explored more extensively in Roth (2003). She describes how white U.S. feminists in the 1970s recognized a need for more women of color in their movement but were not willing to take actions to level the playing field so that black and Latina women could participate equally.

Works Cited

Almeida, Paul D. 2003. "Opportunity Organizations and Threat-Induced Contention: Protest Waves in Authoritarian Settings." *American Journal of Sociology* 109: 345–400.

Alonso, Graciela, and Raúl Díaz. 2002. "Encuentros Nacionales de Mujeres: Pedagogías de viajes y experiencias." In *Hacía una pedagogía de las experiencias de las mujeres,* edited by G. Alonso and R. Díaz, 76–109. Buenos Aires, Argentina: Miño y Dávila.

Alvarez, Sonia E. 1990. *Engendering Democracy in Brazil: Women's Movements in Transition Politics.* Princeton, N.J.: Princeton University Press.

Alvarez, Sonia E., Nalu Faria, and Miriam Nobre. 2003. "Another (Also Feminist) World Is Possible: Constructing Transnational Spaces and Global Alternatives from the Movements." In *World Social Forum: Challenging Empires,* edited by Jai Sen and Peter Waterman, 199–206. Montevideo, Uruguay: Third World Institute.

Auyero, Javier. 2003. *Contentious Lives: Two Argentine Women, Two Protests, and the Quest for Recognition.* Durham, N.C.: Duke University Press.

———. 2007. *Routine Politics and Violence in Argentina: The Gray Zone of State Power.* Cambridge: Cambridge University Press.

Bandy, Joe, and Jackie Smith, eds. 2005. *Coalitions across Borders: Transnational Protest and the Neoliberal Order.* Lanham, Md.: Rowman & Littlefield.

Barvosa-Carter, Edwina. 2001. "Multiple Identity and Coalition Building: How Identity Differences within Us Enable Radical Alliances among Us." In *Forging Radical Alliances across Difference: Coalition Politics for the New Millennium,* edited by Jill M. Bystydzienski and Steven P. Schacht, 21–34. Lanham, Md.: Rowman & Littlefield.

Bellucci, Mabel. 1997. "Women's Struggle to Decide about Their Own Bodies: Abortion and Sexual Rights in Argentina." *Reproductive Health Matters* 10: 99–106.

Blondet, Cecilia. 1995. "Out of the Kitchens and onto the Streets." In *The Challenge of Local Feminisms,* edited by A. Basu, 251–75. Boulder, Colo.: Westview Press.

Borland, Elizabeth. 2004a. "Cultural Opportunities and Tactical Choice in the Argentine and Chilean Reproductive Rights Movements." *Mobilization* 9: 327–39.

———. 2004b. "Growth, Decay, and Change: Organizations in the Contemporary Women's Movement in Buenos Aires, Argentina." Ph.D. dissertation, Department of Sociology, University of Arizona, Tucson.

———. 2006. "The Mature Resistance of Argentina's Madres de Plaza de Mayo." In *Latin American Social Movements: Globalization, Democratization, and Transnational Networks,* edited by Hank Johnston and Paul D. Almeida, 115–30. Boulder, Colo.: Rowman & Littlefield.

———. 2008. "Social Movement Organizations and Coalitions: Comparisons from the Women's Movement in Buenos Aires, Argentina." *Research in Social Movements, Conflicts, and Change* 28: 83–112.

Borland, Elizabeth, and Barbara Sutton. 2007. "Quotidian Disruption and Women's Activism in Times of Crisis, Argentina, 2002–2003." *Gender and Society* 21: 700–722.

Briones, Claudia, and Marcela Mendoza. 2003. *Urban Middle-Class Women's Responses to Political Crisis in Buenos Aires.* Memphis: University of Memphis Center for Research on Women.

Brockett, Charles D. 1991. "The Structure of Political Opportunities and Peasant Mobilization in Central America." *Comparative Politics* 23: 253–74.

Bystydzienski, Jill M., and Steven P. Schacht, eds. 2001. *Forging Radical Alliances across Difference: Coalition Politics for the New Millennium.* Lanham, Md.: Rowman & Littlefield.

Chaneton, July. 1995. "Feminismo y movimiento social de mujeres: Historia de un malentendido." *Feminaria* 8: 15–19.

Coffey, Amanda, and Paul Atkinson. 1996. *Making Sense of Qualitative Data: Complementary Research Strategies.* Thousand Oaks, Calif.: Sage.

Conway, Janet. 2008. "Geographies of Transnational Feminisms: The Politics of Place and Scale in the World March of Women." *Social Politics: International Studies in Gender, State, and Society* 15: 207–31.

Croteau, David, and Lyndsi Hicks. 2003. "Coalition Framing and the Challenge of a Consonant Frame Pyramid: The Case of a Collaborative Response to Homelessness." *Social Problems* 50: 251–72.

Di Marco, Graciela, Héctor Palomino, Susana Méndez, Ramón Altamirano, and Mirta Libchaber de Palomino. 2003. *Movimientos sociales en la Argentina: Asambleas–la politización de la sociedad civil.* Buenos Aires, Argentina: Jorge Baudino Ediciones.

Dufour, Pascale, and Isabelle Giraud. 2007. "The Continuity of Transnational Solidarities in the World March for Women, 2000 and 2005: A Collective Identity-Building Approach." *Mobilization* 12: 307–22.

Ferree, Myra Marx, and Silke Roth. 1998. "Gender, Class and the Interaction between Social Movements: A Strike of West Berlin Day Care Workers." *Gender and Society* 12: 626–48.

Fisher, Jo. 2000. "Gender and the State in Argentina: The Case of the Sindicato de Amas de Casa." In *Hidden Histories in Gender and the State in Latin America,* edited by E. Dore and M. Molyneux, 322–45. Durham, N.C.: Duke University Press.

Flori, Mónica. 1988. "Argentine Women's Organizations during the Transition to Democracy." *Feminist Issues* 8: 53–66.

Fraga, Rosendo. 2002. "Nacieron 272 asambleas luego de los cacerolazos." *Nación,* March 25, 8.

Frohmann, Alicia, and Teresa Valdés. 1995. "Democracy in the Country and in the Home: The Women's Movement in Chile." In *Women's Movements in Global Perspective,* edited by A. Basu, 276–301. New Delhi: Kali Press.

Gallo, Daniel. 2002. "En lo que va del año se realizaron unas 20 protestas callejeras por día." *Nación,* August 22, 8.

Giarracca, Norma, and Miguel Teubal. 2001. "Crisis and Agrarian Protest in Argentina: The Movimiento Mujeres Agropecuarias en Lucha." *Latin American Perspectives* 28: 38–53.

INDEC (Instituto Nacional de Estadística y Censos). n.d. "Tasa de desocupación por aglomerado desde 1974 en adelante." http://www.indec.gov.ar/nuevaweb/cuadros/4/shempleo4.xls. Accessed March 31, 2010.

Jacquette, Jane S. 1991. Introduction to *The Women's Movement in Latin America,* edited by Jane S. Jacquette, 1–17. Boulder, Colo.: Westview Press.

Juris, Jeffrey S. 2008. "Spaces of Intentionality: Race, Class, and Horizontality at the United States Social Forum." *Mobilization* 13: 353–72.

Marshall, Catherine, and Gretchen B. Rossman. 1995. *Designing Qualitative Research.* Thousand Oaks, Calif.: Sage.

McCammon, Holly J., and Karen E. Campbell. 2002. "Allies on the Road to Victory: Coalition Formation between the Suffragists and the Woman's Christian Temperance Union." *Social Forces* 82: 1457–92.

Medina Rosas, Andrea, and Shamillah Wilson. 2003. "The Women's Movement in the Era of Globalisation: Does It Face Extinction?" *Gender and Development* 11: 135–41.

Meyer, David S., and Catherine Corrigall-Brown. 2005. "Coalitions and Political Context: U.S. Movements against Wars in Iraq." *Mobilization* 10: 327–44.

Minkoff, Debra. 1999. "Bending with the Wind: Strategic Change and Adaptation by Women's and Racial Minority Organizations." *American Journal of Sociology* 104: 1666–703.

Molyneux, Maxine. 1998. "Analyzing Women's Movements." *Development and Change* 29: 219–45.

Navarro, Marysa. 2001. "Los encuentros y desencuentros de los estudios de mujeres y el movimiento feminista." *Mora* 7: 106–13.

Obach, Brian K. 2004. *Labor and the Environmental Movement: A Quest for Common Ground.* Cambridge, Mass.: MIT Press.

Ovalles, Eduardo. 2002. "Evolución de los cacerolazos por distrito; Diciembre 2002–Marzo 2002." Centro de Estudios Nueva Mayoria, Buenos Aires.

Rossi, Federico Matías. 2005. "Aparición, auge y declinación de un movimiento social: Las asambleas vecinales y populares de Buenos Aires, 2001–2003." *Revista Europea de Estudios Latinoamericanos y del Caribe* 78: 67–88.

Roth, Benita. 2003. *Separate Roads to Feminism: Black, Chicana, and White Feminists in America's Second Wave.* Cambridge: Cambridge University Press.

Rucht, Dieter. 2004. "Movement Allies, Adversaries, and Third Parties." In *The Blackwell Companion to Social Movements,* edited by David A. Snow, Sarah A. Soule, and Hanspeter Kriesi, 197–216. Malden, Mass.: Blackwell.

Shaffer, Martin. 2000. "Coalition Work among Movement Groups: Who Partici-pates?" *Research in Social Movements, Conflicts, and Change* 22: 111–26.

Staggenborg, Suzanne. 1986. "Coalition Work in the Pro-Choice Movement: Orga-nizational and Environmental Opportunities and Obstacles." *Social Problems* 33: 374–90.

Stephen, Lynn. 1997. *Women and Social Movements in Latin America: Power from Below.* Austin: University of Texas Press.

Van Dyke, Nella. 2003. "Crossing Movement Boundaries: Factors That Facilitate Coalition Protest by American College Students, 1930–1990." *Social Problems* 50: 226–50.

Vezzetti, Hugo. 2002. "Scenes from the Crisis." *Journal of Latin American Cultural Studies* 11: 163–71.

12

Sudden Mobilization: Movement Crossovers, Threats, and the Surprising Rise of the U.S. Antiwar Movement

Ellen Reese, Christine Petit, and David S. Meyer

According to antiwar organizers, in April 2002, more than 100,000 demonstrators gathered in Washington, D.C., to protest against the threat of war in Iraq. Nine months later, on January 18, 2003, millions participated in internationally coordinated protests in at least thirty countries. In the United States, the activist International Action Center (2003) reported that these protests drew 500,000 in Washington, D.C.; 200,000 in San Francisco; and thousands to tens of thousands in cities across the country. Predictably, mainstream media estimates of these events were generally smaller, but it was clear that a mass-based antiwar movement had grown astonishingly quickly and represented a broad array of coalition partners. Groups opposed to the war collaborated through the full range of interorganizational arrangements commonly found within contemporary movement coalitions, including stable and long-lived institutions, such as umbrella organizations, that facilitated discussion of tactics and issues among various groups, as well as much shorter agreements to participate in discrete events (Levi and Murphy 2006).

By the standards of the American peace movement, the protests were cross-generational and cross-racial affairs involving a wide array of political and social groups. As one reporter described, they "attracted a wide spectrum of demonstrators, from sign-toting grandmothers to college students to gay activists to parents with babies in strollers" (Willman and Piller 2003). Nor was all the action in the streets. Broad sectors of the American public engaged in a wide variety of antiwar activities: they launched media campaigns, lobbied, signed petitions, organized public forums, screened films, boycotted classes, built symbolic graveyards, and adorned their bodies, vehicles, and doors with the symbols and slogans of their new movement.

The initial antiwar mobilization was historically unprecedented in terms of both its sudden emergence and the breadth of coalition partners involved. Perhaps because so many different groups participated, the size of protests against the second war in Iraq far exceeded that of demonstrations against the first Gulf War ten years earlier, or the U.S. invasion of Afghanistan in 2001. They even exceeded the size of early protests against the war in Vietnam. Even more remarkable, these mass demonstrations against the second invasion of Iraq occurred before the war began. As Tom Hayden, a leading antiwar activist in the 1960s and later a California state senator, noted, "These numbers are bigger than when we first marched in Washington, when Johnson first sent in the troops in the spring of '65. . . . The official count was only 20,000. And that was seen as unprecedented, enormous" (cited in Willman and Piller 2003). Large-scale demonstrations against the war in Vietnam comparable in size and breadth to those that occurred in 2003 developed after years of war, after tens of thousands of Americans were drafted, sent to war, and killed or maimed, and after the horrors of war were graphically televised across the nation's living rooms.

What accounts for the sudden mobilization against the second war in Iraq and the breadth of coalition participation in antiwar protests? Some observers credit the spread of electronic media (e.g., Neuman 2003), but that technology is now available to activists on virtually all issues in American politics. Further, it is important not to confuse a mechanism with a cause. We want to understand how a mass movement can suddenly appear in response to the crisis of the moment, tracing some of the processes through which organizers mobilize dissent (McAdam, Tarrow, and Tilly 2001).

Combining interviews with activists and information from electronic mailing lists, Web sites, newspaper articles, and public opinion polls, we argue that the sudden growth of the antiwar movement in the United States was due to a combination of favorable political conditions and the effects of "movement spillover" (Meyer and Whittier 1994). Our explanation combines theoretical insights from several strands of social movement research. First, we draw insights from political process models. Scholars in this tradition emphasize the role of expanding political opportunities for stimulating protest (McAdam 1999; Meyer 2004; Tarrow 1998). Following older versions of these models (Eisinger 1973; Tilly 1978) and recent literature, we emphasize the importance of both threats and political opportunities for explaining the rise of social movements (Almeida 2003; Andrews 2002; Goldstone and Tilly 2001; McCammon and Campbell 2002; Meyer 2004; Meyer and Minkoff 2004; Reese 2005; Reese, Giedraitis, and Vega 2005; Van Dyke 2003). Consistent with this, we suggest that high levels of political polarization and the bold leadership style of the George W. Bush administration created multiple threats and grievances, and that the plans to go to war provided a proximate cause to unite a wide range of groups and individuals (Meyer and Corrigall-Brown 2005).

Second, we draw insights from the literature on resource mobilization and on coalitions, arguing that prior mobilization, previously developed inter-organizational and individual networks, and coalition building provided the personnel and organizational resources necessary to mobilize latent opposition against the war rapidly. We use in-depth interviews to explore the particular roles played by "movement crossovers" in building the antiwar movement. Crossovers, because they belong to multiple movements and national and international federations or networks, were strategically positioned to broaden the reach of the antiwar movement, create new antiwar organizations, coordinate national and international protests, and build cross-movement alliances.

We begin by laying out the theoretical premises on which our analysis is based, starting with the political context and then focusing on the relationships among groups and organizers. We trace the process of negotiating cooperation in activism through the efforts of well-established actors, mostly on the left. We trace the dynamics of crossovers in terms of organizations, tactics, and claims. We conclude with a discussion of the long-term process of organization building that makes ostensibly sudden collaborative mobilization possible.

Sudden Mobilization: Theoretical Perspectives

Social movements result from the intersection of structure and agency—that is, opportunities and grievances are coincident with effective organization. Although popular accounts of social movements often emphasize the relatively sudden emergence of protest movements, scholarly accounts commonly emphasize long-standing efforts at organizing and well-established resources (e.g., McCarthy and Zald 1977; Morris 1984). The predominant approach to mobilization focuses attention on the purposive efforts of activists and organizers in building the capacity, including material, cultural, and cognitive dimensions, to mobilize and coordinate collective action. But this approach begs the question of why, if activist efforts are continual and progress gradually, the emergence of collective action sometimes appears so suddenly.

A few scholars have addressed ostensibly sudden mobilization, but they neglect the processes through which it is effected. Piven and Cloward (1977), in arguing that membership organizations dampen protest and its influence, claim that movements of the poor emerge when social–structural conditions develop in such a way as to make quotidian life impossible. (They nonetheless recognize the important organizing role of groups to mobilization, which they describe as cadre organizations). Of course, we know that the maintenance of daily life has become impossible only when we see protest emerge. Walsh (1981), in looking at the apparently rapid mobilization of a large movement against nuclear power, also pointed to exogenous factors, specifically "suddenly imposed grievances" that came with a reactor accident at Three Mile Island. But a coordinated response to this newly salient grievance was possible only because of a decade of political organizing (Gamson 1988). Similarly, Meyer and Corrigall-Brown (2005) looked at the emergence of the Win Without War coalition, which organized against the war in Iraq. In their analysis, the key factor explaining cooperation among diverse groups with distinct interests was the provocation of an imminent war. Corrigall-Brown and Meyer (this volume) emphasize the long-standing relationships among the key actors in this coalition, which allowed organizers to trust one another and respond effectively to the threat of war.

The political process model identifies potential influence of both expanding opportunities and external threats for stimulating collective action and greater cooperation among social movement organizations (Hathaway and Meyer 1997; Kleidman and Rochon 1997; McAdam 1999, x–xi; McCammon and Campbell 2002; Staggenborg 1986; Tarrow 1998, 86; Tilly 1978; Van Dyke 2003). For volatile social movements to emerge, sufficient numbers of people must be convinced that their engagement in unusual efforts is necessary and potentially effective (Meyer 2007). Research on the civil rights movement suggests that this occurs when political opportunities are expanding or partly open, such as when governmental officials are politically divided (Jenkins, Jacobs, and Agnone 2003). If activists believe that they can get what they want without engaging the costs and risks of social movement action, they are likely to rely on conventional forms of political participation, such as electoral campaigns and lobbying. On the other hand, when authorities appear completely resistant to popular influence, groups may respond to threats with resignation (Eisinger 1973; McAdam 1999; Meyer 1999, 2004; Tarrow 1998) or by turning inward to develop ideas and nourish their base, rather than engage in political campaigns likely to be risky and/or futile (Taylor 1989). Recent research has explored the ways in which various kinds of threats can stimulate greater interorganizational collaboration and protest, including repression, state-attributed economic problems, and the erosion of rights (Almeida 2003), the loss of social services and jobs (Reese 2005; Reese, Giedraitis, and Vega 2005), rising war deaths and levels of racial income inequality (Jenkins, Jacobs, and Agnone 2003) and the presence of political antagonists (Van Dyke 2003). In each case, researchers have described how an external political shift has allowed a clear focal point for a variety of nominally distinct but closely related movements to mobilize around.

Clearly, both activist efforts and political opportunities are critical to the emergence of strong protest movements, even those responding to threats. Mobilization that is both sudden and broad occurs when sufficient numbers of people are quickly convinced that their unusual efforts might succeed in bringing something desirable about—or stopping some unwanted policy initiative—but only through political mobilization. Because contemporary American politics includes numerous groups prepared to use protest to advance their claims, large-scale mobilization is a function of uniting diverse groups in common purpose. But rapid mobilization actually takes long-term efforts.

We draw insights from the political process model in an effort to understand the structural, political, and organizational elements that coincided to allow for very rapid mobilization in response to the threat of the imminent, then actual, second Gulf War within the United States. Four contextual factors were particularly salient: (1) highly publicized electoral scandals during the 2000 presidential election; (2) the creation of multiple grievances as the Bush administration carried out bold moves on both domestic and foreign policy fronts that encouraged diverse organizations to cooperate in common struggle; (3) the rise of both significant elite and international opposition to the war; and (4) the absence of apparently viable institutional strategies for opposing the war. Together, these four conditions aided coalition building among left and liberal forces and aided their efforts in reaching a broader public.

We need to stress that external conditions do not create mobilization; rather, they generate the circumstances in which clever activist efforts might meet a responsive audience. Mobilization and coalition building also require organizational resources and bridge builders. To mobilize, discontented groups must have access to organizational resources in order to coordinate action and carry it out effectively. To mobilize broadly and rapidly, they need access to both "micromobilizing" structures, such as churches or social movement organizations, to engage in bloc recruitment of individuals, and mesomobilizing structures, such as coalitions or umbrella groups (Gerhards and Rucht 1992). The United States has a well-developed and institutionalized social movement sector with numerous formal and informal organizations across multiple policy and issue domains (Meyer and Tarrow 1998). Activists drew from this preexisting movement infrastructure to form new antiwar groups and to mobilize against the war. At least three kinds of groups mobilized against the war, contributing to the large size of antiwar protests: (1) newly formed antiwar organizations and coalitions; (2) preexisting organizations, coalitions, and social networks; and (3) emergent activists, or unaffiliated opponents of the war, who showed up to events coordinated by the other two groups.

Like other social movements, this antiwar movement represented a broad coalition of social groups and organizations, united more in opposition to a proximate provocation than a common program for the future (Meyer and Corrigall-Brown 2005). We want to understand how groups with a range of interests and priorities come to cooperate in common cause. Prior research on social movement coalitions emphasizes the role of brokers (McAdam, Tarrow, and Tilly 2001, 142–43; Obach 2004). More commonly, analysts use the metaphor of a bridge, which spans distinct and separate places. Rose (2000, 143) identifies bridge builders as critical to connecting labor organizers with the environmental movement, while Mische (2008) emphasizes the importance of "bridging leaders" who are conversant in the norms of discourse in different institutional contexts in Brazilian civil society. In writing about the civil rights movement, Robnett (1997; see also Kuumba 2001) stresses the importance of bridge leaders in connecting the national rhetoric, leadership, and claims of the movement to grassroots activism.

We can think of these brokers or bridgers as individuals who, by virtue of peculiar commitments and capacities, can create and manage ties among two or more ostensibly distinct social groups, constituencies, or organizations. These people often have common experiences with or ties to the groups and organizations they help to unite (McAdam, Tarrow, and Tilly 2001, 142–43; Mische 2008; Obach 2004, 24; Rose 2000, 143). The entities bridged by these leaders may be separated by location, political analysis, previous political activism, formal organizational barriers, class or ethnic differences, or generation. Here, we identify "movement crossovers," a particular type of bridge builder who brings together two or more social movements, and we explore their roles in coordinating the recent mobilization against the war in Iraq.

To be sure, participation in more than one ostensibly distinct social movement over time, or even simultaneously, is hardly unique (Meyer and Whittier 1994; Mische 2008; Rosenthal et al. 1985). Explicit concern with uniting these distinct movements is less common, however, and absolutely critical to building multi-issue coalitions. Our term, *movement crossovers,* refers to activists involved in multiple political issues and campaigns normally characterized as being part of distinct movements. Movement crossovers straddle movements normally seen as distinct in at least one of four different ways: (1) they informally belong to overlapping social networks or overlapping social movement communities that cross movement boundaries; (2) they participate in two or more movements by virtue of holding multiple organizational memberships; (3) they hold memberships in multi-issue organizations; or (4) they participate in formal or ad hoc cross-movement coalitions (Van Dyke 2003).

Our concept of movement crossovers extends the conceptualization by Rosenthal et al. (1985) of bridgers by including unaffiliated activists and those participating in ad hoc groups that span one or more movements. The term *bridgers* refers to reformers involved in two or more sectors of activity through their membership in formal organizations or institutions. Reformers' activities might include movement participation, but they could simply involve voluntary or professional service or charitable activities. Movement crossovers, on the other hand, have affiliations that span one or more movements and are by definition movement participants.

Individual crossovers are often situated in organizations with broad, multi-issue agendas that encourage them to link issues. Van Dyke's (2003) research on student protest shows that members of such multi-issue organizations often share broad ideological outlooks that facilitate the formation of cross-movement coalitions. Similarly, Obach (2004) found that coalitions between labor and environmental organizations usually involved the leaders of organizations that defined their agenda and roles broadly. Likewise, Rosenthal et al. (1985), in their network analysis of the organizational affiliations of leading women reformers in nineteenth-century New York, found that reformers belonging to multi-issue feminist organizations tended to have multiple and strong ties to organizations involved in various clusters of activity.

We argue that movement crossovers were strategically positioned to organize broad-based opposition to the war rapidly because they could mobilize the ideas, personnel, leaders, and resources of multiple movements. This was particularly true of movement crossovers who belonged to multi-issue groups or to networks organized at the national and international levels. Many single-issue peace activists and emergent activists also mobilized opposition to the war. However, movement crossovers played a larger role in mobilization because they were able to take advantage of their ties to multiple movements to build broad antiwar organizations, such as the International ANSWER (Act Now to Stop War and End Racism) coalition. Others formed more narrowly targeted, identity-based antiwar groups, such as CODEPINK or Latinos Against the War, which helped to draw particular types of movement communities into the antiwar movement. Our analysis highlights multiple kinds of "movement spillover" processes, including the spillover of personnel, organizations, goals, rhetoric, and tactics, which were critical to building new kinds of formal coalition organizations and broad-based protest coalitions against the war in Iraq.

Threats, Opportunities, and Antiwar Mobilization
Multiple Grievances and Elite Dissent

As the political process model suggests, exogenous conditions affect the potential growth of protest movements. The contested presidential election, a controversial president, and unpopular domestic and foreign policies drew diverse actors into an alliance against the president, while elite division around the war legitimated and encouraged popular dissent, and the quick end to congressional debate encouraged dissatisfied people to take their grievances to the streets. The coincidence of these conditions afforded U.S. activists the opportunity to mobilize broadly and rapidly against the proposed and actual second Gulf War.

From the start, the Bush administration suffered from a legitimacy deficit. Bush lost the popular vote in 2000 and won a narrow electoral college victory based on a very small margin in Florida, a state in which a majority of voters clearly intended to vote for his opponent, and the United States Supreme Court stopped a recount in progress. A broad range of liberal and left groups, critical of Bush's policies, organized protests throughout the country to oppose his first inauguration. The largest event was in Washington, D.C., where between 10,000 and 20,000 people protested the inauguration, representing the largest counterinauguration protest since 1973, when an already damaged Richard Nixon took his second oath of office (Helm and Dlouhy 2001; Reinert and Gonzalez 2001).

President Bush did not allow his narrow margin of victory to temper the pursuit of his agenda. Rather, the new president claimed a mandate, boldly pursuing controversial policies popular with his core supporters. Although the Bush agenda initially stalled in Congress and with the public, the administration used the September 11, 2001, attack on the World Trade Center to provide a sense of urgency and exploit the prerogatives of the executive. Beginning with the invasion of Afghanistan, the Bush administration pursued a range of foreign and domestic policies that antagonized as many organized interests as they satisfied.

Central to the administration's agenda was a series of tax cuts heavily weighted to the wealthy, weakening of government regulation of business and the environment, opposition to labor organizing, and the appointment of conservative officials and judges. The administration's social agenda included promoting marriage for welfare recipients while prohibiting it for gays and lesbians, encouraging sexual abstinence for the unmarried at home and abroad, and prohibiting comprehensive birth control counseling by anyone receiving federal funds. The president's education reform program started with extensive mandated testing and recurrent calls for the development of a voucher system. More broadly, the administration called for market-based reforms of health and welfare policies and for the use of faith-based institutions, particularly churches, as agents of federally funded social and educational policies. President Bush used the powers of the executive branch of the government, augmented by the Patriot Act, to detain and prosecute immigrants, and he enhanced surveillance of persons suspected of complicity in terror, broadly defined. The administration also steadfastly refused to embrace policies to ameliorate the recession for poor and working-class people while leaving state and local governments to manage increased expenses (for security and educational testing, for example) and decreased tax revenues mostly by cutting funding for social services. All these initiatives served to increase popular sensitivity to rising military expenditures.

By February 2003, 47 percent of those polled expressed disapproval of Bush's handling of the economy (Associated Press State and Local Wire 2003). Nevertheless, Figure 12.1 shows that national rates of public disapproval of President Bush's overall performance had risen since 2001, but remained relatively low until 2003. There were, however, large sectors of the population, particularly organized groups, with grievances ready to mobilize. The Bush administration's bold policy agenda, and its failure to build political consensus, provided a common enemy that united opponents, who ran the gamut of hard-core leftists to moderate Republicans. The antiwar movement appealed to these multiple grievances by drawing connections between the war in Iraq and the war at home against immigrants, workers, and the poor.

The Bush administration's evident aggressive pursuit of war, and its guarded and ultimately unsuccessful effort to gain United Nations support,

Year	Percentage Who Disapprove
2001	6–39
2002	12–33
2003	26–47
2004	35–51
2005	40–60
2006	54–65

Figure 12.1. Job disapproval ratings for President George W. Bush.
Source: *Gallup Poll and CNN/USA Today/Gallup (PollingReport .com 2006a). These ranges are based on monthly or bimonthly polls for each year. For 2006, this range is for polls taken between January and July. The question asked was "Do you approve or disapprove of the way George W. Bush is handling his job as president?"*

also strengthened opposition to the war. A February 2003 national poll showed that about 70 percent of respondents believed that Colin Powell had provided sufficient evidence that Iraq had weapons of mass destruction. Nevertheless, only 55 percent of respondents favored a military action with some allied backing, but without U.N. approval, the course of action taken by the Bush administration (Barabak 2003). Another national poll, taken a month before the second invasion of Iraq, found that 59 percent of all respondents thought that the United States should wait and give the U.N. weapons inspectors more time rather than take military action fairly soon (Zeller 2003). In Washington, however, the Republican-controlled Congress voted to authorize the president to use force early in the fall of 2002 by large margins. Congressional leaders scheduled the vote to exploit legislators' fears of appearing soft on terrorism on the eve of a national election. This worked to stifle congressional debate. Paul Wellstone (Democrat, Minnesota) was the only senator facing reelection who voted against the authorizing resolution.

Strong and vocal opposition to the war among political and cultural elites and policy experts helped to publicize and legitimate protesters' claims and arouse skepticism about the justification for war; it also provided activists some hope for stopping it. The U.N.'s chief arms inspector, Hans Blix, declared that there was no evidence of weapons of mass destruction in Iraq, while the U.N. Social Security Council rejected the Bush administration's requests for support. Although Congress did not consider authorizing the war again, other legislative bodies began to address the issue: by February 2003, at least seventy-five local legislative bodies had passed some sort of antiwar resolution (McDermott 2003). Visible elite opposition to the war also came from sources with indisputable military or conservative credentials. General Norman Schwarzkopf, commander of American military forces during the first Gulf War, and Congressman James P. Moran, a retired general and former assistant secretary of defense, along with other military officials, voiced opposition to the war (Lamb 2003; Ricks 2003). And CIA and FBI officials publicly expressed skepticism about the justifications for the war, including Bush's claims about the link between Iraq and al-Qaeda (Bennis 2003). Numerous acclaimed actors, writers, and musicians also added to the antiwar fervor.

Bush's drive to war in Iraq followed closely on the heels of several other foreign policies, particularly the U.S. invasion of Afghanistan and continued U.S. support of Israel's occupation of the Palestinian territories. Although these policies were not widely contested, they had mobilized activist groups, mostly on the political left, and led organizers to look for an opportunity to build their visibility and support. Indeed, the national steering committee of the International ANSWER coalition, one of the largest antiwar organizations in the United States, includes members of the Free Palestine Alliance, the national Muslim Student Association, and the Middle East Children's Alliance. These groups were already engaged in organizing, although with limited popular response.

Immediately after the war began, only 25 percent of Americans polled opposed the invasion, compared to 37 percent earlier that month, following a long-standing trend for Americans to support American troops in battle, at least initially (Mueller 1973). However, Gallup poll analysts reported that "many of those who shifted in favor of the war continue[d] to have doubts about the merits of it, but want[ed] to show their support for the troops" (Saad 2003). Although the decline in protest activity after the start of war wasn't surprising, the extent to which activists continued to press their claims in the streets was. For example, more than 500,000 marched in the streets outside of the 2004 Republican National Convention to express their opposition to the war and the Bush administration.

Movement Crossovers and Movement Spillover

Grievances and political opportunities, by themselves, do not produce a massive protest movement; organizers do, and they use preexisting mobilizing structures to do it. Activists of various political stripes formed new kinds of movement organizations and politicized preexisting ones, providing the vehicles for mass mobilization and coalition building. Here, we explore the particular roles played by movement crossover agents in the growth of the antiwar movement, heeding Obach's (2004, 234) caution that "in the final analysis, the study of coalitions must examine the key personnel who actually pull organizations into coalition activity. It is they who carry out the mundane, but necessary task of interorganizational outreach."

Data and Methods

Our research is based on semistructured interviews with ten antiwar activists in the Los Angeles area, where some of the largest antiwar demonstrations in the country were held. We relied on a purposive sample of interviewees. We chose interviewees both because they mobilized people against the war in Iraq in ways that crossed movement boundaries and because they played leading roles in a variety of other social movements. All of our interviewees were staff, leaders, or active members of organizations associated with another social movement besides the antiwar movement. With a few exceptions, our links to these interviewees were made through our participation in the antiwar movement in Los Angeles. In addition to participation within citywide protest events, one of the coauthors (C.P.) participated in meetings and events organized by CODEPINK and ANSWER, while another coauthor (E.R.) participated in those organized by a neighborhood peace and justice group and Coalition for World Peace, an affiliate of United for Peace and Justice.

Figure 12.2 summarizes the movement and organizational affiliations of our interviewees. We use the term "antiwar organizations" to refer to those organizations that identified stopping the second Gulf War as a primary goal;

Other Movements	Antiwar Organizations	Other Organizations
1. Labor, human rights	U.S. Labor Against the War, Students and Educators Against the War, Coalition for World Peace	United Teachers of Los Angeles, American Federation of Teachers, Central Labor Council, National Association of Educators
2. Socialist, immigrant rights	San Gabriel Valley Neighbors for Peace and Justice	International Socialist Organization
3. Korean sovereignty, Korean American rights, immigrant rights	Coalition for World Peace	Young Koreans United
4. Human rights, civil liberties	Coalition for World Peace	Committee in Solidarity with the People in El Salvador, National Lawyers' Guild
5. Human rights	Interfaith Communities United for Justice and Peace, American Friends Service Committee	None
6. Progressive Democrat	None	Democracy for America So Cal Grassroots
7. Global justice (respondent 1)	CODEPINK	
8. Global justice (respondent 2)	Radical Teen Cheer	None
9. Anti-Bush, gay rights, immigrant rights	World Can't Wait, Drive Out the Bush Regime	South Central Farm Support Committee, Global Women's Strike
10. Anti-imperialism, antiracism/Arab American/ Palestinian rights	ANSWER	Free Palestine Alliance

Figure 12.2. Interviewees' movement and organizational affiliations.

many of these groups were multi-issue organizations that pursued other concerns at the same time. "Other organizations" sometimes mobilized against the war but devoted most of their efforts to other goals. So Cal Grassroots, for example, was mainly concerned with revitalizing and reshaping the Democratic Party and voter mobilization; its members pressed elected Democrats to oppose the war as part of its multi-issue progressive agenda. Thus, we distinguish between antiwar organizations and other organizations in terms of the extent to which they prioritized stopping the war and their level of involvement in antiwar activities. Each interview lasted about seventy-five minutes and explored how and why our interviewees mobilized against the war, their target constituents, their participation in social movement organizations and coalitions, and their roles as bridge activists.

In what follows, we seek to identify particular kinds of movement spillover processes through which multiple social movements interacted and fed the sudden rise of the antiwar movement. We first focus on how organizations and personnel from various movements spilled over into the antiwar movement and vice versa. We identify the particular organizational mechanisms through which movement crossovers built links between the antiwar movement and other social movements. Next, we focus on how movement crossovers mobilized particular groups against the war by drawing on the rhetoric and tactics associated with other social movements. Corrigall-Brown and Meyer (this volume) note that long-standing relationships among activists facilitated new alliances in the moment. Here, we focus on the direct responses to the impending war by an array of movement crossovers and the various strategies and organizational forms through which they broadened the reach of the antiwar movement.

Spillover of Organizations, Personnel, and Goals

In looking at the sudden mobilization against the war, it is critical to recognize less visible organizing that had been taking place for many years on different, often apparently unrelated issues. The groups and activists involved in prior organizing provided infrastructure for rapid mobilization against the war. Our interviews with antiwar activists revealed that many drew on personal or informal ties to activists involved in other movements to mobilize against the war. More commonly, they used bridging mechanisms that involved formal organizations or coalitions to cross between movements and broaden the reach of the antiwar movement. Three such organizational mechanisms were particularly important. First, some worked within new or preexisting multi-issue organizations or coalitions whose agendas crossed movement boundaries, sometimes holding particular positions within such groups, such as participating in task forces that bridged several movements commonly seen as distinct. Second, they formed or joined targeted organizations or coalitions that mobilized members of particular movement communities against the war. Finally, they held multiple organizational memberships and used organizational resources from another movement to build antiwar organizations and mobilize popular opposition to the war.

These three organizational mechanisms for bridging the antiwar movement with another social movement were not mutually exclusive. As Figure 12.3 indicates, most of our interviewees used more than one of these three organizational mechanisms to build links between the antiwar movement and other social movements. Most were involved in multiple social movement organizations and sometimes more than one formal coalition. Organizations themselves also combined elements of these three organizational mechanisms to mobilize constituents. For example, our interviewee employed in the American Friends Service Committee described how committee staff used the organizational resources of this long-standing multi-issue peace and

Other Movements	Multi-issue Organization	Targeted or Broad Antiwar Organization	Cross-Movement Antiwar Coalition
1. Labor	Yes	Targeted	Yes
2. Socialist, immigrant rights	Yes	Targeted	No
3. Korean American rights, Korean sovereignty, immigrant rights	Yes	Broad	No
4. Peace and Justice in Central America	Yes	Broad	No
5. Human rights, civil liberties	Yes	Targeted	Yes
6. Progressive Democrat	Yes	Neither	No
7. Global justice (respondent 1)	Yes	Targeted	No
8. Global justice (resondent 2)	Yes	Targeted	No
9. Anti-Bush, gay rights, immigrant rights	Yes	Targeted	No
10. Anti-imperialism, antiracism/ Arab American/Palestinian rights	Yes	Broad	Yes

Figure 12.3. Interviewees' cross-movement organizational bridging mechanisms.

justice organization to mobilize opposition to the war in Iraq. Some of the volunteers it mobilized belonged to AFSC's Middle East Peace and Education Program, members of which were involved in the international solidarity movement for Palestine. This same interviewee was also an active member of Interfaith Communities United for Justice and Peace, a multi-issue coalition that targeted its antiwar mobilization among faith-based groups.

The global justice movement, which rose in the early 1990s, was pivotal in building cross-movement coalitions among activists in the labor, environmental, women's, antiracist, and human rights campaigns in the United States. This movement addressed multiple issues, brokering broad differences in analysis among its supporters. It coordinated large and volatile protests against the World Trade Organization, International Monetary Fund, and World Bank and attracted support from a wide range of activists, strengthening cross-movement alliances at local, national, and international levels. In 2000, U.S. activists involved in this movement focused on challenging electoral politics, organizing mass protests during the Republican and Democratic conventions and presidential inauguration (Klein 2002; Smith 2001; Starr 2000). Because it combined multiple issues, organizations, and tactics, the global justice movement provided a great deal of the organizational infrastructure—personnel, organizations, coalition structures, and informal networks among activists—that were used to build new antiwar movement organizations and coordinate protests. For example, workshops held at the 2003 World Social Forum were used to coordinate the international protests against the war that occurred a few months later when the war began (Reitan 2007).

Global justice activists established several antiwar groups represented in our study, including CODEPINK and radical cheerleading squads. Many of CODEPINK's initial organizers, such as Medea Benjamin, Starhawk, Jodie Evans, and Diane Wilson, were active in the global justice movement and used their ties from that movement (among others) to recruit members (CODE-PINK 2005; Petit 2005). Since CODEPINK's initial call to "unreasonable women" for action in November 2002, over a hundred chapters have been formed across the United States. Although some men participate in CODE-PINK activities, the group mainly appealed to women, who make up the bulk of its membership and leadership. Global justice activists also founded radical cheerleading squads, multi-issue organizations that drew thousands of teenage women in the United States and Canada into the antiwar movement. Los Angeles' Radical Teen Cheerleaders' first performance was at an antisweatshop protest. In response to the impending war and the invasion of Iraq, Radical Teen Cheerleaders shifted its focus and performed at numerous antiwar protests and marches. Our interviewee stressed that because they are young, their members are often not taken seriously by other organizations. Radical Teen Cheerleaders sought to create a fun and autonomous organization for radical youth, especially girls and young women.

Other movement crossovers in our study also used organizational resources from various social movements to build new antiwar organizations. Union activists, seeking to mobilize members of labor organizations against the war, formed U.S. Labor Against the War. Its first national conference in Chicago, held on January 11, 2003, drew more than 100 delegates, representing 76 national, regional, and local labor organizations. By 2006, the organization claimed over 140 affiliated organizations, including state and regional labor federations. USLAW's rapid growth was predicated on the spread of social movement unionism by leftists within the labor movement. Efforts to revitalize the labor movement, underway for decades, intensified in the 1990s after John Sweeney gained leadership of the AFL-CIO. Under his leadership, and in response to declining membership and worsening conditions for organized labor, many unions devoted more resources for organizing in the 1990s. Although the spread of social movement unionism or community unionism was uneven, many unions began to tie their struggles to other issues and organizers; they built alliances with community groups and called for social justice beyond the workplace (Clawson 2003; Voss and Sherman 2000).

Socialist activists played leading roles in building the three largest antiwar organizations in the United States, themselves coalitions of numerous smaller groups: International ANSWER, Not in Our Name, and United for Peace and Justice. These three groups dominated the national coordination of mass protests against the war in Iraq, particularly initially. Unlike targeted antiwar organizations, these broad antiwar organizations sought to attract a wide array of social groups. Activists affiliated with Workers' World Party, and later the Party for Liberation and Socialism, founded ANSWER; activists affiliated with the Revolutionary Communist Party helped to found Not in Our Name, and members of the Committees of Correspondence for Democracy and Socialism, Freedom Road Socialist Organization, and Solidarity helped to found United for Peace and Justice.

Although the politics, rhetoric, or allies of some of these early antiwar activists generated criticism (Green 2004; Weinberg 2005), it is critical to recognize the experience, efforts, and organizational resources of left activists in providing an infrastructure for a broader antiwar mobilization. National and international federated socialist organizations, already active in multiple social movements, were well prepared to form national antiwar organizations and coordinate protests across cities. Although the antiwar movement was able to draw support from larger more mainstream organizations, such as the National Association for the Advancement of Colored People (NAACP) and the National Organization for Women (NOW), left organizations played a critical role in forging movement coalitions. From the start, these small groups expressed an inherently multi-issue ideological orientation, comfort and experience with disruptive tactics, and financial independence from powerful sponsors (which was made possible by their small size). These characteristics enabled left groups to make both sudden and dramatic shifts in their organizational energy and resources to antiwar activity and encouraged them to organize mass protests. Larger and more bureaucratic organizations enjoyed more extensive resources, but they were also more constrained in their capacity to shift resources into antiwar activity because of ongoing issue commitments and real and imagined restrictions from large donors or granting agencies. Partly as a result, the larger organizations were less interested and less suited for the mass mobilization strategies to which left groups were ideologically committed.

Many of our interviewees led other types of multi-issue organizations, which expanded their agenda to include stopping the war. For example, Young Koreans United opposed the war in Iraq because they were concerned that the war against terrorism would spread into North Korea, increase discrimination against Korean Americans, and use up money that could pay for services for their community. Similarly, the American Friends Service Committee was quick to mobilize opposition to the war in Iraq because this goal fit with its long-standing mission of promoting peace as well as its local chapters' focus on the Middle East. So Cal Grassroots, formed to revitalize the Democratic Party, elect progressive candidates, and advocate on behalf of a progressive agenda, agreed to support antiwar resolutions in Congress. Differences in these various groups' tactics and rhetoric illustrated other movement spillover processes.

Targeted Appeals: Rhetorical and Tactical Spillover

As Maney, Woehrle, and Coy (2005) suggest, movement organizations often frame their claims strategically, aiming to reach particular target audiences. Framing can also reflect organizational interests and ideological commitments. In mobilizing opposition to the war, movement crossovers borrowed rhetoric, symbols, and tactics from other social movements in an effort to appeal to particular social groups and movement communities and involve them in new protest coalitions. International ANSWER, for example, consistently framed its antiwar messages in anti-imperialist terms, in line with its commitments on other issues, and linked opposition to the war in Iraq to opposition to U.S. foreign policies toward other countries, including Palestine, Haiti, and Venezuela. In contrast, Coalition for World Peace, which, according to our interviewee, included "a broad spectrum all the way from liberal to radical left," avoided such language. Instead, its members drew on the language of rights popularized by other social movements. As one of the founding members of the group explained:

> It was the center of our population in this country that needed to be addressed, so we did not use words like imperialism. We didn't use rhetoric that would scare people. We tried to conceptualize this as a "peace issue," as a "human and civil rights" issue, as a "rights for immigrants" issue, and as a defense of the Bill of Rights.

Another interviewee, a member of Interfaith Communities United for Justice and Peace, described how its "basic motto is, 'religious communities must stop blessing war.'" As a Quaker and a pacifist, he found Interfaith Communities United for Justice and Peace's message particularly appealing because "you won't find any demonizing." He contrasted this to the often more strident rhetoric of other antiwar organizations, such as ANSWER or Not in Our Name, which aggressively criticized their opponents. Radical Teen Cheer offered radical politics in a different voice, combining leftist language with irony and humor to present punchy, radical critiques of the war and other social ills; their cheers frequently tackled multiple issues, challenging capitalism, war, environmental degradation, police brutality, and violence against women simultaneously.

Other interviewees drew on ethnic- or class-based framings that were commonly used by their organizations to mobilize on other issues. For example, Young Koreans United highlighted the particular dangers that the war posed to Korean Americans, wrote opinion editorials for Korean newspapers, and organized vigils and other events for the Korean American community. As our interviewee described, "There was a Korean businessman who went to Iraq and got captured and beheaded and executed . . . so we had the vigil for him in Koreatown right after that. There was good video coverage of that by the Korean media and even the mainstream media too." Similarly, they drew attention to a Korean American immigrant who served in the military to obtain his citizenship and was killed. At citywide marches, Young Koreans United members marched with Korean drums to express pride in their cultural heritage and to create a visible presence at antiwar demonstrations.

Working inside the labor movement, USLAW brought a "working family" voice to the antiwar movement. To mobilize union members against the war, USLAW distributed a series of flyers that emphasized the specific effects of the war on workers in a variety of industries, including education, steel, and health care. Its organizers also held workshops on the economic effects of the war. To build international labor solidarity, USLAW organized a twenty-five-city tour of Iraqi labor leaders. USLAW also used a traditional tactic of unions to publicize their opposition to the war; they coordinated the passage of hundreds of antiwar resolutions by unions, including one from the largest labor federation, the AFL-CIO. These antiwar resolutions highlighted the burdens of the war for working families, linking spiraling military costs to social service cutbacks; some also drew attention to the class-based nature of military recruitment and death tolls. USLAW also organized labor contingents at citywide and national antiwar demonstrations; as many as 20,000 trade unionists from across the country marched in a labor contingent at United for Peace and Justice's national antiwar march in April 2006 (USLAW 2006; USLAW Steering Committee 2005).

In contrast, CODEPINK cleverly drew on the language and symbols of both feminism and femininity to mobilize women against the war. For example, it called "a code pink alert signifying extreme danger to all the values of nurturing, caring, and compassion that women and loving men have held" (CODEPINK 2005). In January 2004, CODEPINK activists in Los Angeles delivered a forty-five-foot pink slip to Dick Cheney in protest of the Iraq war, including the profits being made by his former company, Halliburton, as a result. The banner, in the shape of a woman's dress slip, frills and all, read, "Dick's in bed with Halliburton, but we got screwed! Cheney, you're fired." In addition to issuing pink slips, tactics used by CODEPINK in Los Angeles have included handing out hundreds of pink flowers during a funeral procession in mourning for the civilians and troops lost to the war at a protest marking one year since the invasion of Iraq; organizing a Mother's Day for Peace event at Santa Monica beach; and encouraging holiday shoppers to buy nonviolent toys. A founding member stressed the importance of CODEPINK's distinct identity: "Being able to have it be about women [who are] called, creates a focus that's important. So within the focus of antiwar activism to be the women's group creates an identity [and is] a strength for an organization."

Our findings on how movement crossovers and their organizations framed their opposition to war by drawing on the rhetoric of other identity-based movements dovetail with the conclusions of Maney, Woehrle, and Coy (2005). They analyze nine antiwar organizations' official statements and find that the organizations "see social identity-based mobilization as one of the means to expand membership and to make the concerns expressed in the organizational discourse meaningful to potential participants" (371). This type of framing, especially when it challenged social structural inequalities or emphasized the cost of war to minority groups, was most commonly used by "organizations whose identities are linked to issues of race, class, and gender." However, they also find that "social identities were not their primary framing devices" in their official statements, which frequently appropriated salient emotions and themes found in the dominant culture in an effort to appeal to a broad audience and counter potential criticisms of opposing war in a time of heightened nationalism (374).

More generally, we see that social movement organizations, mostly on the political left, were able to build on their efforts on other issues to organize against the war in Iraq. Each group had special access to groups and individuals from earlier campaigns, a kind of activist social capital, as well as a distinct niche defined by some combination of constituents, resources, political experience, or tactics. This gave the larger antiwar movement not only a preexisting infrastructure tied into activist communities, but also a broader profile with reach into diverse social and political audiences (Hathaway and Meyer 1997; Rosenthal et al. 1985; Staggenborg 1986). In reaching these groups, the movement as a whole engaged mobilizers and built bridges to other activist groups. Thus, mobilization could appear to emerge suddenly, even as diverse actors had been building largely invisible resources and political momentum for years.

Conclusion

The Bush administration's plans to invade Iraq provided a common threat to a wide range of activist groups with diverse litanies of grievances against the administration. Feminists, environmentalists, global justice advocates, gays and lesbians, and many others each had their own sometimes overlapping targets and provocations in administration policy; the war provided an overarching link for their efforts. To be sure, President Bush's bold style made it easier for opposition activists to recognize and negotiate links with other groups. By facing a common antagonist and an imminent threat, new coalitions among ostensibly distinct movements formed and preexisting alliances deepened. This sudden mobilization, however, depended on the long-term and largely invisible development of movement infrastructure and the coalition-building work of many activists. Although they were certainly not the only kinds of activists fostering the growth of the antiwar movement, we believe that movement crossovers played a critical role in these organizational processes.

Although the large and diverse campaign against the war in Iraq seemed to spring spontaneously from the body politic in response to the war, like other social movements, it had much deeper roots (Morris 1984; Taylor 1989). In fact, this new mobilization stood atop often less visible and ostensibly unconnected organizing efforts, including opposition to corporate globalization, movements on behalf of environmental protection, and disgruntled mainstream Democrats seeking some effective venue for political participation. President Bush's political management of both the war and domestic conflicts encouraged his opponents to cooperate, but it is critical to recognize activists' efforts in building a broad and volatile social movement. The new mobilization against the war was less a new movement than a new focus for various preexisting social movements and an emergent anti-Bush coalition. This overnight sensation was many years in the making.

Our case raises important alerts for analysts of social movements. First, researchers should recognize the often submerged links among movements and activists that surface suddenly in the context of new political grievances. Although scholars separate movements by distinct issues, activists are often far more inclined to see connections (Meyer and Whittier 1994; Mische 2008). Movement politics are based on alliances and contingencies that stretch and challenge the definitions of most analytical frameworks. Nonetheless, we find the concept of *movement crossovers*—that is, activists involved, formally or informally, in more than one ostensibly distinct movement—useful for understanding and distinguishing the precise roles played by a specific type of movement broker (McAdam, Tarrow, and Tilly 2001; Obach 2004), bridger (Rosenthal et al. 1985), or bridge builder (Rose 2000). This concept, and the four types of movement crossovers (identified above), are especially relevant to studies of various kinds of cross-sectoral movement phenomena, including community–labor alliances, the global justice movement, and the World Social Forum.

This case also calls for us to take a longer time frame into consideration in assessing the development of social movements, recognizing connections among apparently discrete events and campaigns, and searching for the activists during apparently quiescent times (Taylor 1989). Here, we must recognize that analytical approaches that date movement emergence from first appearance in mass media, for example, are getting to the story late. The case also calls for us to consider political circumstances and resources simultaneously. Many committed activists and organizations were working to reach a broad public and mobilize support well before the war and even the Bush presidency. Changed political circumstances afforded them greater opportunities to do so, and activists were opportunistic in picking issues and ways to frame them likely to win support.

We cannot, of course, predict with any certainty what comes next. The antiwar movement has already fragmented and declined significantly since the start of the war (Figure 12.1). The antiwar coalitions described above have proved fragile and contingent as new issues and strategies constantly emerge and draw in activists. John Kerry's unsuccessful 2004 presidential campaign and Barack Obama's successful 2008 campaign both drew support from many antiwar activists. Similarly, although opposition to the war served as a litmus test for liberal support in the Democratic primaries in 2008, the eventual nominee, seeking the political center, backed away from a clear exit from the war. Nonetheless, in both elections, many activists devoted their time and money to what seemed like their best bet to counter the Bush agenda.

Fragile public support for the war eroded as the Bush administration demonstrated both strategic and public relations mismanagement of the occupation of Iraq (Pollingreport.com 2006b). At the same time, other issues have become more salient for many activists, and certainly for the public at large. But the organizations and activists animating the antiwar movement remain, and movement crossovers may still reshape American politics in unpredictable ways.

Note

We thank Katrina Paxton and Darragh White for their assistance in collecting data for this project. We didicate this chapter to the memory of Don White, whose capacities as a "movement crossover" were inspiring.

Works Cited

Almeida, Paul D. 2003. "Opportunity Organizations and Threat-Induced Contention: Protest Waves in Authoritarian Settings." *American Journal of Sociology* 109: 345–400.

Andrews, Kenneth T. 2002. "Movement–Countermovement Dynamics and the Emergence of New Institutions: The Case of 'White Flight' Schools in Mississippi." *Social Forces* 80: 911–36.

Associated Press State and Local Wire. 2003. "Poll Finds Few Americans Favor War Unless U.N. Approves." *Associated Press State and Local Wire*, February 4.

Barabak, Mark Z. 2003. "Showdown with Iraq; The Times Poll; Many Desire U.N. Backing for War on Iraq; Most Americans Believe Colin L. Powell Was Persuasive, but Support for Action Falls from 62% with Security Council Backing to 55% Without." *Los Angeles Times*, February 9, A1.

Bennis, Phyllis. 2003. "Powell's Dubious Case for War." February 5. *Foreign Policy in Focus*. http://www.fpif.org/articles/powells_dubious_case_for_war. Accessed April 15, 2010.

Clawson, Dan. 2003. *The Next Upsurge: Labor and New Social Movements.* Ithaca, N.Y.: ILR Press.

CODEPINK. 2005. CODEPINK: Women for Peace. http://www.codepink4peace .org/. Accessed March 10, 2010.

Eisinger, Peter K. 1973. "The Conditions of Protest Behavior in American Cities." *American Political Science Review* 67: 11–28.

Gamson, William A. 1988. "Political Discourse and Collective Action." In *From Structure to Action: Social Movement Participation across Cultures,* edited by Bert Klandermans, Hanspeter Kriesi, and Sidney Tarrow, 219–44. Greenwich, Conn.: JAI Press.

Gerhards, Jurgen, and Dieter Rucht. 1992. "Mesomobilization: Organizing and Framing in Two Protest Campaigns in West Germany." *American Journal of Sociology* 98: 555–95.

Goldstone, Jack, and Charles Tilly. 2001. "Threat (and Opportunity): Popular Action and State Response in the Dynamics of Contentious Action." In *Silence and Voice in the Study of Contentious Politics,* edited by Ronald R. Aminzade, Doug McAdam, Elizabeth J. Perry, William H. Sewell Jr., Sidney Tarrow, and Charles Tilly, 179–94. Cambridge: Cambridge University Press.

Green, Robert. 2004. "Give Protests a Chance: The Peace Movement That Couldn't Stop a War." *L.A. Weekly,* August 27–September 2, 26, 29–31. http://www .laweekly.com/2004-08-26/news/give-protests-a-chance/. Accessed April 15, 2010.

Hathaway, Will, and David S. Meyer. 1997. "Competition and Cooperation in Movement Coalitions: Lobbying for Peace in the 1980s." In *Coalitions and Political Movements: The Lessons of the Nuclear Freeze,* edited by T. R. Rochon and D. S. Meyer, 61–79. Boulder, Colo.: Lynne Rienner.

Helm, Mark, and Jennifer Dlouhy. 2001. "Jeers of Protest amid the Cheers as Thousands Voice Discontent." *Times Union,* January 21, A6.

International Action Center. 2003. "Media Coverage of January 18–19, 2003, Anti-War Actions." http://www.iacenter.org/archive2003/J18_media.html. Accessed April 15, 2010.

Jenkins, J. Craig, David Jacobs, and Jon Agnone. 2003. "Political Opportunities and African-American Protest, 1948–1997." *American Journal of Sociology* 109: 277–303.

Kleidman, Robert, and Thomas R. Rochon. 1997. "Dilemmas of Organization in Peace Campaigns." In *Coalitions and Political Movements: The Lessons of the Nuclear Freeze,* edited by T. R. Rochon and D. S. Meyer, 47–60. Boulder, Colo.: Lynne Rienner.

Klein, Naomi. 2002. *Fences and Windows: Dispatches from the Front Lines of the Globalization Debate,* edited by Debra Ann Levy. New York: Picador USA.

Kuumba, M. Bahati. 2001. *Gender and Social Movements.* Walnut Creek, Calif.: Alta Mira Press.

Lamb, David. 2003. "Federal Bastion Raises a Peace Flag." *Los Angeles Times,* February 12, A1.

Levi, Margaret, and Gillian H. Murphy. 2006. "Coalitions of Contention: The Case of the WTO Protests in Seattle." *Political Studies* 54: 651–70.

Maney, Gregory M., Lynne M. Woehrle, and Patrick G. Coy. 2005. "Harnessing and Challenging Hegemony: The U.S. Peace Movement after 9/11." *Sociological Perspectives* 48: 357–81.

McAdam, Doug. 1999 [1982]. *Political Process and the Development of Black Insurgency, 1930–1970.* Chicago: University of Chicago Press.

McAdam, Doug, Sidney Tarrow, and Charles Tilly. 2001. *Dynamics of Contention.* New York: Cambridge University Press.

McCammon, Holly J., and Karen E. Campbell. 2002. "Allies on the Road to Victory: Coalition Formation between the Suffragists and the Woman's Christian Temperance Union." *Mobilization* 7: 231–51.

McCarthy, John D., and Mayer N. Zald. 1977. "Resource Mobilization and Social Movements: A Partial Theory." *American Journal of Sociology* 82: 1212–41.

McDermott, Kevin. 2003. "Oak Park Village Board Passes Broad Peace Resolution." Press release, February 10. http://www.opctj.org/news/opctj-02-11-2003-010640 .html. Accessed April 15, 2010.

Meyer, David S. 1999. "Tending the Vineyard: Cultivating Political Process Research." *Sociological Forum* 14: 79–92.

———. 2004. "Protest and Political Opportunity." *Annual Review of Sociology* 30: 125–40.

———. 2007. *The Politics of Protest: Social Movements in America.* New York: Oxford University Press.

Meyer, David S., and Catherine Corrigall-Brown. 2005. "Coalitions and Political Context: U.S. Movements against Wars in Iraq." *Mobilization* 10: 327–44.

Meyer, David S., and Debra C. Minkoff. 2004. "Conceptualizing Political Opportunity." *Social Forces* 82: 1457–92.

Meyer, David, and Sidney Tarrow, eds. 1998. *The Social Movement Society: Contentious Politics for a New Century.* Lanham, Md.: Rowman & Littlefield.

Meyer, David S., and Nancy Whittier. 1994. "Social Movement Spillover." *Social Problems* 41: 277–98.

Mische, Ann. 2008. *Partisan Publics: Communication and Contention across Brazilian Youth Activist Networks.* Princeton, N.J.: Princeton University Press.

Morris, Aldon D. 1984. *The Origins of the Civil Rights Movement.* New York: Free Press.

Mueller, John E. 1973. *War, Presidents, and Public Opinion.* New York: Wiley.

Neuman, Johanna. 2003. "A Battle for the Hearts and Minds of America: With War Support High, Activists Hope to Marshal the Middle Class in Time to Prevent Hostilities." *Los Angeles Times,* February 14, A15. http://articles.latimes.com/2003/feb/14/nation/na-antiwar14. Accessed April 15, 2010.

Obach, Brian K. 2004. *Labor and the Environmental Movement: The Quest for Common Ground.* Cambridge, Mass.: MIT Press.

Petit, Christine. 2005. "Feminist Activism or Feminine Activism? CODEPINK and the Politics of Femininity." Master's thesis, Sociology Department, University of California, Riverside.

Piven, Frances Fox, and Richard A. Cloward. 1977. *Poor People's Movements.* New York: Vintage

PollingReport.com. 2006a. "President Bush—Overall Job Rating." http://www.pollingreport.com/BushJob.htm. 2006. Accessed March 31, 2010.

———. 2006b. "Iraq." http://www.pollingreport.com/iraq.htm. 2006. Accessed March 31, 2010.

Reitan, Ruth. 2007. *Global Activism.* London: Routledge.

Reese, Ellen. 2005. "Policy Threats and Social Movement Coalitions: California's Campaign to Restore Legal Immigrants' Rights to Welfare." In *Routing the Opposition: Social Movements, Public Policy, and Democracy,* edited by Helen Ingram, Valerie Jenness, and David Meyer, 259–87. Minneapolis: University of Minnesota Press.

Reese, Ellen, Vincent Giedraitis, and Eric Vega. 2005. "Mobilization and Threat: Campaigns against Welfare Privatization in Four Cities." *Sociological Focus* 38: 287–307.

Reinert, Patty, and John W. Gonzalez. 2001. "The Inauguration of George W. Bush: Bush Takes Jabs from Protesters; Everything from Contested Election to His Cabinet Choices Is Criticized." *Houston Chronicle,* January 21, A17.

Ricks, Thomas E. 2003. "Desert Caution: Once 'Stormin' Norman,' Gen. Schwarzkopf Is Skeptical about U.S. Action in Iraq." *Washington Post,* January 28, C1. http://www.washingtonpost.com/ac2/wp-dyn/A52450-2003Jan27?language=printer. Accessed April 15, 2010.

Robnett, Belinda. 1997. *How Long? How Long? African-American Women in the Struggle for Civil Rights.* New York: Oxford University Press.

Rose, Fred. 2000. *Coalitions across the Class Divide: Lessons from the Labor, Peace, and Environmental Movements.* Ithaca, N.Y. Cornell University Press.

Rosenthal, Naomi, Meryl Fingrutd, Michele Ethier, Roberta Karant, and David McDonald. 1985. "Social Movements and Network Analysis: A Case Study of Nineteenth-Century Women's Reform in New York State." *American Journal of Sociology* 90: 1022–54.

Saad, Lydia. 2003. "Iraq War Triggers Major Rally Effect; Falls Just Short of 1991

Surge in Public Attitudes." *Gallup News Service,* March 25. http://www.gallup
.com/poll/8074/iraq-war-triggers-major-rally-effect.aspx. Accessed April 15, 2010.

Smith, Jackie. 2001. "Globalizing Resistance: The Battle of Seattle and the Future
of Social Movements." *Mobilization* 6: 1–19.

Staggenborg, Suzanne. 1986. "Coalition Work in the Pro-Choice Movement: Organizational and Environmental Opportunities and Obstacles." *Social Problems*
33: 374–90.

Starr, Amory. 2000. *Naming the Enemy: Anti-Corporate Movements Confront Globalization.* London: Zed Books.

Tarrow, Sidney. 1998. *Power in Movement: Social Movements and Contentious Politics, Second Edition.* Cambridge: Cambridge University Press.

Taylor, Verta A. 1989. "Social Movement Continuity: The Women's Movement in
Abeyance." *American Sociological Review* 54: 761–75.

Tilly, Charles. 1978. *From Mobilization to Revolution.* Reading, Mass.: Addison-Wesley.

USLAW (U.S. Labor Against the War). 2006. "Hundreds of Thousands in New
York City March against the War." May 10. http://www.uslaboragainstwar.org/.
Accessed July 31, 2006.

USLAW (U.S. Labor Against the War) Steering Committee. 2005. "Statement of
USLAW Steering Committee, Adopted 12/3/05." http://archives.econ.utah
.edu/archives/marxism/2005w49/msg00105.htm. Accessed April 15, 2010.

Van Dyke, Nella. 2003. "Crossing Movement Boundaries: Factors That Facilitate
Coalition Protest by American College Students, 1930–1990." *Social Problems*
50: 226–50.

Voss, Kim, and Rachel Sherman. 2000. "Breaking the Iron Law of Oligarchy: Union
Revitalization in the American Labor Movement." *American Journal of Sociology* 106: 303–49.

Walsh, Edward. 1981. "Resource Mobilization and Citizen Protest in Communities
around Three Mile Island." *Social Problems* 29: 1–21.

Weinberg, Bill. 2005. "The Politics of the Antiwar Movement: The Question of
International ANSWER." *Non-Violent Activist: The Magazine of the War Resisters
League,* November–December. http://www.warresisters.org/nva1105-1.htm.
Accessed April 15, 2010.

Willman, David, and Charles Piller. 2003. "Antiwar Activists Join Forces: Tens of
Thousands Rally in Washington, San Francisco and Elsewhere against Policy
on Iraq." *Los Angeles Times,* January 19, A1.

Zeller, Tom. 2003. "The Nation: Reading the Polls on Iraq." *New York Times,* February 23, 5. http://www.nytimes.com/2003/02/23/weekinreview/the-nation-
reading-the-polls-on-iraq.html?pagewanted=1. Accessed April 15, 2010.

13

Applying Qualitative Comparative Analysis to Empirical Studies of Social Movement Coalition Formation

Holly J. McCammon and Nella Van Dyke

Although scholars have long recognized the importance of organization to collective action (e.g., McCarthy and Zald 1977; Tilly 1978), only recently have coalitions among those organizations received attention from sociologists. A spate of recent research has identified a number of factors that influence coalition formation, including both organizational characteristics that lead activists to form coalitions and contextual circumstances that set the stage for such alliances. Scholars have demonstrated that congruent organizational ideologies and identities, shared social ties, a resource-rich environment, and political threats and opportunities play a role in coalition formation. In our introduction to this volume, we discuss in detail the various types of social movement coalitions.

A critical question arises, however, concerning whether these elements are essential in all instances of movement organizational coalition formation or whether they are important causal factors only under certain conditions. We also wonder whether some of these causal elements play a more prominent role in movement coalition formation than others. In short, although existing research reveals that various organizational and contextual factors produce movement organizational alliances, little research explores the interplay between these different factors and the contingent conditions under which organizational partnerships are likely to form (see Borland 2008 for a rare exception). For instance, it may be that political opportunity fosters coalitions between social movement organizations typically only when resources are abundant and the interests and ideological orientations of the groups align. Perhaps social ties are more necessary in some situations than others.

Although we know these factors matter to coalition formation, scholarship has yet to explore when each of them is most likely to facilitate collaboration.

In addition, the results of recent studies are mixed. A variety of investigations demonstrate that favorable environmental conditions, such as political opportunities presented by state actor allies (Stearns and Almeida 2004) or a relatively conflict-free social environment (Bandy and Smith 2005), support coalition formation. However, recent research suggests that an adverse social environment, such as threats from antagonistic political actors, also sometimes facilitates coalition formation (McCammon and Campbell 2002; Reese 2005; Reger 2002; Van Dyke 2003). Also, early investigations of coalitions found that environments in which resources are relatively plentiful spur coalitions (Williams 1999; Zald and McCarthy 1987). However, studies also suggest that groups sometimes pool their resources to overcome resource limitations (Almeida and Stearns 1998; Staggenborg 1986). Although we cannot decisively resolve these debates here, we can explore whether factors that influence coalition formation act in concert and whether the influence of one element of the environment is contingent on the presence of another.

To explore the relative importance and the combined effects of threats to the movement, political opportunity, organizational resources, ideological alignment, and prior social ties (or the primary factors demonstrated in the scholarly literature to foster movement coalitions), we use qualitative comparative analysis (QCA) (Ragin 1987) as part of our meta-analysis of the literature on social movements. An overview of the existing empirical literature on coalition formation among social movement groups allows us to identify recurring findings in the literature and to draw tentative conclusions about which of the key causal factors is most frequently identified in the literature as contributing to coalition formation. To facilitate a more systematic examination of the literature, however, we use QCA. QCA allows us to go a step further and systematically explore combinations of causal factors appearing in the empirical literature (Ragin 1987). For instance, QCA can help us see whether organizational ideological alignment and political opportunities commonly occur together as causal factors or whether, when scholarly studies are considered in the aggregate, we find that coalitions sometimes emerge where ideological congruence exists but where political opportunities do not. Moreover, as we discuss more fully below, QCA also allows for the possibility that there may be several combinations of causal factors, or paths, that lead to coalition outcomes. For instance, perhaps the combination of ideological alignment and political opportunity is a common circumstance in which a movement organizational coalition is likely to emerge, but the combination of ideological alignment and political threats is also a circumstance in which coalitions are built. Again, QCA allows us to analyze the literature systematically and identify the potential variety of routes to social movement organizational partnerships.

We begin our discussion below with our broad overview of the social movement coalition literature to generate hypotheses concerning the ways in which the key causal factors may combine to produce coalitions among social movement groups. We then turn to our analysis.

Key Causal Influences on Movement Coalition Formation
Interests, Identities, and Ideology

It almost goes without saying that two organizations will not work in coalition with one another unless they share at least some common interests and goals, or unless their ideologies or group identities align at least to some degree. Rarely do we see coalitions among organizations with diametrically opposing views, although one exception is an alliance in the 1980s between feminists and conservatives in a fight against pornography (West 1987). A significant body of research, however, demonstrates the importance of shared interests, ideologies, and identities to organizational collaboration (see, e.g., Lichterman 1995). Bandy and Smith (2005), in their overview of research on transnational coalitions, discuss how cultural similarities make it easier for groups from different nations to work together. Gerhards and Rucht (1992) point out that organizations typically need to be integrated ideologically before they are willing to work together to stage protest events. And Bell and Delaney (2001) present a case where even in the presence of abundant resources and political allies, ideological and cultural differences were enough to prevent coalition work.

However, in spite of sharing a common goal or in spite of similar collective identities, many groups never work together. This raises the question of whether a shared set of beliefs and goals or whether a similar ideology is sufficient for groups to work in coalition. Some studies show that organizations often do not work in coalition, even when they share common interests (Barkan 1986), suggesting that congruent ideology in and of itself will not result in coalition formation. However, few researchers consider which organizational and environmental conditions work in combination with shared interests, goals, and ideologies to facilitate coalition formation. In one attempt to explore such a relationship, McCammon and Campbell (2002) use an interaction term in a regression analysis and show that the U.S. Woman's Christian Temperance Union was willing to coalesce with the woman suffrage movement when the two groups could agree on more traditional claims for giving women the vote (for example, women could better protect the home if they had the ballot) and when the Woman's Christian Temperance Union faced the political threat of failed prohibition legislation. But further research considering how ideological alignment or shared interests combine with other factors (such as a political threat) to produce a coalition is needed.

It is also possible that a shared ideology or overlapping identities or goals are *necessary* for groups to work in collaboration. That is, no matter what other conditions may be, the presence of shared values and beliefs is required for an alliance to form. We know that groups must agree on at least some basic goal around which the coalition is being formed. And certain environmental conditions—for example, serious threats to groups' goals—may inspire collaboration even among groups that previously had little in common, creating a shared adversary that enables groups to collaborate without sharing a broader ideology. Our review of the literature will explore these possible circumstances.

Often it is difficult to separate group interests from the surrounding social circumstances, including circumstances that threaten group interests. For example, Reger (2002) finds that class differences prevented local NOW chapters in the Cleveland area from working together, until the common threat produced by attacks on local abortion clinics inspired them to overcome their differences. Thus, organizations that had a great deal in common in terms of ideology, all being chapters of the same national organization, did not feel motivated to overcome other group differences until contextual circumstances took a turn for the worse, creating a shared common interest in collaboration. Similarly, Van Dyke and Cress (2006) demonstrate that gay men and lesbians worked together more during the 1980s than during other decades because of their shared position as targets of the Christian right, especially during the initial HIV crisis, as well as in response to the mortal threats to self and loved ones generated by the disease. Political and mortal threats generated shared interests and an urgency to collaborate. If groups are more likely to work together when faced with political threats, this may be due to a new sense of common interests brought on by the threat, or it may be due to the threat heightening the intensity of an existing set of common interests. As Staggenborg (1986, 382) states in her classic study of the pro-choice movement, "Exceptional environmental conditions may cause organizations to set aside ideological differences." However, clearly, without common social positions, identity elements, and/or interests, political events will have a difficult time inspiring collaboration.

Although we recognize the complex interconnectedness of external social circumstances and individual and group identities and beliefs, it is still possible to examine the extent to which common interests and identities may be sufficient and even necessary to inspire collaboration in the absence of immediate threats or opportunities present in the surrounding social environment. But we also examine whether other circumstances are required, in addition to group ideological alignment and shared goals, to produce a coalition, such as a political threat or preexisting social ties. Below, using QCA, we explore the degree to which a shared ideology or common interests are present in studies that look at coalitions across a variety of social conditions. We consider the following two propositions as we pursue our examination of the studies:

> PROPOSITION 1. *Ideological congruence and/or shared interests and identities can be sufficient to inspire organizational collaboration.*
> PROPOSITION 2. *Ideological congruence and/or shared interests and identities are necessary for organizational collaboration.*

Political Threats and Opportunities

The literature on coalitions suggests that such alliances may mobilize in response to changes in the political context, including either new political threats or political opportunities. A threat to a movement group's goal may come about with the passage of new policy that threatens the group's interests or rights, or it may come about when a legislative bill the group has long supported is defeated. Threats may also take the form of an economic downturn, or, as Levi and Murphy (2006) and Gerhards and Rucht (1992) demonstrate, a visit from a representative of a threatening organization, such as the World Trade Organization or the president of the United States, which can put a group's goals in peril. A political opportunity, on the other hand, may take the form of divided political elites, the possibility of positive political change, or elite allies (McAdam 1996). Staggenborg (1986) finds that abortion rights groups formed coalitions to take advantage of new opportunities, such as when several states repealed their antiabortion laws, but these groups also joined together when threatened with new legislation cutting Medicaid funding for abortions, a clear threat to the movement's goals. Others also uncover a similar pattern where both threats and opportunities are at work. Juska and Edwards (2005), for instance, find that in the global justice movement, animal rights activists and Polish farmers worked together as a response to both the threat of economic restructuring in the pork industry and the opportunity provided by the Polish government's interest in entering the European Union and the need for new regulations to prepare for its entry. Clearly, threats and opportunities can coexist at a given point in time.

But Staggenborg (1986) notes that times of unusual opportunities or threats may mobilize movement constituents specifically because of the way in which these contexts interact with resources. Financial resources tend to be more plentiful when there is the chance for victory because supporters are motivated to provide funding to aid in the effort. During these times, organizational competition for resources is less divisive and common interests become more salient. Staggenborg also suggests that the same may hold true during times of political threat. Donations to movement organizations may increase when supporters fear a loss, and this too can reduce interorganizational competition. Thus, political circumstances and resources may work together to trigger coalitions.

A number of studies suggest, however, that threats may more predictably enable groups to overcome barriers to cooperation than will political opportunities. For instance, returning to McCammon and Campbell's (2002) study of alliances between the Woman's Christian Temperance Union and the suffragists, we see that during periods of political opportunity when the political climate seemed ripe for woman's suffrage success, coalition work between these two groups fell off. However, during periods when the goals of the Woman's Christian Temperance Union were threatened, ties between the groups emerged. These researchers argue that when the political climate is favorable, movement actors are less likely to turn to new strategies, such as forming a coalition. Rather, they will stick to existing tactics because such tactics seem to be working. Scholarship in social psychology suggests a related logic. Tversky and Kahneman (1981) indicate that individuals respond more powerfully to a threatened loss of some good than they do to the presentation of a new benefit. The threat of new legislation that restricts rights or negatively affects quality of life (as in NIMBY—"not in my backyard"—mobilizations) will motivate groups to engage in new and even more aggressive actions, including coalition work. In fact, it may be that severe enough threats will cause groups to overlook ideological differences, leading them to form coalitions with otherwise unlikely partners. Reese (2005) shows, for instance, that the threats posed by new federal welfare legislation in 1996 brought a number of ethnic, immigrant, and community organizations together in California, even where noticeable cultural differences and varying levels of professionalization among the groups existed. We thus consider the following propositions:

PROPOSITION 3. *Political threats can be sufficient to inspire organizational collaboration.*

PROPOSITION 4. *Political threats are necessary for organizational collaboration.*

PROPOSITION 5. *Political opportunities will facilitate coalition formation, but they will be neither necessary nor sufficient for collaboration.*

Prior Social Ties

Like the social movements literature generally, which demonstrates that social ties are the factor most likely to lead an individual to join a social movement (e.g., Diani 2004), coalition scholars have demonstrated that social ties facilitate coalition formation. Several studies illustrate the importance of the presence of individuals with ties across organizations, what scholars have called coalition brokers or bridge builders. For example, Rose (2000) finds that bridge builders played a critical role in helping environmental, labor, and peace organizations overcome class divides that made it difficult for them to collaborate. Similarly, Grossman (2001) demonstrates that similar "bridge" individuals enabled a Native American group and a rural white outdoors organization to overcome the culture, race, and class differences that had previously divided them, allowing the groups to fight to protect natural resources in Wisconsin together. What remains unexplored, however, is whether social ties facilitate coalitions equally in all social conditions. That is, we know little about how prior social ties interact with conditions internal to social movement groups and with broader social environmental circumstances to facilitate coalition formation. For instance, while ties may allow us to predict which groups are likely to forge a tighter bond, does it take an opportunity or threat in the broader political context to prompt the coalition?

On the basis of our review of the literature, we predict that social ties will help pave the way for coalitions in many social circumstances, but that social ties alone do not provide the impetus for coalition formation. As others (e.g., Hula 1995) have pointed out, coalition work has certain benefits, including increased chances of success. However, coalitions also involve considerable potential costs, such as forfeiting control over a broader agenda, not receiving full credit for work done, or even losing members to other groups in the coalition. Research suggests that shared members or ties between organizations can aid in communication between groups, promote trust, and facilitate the development of a shared ideology and goals that can help reduce the costs associated with collaboration (Levi and Murphy 2006). But it may be that without a shift in the political opportunity structure to prompt coalition work, or without an abundance of organizational resources to reduce some of the potential risks of coalescing, movement groups, even those with strong ties, will be unwilling to form an alliance. Therefore, we expect social ties alone are unlikely to produce coalition work, but that such ties will work in conjunction with a changed context or increasing resources to produce a coalition. We predict that social ties are not a sufficient (or necessary) condition for coalition formation, but that political threats, opportunities, abundant resources, or a common ideological orientation must also be present.

PROPOSITION 6. *Prior social ties will facilitate coalition formation, but they will be neither necessary nor sufficient for collaboration.*

Organizational Resources

Many studies have shown that groups will not mobilize for collective action unless they enjoy a certain level of resources (McCarthy and Zald 1977; Zald 1992). Organizations require various resources to maintain themselves, including financial resources, meeting space, and human resources such as time, knowledge, and skill. Van Dyke (2003) argues that limited resources inhibit coalition formation because groups struggling for survival may find it difficult to cooperate with their competitors or because they need to maintain a unique identity to justify support. In addition, when resources are scarce, conflicts within coalitions may arise because some coalition members may think that other individual organizations are not contributing equally to the resource needs of the coalition. Barkan (1986) finds that rivalry among civil rights movement organizations for both funding and media coverage impeded coalition work in that movement. Cornfield and Canak (2007) argue that a lack of cultural and organizational resources stand in the way of viable labor–immigrant coalitions in some cities. Therefore, we would expect in our analysis of the literature to find coalitions occurring more often when organizational resources are plentiful (Williams 1999; Zald and McCarthy 1987).

But will plentiful resources be sufficient to inspire coalition formation, regardless of the sociopolitical conditions? Organizations will participate in coalitions if they view doing so to be in their strategic interests. As we already noted, there are almost always benefits to coalition work, but certain costs can also exist. Organizations with limited resources may find benefits in pooling their resources with those of other organizations (Bickel 2001). Some research suggests that coalitions are able to mobilize larger crowds for demonstrations and other forms of collective action than single organizations can (Gerhards and Rucht 1992; Jones et al. 2001), and this may inspire organizations to join in coalitions at certain times. As we noted above in our discussion of political opportunities and threats, periods of opportunity or urgency may cause groups to join coalitions, but only when they have sufficient access to resources. Also, groups tend to work together on a campaign if they share certain goals, agree on how to frame the issues, and share a strategic orientation with their potential collaborators. It may be that plentiful resources facilitate coalition formation, but only among organizations that share consistent ideologies. In sum, then, we expect that resource availability alone is not a predictor of the formation of movement coalitions. Rather, available resources combine with other circumstances, such as political opportunities, threats, or ideological alignment, to produce coalition work.

PROPOSITION 7. *Resources will facilitate coalition formation, but will be neither necessary nor sufficient for collaboration.*

Method of Analysis

To conduct a qualitatiave comparative analysis of the empirical literature on coalition formation, we identified potential empirical studies to include in the analysis by combing the reference lists of coalition research monographs and scholarly articles and book chapters already known to us on the topic and by using electronic search tools to locate additional sources on movement coalitions. We then examined the various studies to see whether they focused on coalition formation. We included investigations only if a central focus of the work was an empirical examination of the factors giving rise to collective action coalitions—either alliances between or among groups within a single movement, or organizational partnerships across social movements. Thus, we did not include studies that examined coalition-actor behavior once a coalition had been formed or that explored the consequences of movement–group alliances. In total, we included twenty-four studies in our analysis. Coalitions take multiple forms in these studies, including both longer-term and event-specific alliances, and both multigroup umbrella coalition organizations and partnerships between just two groups. In four of the investigations included here, the authors of the studies consider the factors that *prevent* coalitions from emerging (Barkan 1986; Diaz-Veizades and Chang 1996; Ferree and Roth 1998; Lichterman 1995).

We then content analyzed each book, article, or chapter to discern which factors were identified by the authors as influencing coalition formation. We created variables indicating whether the authors provided empirical evidence that one of the five circumstances discussed above led to coalition formation: (1) shared common interests, ideologies, and/or identities among the movement groups; (2) prior social ties between groups, such as bridge leaders, coalition brokers, or overlapping memberships; (3) plentiful resources, either financial or human capital, present in the surrounding social environment; (4) political threats, such as the imposition of legislation that would adversely affect movement goals; and (5) political opportunities, such as the passage of beneficial legislation or the emergence of new political allies. Each variable was coded trichotomously: "1" if the study's authors found that the circumstance led to coalition formation, "0" if the authors found that the circumstance either did not affect coalition formation or had a negative influence on coalition work (that is, "0" indicates the absence of a positive influence), and "don't care" if the authors of the study did not consider the circumstance in their study. QCA allows this third classification when the QCA analyst, for whatever reason, cannot code the case as having or not having the condition. We used the "don't care" classification for studies in which the authors did not discuss whether the particular circumstance (e.g., social ties or ideological alignment) influenced coalition formation, because for the particular study, we do not know whether the condition helped to produce a coalition.

Augmenting our overview of the literature with QCA is beneficial for our purposes because it allows us systematically to examine the coalition empirical literature to explore what the literature reveals about social movement coalition formation. QCA permits analysts to move beyond additive models of causality to explore combinatorial explanations, or models that highlight the interactions among explanatory factors. In addition, results from a QCA can reveal multiple causal processes, or paths, resulting in coalition formation. Unlike regression-based statistical analyses that produce a single explanatory model, QCA allows the possibility that multiple explanatory models will be revealed in the data.

Although most researchers who utilize QCA do so to discover causal patterns in empirical data for a set of cases (e.g., Griffin et al. 1997; McCammon et al. 2008), our purpose is different. We use QCA to compare completed empirical studies of coalition formation; that is, we rely on QCA to help us systematically sift through these studies to find common patterns of causation among them. At a minimum, this means we cannot say that "the data reveal . . . " because we are not analyzing the data per se. Rather, we must conclude that "the aggregate literature shows a common route to coalitions is. . . . " Also, some of the studies we include are case studies focusing on a single coalition (or the absence of a single coalition). Other studies include multiple cases with multiple coalitions, such as the quantitative studies by McCammon and Campbell (2002) and Van Dyke (2003). In the interest of parsimony, our QCA investigation does not weigh the case studies differently than the multicase studies. The findings from each individual study are treated as one case in our qualitative comparison.

A shortcoming in the use of QCA is that the data requirements necessitate the use of broad categories for our measures of the likely causes of coalition formation, such as resource availability and ideological alignment. As Amenta and Poulsen (1994) discuss, including a large number of explanatory measures in QCA can produce an unwieldy list of possible causal configurations. Thus, rather than including separate measures, for instance, for different types of resources (e.g., one measure to indicate the presence of bountiful economic resources and another for a large and skilled volunteer pool), we simply use a general measure of resources. This can mean that important nuances in discerning the role different types of resources play in coalition formation are lost. The loss of detail is unfortunate; however, we think that QCA nonetheless provides us with a useful assessment of patterns in the literature.

We present the list of the twenty-four studies of coalition formation that we uncovered in the literature, along with the factors that each of these studies found to be causally relevant (Table 13.1 and Figure 13.1). Our QCA results are then presented (Figures 13.2 and 13.3).

Findings

Table 13.1 presents the detailed results of our meta-analysis. Each study in the table and the factors the study's authors found to be important causes of coalitions among social movement groups are listed, with a "1" indicating that the authors found the factor to be important in facilitating coalition formation, a "0" indicating that the circumstance either had a negative effect on coalition formation or it had no effect, and a dash indicating that the authors did not consider the factor in their analysis.

As the results in Table 13.1 show, there is strong evidence in the empirical literature that all five factors play a role in coalition formation. That is, there are quite a few "1"s in the table, with ideological alignment being considered most frequently among the twenty-four studies. As the summary figures in Figure 13.1 show, twenty-one out of the total twenty-four studies considered whether ideological congruence between movement groups played a role in coalition formation, and 90 percent of the investigations that considered the role of ideology found that it had a positive impact (nineteen of twenty-one studies; two studies showed no effect for ideology). Threats to movement goals were considered in sixteen of the investigations. Ninety-four percent of the time (fifteen of sixteen studies), the investigations revealed that threats prompted coalition work. (One study found a negative effect.) Political opportunities were examined in eleven studies (the smallest number of studies for the five factors), and eight of these eleven studies (73 percent) found a positive effect. (Two studies found no effect and one study found a negative impact of political opportunities.) Prior ties among movement groups were considered in fourteen analyses, and thirteen of these (93 percent) revealed that previous ties facilitated a coalition. (One study revealed no effect.) Finally, seventeen studies evaluated the role of resources in coalition formation,

Table 13.1. Factors Leading to Coalition Formation in Twenty-four Empirical Studies

Study	Ideological Alignment	Political Threats	Political Opportunity	Prior Social Ties	Plentiful Resources
Barkan (1986)	1	—	—	—	1
Bevacqua (2001)	0	1	—	—	—
Bickel (2001)	—	1	—	1	0
Borland (2008)	1	—	—	—	1
Cullen (2005)	1	—	—	—	0
Diani (2004)	1	1	1	—	1
Diaz-Veizades and Chang (1996)	1	—	1	—	1
Dolgon (2001)	—	1	—	1	—
Ferree and Roth (1998)	1	—	—	1	—
Grossman (2001)	1	1	—	1	1
Hathaway and Meyer (1993)	—	1	0	—	1
Juska and Edwards (2005)	1	1	1	0	1
Levi and Murphy (2006)	1	—	—	1	1
Lichterman (1995)	1	—	—	—	—
Maney (2000)	1	0	1	1	1
McCammon and Campbell (2002)	1	1	0	—	1
Meyer and Corrigall-Brown (2005)	1	1	0	1	—
Obach (2004)	1	1	1	1	1
Reese (2005)	0	1	1	1	1
Rose (2000)	1	1	1	1	1
Shaffer (2000)	1	—	—	1	—
Sonenshein (1989)	1	1	—	1	—
Staggenborg (1986)	1	1	1	—	0
Van Dyke (2003)	1	1	—	1	1

and 82 percent of these investigations found a positive role for the availability of resources (fourteen of seventeen analyses; two studies found a negative influence, and one study found no effect).

But how do these causal factors combine to produce coalition work? We use the data from Table 13.1 and conduct two separate qualitative comparative analyses. In the first, we code all missing data in Table 13.1 (i.e., the dashes or "don't cares") as "0." This allows us to assume that if the authors of a study do not discuss one or more of the factors in their investigation, then the factor or factors had no influence on a coalition outcome, and thus we code it "0" in our first analysis. In a second QCA, we enter the data in

Characteristic	Ideological Alignment	Political Threats	Political Opportunity	Prior Social Ties	Plentiful Resources
Number of studies considering the factor	21	16	11	14	17
Percentage of studies considering factor that find positive effect	90%	94%	73%	93%	82%
Number of studies considering factor that find positive effect	19	15	8	13	14

Figure 13.1. Summary of findings for twenty-four coalition studies in Table 13.1.

Table 13.1 into QCA just as it is shown. That is, where the authors did not consider a particular potential causal factor in their analysis (such as political threats in the study by Barkan 1986), we code the factor for the study as "don't care" for our analysis, allowing QCA to treat these cases either as if the causal element had a positive effect and thus is considered equal to "1," or as if the causal factor had a negative effect or no effect at all and thus is considered equal to "0." Thus, we tell the program we do not care how the factor is included in the analysis, and QCA itself then decides how to code it so as to find the most parsimonious causal solution possible (Ragin 2008). We report our findings for the first analysis (where dashes are combined with our other "0"s) in Figure 13.2. As is customary in reporting QCA results, "*" indicates "and," and "+" represents "or." A variable name written in all capital letters indicates the causal factor has a positive influence on coalition formation; for example, IDEOLOGY means that a common set of beliefs helps foster coalition work. A variable name in all lowercase letters implies that the factor had no influence on coalition work, had a negative effect, or was not discussed by the authors, and thus we assume the factor had no effect in this analysis. Finally, the absence of a term in a causal configuration implies that the factor is irrelevant in the causal process. The numbers listed on the right-hand side of Figure 13.2 reveal how many empirical studies from our list in Table 13.1 are represented by each causal combination.

The results in Figure 13.2 show that our studies can be summarized by six different routes to a movement coalition, demonstrating that not all movement coalitions come about in the same way. Rather, a variety of causal processes are at work in creating these alliances among movement organizations, although the numbers on the right-hand side of the figure suggest that these

IDEOLOGY *		RESOURCES			+	(12)
IDEOLOGY *	threat *			pol opp	+	(7)
IDEOLOGY *	THREAT *		ties *	POL OPP	+	(3)
ideology *	THREAT *		ties *	pol opp	+	(1)
	THREAT *	RESOURCES *	TIES *	POL OPP	+	(2)
	THREAT *	resources *	TIES *	pol opp		(4)

Figure 13.2. Results from a qualitative comparative analysis with "don't care" or a dash coded as 0. Note: "" equals "and," and "+" equals "or." A variable name written in all capital letters indicates that the factor had a positive influence on coalition formation, while a lowercase variable name indicates the factor had no influence, the factor had a negative effect, or the author did not discuss the factor's role in coalition formation. The absence of a term in a causal configuration indicates that it is not relevant to that causal configuration.*

processes are not necessarily followed evenly. For instance, a number of studies reveal that IDEOLOGY and RESOURCES combine to produce coalitions, while only one study shows that THREATS and the absence of a number of other factors result in a movement alliance.

Some of the different causal configurations in Figure 13.2 can be grouped together. For instance, in the first three paths, the presence of the term IDEOLOGY indicates, for the studies characterized by these causal configurations, that where movement groups share a common ideological orientation, an alliance among groups occurs. For the last four combinations in the figure (one of which overlaps with the IDEOLOGY configurations), the presence of the term THREAT indicates that for these studies a threat was a causal agent in coalition formation. Taken together, the QCA results reveal that the presence of aligned organizational ideologies or the presence of a threat to movement goals is needed to spark coalition work, given that each path contains at least one of these elements. For researchers, these findings suggest that the role of ideology and threats should be at the top of the list of factors to be considered in the study of coalition formation.

Before discussing the additional findings in Figure 13.2, however, we present the results of our second QCA. In this analysis, we entered the data in Table 13.1 into QCA just as it appears in the table. That is, we coded potential causal factors where the authors did not consider the factor in their discussion (again, such as political threats in the study by Barkan 1986) as "don't care" in QCA, allowing the program to treat these factors either as if the causal element had a positive effect and thus is considered equal to "1," or as if the causal factor had a negative effect or no effect and thus is considered equal to "0." We, in effect, let the program decide how to treat these cases, allowing QCA to find the most parsimonious solution possible. We report the results of this second QCA in Figure 13.3.

As can readily be seen, our second set of QCA results is simple. Here, two main routes to organizational collaboration emerge from the empirical literature. Either an ideological alignment is present among groups (IDEOLOGY) or a threat to the groups' goal exists (THREAT). The numbers on the right-hand side of Figure 13.3 reveal that ideological congruence played a role in the emergence of a movement coalition in nineteen studies, and threats to movement goals appear in fifteen (which echoes our summary figures in Figure 13.1). As one can see, however, the paths are not mutually exclusive (i.e., the numbers do not sum to twenty-four). A perusal of Table 13.1 shows that IDEOLOGY and THREAT appear together as causal factors in ten studies.

Although the Figure 13.3 results are simple, they repeat themes found in our first QCA in Figure 13.2. The findings for the first round of QCA could be grouped into paths indicating the importance of ideological congruence and those indicating the importance of a threat to the movement's goals (or a few studies that indicated that both were important). Our second set of QCA results also suggests that these two causal factors play a pivotal role in coalition formation. There is thus evidence in the QCA results indicating that shared interests or identities on the one hand, or a threat to movement goals such as the erosion of rights, a disadvantageous policy, or economic difficulties on the other, each in and of itself might be considered a sufficient cause of coalition work, providing support for propositions 1 and 3.

Some of the studies also provide support for these factors being named sufficient conditions. Returning to Table 13.1, one can see that Bevacqua (2001) found that a threat alone produced a partnership among movement groups, and both Cullen (2005) and Lichterman (1995) conclude that ideological alignment can be a singular cause of organizational collaboration. In addition, two of the QCA routes to coalition formation in Figure 13.2 offer a similar conclusion. In the second path in Figure 13.2, a positive effect for IDEOLOGY is present, and a lack of an effect (or a negative effect) is found for both threat and political opportunity. The other factors (resources and ties)

IDEOLOGY +   (19)
THREAT   (15)

Figure 13.3. Results from a qualitative comparative analysis with "don't care" or a dash coded as a dash. Note: "+" equals "or." A variable name written in all capital letters indicates that the factor had a positive influence on coalition formation. The absence of a term in a causal configuration indicates that it is not relevant to that causal configuration.

are irrelevant in this causal configuration. In the fourth path in Figure 13.2, THREAT is the only factor for which a positive effect is evident in the combination; the other factors are either lowercase or not relevant. A threat, in particular, may help groups overcome the difficulties created by a shortage of resources or even the divisiveness of differences in ideology. For instance, Staggenborg's (1986) study of coalitions in the pro-choice movement finds that resource-poor groups collaborate when changes in policy severely threaten the movement's goals.

All this said, however, to conclude that ideological congruence or threats to movement goals are indeed sufficient causes of social movement coalition may overstate matters. It is important to note that as nuanced and careful as these various studies are, in all likelihood some important causal factors may have gone unmeasured. It is quite probable that some of the studies are under-specified, and if additional measures were included in our QCA, our results in Figure 13.3 would be more complex. Also, as we mentioned earlier, because QCA works best when the number of explanatory measures included in the analysis are limited in number, highly general rather than specific measures underpin the figures above. It is highly probable that if more detailed, dis-aggregated measures of the causal factors were used, our results would be more complex. We also note that in most of the twenty-four studies examined here, threats and ideology combine with other causal agents to bring about coalitions (e.g., a congruent ideology and plentiful resources often together result in coalition formation). This is also evidence that placing too much emphasis on threat and ideology as sufficient causes may overstate our case. We conclude that our findings reveal that threats and ideological alignment are highly important potential causes of social movement coalitions—potential causes that should be considered carefully by researchers attempting to understand movement coalition formation.

Given that neither IDEOLOGY nor THREAT appears in all the causal combinations produced by QCA, our results also show that neither of them is *necessary* for movement coalitions. That is, ideological congruence or a political threat is not required for a coalition to form. We thus repeat Staggenborg's (1986, 382) observation that unusual circumstances (such as a threat) may lead groups to ignore or downplay ideological differences to work together to confront a serious and common challenge. Or ideological similarities may mean that groups join together in a coalition, even though nothing specific threatens their stated goals. Thus, propositions 2 and 4 characterizing these causes as necessary conditions are not supported.

We now delve more deeply into our QCA findings. Although ideological or identity congruence among groups and threats to their goals may each be critical in mobilizing a coalition, many of the studies we review show that other causal elements also play a role in coalition formation. For instance, the numbers on the right-hand side of Figure 13.2 indicate that many of the studies can be represented by the causal combination in which ideological congruence and the availability of resources work together to create coalitions. Twelve of the studies we examined fall into this category. For instance, Grossman (2001) explains how rural whites and Native Americans in Wisconsin came together in an environmental coalition because they shared a common sense of the land as sacred, but they did so when casinos and the emergence of a gaming economy surrounding the casinos injected new resources into the Native American community and, at least to a degree, equalized the economic relations between rural whites and the Ojibwe tribe. Grossman's findings indicate that the confluence of a common belief and growing resources paved the way for these two groups to work together. Maney's (2000) research, on the other hand, points to a negative case, where differences in political ideology, conflicting identities, and resource shortages prevented ties from emerging among groups supporting civil rights in Northern Ireland in the late 1960s and early 1970s. Both studies, however, highlight the combined roles of ideology and resources in promoting (or hindering) coalition work. Given that many of the studies examined here point to a combination of IDEOLOGY and RESOURCES in prompting coalition work, researchers should give careful attention to this potential combination of causal factors.

The results in Figure 13.2 also show that political opportunities, prior social ties, and/or the availability of resources combine with threats to produce coalition partnerships (see paths 3, 4, 5, and 6). And, as noted, in a number of cases, threats combine with ideological congruence to foster organizational collaboration (see the third path in Figure 13.2). Threats can create an urgency for activists to form partnerships, and where another potential causal element also occurs, a coalition may appear quite compelling for activists. For instance, Reese (2005) describes how broad policy threats (the passage of a detrimental welfare law for immigrants) coupled with supportive political allies (a political opportunity) facilitated immigrant welfare rights coalitions in California in the 1990s. This occurred in the face of significant ideological disagreements among the groups. Thus, threats and opportunities are not flip sides of the same coin. Rather, they can occur simultaneously and prompt movement actors to coordinate efforts. Moreover, the combination of a common political threat side by side with a political opportunity may allow groups to overcome significant differences in beliefs and values to band together to resist potential harm to their interests.

Additionally, Sonenshein's (1989) study of a biracial coalition between blacks and liberal whites in Los Angeles in the 1960s finds that a political threat combined with preexisting social ties to facilitate the cross-race partnership. Blacks and liberal whites both campaigned to elect Tom Bradley to the Los Angeles city council in 1961, and thus the groups had prior knowledge of and a preexisting connection with one another. When the current mayor, Sam Yorty, threatened black interests later by failing to respond to their demands for police accountability, the prior ties between blacks and whites, along with the political threat, fostered a coalition alliance between the two racial groups to challenge the mayor's refusal to accommodate requests for restraints on police. Again, a threat combined with another causal factor, this time prior social ties between groups, resulted in a viable coalition.

Hathaway and Meyer (1993, 69) provide a case in which threats and the availability of resources fuel movement–group collaboration. In their study of nuclear freeze coalitions, these researchers find that in the early years of the Reagan administration's arms buildup and the threat this posed to peace, a growth in resources to the peace movement brought about a rapid increase in the number of coalition partners, including a jump from seven groups in the Monday Lobby Group in 1981 to forty-one groups by 1986.

We conclude that propositions 5, 6, and 7 are supported. These propositions state that political opportunities, prior social ties, and available resources will facilitate coalition formation, but none of these factors will be either necessary or sufficient for the emergence of a collaboration. The evidence from the studies themselves and our QCA of the studies show that the three factors tend to combine with either ideological congruence or threats to induce movement actors to build coalitions. The scholarly literature on coalitions points to each—opportunities, ties, and resources—as playing an important role in movement alliances, and although our analysis does not suggest that they are critical for coalition formation, our results do indicate that there is substantial evidence that, when paired with common interests and ideologies among movement organizations or with an external threat to movement goals, any of these three factors can also contribute to the emergence of a movement coalition.

Conclusion

Our examination of twenty-four studies in the social movement literature on coalition formation among movement groups reveals that various paths to organizational alliance exist. Clearly, one explanation does not suffice to capture the variety of ways in which coalitions come into being. However, although there is diversity in the causal processes resulting in movement group coalition work, a number of paths can be pointed to as being at least somewhat well trod by activists who seek coalition partners. For instance, our findings suggest that a common set of beliefs, values, identities, or even strategic orientations among movement organizations is a circumstance that itself is often sufficient to result in an alliance. Other causal elements may not necessarily be required to prompt collaboration when the groups' ideological stances are reasonably well aligned. Ideological alignment, our results indicate, is very important for the mobilization of movement coalitions. Nineteen out of our twenty-four studies reported that groups entering into partnerships shared similar ideologies and/or identities.

Our results show that threats, too, may in some cases be a sufficient condition for coalition formation. When movement actors believe their interests are in peril, they may overlook competition for scarce resources or even differences in beliefs, or they may not need preexisting social ties with another group to come together in a coalition. Our finding that either ideological alignment or a political threat may be a sufficient condition for the mobilization of a social movement coalition conveys the greater importance of these two casual factors compared to other causal elements in the study of coalition formation. Although both often occur in tandem with other influential factors, at other times, they are the sole factor inspiring collaboration.

Other causal routes to coalition formation are more complex, involving a combination of factors. For instance, many of our studies reveal that movement organizations with congruent ideological orientations are likely to begin working together in a coalition when resources in the broader environment are more plentiful, when a scarcity of resources does not compel groups to compete with one another for material or human resources. In addition, developments in the broader context that threaten the goals of movement groups, our results also show, often combine with other factors to spur movement coalitions. Threats and political opportunities, preexisting social ties among groups, and/or a resource-rich environment combine in various ways to produce coalitions. Thus, a coalition is likely to emerge when groups feel their interests are threatened by, for example, a new social policy that circumscribes rights or that reduces state-sponsored benefits *and* where these groups have previous working knowledge of one another. Bridge leaders can pave the way for a new coalition when interests are threatened, and previously established trust can help foster the alliance.

Although the results of our QCA meta-analysis allow us to extract from the scholarly and empirical literature the broad causal processes leading to alliances among social movement groups, we have painted our picture with a broad brush—perhaps overly broad. Future research should begin to explore in a more nuanced fashion the dynamics underlying the broad causal processes we have identified here. For instance, when resources and a common ideological orientation combine to produce a coalition, as the literature tells us they do in many cases, additional research can begin to explore which resources are most important to actors contemplating coalition building. How must ideologies or identities align, and when do differences create divisions that are impossible to overcome? Moreover, how urgent must a political threat to a group's goals be for the threat alone to send a group in search of coalition partners? What types of threats require bridge leaders, a common core identity, or high levels of movement group funding to produce a coalition? Also, it may be that threats are more likely to influence the timing of coalition emergence, whereas ideological convergence influences the choice of coalition partners. Finally, we have paid little attention here to the effect of different types of movement targets on coalition formation. In the future, researchers should explore how the nature of the target (for instance, whether the institution being challenged is the state, a multinational corporation, or a religious body) influences coalition formation processes. Answering these and many additional questions will allow us to understand movement coalitions far more fully.

Our results also have important implications for cross-border organizing. Our finding that threats can be enough to inspire groups to overcome their differences to work in collaboration is borne out by the global justice movement. As others have noted, the event that marked the entrance of the global justice movement onto an international stage, the World Trade Organization protests in Seattle in 1999, involved hundreds of organizations from a variety of movements, including some that we would not ordinarily expect to work together, such as labor unions and environmentalists. The broad threat to a variety of interests generated by the World Trade Organization enabled groups to overcome their differences. Wiest's chapter in this volume also presents findings consistent with those observed here: sometimes a threat in combination with prior social ties inspires cross-national collaboration. On the other hand, work by scholars such as Bob (2005) provides an important caution: there are hundreds of international movements and organizations, many of which never come to work in collaboration with international nongovernmental organizations; their access to resources, the media, and their ability to frame issues in a way that resonates all influence their ability to do so. Thus, cross-national organizing may present even greater barriers to coalition work than does coordination among groups within one nation. Forums that provide a space for the generation of social ties, such as the World Social Forums, may play a crucial role. Resources may be crucially important as well.

Given the prominence of the new brand of transnational organizing represented by the global justice movement, these are questions that call out for future research.

Much remains to be done as we try to understand how and why social movement coalitions come into being. In today's world, however, where many movements have become global movements with ties across borders and around the world, understanding how and why movement alliances emerge is all that much more important.

Works Cited

Almeida, Paul, and Linda Brewster Stearns. 1998. "Political Opportunities and Local Grassroots Environmental Movements: The Case of Minamata." *Social Problems* 45: 37–60.

Amenta, Edwin, and Jane D. Poulsen. 1994. "Where to Begin: A Survey of Five Approaches to Selecting Independent Variables for Qualitative Comparative Analysis." *Sociological Methods and Research* 23: 22–53.

Bandy, Joe, and Jackie Smith, eds. 2005. *Coalitions across Borders: Transnational Protest and the Neoliberal Order.* Lanham, Md.: Rowman & Littlefield.

Barkan, Steven. 1986. "Interorganizational Conflict in the Southern Civil Rights Movement." *Sociological Inquiry* 56: 190–209.

Bell, Sandra J. and Mary E. Delaney. 2001. "Collaborating across Difference: From Theory and Rhetoric to the Hard Reality of Building Coalitions." In *Forging Radical Alliances across Difference: Coalition Politics for the New Millennium,* edited by Jill M. Bystydzienski and Steven P. Schacht, 63–76. Lanham, Md.: Rowman & Littlefield.

Bevacqua, Maria. 2001. "Anti-Rape Coalitions: Radical, Liberal, Black, and White Feminists Challenging Boundaries." In *Forging Radical Alliances across Difference: Coalition Politics for the New Millennium,* edited by Jill M. Bystydzienski and Steven P. Schacht, 163–76. Lanham, Md.: Rowman & Littlefield.

Bickel, Christopher. 2001. "Reasons to Resist: Coalition Building at Indiana University." In *Forging Radical Alliances across Difference: Coalition Politics for the New Millennium,* edited by Jill M. Bystydzienski and Steven P. Schacht, 207–19. Lanham, Md.: Rowman & Littlefield.

Bob, Clifford. 2005. *The Marketing of Rebellion.* New York: Cambridge University Press.

Borland, Elizabeth. 2008. "Social Movement Organizations and Coalitions: Comparisons from the Women's Movement in Buenos Aires, Argentina." *Research in Social Movements, Conflicts, and Change* 28: 83–112.

Cornfield, Daniel B., and William Canak. 2007. "Immigrants and Labor in a Globalizing City: Prospects for Coalition Building in Nashville." In *Labor in the New*

Urban Battlegrounds: Local Solidarity in a Global Economy, edited by Lowell Turner and Daniel B. Cornfield, 163–77. Ithaca, N.Y.: ILR Press.

Cullen, Pauline P. 2005. "Conflict and Cooperation within the Platform of European Social NGOs." In *Coalitions across Borders: Transnational Protest and the Neoliberal Order,* edited by Joe Bandy and Jackie Smith, 71–94. Lanham, Md.: Rowman & Littlefield.

Diani, Mario. 2004. "Networks and Participation." In *The Blackwell Companion to Social Movements,* edited by David A. Snow, Sarah A. Soule, and Hanpeter Kriesi, 339–59. Malden, Mass.: Blackwell.

Diaz-Veizades, Jeannette, and Edward T. Chang. 1996. "Building Cross-Cultural Coalitions: A Case-Study of the Black-Korean Alliance and the Latino-Black Roundtable." *Ethnic and Racial Studies* 19: 680–700.

Dolgon, Corey. 2001. "Building Community amid the Ruins: Strategies for Struggle from the Coalition for Justice at Southampton College." In *Forging Radical Alliances across Difference: Coalition Politics for the New Millennium,* edited by Jill M. Bystydzienski and Steven P. Schacht, 220–32. Lanham, Md.: Rowman & Littlefield.

Ferree, Myra Marx, and Silke Roth. 1998. "Gender, Class and the Interaction between Social Movements." *Gender and Society* 12: 626–48.

Gerhards, Jürgen, and Dieter Rucht. 1992. "Mesomobilization: Organizing and Framing in Two Protest Campaigns in West Germany." *American Journal of Sociology* 98: 555–95.

Griffin, Larry J., Christopher Caplinger, Kathryn Lively, Nancy L. Malcom, Darren McDaniel, and Candice J. Nelson. 1997. "Comparative-Historical Research and Scientific Inference: Disfranchisement in the U.S. South as a Test Case." *Historical Methods* 30: 13–27.

Grossman, Zoltan. 2001. "'Let's not create evilness for this river': Interethnic Environmental Alliances of Native Americans and Rural Whites in Northern Wisconsin." In *Forging Radical Alliances across Difference: Coalition Politics for the New Millennium,* edited by Jill M. Bystydzienski and Steven P. Schacht, 146–59. Lanham, Md.: Rowman & Littlefield.

Hathaway, Will, and David S. Meyer. 1993. "Competition and Cooperation in Social Movement Coalitions: Lobbying for Peace in the 1980s." *Berkeley Journal of Sociology* 38: 156–83.

Hula, Kevin. 1995. "Rounding Up the Usual Suspects: Forging Interest Group Coalitions in Washington." In *Interest Group Politics,* 4th ed., edited by A. J. Cigler and B. A. Loomis, 239–58. Washington, D.C.: CQ Press.

Jones, Andrew W., Richard N. Hutchinson, Nella Van Dyke, Leslie Gates, and Michele Companion. 2001. "Coalition Form and Mobilization Effectiveness in Local Social Movements." *Sociological Spectrum* 21: 207–31.

Juska, Arunas, and Bob Edwards. 2005. "Refusing the Trojan Pig: The U.S.–Poland Coalition against Corporate Pork Production." In *Coalitions across Borders: Transnational Protest and the Neoliberal Order,* edited by Joe Smith and Jackie Smith, 187–207. Lanham, Md.: Rowman & Littlefield.

Levi, Margaret, and Gillian H. Murphy. 2006. "Coalitions of Contention: The Case of the WTO Protests in Seattle." *Political Studies* 54: 651–70.

Lichterman, Paul. 1995. "Piecing Together Multicultural Community: Cultural Differences in Community Building among Grass-Roots Environmentalists." *Social Problems* 42: 513–34.

Maney, Gregory M. 2000. "Transnational Mobilization and Civil Rights in Northern Ireland." *Social Problems* 47: 153–79.

McAdam, Doug. 1996. "Conceptual Origins, Current Problems, Future Directions." In *Comparative Perspectives on Social Movements: Political Opportunities, Mobilizing Structures, and Cultural Framings,* edited by Doug McAdam, John D. McCarthy, and Mayer N. Zald, 23–40. New York: Cambridge University Press.

McCammon, Holly J., and Karen E. Campbell. 2002. "Allies on the Road to Victory: Coalition Formation between the Suffragists and the Woman's Christian Temperance Union." *Mobilization* 7: 231–51.

McCammon, Holly J., Soma Chaudhuri, Lyndi N. Hewitt, Courtney Sanders Muse, Harmony D. Newman, Carrie Lee Smith, and Teresa M. Terrell. 2008. "Becoming Full Citizens: The U.S. Women's Jury Rights Campaigns, the Pace of Reform, and Strategic Adaptation." *American Journal of Sociology* 113: 1104–47.

McCarthy, John D., and Mayer N. Zald. 1977. "Resource Mobilization and Social Movements: A Partial Theory." *American Journal of Sociology* 82: 1212–41.

Meyer, David S., and Catherine Corrigall-Brown. 2005. "Coalitions and Political Context: U.S. Movements against the War in Iraq." *Mobilization* 10: 327–44.

Obach, Brian K. 2004. *Labor and the Environmental Movement: A Quest for Common Ground.* Cambridge, Mass.: MIT Press.

Ragin, Charles C. 1987. *The Comparative Method: Moving beyond Qualitative and Quantitative Strategies.* Berkeley: University of California Press.

———. 2008. *User's Guide to Fuzzy-Set/Qualitative Comparative Analysis 2.0.* Tucson: Department of Sociology, University of Arizona.

Reese, Ellen. 2005. "Policy Threats and Social Movement Coalitions: California's Campaign to Restore Legal Immigrants' Rights to Welfare." In *Routing the Opposition: Social Movements, Public Policy, and Democracy,* edited by David S. Meyer, Valerie Jenness, and Helen Ingram, 259–87. Minneapolis: University of Minnesota Press.

Reger, Jo. 2002. "Organizational Dynamics and Construction of Multiple Feminist Identities in the National Organization for Women." *Gender and Society* 16: 710–27.

Rose, Fred. 2000. *Coalitions across the Class Divide: Lessons from the Labor, Peace, and Environmental Movements.* Ithaca, N.Y.: Cornell University Press.

Shaffer, Martin B. 2000. "Coalition Work among Environmental Groups: Who Participates?" *Research in Social Movements, Conflict and Change* 22: 111–26.

Sonenshein, Raphael J. 1989. "The Dynamics of Bi-Racial Coalitions: Crossover Politics in Los Angeles." *Western Political Quarterly* 42: 333–53.

Staggenborg, Suzanne. 1986. "Coalition Work in the Pro-Choice Movement: Organizational and Environmental Opportunities and Obstacles." *Social Problems* 33: 374–90.

Stearns, Linda Brewster, and Paul D. Almeida. 2004. "The Formation of State Actor–Social Movement Coalitions and Favorable Policy Outcomes." *Social Problems* 51: 478–504.

Tilly, Charles. 1978. *From Mobilization to Revolution.* Reading, Mass.: Addison-Wesley.

Tversky, Amos, and Daniel Kahneman. 1981. "The Framing of Decisions and the Psychology of Choice." *Science* 211: 453–58.

Van Dyke, Nella. 2003. "Crossing Movement Boundaries: Factors That Facilitate Coalition Protest by American College Students, 1930–1990." *Social Problems* 50: 226–50.

Van Dyke, Nella, and Ronda Cress. 2006. "Political Opportunities and Collective Identity in Ohio's Gay and Lesbian Movement, 1970–2000." *Sociological Perspectives* 49: 503–26.

West, Robin. 1987. "The Feminist–Conservative Anti-Pornography Alliance and the 1986 Attorney General's Commission on Pornography Report." *American Bar Foundation Research Journal* 4: 687–711.

Williams, Heather L. 1999. "Mobile Capital and Transborder Labor Rights Mobilization." *Politics and Society* 27: 139–66.

Zald, Mayer N. 1992. "Looking Backward to Look Forward: Reflections on the Past and Future of the Resource Mobilization Research Paradigm." In *Frontiers in Social Movement Theory,* edited by A. D. Morris and C. McClurg Mueller, 326–48. New Haven, Conn.: Yale University Press.

Zald, Mayer N., and John D. McCarthy. 1987. "Social Movement Industries: Competition and Conflict among SMOs." In *Social Movements in an Organizational Society: Collected Essays,* edited by Mayer N. Zald and John D. McCarthy, 161–80. New Brunswick, N.J.: Transaction.

Conclusion:
Research on Social Movement Coalitions

Suzanne Staggenborg

Coalitions seem obviously important to both social movement scholars and activists; by combining resources and coordinating strategies, movements and their allies are bound to be more effective in achieving goals and creating social changes in culture, institutions, and public policy. Scholarly research on movement coalitions has increased steadily in the past twenty years, and the present volume makes important contributions to the growing body of coalition research. Researchers generally agree that the rise and effectiveness of coalitions are influenced by a combination of environmental, organizational, and ideological factors. Beyond recognizing these key influences, new research in this volume and elsewhere examines coalition dynamics in historical and comparative perspective. Coalitions involve interactions over time among groups and individuals, which are influenced by historical relations and by current opportunities and constraints. Ongoing empirical and theoretical work aims to develop our understanding of the processes that facilitate and impede coalitions and their impacts.

In this conclusion, I begin by discussing the different types of coalition work identified by scholars, noting some of the major research questions involved in studying various types of cooperative efforts. I then discuss important arguments in the literature, including the contributions in this volume, regarding the mobilization of coalitions. I end by suggesting some directions for future research.

Types of Coalitions and Partnerships

As the chapters in this book illustrate, scholars have considered a wide range of cooperative efforts under the rubric of "coalitions." Forms of coalition work range from loosely coupled activities aimed at similar goals to formal or informal organizations of movement groups to mergers of institutionalized organizations. Coalition partners in these various forms of cooperative work may include individual activists, movement organizations, other types of organizations or institutions, and even elite supporters such as government officials or agencies. Coalitions may bridge organizational or movement boundaries, geographical and national borders, and various social divisions, such as class, race, ethnicity, and gender. Different types of coalitions involve different forms of interaction among social movement organizations (SMOs) and other actors in multiorganizational fields (Curtis and Zurcher 1973). Depending on the types of organizations involved and the nature of the coalition work, activists face varying challenges and scholars are confronted with a diverse set of research questions.

The most common forms of coalitions, reflected by the work in this volume, involve alliances among movement activists. These include formal and informal coalition organizations of varying duration that bring together different types of actors, including individuals and SMOs within and across movements, activists and organizations from different nations and regions, movements and political parties or other extramovement organizations, and different social classes and ethnic groups. However, coalition work among groups with common goals is far from inevitable; the various forms of interaction possible among SMOs include competition, ideological conflict, and factionalism as well as cooperation (Zald and McCarthy 1980). In this volume, researchers ask a number of key questions: What makes cooperation rather than competition possible, often among actors with unequal resources and different ideological approaches? How can coalition organizations be structured and issues framed to avoid conflict and encourage inclusiveness? How are coalitions maintained beyond a period of intense activity? What makes coalitions effective?

Many coalitions, whether ad hoc or formal, are focused on particular events or campaigns. As Diani, Lindsay, and Purdue (this volume) argue, campaigns around events often give rise to coalitions, and numerous coalition campaigns provide opportunities for the sustained interactions that constitute ongoing social movements. Cross-movement coalitions are likely to be involved in movement campaigns, which require extensive resources. Coalitions focused on particular events may be especially vulnerable to dissolution after the initial threat subsides and as other issues and threats draw the attention of activists with multiple interests (see Reese, Petit, and Meyer, this volume). Key research questions related to campaign coalitions have to do with the conditions that make coalition work particularly attractive during campaigns, including the types of tactics and frames used (see Gerhards and Rucht 1992; Van Dyke 2003), and the effects on coalitions once a campaign comes to an end.

Whether focused on a particular event or campaign or created as a longer-term, more formalized organization, coalitions face different challenges depending on the types of actors they bring together and the types of barriers they attempt to overcome. Important research questions linked to mobilization of coalitions among diverse groups include how coalitions can be structured to reduce conflict and encourage wide participation, and how heterogeneous coalitions are able to enhance movement effectiveness. In the case of cross-movement coalitions, researchers examine the processes through which ideological and social differences among activists, often from different social classes and ethnic groups, can be bridged. Studies of transregional and transnational coalitions, particularly those including activists and organizations from both the global north and south, examine how cultural differences and resource inequalities make it difficult to create coalitions in which participants from less privileged regions or nations are equal partners (see Bandy and Smith 2005).

Some coalitions are so successful in overcoming ideological differences that organizational mergers occur. Cornfield and McCammon (this volume) provide evidence of growing ideological convergence in the case of the AFL-CIO merger, particularly through the broadening of the AFL agenda to facilitate a merger. This contrasts with the case of feminists of the 1970s examined by Roth in her chapter, where ideology prevented coalition work, despite similar public policy goals. Important research questions focus on the conditions under which ideological similarities and common goals provide the basis for coalitions and the ways in which institutionalized organizations such as established labor unions differ from outside challengers such as early feminists in their propensity for coalition work.

When there is little if any organization among partners or little in the way of formal agreement, groups may act in "coalition" insofar as they are working toward common goals. As Isaac describes in this volume, coalitions can consist of a temporary merging of forces and might include movement–state coalitions and countermovement–state coalitions (Stearns and Almeida 2004) as well as coalitions within and between movements. In these cases, we can ask what causes simultaneous work by multiple types of actors and what forms of contact and coordination occur among the actors. If no contact or coordination occurs, we might hesitate to label actions oriented toward similar goals coalitions, but common interests may ultimately forge coordinated alliances (McCammon and Van Dyke, this volume). Key questions for social movement research include how movement goals become shared by other actors, such as state agencies and political parties (see Almeida, this volume); how the characteristics of movements and SMOs affect elite interest in the movement agenda; how elite willingness to work for movement concerns can be maintained; and how such alliances affect movements and SMOs.

In some cases, institutional actors compete with movement partners in framing issues and shaping outcomes, and alliances with state actors may have negative impacts on movements. Movement organizations that act in coalition with elites risk losing legitimacy with constituents, and as Zald and McCarthy (1980, 8) point out, SMOs that have not been accepted by authorities might openly attack those recognized as legitimate. Moreover, SMOs may experience difficulty recruiting participants when elites take up their cause because movement action no longer seems so urgent to adherents. If government agencies are addressing environmental concerns, for example, constituents may see little need to donate money to environmental movement organizations. Thus, key questions about coalitions with elites include both the processes by which these alliances form and their impacts on movements and SMOs.

Explaining the Mobilization of Coalitions

Researchers are making significant progress in explaining the conditions under which coalitions mobilize. The present volume examines many key factors involved in the formation of different types of coalitions, showing how environmental, organizational, and ideological dynamics all influence coalition work in social movements. In this section, I attempt to summarize some of the major findings regarding how these processes influence the mobilization of coalitions, drawing on the contributions in this volume as well as other literature on movement coalitions.

Environmental Influences

Numerous analyses of coalitions suggest that they are most likely to organize under particular environmental conditions. Coalitions are especially likely to form in periods of threat or crisis, as participants put aside differences to face an immediate threat or focus on a specific target (McCammon and Campbell 2002; Meyer and Corrigall-Brown 2005; Staggenborg 1986; Van Dyke 2003). Political opportunities also stimulate coalition work insofar as movement organizations are motivated to enhance their resources in order to take advantage of opportunities for gain (Cullen 1999; Hathaway and Meyer 1993–94; Staggenborg 1986). McCammon and Campbell (2002) argue, however, that opportunities are less likely than threats to motivate coalitions because political opportunities increase the chances of movement success, making coalitions less necessary. McCammon and Van Dyke (this volume) demonstrate that threats are indeed more central than opportunities in analyses of coalition work, but they also note that both threats and opportunities may be involved simultaneously in stimulating particular coalitions. Importantly, McCammon and Van Dyke encourage researchers to examine the different paths to coalition work, which almost always involve some environmental threats or opportunities combined with organizational and ideological factors. The challenge for social movement theorists is to uncover the mechanisms and processes through which these factors produce coalitions.

Shared interests and identities are critical to coalition work, as McCammon and Van Dyke show, but they often combine with environmental factors in paths to coalition work. A number of studies find that coalitions are most likely to form when movement participants not only share interests, but also encounter threats to their common interests and expected gains. For example, political defeats stimulated coalition work by temperance and suffrage activists (McCammon and Campbell 2002), and countermovement efforts to overturn legal abortion and cut government funding of abortions for poor women led abortion rights activists to band together (Staggenborg 1986). Different types of threats may stimulate different forms of coalitions. Comparing within-movement coalitions with cross-movement coalitions, Van Dyke (2003) finds that local threats are enough to inspire within-movement coalitions, but that larger threats are needed to stimulate cross-movement coalitions, which involve multiple constituencies with more broadly defined identities.

The essays in this volume allow us to further specify how different types of threats stimulate coalitions. Borland finds that the 2001 economic and political crisis in Argentina helped to overcome some barriers to coalitions within the women's movement, such as differences in social class and sexual orientation. She shows how the threats activated preexisting networks and motivated feminists to focus on common ideology rather than differences. Although the external crisis served as a catalyst for these internal dynamics, Borland demonstrates that threats do not automatically produce coalitions. Activists need to work to overcome boundaries, and not all barriers can be overcome, as shown by the persistent divisions between popular women's groups and feminists in Argentina, divisions often rooted in class differences. In addition to uncovering the dynamics underlying coalition formation among those with shared ideological perspectives during a period of crisis, Borland suggests that there may be connections between the types of threats that stimulate coalition work and the types of problems that coalitions encounter. In her case, the economic threats made some feminist concerns appear unimportant to women's groups preoccupied with poverty and unemployment. Thus, coalitions may be forced to tailor their frames to the nature of the threat that facilitates coalition work.

Other chapters also add to our understanding of how environmental changes affect coalition work. Wiest shows that financial and environmental crises and threats in the 1990s spurred cross-national coalitions in Southeast Asia. In this case, the financial threat combined with the institutional context to strengthen transnational ties and stimulate coalition work. Okamoto finds an environmental spur to coalition work in the form of interracial economic competition and anti-Asian attacks. Describing how cross-ethnic coalition events were organized by community groups in response to precipitating events (anti-Asian attacks), Okamoto's work draws attention to the dynamics of interaction and the emergent properties of coalitions. Corrigall-Brown and Meyer show how groups with preexisting ties organized the Win Without War coalition during the threats involved in the lead-up to the war on Iraq. They suggest that past campaigns create ties, which are activated by new threats for subsequent coalitions. Reese, Petit, and Meyer elaborate on how grievances and threats spurred coalition work against the Iraq war and helped activists connect with a broader public. Their work raises the question of the stability of coalitions that emerge in response to threats, suggesting that alliances may be difficult to maintain when threats subside and new issues become more pressing for activists.

In addition to reacting to external threats and critical events, movements can also help create a sense of threat or urgency, changing the environment so as to increase the possibility of certain types of alliances. In some instances, movements influence public opinion to the extent that elected officials are forced to address movement issues. As Isaac notes in his chapter, movement size increases both public pressure for state acknowledgment and the likelihood of movement–state coalitions. In late nineteenth-century America, Isaac finds that a nonrestrictive legal environment, shared framing regarding the threat from a labor uprising, and the elite-based organizational forms of private militias facilitated coalitions with local governments.

In these and other cases, environmental threats and opportunities interact with organizational and ideological influences. Often, threats activate preexisting networks within and across movements, and make participants aware of the urgency of solidarity with ideological allies. The mobilization of coalitions is an ongoing process; as coalitions form in response to environmental developments, they organize specific events or campaigns, which may create internal solidarity and strengthen ties for future coalition work as well as potentially influencing external audiences and targets.

Organizational Dynamics

Organizational factors, which influence the ability of activists to react to environmental threats and opportunities, include the types of connections and structures that exist within and across movement communities as well as internal dynamics within SMOs. Preexisting networks among groups, and positive experiences working in previous coalitions, facilitate coalition work when new threats and opportunities arise. Within movements, overlaps in memberships among inclusive SMOs are likely to increase cooperation by increasing communication (Zald and McCarthy 1980). Heterogeneous coalitions have to bridge different identities, ideologies, and styles of activism. Borland (this volume) finds "bridge-building" activists, and organizational efforts to recognize and find places in coalitions for activists from different backgrounds, helped bridge barriers of sexual orientation, age, and organizational form among feminists in Argentina. In the East German women's movement, Guenther (this volume) reports that personal networks and a history of cooperation facilitated transregional coalitions. Across movements, "movement crossovers" straddle movements and promote coalition work (Reese, Petit, and Meyer, this volume). In a study of overlaps among movement organizations in Vancouver, Carroll and Ratner (1996, 616) show that activists who share a "broadly resonant master frame" are likely to be enmeshed in cross-movement networks that facilitate coalition work.

In international coalitions and in cross-movement coalitions, cultural differences and inequalities among participants create significant impediments to coalition work. Leadership and experience in cooperative campaigns help to create solidarity within cross-class coalitions, and cross-movement alliances typically rely on brokers to create trust and communication (Obach 2004; Rose 2000). Rose (2000) points to the role of leaders who serve as "bridge builders" between the cultures of middle-class peace and environmental activists and working-class labor activists, and he emphasizes the importance of working together to create bonds of trust for subsequent coalition work. Obach (2004) similarly argues that "coalition brokers" play a key role in bringing together environmentalists and unionists, and that the experience of working together builds trust and understanding, which facilitates further coalition work. Although brokers are often individual leaders who participate in two or more movements, in some cases, "bridging organizations," such as the Coalition of Labor Union Women, create connections between movements (Roth 2003).

Linkages between movements may, however, be restricted by institutional structures. In this volume, Obach argues that the U.S. government channels organizations away from coalition work by creating distinct policy domains, which limit cross-movement contacts, and by restricting opportunities for cross-movement electoral participation through tax laws regulating the activities of nonprofit organizations. Thus, Obach shows how structural barriers created by the state can prevent coalition brokers from ever having the opportunity to bridge cultural divides. His work raises the question of the extent to which movements are able to get around these barriers and create interactional spaces that allow coalition brokers to bring together activists from different movements.

Research suggests that coalitions can be organized in ways that help overcome barriers among participants and facilitate cooperation rather than conflict. Internal organizational structures are important in maintaining participation in both individual SMOs and coalition organizations. Organizations with structures that allow for the development of leadership, completion of maintenance tasks, and meaningful participation of activists are likely to enhance their strategic capacity and sustain themselves over time (Ganz 2000; Polletta 2002; Reger and Staggenborg 2006). Coalition organizations need structures that allow for input from different types of members and that avoid competition with member organizations for leadership and resources. Coalitions and SMOs that lack participatory structures may engage in actions that do not benefit all of their members equally. In a rare study of the unequal impacts of coalition work on members, Kowalchuk (2003) shows how land-seeking peasants were marginalized in a coalition representing both landless peasants and others in El Salvador. The centralized structures of peasant organizations in the coalition allowed leaders to involve landless peasants in coalition protests from which they had little to gain, while land-related protest was put on hold.

Regarding transnational coalition work, Wood (2005) shows in the case of the People's Global Action that a decentralized structure helped the coalition avoid domination by participants from northern countries, who had far greater resources than participants from southern nations. In addition, the strategy of working together on "living documents" that were continually revised provided a mechanism for creating collective identity, which helped to maintain the coalition (Wood 2005, 110). In a study of the Coalition for Justice in the Maquiladoras, Bandy (2004, 417) argues that the coalition created a "culture of solidarity" by developing "regular fora for communication and education," such as workshops, conferences, protests, Web sites, and worker exchanges among participants in Mexico, Canada, and the United

States (see also Williams 1999). Just as movement organizations increase their strategic capacity by developing forums for "regular, open, and authoritative deliberation" (Ganz 2000:1016), coalition organizations might be structured in ways that give coalition partners equal voice while still allowing for effective leadership.

Competition among movement organizations for funding, membership, and legitimacy is perhaps the major organizational challenge for movement coalitions. Coalitions need to organize in ways that do not threaten the resources and visibility of member organizations. Obach (2004, 23) describes the "coalition contradiction" faced by SMOs; although they need to be distinctive to attract resources and maintain themselves, "distinctiveness reduces issue overlap with other organizations and inhibits the potential for coalition work." One solution to this dilemma is for SMOs working in coalition to engage only in particularly expensive tactics, such as legislative lobbying, saving resources for individual SMOs and allowing them to distinguish themselves with other tactics (Staggenborg 1986). As SMOs work together in coalition, they learn to trust one another and to expand their concerns as a result of their interactions (Obach 2004). Although SMOs may lose visibility, and consequently resources, by working in coalition, they stand to gain legitimacy in new areas and to make valuable contacts. Coalition work may allow SMOs to reach new audiences and to spread their concerns to other SMOs or movements. For example, Canadian feminists active in the Just Income Coalition around minimum wages gained new access to policy experts and were able to disseminate information about their own goals and activities through the coalition (Grace 2006, 158). By working through the Coalition of Labor Union Women, American feminists were able to put feminist issues on the labor movement agenda (Roth 2003).

Ideology and Framing

Ideology, as McCammon and Van Dyke show, is central to the study of coalitions. Ideological conflict is clearly an important impediment to coalition work, while ideological compatibility and shared collective identity promote coalitions. The studies by Borland, Guenther, and others in this volume raise the important question of how activists can be coaxed outside their ideological comfort zones for coalition work. External threats may be necessary to provide sufficient incentive for coalition work when ideological differences exist. But Roth's analysis (this volume) of how U.S. feminists in the 1960s and 1970s deliberately did not pursue coalition work across race and ethnic lines because they shared an ethos of "organizing one's own" suggests that ideological impediments to coalitions must be seen in a larger cultural and political context. For Roth's activists, the broader politics of the women's movement and other social movements during these years may have fostered this ethos within specific women's organizations. Although race and class barriers are difficult to surmount, diverse coalitions will need to overcome these barriers to succeed.

Leaders or organizational "mesomobilization actors" play an important role in overcoming ideological barriers by framing issues so that a variety of groups can connect their concerns to a master frame (Gerhards and Rucht 1992). Within movements, coalitions may use unsuccessful frames because leadership is too centralized and constituents are not widely consulted (see Dugan 2004). In cross-movement coalitions, where participants may come from different backgrounds and have different goals, the creation of a common identity, in part through framing, is particularly important. Work on cross-class coalitions suggests that bridge leaders and organizations are critical and that, when groups work together, they are likely to learn to expand their concerns to include those of coalition partners (Obach 2004). In contrast, groups that occupy unconnected realms will have difficulty finding a unifying frame that facilitates coalition work (Ferree and Roth 1998).

Research shows that multi-issue organizations are most likely to participate in both intramovement and cross-movement coalitions (Van Dyke 2003). Movement organizations that are connected to one another through overlapping leaders and social networks are likely to share master frames and to participate in coalitions based on common framing of issues (Carroll and Ratner 1996; Gerhards and Rucht 1992). Overlaps in leadership or membership are also one mechanism by which movement ideologies and goals are spread to extramovement organizations. Movement personnel may, for example, work within government agencies or political parties, or win election to public office, during or after their tenure in movement organizations and campaigns. Almeida (this volume) finds that movement–party coalitions in Latin America were encouraged by overlaps in participation and party encouragement of movement participation, as well as common interests. Cornfield and McCammon (this volume) show that ideological convergence facilitated merger in the AFL-CIO.

Directions for Future Research

The essays in this volume, together with other recent work on coalitions, suggest a number of directions for future research. We know that environmental, organizational, and ideological factors all affect the formation of coalitions, but we need to better understand the processes involved in various paths to coalition work. Threats are clearly an important incentive for

coalitions, but more studies are needed to examine the ways in which different types of threats are perceived by different types of movement actors and
the processes by which threats are used to mobilize coalitions. And although
threats may be more potent motivators than opportunities, researchers also
need to specify the types of opportunities—sometimes mixed with threats—
that are likely to stimulate coalitions and to examine the conditions under
which different types of movements perceive and act on opportunities by
engaging in coalition work.

An understanding of the perceptions and uses of threats and opportunities requires better understanding of the characteristics of the movement
communities in which coalitions form. In locales with highly developed "general" social movement communities that feature cross-movement overlaps
(Staggenborg 1998), visible local threats may be enough to stimulate cross-
movement coalitions. In communities where dense networks connect activists,
shared frames are also likely to exist (Carroll and Ratner 1996) to facilitate
coalition work. In communities with a history of successful multiorganizational and cross-movement campaigns, bonds of trust are likely available to
sustain coalition organizations and subsequent coalition campaigns. Where
community bonds are less strong, leadership is likely to be more important
in creating bridges and framing issues so that diverse groups can be brought
together. More studies are needed to examine the processes of coalition bro-
kerage that bring different types of organizations together in different types
of communities and at different levels (Obach 2004; Tarrow 2005).

In terms of organizational dynamics, coalition work is notoriously difficult because of perceived and real costs to organizations. Groups working in
coalition may get less media exposure and visibility than groups working alone,
and they may have trouble attracting members as a result. Conflicts among
different types of activists may also sap their energies during coalition work.
Coalitions may drain resources from member organizations. Yet movement
organizations also have much to gain from coalition participation. Coalitions
can expand the range of movement organization goals and allow groups to
engage in more ambitious activities than they could otherwise manage. The
ability to stage visible tactics and pursue ambitious goals may attract constituents, enhancing the legitimacy of movement organizations, and the tactics may heighten the chances of achieving victory. Although studies have
identified many of the difficulties with coalition work, more studies of coalitions are needed to show how participants can benefit from coalition work.

Because coalitions involve daunting challenges in bringing together diverse activists and organizations, more detailed empirical studies are needed

to show how this might be accomplished. To understand the structural dynamics of coalitions as well as the impacts of coalitions on their members, further study of internal organizational processes in both member organizations and coalition organizations is needed. Just as movement organizations need to create structures that allow for the mobilization of resources from diverse constituencies, the development of leadership teams, and deliberations about strategy (Ganz 2000), coalition organizations need to develop structures that will allow leaders from member groups to work together to develop strategies that involve and benefit their various constituents without straining the resources of coalition partners and creating tensions within the coalition. Because ideology is central to coalitions, further research is needed to show how cooperation can be initiated among ideologically diverse groups, with the goal of creating common understandings and bases for ongoing coalition work.

Finally, more research needs to assess the outcomes of coalition work. The research reported in this volume, like most other work on coalitions, concentrates on questions of how and why coalitions form and what dilemmas coalitions face. Just as study of the outcomes of social movements has lagged behind research on movement emergence and mobilization, analyses of coalitions have focused primarily on their formation and (to a lesser extent) maintenance, but little attention has been paid to their effectiveness in achieving goals. Among the few scholars who attend to the outcomes of coalitions, some focus on the impact of coalitions for internal movement dynamics. Murphy (2005, 247) looks at the consequences of coalition foundings for the formation of new organizations in the environmental movement, and Heaney and Rojas (2008) analyze the effects of coalition dissolution on ties among SMOs in the contemporary American antiwar movement. Fewer studies examine the impacts of coalition work on targets and goals, and those that attend to outcomes at all often do so while focusing primarily on the internal dynamics of coalitions. Williams (1999), for example, analyzes tensions in the Coalition for Justice in the Maquiladoras and also observes that coalition strategies resulted in positive responses from targeted corporations. Guenther (this volume), while analyzing the mobilization of German feminist coalitions, suggests that even weak or informal coalitions can have important impacts. And Almeida (this volume) finds that social movement–political party coalitions in Latin American nations resulted in positive political outcomes for both the parties and the movements. These and other studies point to the importance of looking at how coalition structures and strategies affect outcomes. However, more studies are needed to systematically investigate the extent to which coalition work, either along with or in the absence of political opportunities, enhances the political, cultural, and economic impacts of social movements.

Works Cited

Bandy, Joe. 2004. "Paradoxes of Transnational Civil Societies under Neoliberalism." *Social Problems* 51: 410–31.

Bandy, Joe, and Jackie Smith, eds. 2005. *Coalitions across Borders: Transnational Protest and the Neoliberal Order.* Lanham, Md.: Rowman & Littlefield.

Carroll, William K., and R. S. Ratner. 1996. "Master Framing and Cross-Movement Networking in Contemporary Social Movements." *Sociological Quarterly* 37: 601–25.

Cullen, Pauline P. 1999. "Coalitions Working for Social Justice: Transnational Non-Governmental Organizations and International Governance." *Contemporary Justice Review* 2: 159–77.

Curtis, Russell L., Jr., and Louis Zurcher Jr. 1973. "Stable Resources of Protest Movements: The Multi-organizational Field." *Social Forces* 52: 53–61.

Dugan, Kimberly B. 2004. "Strategy and 'Spin': Opposing Movement Frames in an Anti-Gay Voter Initiative." *Sociological Focus* 37: 213–33.

Ferree, Myra Marx, and Silke Roth. 1998. "Gender, Class, and the Interaction between Social Movements: A Strike of West Berlin Day Care Workers." *Gender and Society* 12: 626–48.

Ganz, Marshall. 2000. "Resources and Resourcefulness: Strategic Capacity in the Unionization of California Agriculture, 1959–1966." *American Journal of Sociology* 105: 1003–62.

Gerhards, Jurgen, and Dieter Rucht. 1992. "Mesomobilization: Organizing and Framing in Two Protest Campaigns in West Germany." *American Journal of Sociology* 98: 555–95.

Grace, Joan. 2006. "Dueling for Dollars: Feminist Activism and Minimum Wage Coalition Politics." *Canadian Women's Studies* 25: 154–59.

Hathaway, Will, and David S. Meyer. 1993–94. "Competition and Cooperation in Social Movement Coalitions: Lobbying for Peace in the 1980s." *Berkeley Journal of Sociology* 38: 157–83.

Heaney, Michael T., and Fabio Rojas. 2008. "Coalition Dissolution, Mobilization, and Network Dynamics in the U.S. Antiwar Movement." *Research in Social Movements, Conflicts and Change* 28: 39–82.

Kowalchuk, Lisa. 2003. "Asymmetrical Alliances, Organizational Democracy and Peasant Protest in El Salvador." *Canadian Review of Sociology and Anthropology* 40: 291–309.

McCammon, Holly J., and Karen E. Campbell. 2002. "Allies on the Road to Victory:

Coalition Formation between the Suffragists and the Woman's Christian Temperance Union." *Mobilization* 7: 231–51.

Meyer, David S., and Catherine Corrigall-Brown. 2005. "Coalitions and Political Context: U.S. Movements against Wars in Iraq." *Mobilization* 10: 327–44.

Murphy, Gillian. 2005. "Coalitions and the Development of the Global Environmental Movement: A Double-Edged Sword." *Mobilization* 10: 235–50.

Obach, Brian K. 2004. *Labor and the Environmental Movement: The Quest for Common Ground.* Cambridge, Mass.: MIT Press.

Polletta, Francesca. 2002. *Freedom Is an Endless Meeting: Democracy in American Social Movements.* Chicago: University of Chicago Press.

Reger, Jo, and Suzanne Staggenborg. 2006. "Patterns of Mobilization in Local Movement Organizations: Leadership and Strategy in Four National Organization for Women Chapters." *Sociological Perspectives* 49: 297–323.

Rose, Fred. 2000. *Coalitions across the Class Divide: Lessons from the Labor, Peace, and Environmental Movements.* Ithaca, N.Y.: Cornell University Press.

Roth, Silke. 2003. *Building Movement Bridges: The Coalition of Labor Union Women.* Westport, Conn.: Praeger.

Staggenborg, Suzanne. 1986. "Coalition Work in the Pro-Choice Movement: Organizational and Environmental Opportunities and Obstacles." *Social Problems* 33: 374–90.

———. 1998. "Social Movement Communities and Cycles of Protest: The Emergence and Maintenance of a Local Women's Movement." *Social Problems* 45: 180–204.

Stearns, Linda Brewster, and Paul D. Almeida. 2004. "The Formation of State Actor–Social Movement Coalitions and Favorable Policy Outcomes." *Social Problems* 51: 478–504.

Tarrow, Sidney. 2005. *The New Transnational Activism.* New York: Cambridge University Press.

Van Dyke, Nella. 2003. "Crossing Movement Boundaries: Factors That Facilitate Coalition Protest by American College Students, 1930–1990." *Social Problems* 50: 226–50.

Williams, Heather L. 1999. "Mobile Capital and Transborder Labor Rights Mobilization." *Politics and Society* 27: 139–66.

Wood, Lesley J. 2005. "Bridging the Chasms: The Peoples' Global Action." In *Coalitions across Borders: Transnational Protest and the Neoliberal Order,* edited by Joe Bandy and Jackie Smith, 95–117. Lanham, Md.: Rowman & Littlefield.

Zald, Mayer N., and John D. McCarthy. 1980. "Social Movement Industries: Competition and Cooperation among Movement Organizations." *Research in Social Movements, Conflicts, and Change* 3: 1–20.

Contributors

PAUL ALMEIDA is associate professor of sociology at the University of California, Merced. His research centers on collective mobilization in response to political and economic transitions in the developing world. He is author of *Waves of Protest: Popular Struggle in El Salvador, 1925–2005* (Minnesota, 2008) and coeditor (with H. Johnston) of *Latin American Social Movements: Globalization, Democratization, and Transnational Networks.*

ELIZABETH BORLAND is assistant professor of sociology at The College of New Jersey, where she teaches courses on gender and social movements. She has published several journal articles about women's activism in Argentina, and her recent research explores grandmother activist organizations around the world.

DANIEL B. CORNFIELD is professor of sociology at Vanderbilt University and editor of *Work and Occupations.* He writes about the rise, decline, and revitalization of labor movements and is author or editor of eight books, including *Becoming a Mighty Voice: Conflict and Change in the United Furniture Workers of America* and *Labor in the New Urban Battlegrounds: Local Solidarity in a Global Economy.*

CATHERINE CORRIGALL-BROWN is a postdoctoral fellow at the University of British Columbia. Her research focuses on social movements, political sociology, and social psychology. She is working on a book project about individual participation in social movements, examining the multiple trajectories of participation individual engagement can take over the life course.

MARIO DIANI is ICREA Research Professor in the Department of Political and Social Sciences of the Universitat Pompeu Fabra, Barcelona. He is the author of *Green Networks* and (with D. della Porta) *Social Movements,* and coeditor (with D. McAdam) of *Social Movements and Networks* and (with B. Edwards and M. Foley) *Beyond Tocqueville.*

KATJA M. GUENTHER is assistant professor of sociology at the University of California, Riverside. Her research interests include gender and other social inequalities; qualitative epistemologies; political sociology; and German, European, and postsocialist studies. She is author of *Making Their Place: Feminism after Socialism in Eastern Germany.*

LARRY ISAAC is Distinguished Professor of Sociology, affiliate professor of American studies, and research fellow at the Center for Nashville Studies, Vanderbilt University. He is the author of numerous articles on social movements, politics, labor, and historical sociology of social change. He is working on two major projects: an analysis of the political culture of private bourgeois militias and their role in countering the Gilded Age labor movement, supported by the National Endowment for the Humanities; and a collaborative study of the early Nashville civil rights movement.

ISOBEL LINDSAY has published work on voluntary sector leadership in Scotland and on the role of Scottish civic institutions. She has been actively engaged in voluntary sector work. She recently retired from the Department of Geography and Sociology at Strathclyde University.

HOLLY J. MCCAMMON is professor of sociology at Vanderbilt University. She studies U.S. women's activism, particularly early twentieth-century women's efforts to gain the right to sit on juries and their efforts in the nineteenth century to gain property rights for married women. She is writing a book on strategic adaptation among social movement organizations seeking political reform.

DAVID S. MEYER is professor of sociology, political science, and planning, policy, and design at the University of California, Irvine. He has published numerous articles on social movements and social change, and is author or coeditor of six books, most recently *The Politics of Protest: Social Movements in America.* He is most interested in the connections among institutional politics, public policy, and social movements, particularly in regard to issues of war and peace.

BRIAN OBACH is associate professor of sociology at the State University of New York at New Paltz. He studies social movements, environmental sociology, and political economy. He is author of *Labor and the Environmental Movement: The Quest for Common Ground*, and his research focuses on the organic agriculture movement and on the political economy of ecological degradation.

DINA G. OKAMOTO is associate professor of sociology at the University of California, Davis. Her research focuses on the social conditions that generate Asian American panethnicity in the United States and collective action among contemporary immigrants in new destination cities. Her work develops a theoretical framework for understanding group formation, collective identity, and boundary change, and contributes to research in the areas of race and ethnicity, immigration, and social movements.

CHRISTINE PETIT is a graduate student at the University of California, Riverside. Her research interests include social movements, the law and legal repression, and inequality. She is studying the World Social Forums, and the use of and resistance to legal means of repression.

DERRICK PURDUE is a member of the Faculty of Economics and Social Sciences and a research fellow in the Cities Research Centre, University of the West of England, Bristol, United Kingdom. He is author of *Anti-Genetix: The Emergence of a Global Movement against GM Food* and editor of *Civil Societies and Social Movements*. He is investigating environmental networks, environmental risk, civil society, social exclusion, and governance.

ELLEN REESE is associate professor of sociology at the University of California, Riverside. Her research focuses on poverty, welfare state development, urban politics, and social movements. She is author of *Backlash against Welfare Mothers: Past and Present* and coeditor (with A. Cabezas and M. Waller) of *The Wages of Empire: Neoliberal Policies, Repression, and Women's Poverty.*

BENITA ROTH is associate professor of sociology and women's studies at the State University of New York, Binghamton. Her book *Separate Roads to Feminism: Black, Chicana, and White Feminist Movements in America's Second Wave* received the Distinguished Book Award in 2006 from the Sex and Gender section of the American Sociological Association. Her research involves the nexus of gender, protest, race and ethnicity, and nationality in the U.S. postwar period.

SUZANNE STAGGENBORG is professor of sociology at the University of Pittsburgh. She is author of *The Pro-Choice Movement; Gender, Family, and Social Movements;* and *Social Movements.* She is coeditor (with Bert Klandermans) of *Methods of Social Movement Research* (Minnesota, 2002).

NELLA VAN DYKE is associate professor of sociology at the University of California, Merced. Her research focuses on social movements and hate crime, with an emphasis on how characteristics of the social context influence levels of collective action. She is studying college student labor activism, hate crimes on college campuses, and the LGBT marriage rights movement.

DAWN WIEST is assistant professor of sociology at the University of Memphis. She was formerly assistant director of the Center for the Study of Social Movements and Social Change at the University of Notre Dame. She is coauthor (with J. Smith and K. Tsutsui) of *Networked for Change: Transnational Activism in a Global Era.*

Index

(series page continued from p. ii)